BAKUMAN。

Volume 19

SHONEN JUMP Manga Edition

Story by **TSUGUMI OHBA**
Art by **TAKESHI OBATA**

Translation | **Tetsuichiro Miyaki**
Touch-up Art & Lettering | **James Gaubatz**
Design | **Fawn Lau**
Editor | **Alexis Kirsch**

BAKUMAN。© 2008 by Tsugumi Ohba, Takeshi Obata
All rights reserved.
First published in Japan in 2008 by SHUEISHA Inc., Tokyo.
English translation rights arranged by SHUEISHA Inc.

The rights of the author(s) of the work(s) in this publication to be
so identified have been asserted in accordance with the Copyright,
Designs and Patents Act 1988. A CIP catalogue record for this book
is available from the British Library.

The stories, characters and incidents mentioned in this publication are
entirely fictional.

Printed in the U.S.A.

Published by VIZ Media, LLC
P.O. Box 77010
San Francisco, CA 94107

10 9 8 7 6 5 4 3 2 1
First printing, May 2013

I owned birds as pets until two years ago. But I would get so sad when they died that I can't have them anymore.

-Tsugumi Ohba

The sketch and the final cover art are different for this volume. Sometimes things change during the process.

-Takeshi Obata

SNAP

Tsugumi Ohba
Born in Tokyo, Tsugumi Ohba is the author of the hit series *Death Note*. His latest series *Bakuman.* was serialized in *Weekly Shonen Jump*.

Takeshi Obata
Takeshi Obata was born in 1969 in Niigata, Japan, and is the artist of the wildly popular SHONEN JUMP title *Hikaru no Go*, which won the 2003 Tezuka Osamu Cultural Prize: Shinsei "New Hope" award and the 2000 Shogakukan Manga award. Obata is also the artist of *Arabian Majin Bokentan Lamp Lamp*, *Ayatsuri Sakon*, *Cyborg Jichan G.*, and the smash hit manga *Death Note*. His latest series *Bakuman.* was serialized in *Weekly Shonen Jump*.

BAKUMAN。

19

DECISION and JOY

STORY BY TSUGUMI OHBA

ART BY TAKESHI OBATA

SHONEN JUMP MANGA

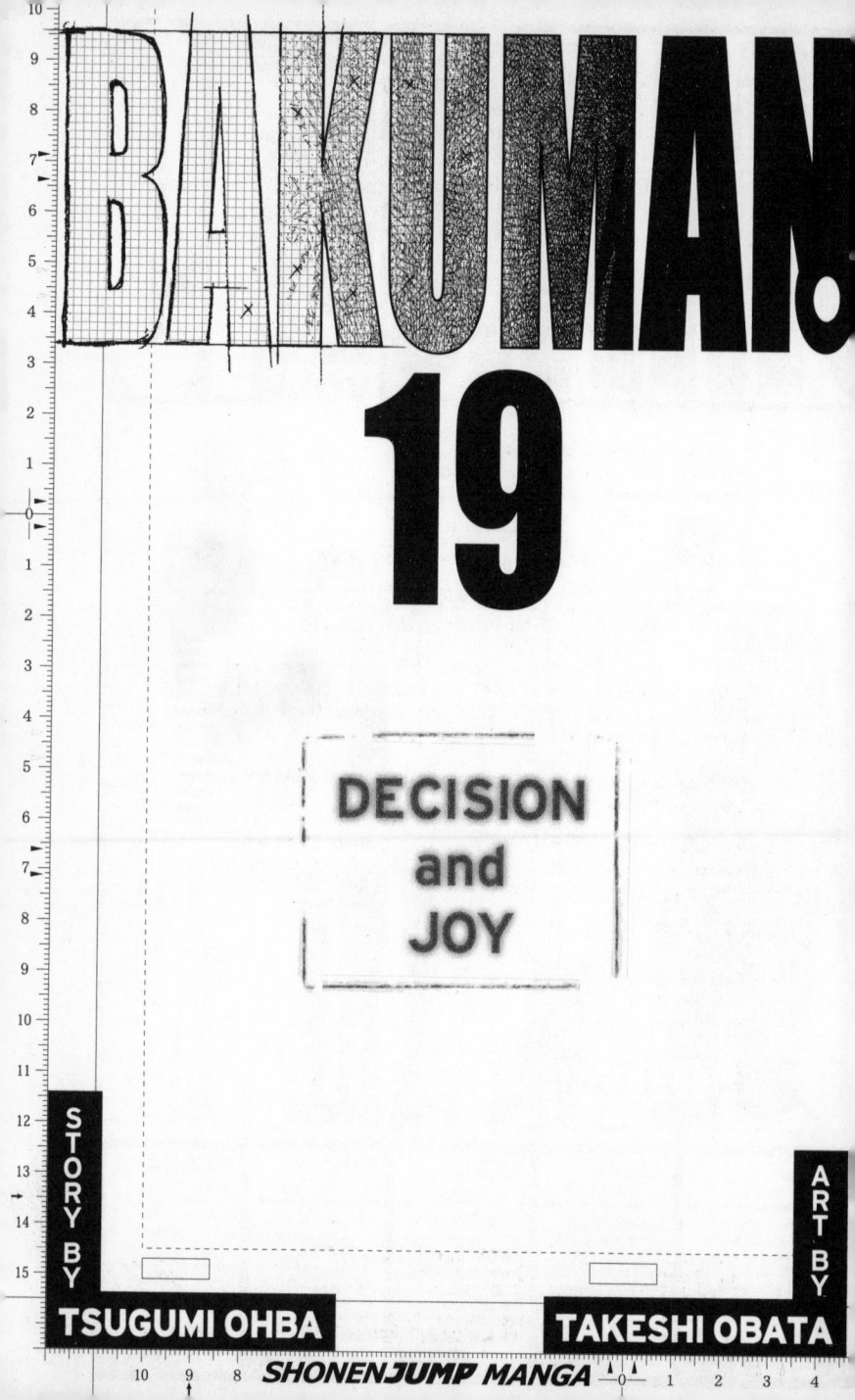

バクマン。 ...UMAN。 vol.19

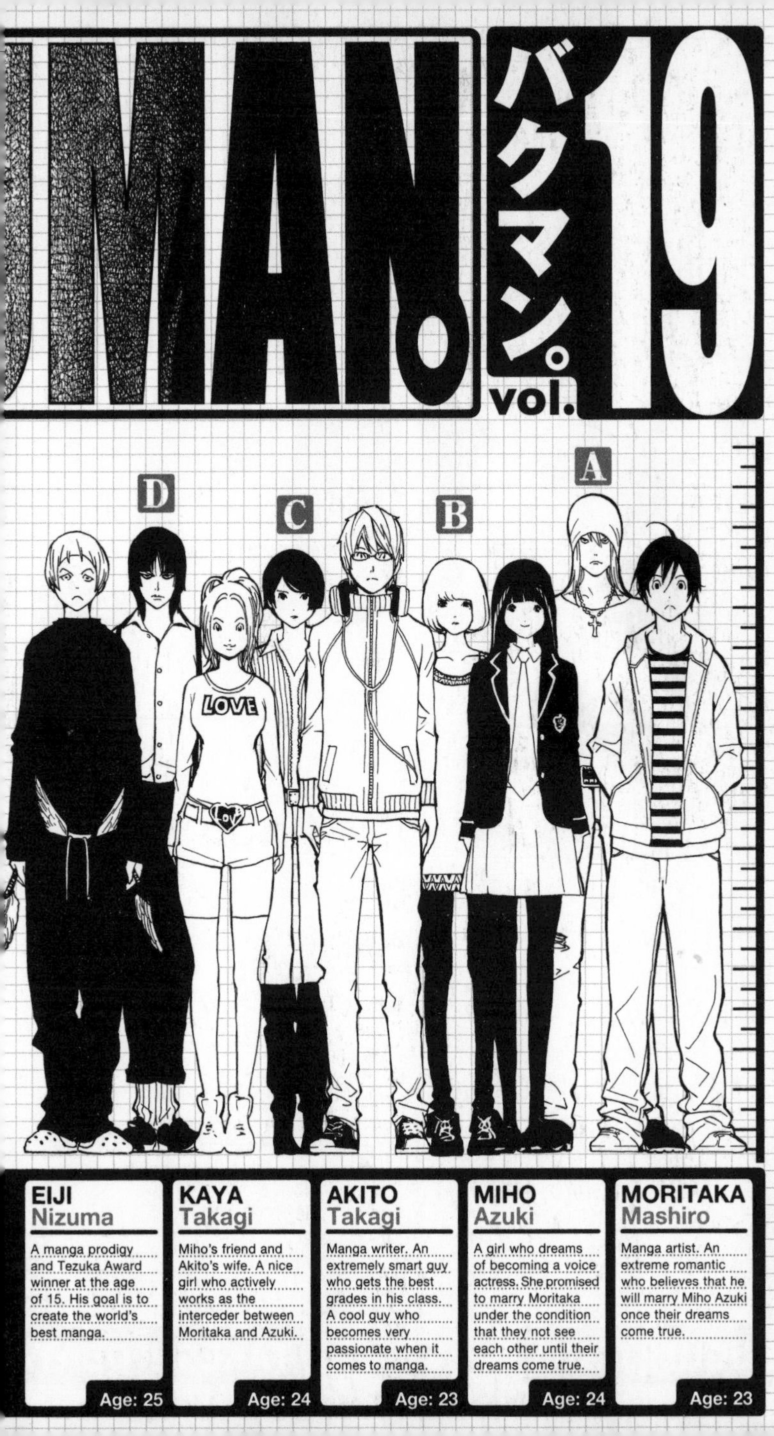

A
B
C
D
LOVE

EIJI
Nizuma

A manga prodigy and Tezuka Award winner at the age of 15. His goal is to create the world's best manga.

Age: 25

KAYA
Takagi

Miho's friend and Akito's wife. A nice girl who actively works as the interceder between Moritaka and Azuki.

Age: 24

AKITO
Takagi

Manga writer. An extremely smart guy who gets the best grades in his class. A cool guy who becomes very passionate when it comes to manga.

Age: 23

MIHO
Azuki

A girl who dreams of becoming a voice actress. She promised to marry Moritaka under the condition that they not see each other until their dreams come true.

Age: 24

MORITAKA
Mashiro

Manga artist. An extreme romantic who believes that he will marry Miho Azuki once their dreams come true.

Age: 23

*These ages are from November 2017.

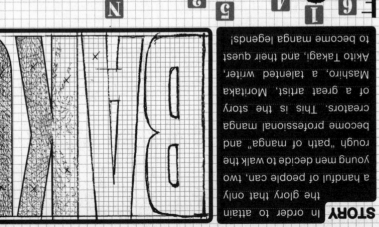

STORY

In order to attain the glory that only a handful of people can, two young men decide to walk the rough "path of manga" and become professional manga creators. This is the story of a great artist, Moritaka Mashiro, a talented writer, Akito Takagi, and their quest to become manga legends!

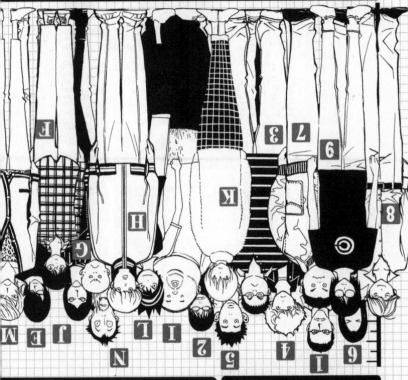

WEEKLY SHONEN JUMP Editorial Department

1. Ex-Editor in Chief Sasaki
2. Editor in Chief Heishi
3. Deputy Editor in Chief Aida
4. Yujiro Hattori
5. Akira Hattori
6. Koji Yoshida
7. Goro Miura
8. Masakazu Yamahisa
9. Kosugi

The MANGA ARTISTS and ASSISTANTS

A. SHINTA FUKUDA
B. KO AOKI
C. AIKO IWASE
D. KAZUYA HIRAMARU
E. RYU SHIZUKA
F. NATSUMI KATO
G. YASUOKA
H. SHOYO TAKAHAMA
I. TAKURO NAKAI
J. SHUICHI MORIYA
K. SHUN SHIRATORI
L. ICHIRIKI ORIHARA
M. TOHRU NANAMINE
N. MIKIHIKO AZUMA

BAKUMAN。

VOL. 19

CONTENTS

(DECISION AND JOY)

CH. 161 BREATHER and PARTY ... 7

CH. 162 HOT SPRING and CHOICES ... 27

CH. 163 CONFIRMATION and CONSENT ... 47

CH. 164 DECISION and JOY ... 67

CH. 165 PRACTICE and RECHARGE ... 89

CH. 166 RUMOR and ARTICLE ... 111

CH. 167 NONSENSE and A WORD ... 131

CH. 168 CORRECTION and DECLARATION ... 151

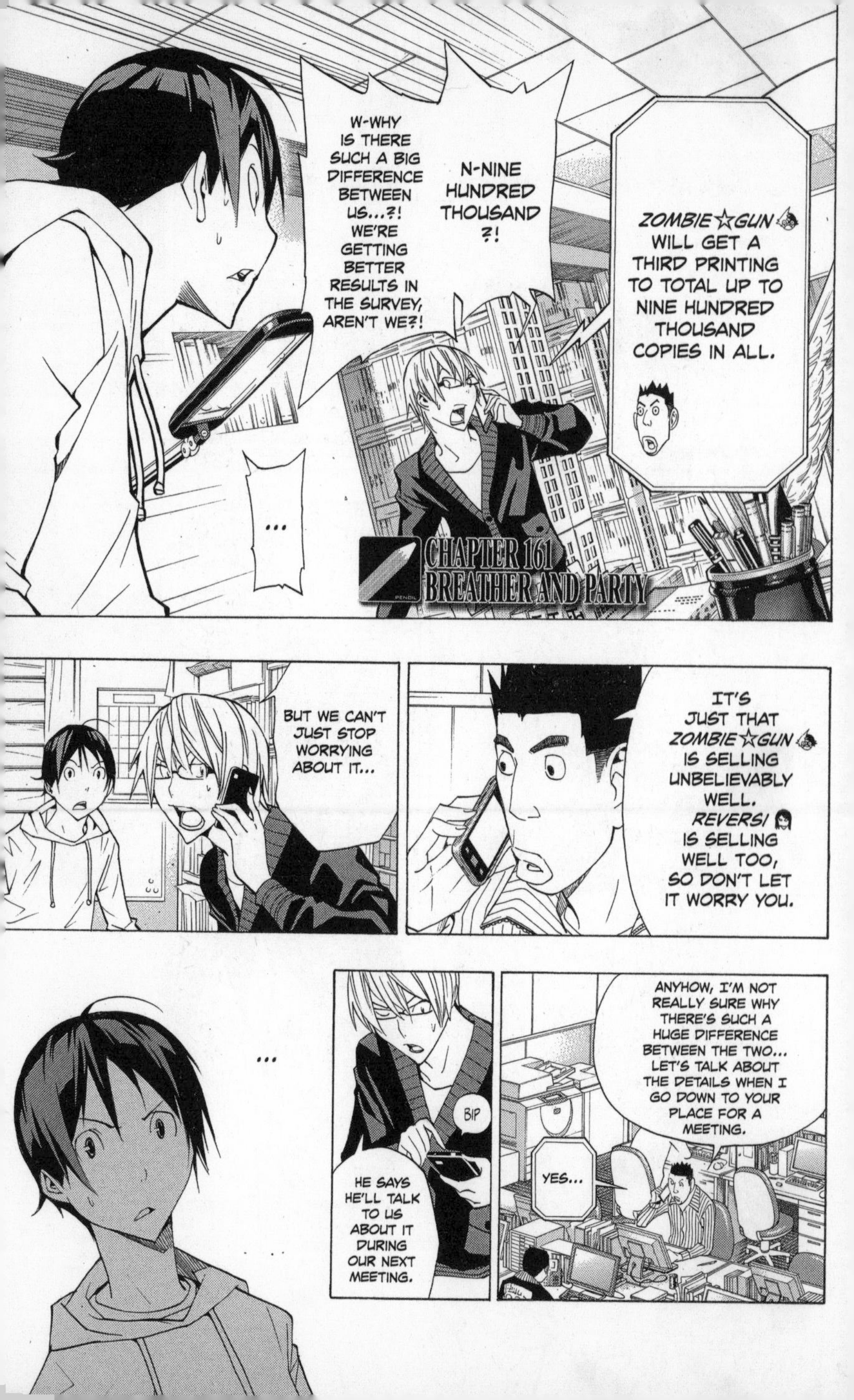

ZOMBIE☆GUN WILL GET A THIRD PRINTING TO TOTAL UP TO NINE HUNDRED THOUSAND COPIES IN ALL.
N-NINE HUNDRED THOUSAND ?!
W-WHY IS THERE SUCH A BIG DIFFERENCE BETWEEN US...?! WE'RE GETTING BETTER RESULTS IN THE SURVEY, AREN'T WE?!
...
CHAPTER 161
BREATHER AND PARTY
PENCIL
IT'S JUST THAT ZOMBIE☆GUN IS SELLING UNBELIEVABLY WELL. REVERSI IS SELLING WELL TOO, SO DON'T LET IT WORRY YOU.
BUT WE CAN'T JUST STOP WORRYING ABOUT IT...
ANYHOW, I'M NOT REALLY SURE WHY THERE'S SUCH A HUGE DIFFERENCE BETWEEN THE TWO... LET'S TALK ABOUT THE DETAILS WHEN I GO DOWN TO YOUR PLACE FOR A MEETING.
YES...
BIP
HE SAYS HE'LL TALK TO US ABOUT IT DURING OUR NEXT MEETING.
...

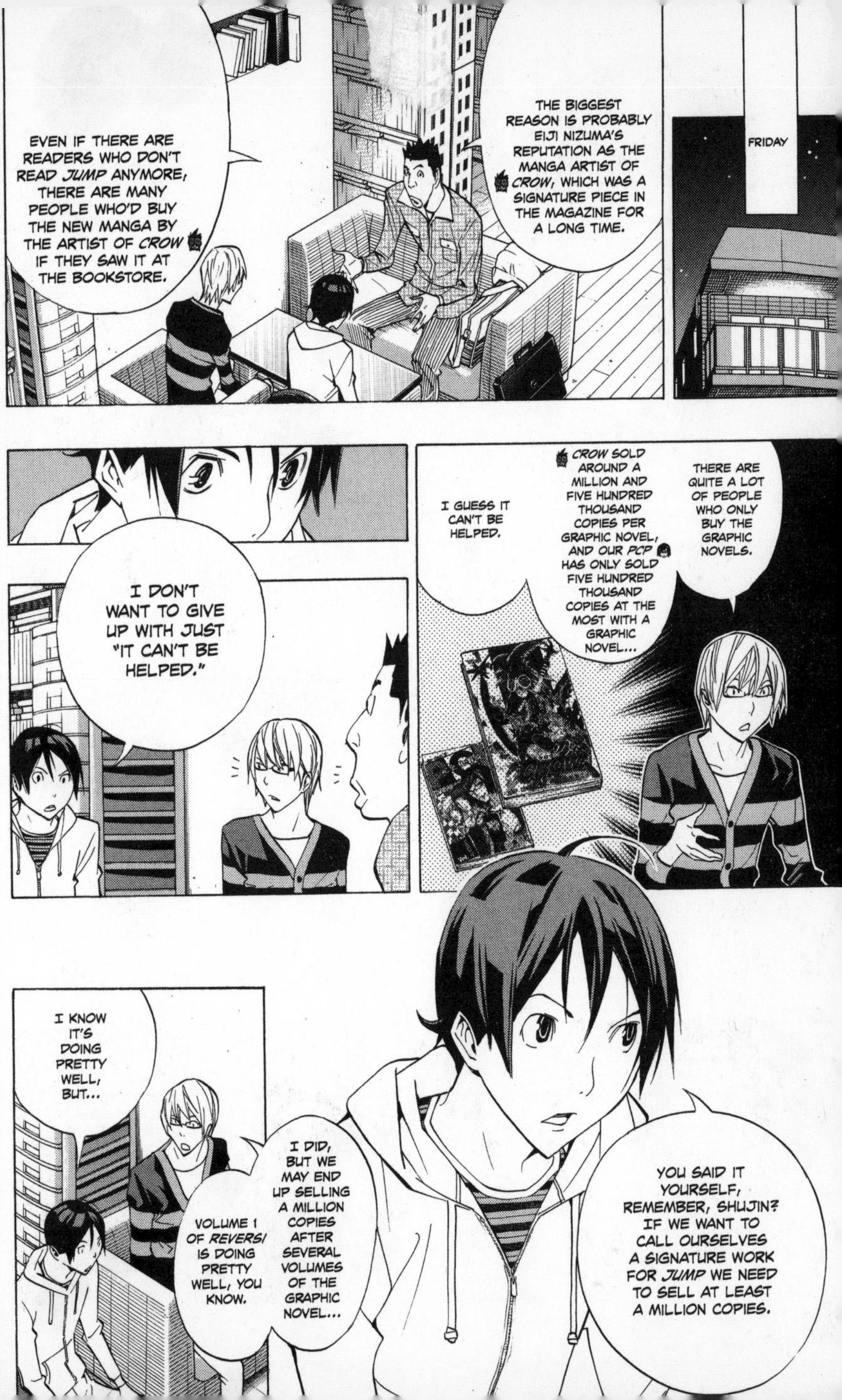
FRIDAY
THE BIGGEST REASON IS PROBABLY EIJI NIZUMA'S REPUTATION AS THE MANGA ARTIST OF *CROW*, WHICH WAS A SIGNATURE PIECE IN THE MAGAZINE FOR A LONG TIME.
EVEN IF THERE ARE READERS WHO DON'T READ *JUMP* ANYMORE, THERE ARE MANY PEOPLE WHO'D BUY THE NEW MANGA BY THE ARTIST OF *CROW* IF THEY SAW IT AT THE BOOKSTORE.
THERE ARE QUITE A LOT OF PEOPLE WHO ONLY BUY THE GRAPHIC NOVELS.
CROW SOLD AROUND A MILLION AND FIVE HUNDRED THOUSAND COPIES PER GRAPHIC NOVEL, AND OUR *PCP* HAS ONLY SOLD FIVE HUNDRED THOUSAND COPIES AT THE MOST WITH A GRAPHIC NOVEL...
I GUESS IT CAN'T BE HELPED.
I DON'T WANT TO GIVE UP WITH JUST "IT CAN'T BE HELPED."
YOU SAID IT YOURSELF, REMEMBER, SHUJIN? IF WE WANT TO CALL OURSELVES A SIGNATURE WORK FOR *JUMP* WE NEED TO SELL AT LEAST A MILLION COPIES.
I DID, BUT WE MAY END UP SELLING A MILLION COPIES AFTER SEVERAL VOLUMES OF THE GRAPHIC NOVEL...
VOLUME 1 OF *REVERSI* IS DOING PRETTY WELL, YOU KNOW.
I KNOW IT'S DOING PRETTY WELL, BUT...

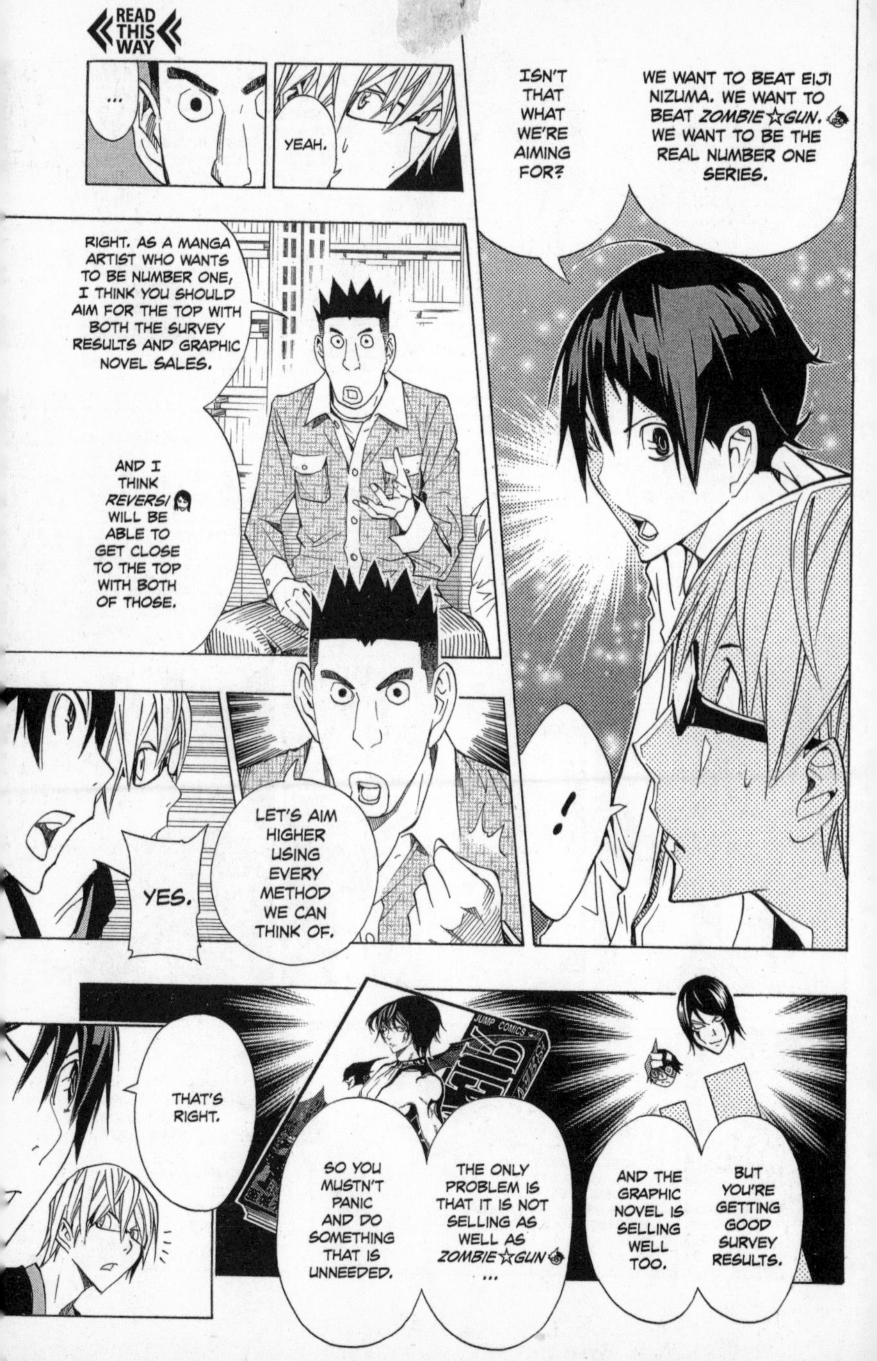
READ THIS WAY
WE WANT TO BEAT EIJI NIZUMA. WE WANT TO BEAT *ZOMBIE☆GUN*. WE WANT TO BE THE REAL NUMBER ONE SERIES.
ISN'T THAT WHAT WE'RE AIMING FOR?
!
YEAH.
...
RIGHT. AS A MANGA ARTIST WHO WANTS TO BE NUMBER ONE, I THINK YOU SHOULD AIM FOR THE TOP WITH BOTH THE SURVEY RESULTS AND GRAPHIC NOVEL SALES.
AND I THINK *REVERSI* WILL BE ABLE TO GET CLOSE TO THE TOP WITH BOTH OF THOSE.
LET'S AIM HIGHER USING EVERY METHOD WE CAN THINK OF.
YES.
BUT YOU'RE GETTING GOOD SURVEY RESULTS.
AND THE GRAPHIC NOVEL IS SELLING WELL TOO.
THE ONLY PROBLEM IS THAT IT IS NOT SELLING AS WELL AS *ZOMBIE☆GUN*...
SO YOU MUSTN'T PANIC AND DO SOMETHING THAT IS UNNEEDED.
THAT'S RIGHT.
JUMP COMICS

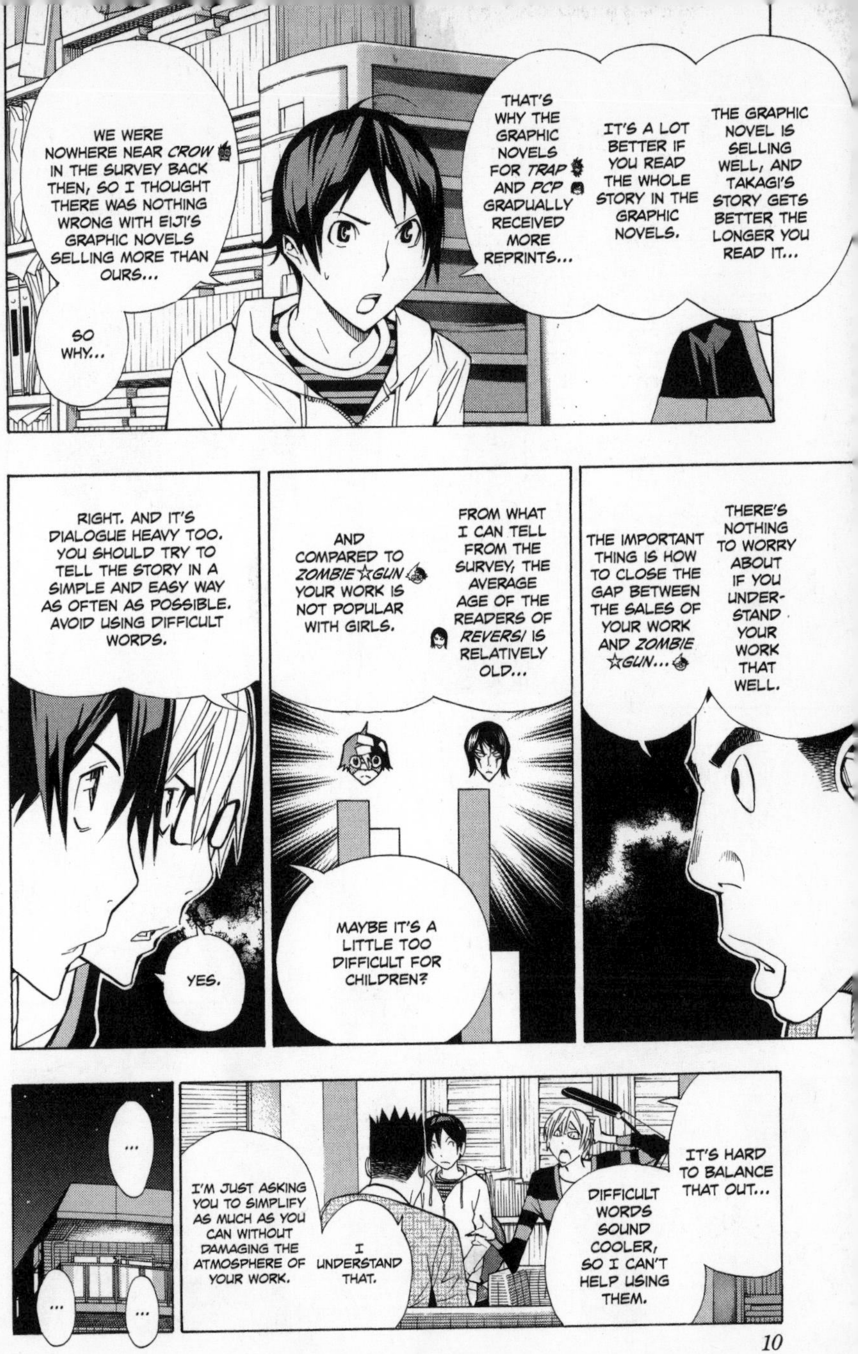
THE GRAPHIC NOVEL IS SELLING WELL, AND TAKAGI'S STORY GETS BETTER THE LONGER YOU READ IT...
IT'S A LOT BETTER IF YOU READ THE WHOLE STORY IN THE GRAPHIC NOVELS.
THAT'S WHY THE GRAPHIC NOVELS FOR *TRAP* AND *PCP* GRADUALLY RECEIVED MORE REPRINTS...
WE WERE NOWHERE NEAR *CROW* IN THE SURVEY BACK THEN, SO I THOUGHT THERE WAS NOTHING WRONG WITH EIJI'S GRAPHIC NOVELS SELLING MORE THAN OURS...
SO WHY...
THERE'S NOTHING TO WORRY ABOUT IF YOU UNDER-STAND YOUR WORK THAT WELL.
THE IMPORTANT THING IS HOW TO CLOSE THE GAP BETWEEN THE SALES OF YOUR WORK AND *ZOMBIE ☆GUN*...
FROM WHAT I CAN TELL FROM THE SURVEY, THE AVERAGE AGE OF THE READERS OF *REVERSI* IS RELATIVELY OLD...
AND COMPARED TO *ZOMBIE☆GUN* YOUR WORK IS NOT POPULAR WITH GIRLS.
MAYBE IT'S A LITTLE TOO DIFFICULT FOR CHILDREN?
RIGHT. AND IT'S DIALOGUE HEAVY TOO. YOU SHOULD TRY TO TELL THE STORY IN A SIMPLE AND EASY WAY AS OFTEN AS POSSIBLE. AVOID USING DIFFICULT WORDS.
YES.
IT'S HARD TO BALANCE THAT OUT...
DIFFICULT WORDS SOUND COOLER, SO I CAN'T HELP USING THEM.
I UNDERSTAND THAT.
I'M JUST ASKING YOU TO SIMPLIFY AS MUCH AS YOU CAN WITHOUT DAMAGING THE ATMOSPHERE OF YOUR WORK.
...
...
...

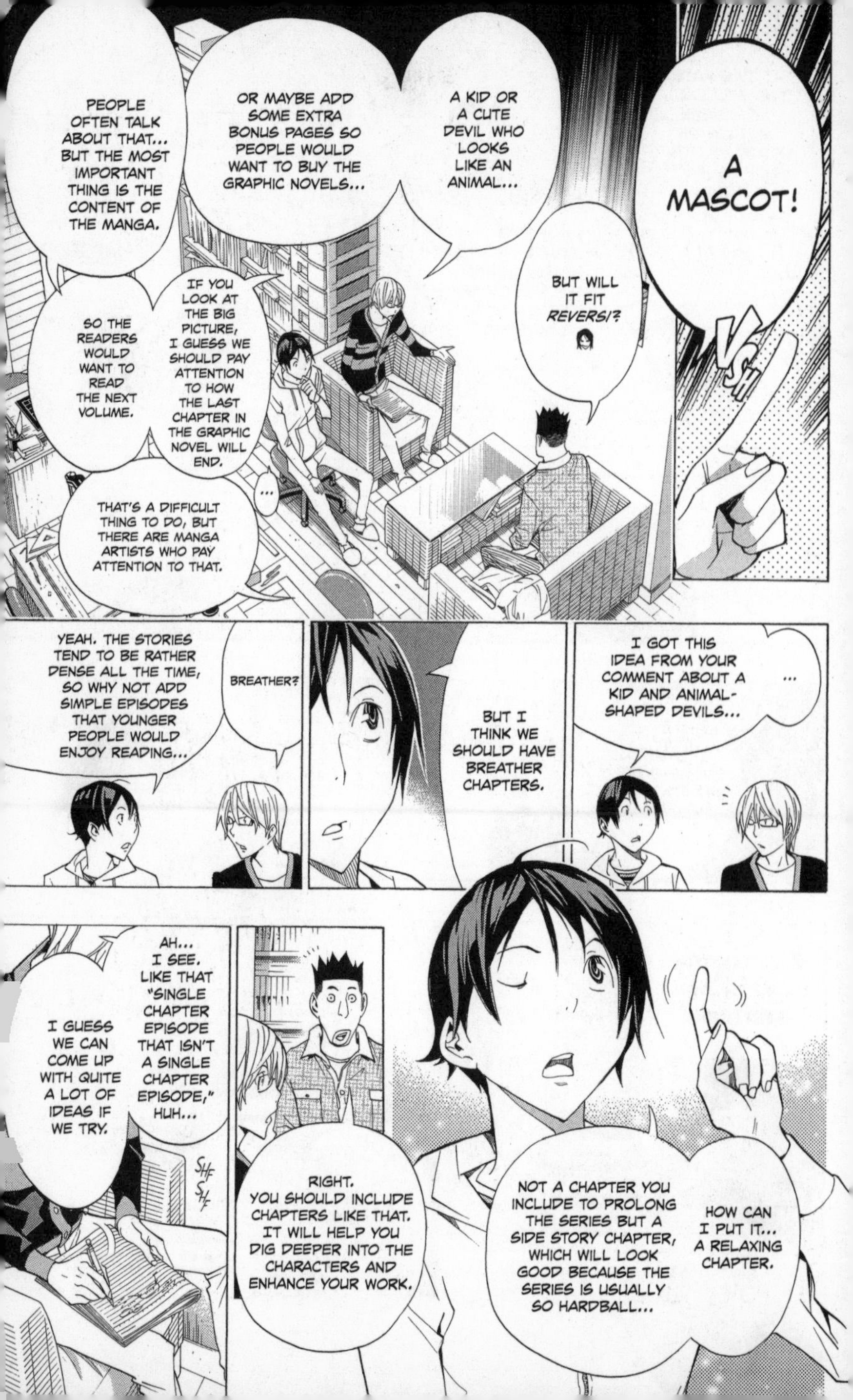
A MASCOT!
VSH
A KID OR A CUTE DEVIL WHO LOOKS LIKE AN ANIMAL...
OR MAYBE ADD SOME EXTRA BONUS PAGES SO PEOPLE WOULD WANT TO BUY THE GRAPHIC NOVELS...
PEOPLE OFTEN TALK ABOUT THAT... BUT THE MOST IMPORTANT THING IS THE CONTENT OF THE MANGA.
BUT WILL IT FIT *REVERSI*!?
IF YOU LOOK AT THE BIG PICTURE, I GUESS WE SHOULD PAY ATTENTION TO HOW THE LAST CHAPTER IN THE GRAPHIC NOVEL WILL END.
SO THE READERS WOULD WANT TO READ THE NEXT VOLUME.
...
THAT'S A DIFFICULT THING TO DO, BUT THERE ARE MANGA ARTISTS WHO PAY ATTENTION TO THAT.
I GOT THIS IDEA FROM YOUR COMMENT ABOUT A KID AND ANIMAL-SHAPED DEVILS...
...
BUT I THINK WE SHOULD HAVE BREATHER CHAPTERS.
BREATHER?
YEAH. THE STORIES TEND TO BE RATHER DENSE ALL THE TIME, SO WHY NOT ADD SIMPLE EPISODES THAT YOUNGER PEOPLE WOULD ENJOY READING...
HOW CAN I PUT IT... A RELAXING CHAPTER.
NOT A CHAPTER YOU INCLUDE TO PROLONG THE SERIES BUT A SIDE STORY CHAPTER, WHICH WILL LOOK GOOD BECAUSE THE SERIES IS USUALLY SO HARDBALL...
RIGHT. YOU SHOULD INCLUDE CHAPTERS LIKE THAT. IT WILL HELP YOU DIG DEEPER INTO THE CHARACTERS AND ENHANCE YOUR WORK.
AH... I SEE. LIKE THAT "SINGLE CHAPTER EPISODE THAT ISN'T A SINGLE CHAPTER EPISODE," HUH...
SHF SHF
I GUESS WE CAN COME UP WITH QUITE A LOT OF IDEAS IF WE TRY.

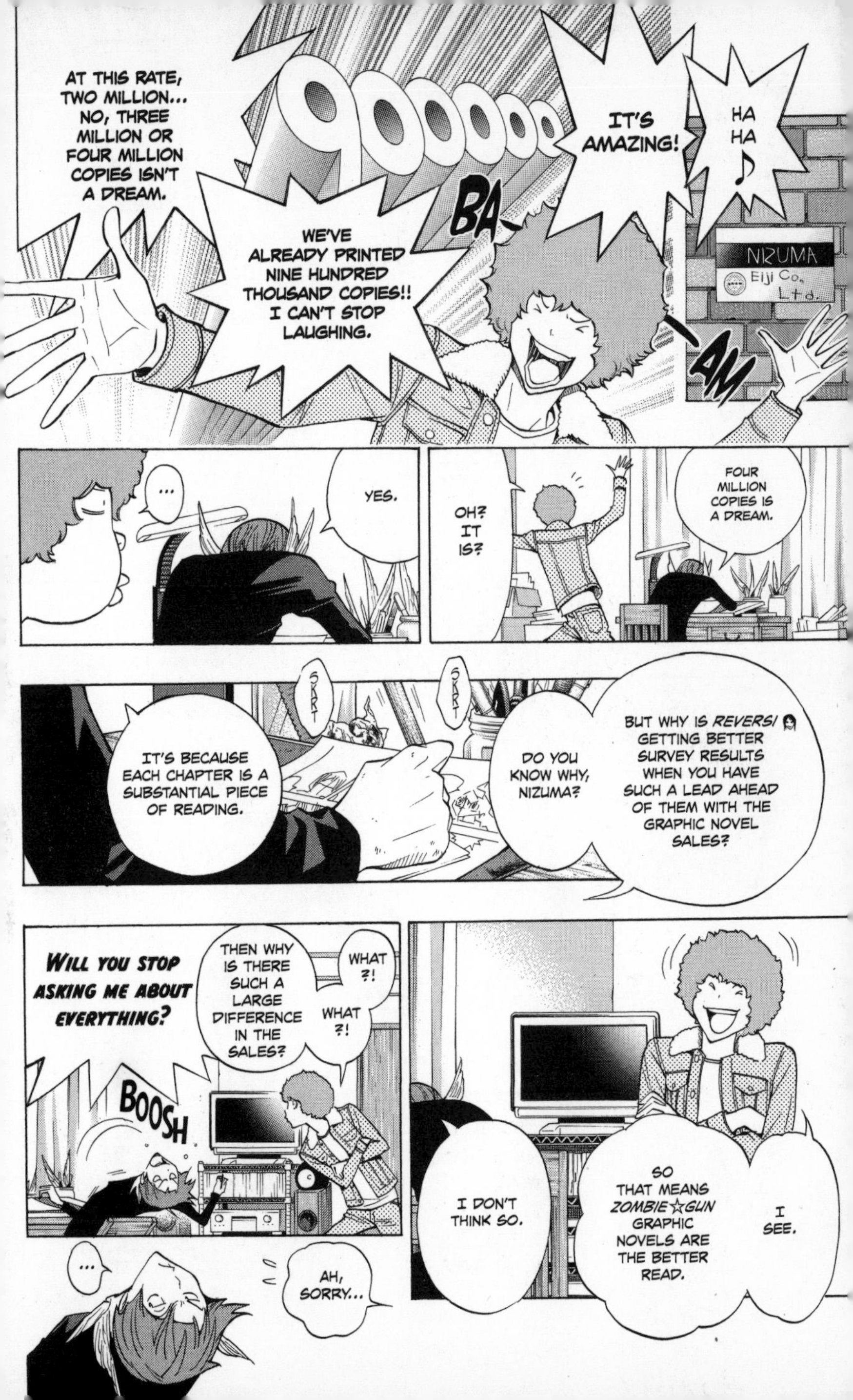
HA HA ♪
IT'S AMAZING!
NIZUMA
Eiji Co., Ltd.
BA-AM
WE'VE ALREADY PRINTED NINE HUNDRED THOUSAND COPIES!! I CAN'T STOP LAUGHING.
AT THIS RATE, TWO MILLION... NO, THREE MILLION OR FOUR MILLION COPIES ISN'T A DREAM.
FOUR MILLION COPIES IS A DREAM.
OH? IT IS?
YES.
...
BUT WHY IS REVERSI GETTING BETTER SURVEY RESULTS WHEN YOU HAVE SUCH A LEAD AHEAD OF THEM WITH THE GRAPHIC NOVEL SALES?
DO YOU KNOW WHY, NIZUMA?
SKRT
SKRT
IT'S BECAUSE EACH CHAPTER IS A SUBSTANTIAL PIECE OF READING.
I SEE.
SO THAT MEANS ZOMBIE☆GUN GRAPHIC NOVELS ARE THE BETTER READ.
I DON'T THINK SO.
WHAT ?!
WHAT ?!
THEN WHY IS THERE SUCH A LARGE DIFFERENCE IN THE SALES?
WILL YOU STOP ASKING ME ABOUT EVERYTHING?
BOOSH
AH, SORRY...
...

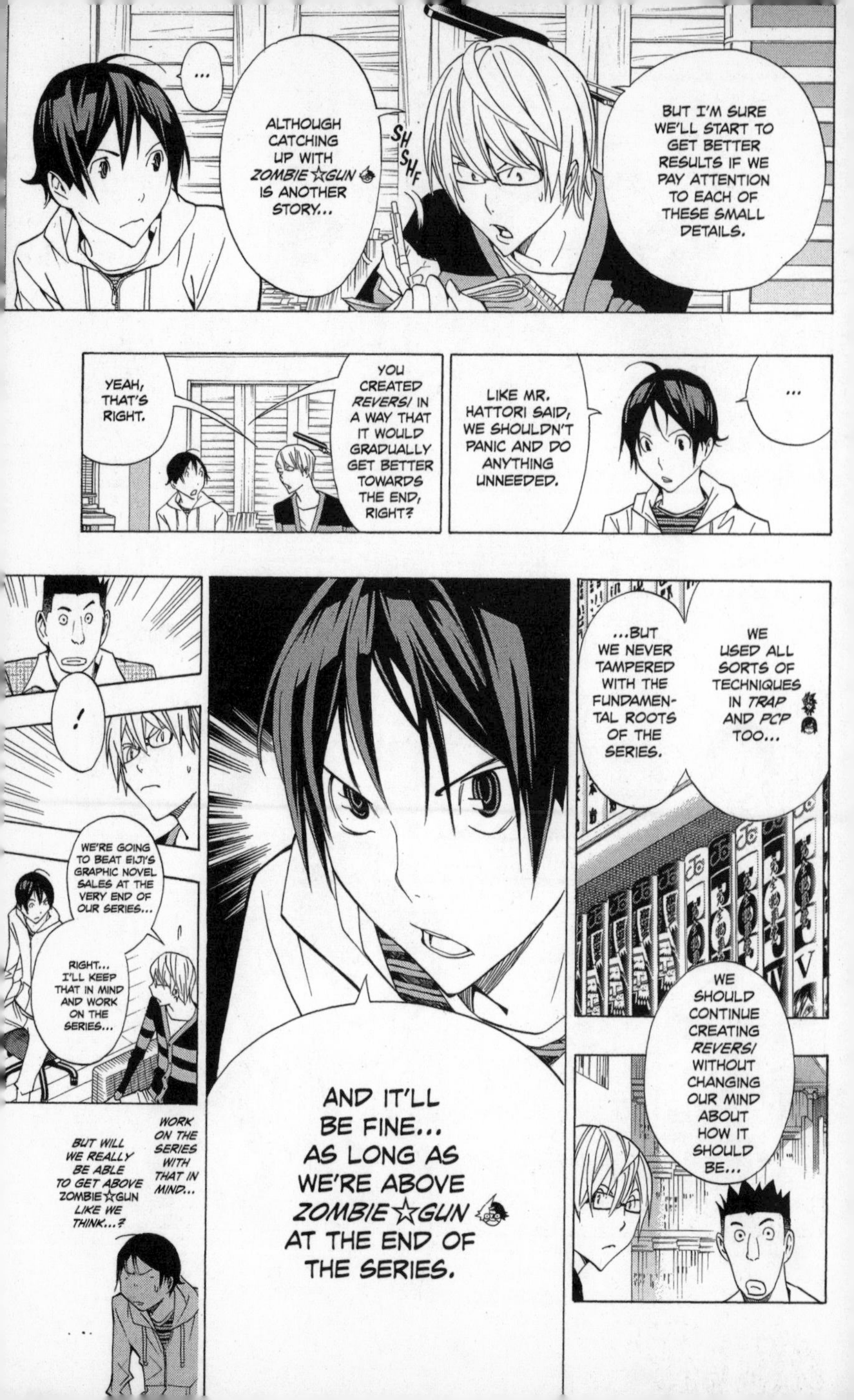
BUT I'M SURE WE'LL START TO GET BETTER RESULTS IF WE PAY ATTENTION TO EACH OF THESE SMALL DETAILS.
SH SHF
ALTHOUGH CATCHING UP WITH ZOMBIE☆GUN IS ANOTHER STORY...
...
...
LIKE MR. HATTORI SAID, WE SHOULDN'T PANIC AND DO ANYTHING UNNEEDED.
YOU CREATED REVERSI IN A WAY THAT IT WOULD GRADUALLY GET BETTER TOWARDS THE END, RIGHT?
YEAH, THAT'S RIGHT.
WE USED ALL SORTS OF TECHNIQUES IN TRAP AND PCP TOO...
...BUT WE NEVER TAMPERED WITH THE FUNDAMENTAL ROOTS OF THE SERIES.
WE SHOULD CONTINUE CREATING REVERSI WITHOUT CHANGING OUR MIND ABOUT HOW IT SHOULD BE...
AND IT'LL BE FINE... AS LONG AS WE'RE ABOVE ZOMBIE☆GUN AT THE END OF THE SERIES.
!
WE'RE GOING TO BEAT EIJI'S GRAPHIC NOVEL SALES AT THE VERY END OF OUR SERIES...
RIGHT... I'LL KEEP THAT IN MIND AND WORK ON THE SERIES...
WORK ON THE SERIES WITH THAT IN MIND...
BUT WILL WE REALLY BE ABLE TO GET ABOVE ZOMBIE☆GUN LIKE WE THINK...?
...

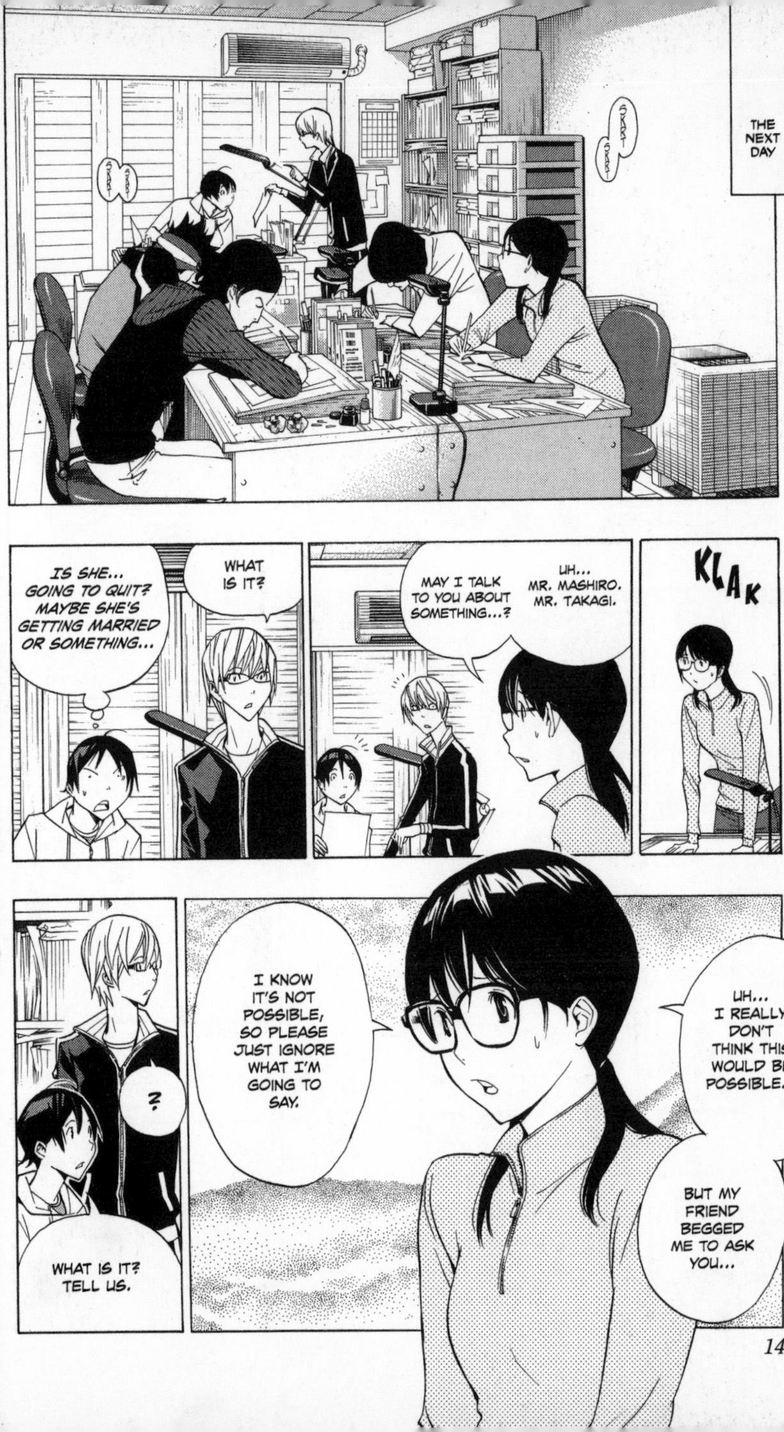
THE NEXT DAY
SKRT SKRT
SKRT SKRT
KLAK
UH... MR. MASHIRO. MR. TAKAGI.
MAY I TALK TO YOU ABOUT SOMETHING...?
WHAT IS IT?
IS SHE... GOING TO QUIT? MAYBE SHE'S GETTING MARRIED OR SOMETHING...
UH... I REALLY DON'T THINK THIS WOULD BE POSSIBLE...
BUT MY FRIEND BEGGED ME TO ASK YOU...
I KNOW IT'S NOT POSSIBLE, SO PLEASE JUST IGNORE WHAT I'M GOING TO SAY.
?
WHAT IS IT? TELL US.

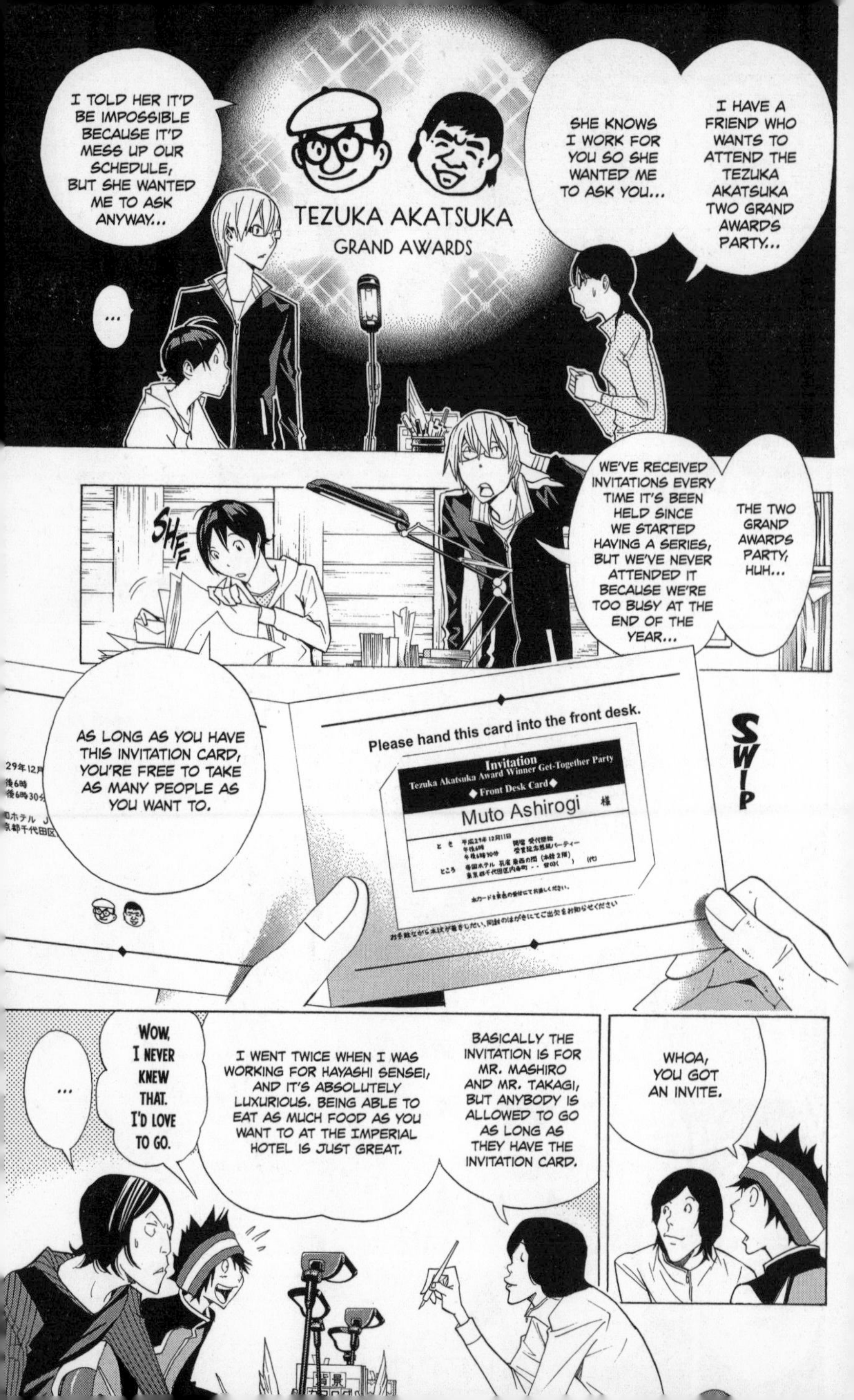
I HAVE A FRIEND WHO WANTS TO ATTEND THE TEZUKA AKATSUKA TWO GRAND AWARDS PARTY...
SHE KNOWS I WORK FOR YOU SO SHE WANTED ME TO ASK YOU...
TEZUKA AKATSUKA
GRAND AWARDS
I TOLD HER IT'D BE IMPOSSIBLE BECAUSE IT'D MESS UP OUR SCHEDULE, BUT SHE WANTED ME TO ASK ANYWAY...
...
THE TWO GRAND AWARDS PARTY, HUH...
WE'VE RECEIVED INVITATIONS EVERY TIME IT'S BEEN HELD SINCE WE STARTED HAVING A SERIES, BUT WE'VE NEVER ATTENDED IT BECAUSE WE'RE TOO BUSY AT THE END OF THE YEAR...
SHFF
SWIP
Please hand this card into the front desk.
Invitation
Tezuka Akatsuka Award Winner Get-Together Party
◆Front Desk Card◆
Muto Ashirogi 様
AS LONG AS YOU HAVE THIS INVITATION CARD, YOU'RE FREE TO TAKE AS MANY PEOPLE AS YOU WANT TO.
WHOA, YOU GOT AN INVITE.
BASICALLY THE INVITATION IS FOR MR. MASHIRO AND MR. TAKAGI, BUT ANYBODY IS ALLOWED TO GO AS LONG AS THEY HAVE THE INVITATION CARD.
I WENT TWICE WHEN I WAS WORKING FOR HAYASHI SENSEI, AND IT'S ABSOLUTELY LUXURIOUS. BEING ABLE TO EAT AS MUCH FOOD AS YOU WANT TO AT THE IMPERIAL HOTEL IS JUST GREAT.
WOW, I NEVER KNEW THAT. I'D LOVE TO GO.
...

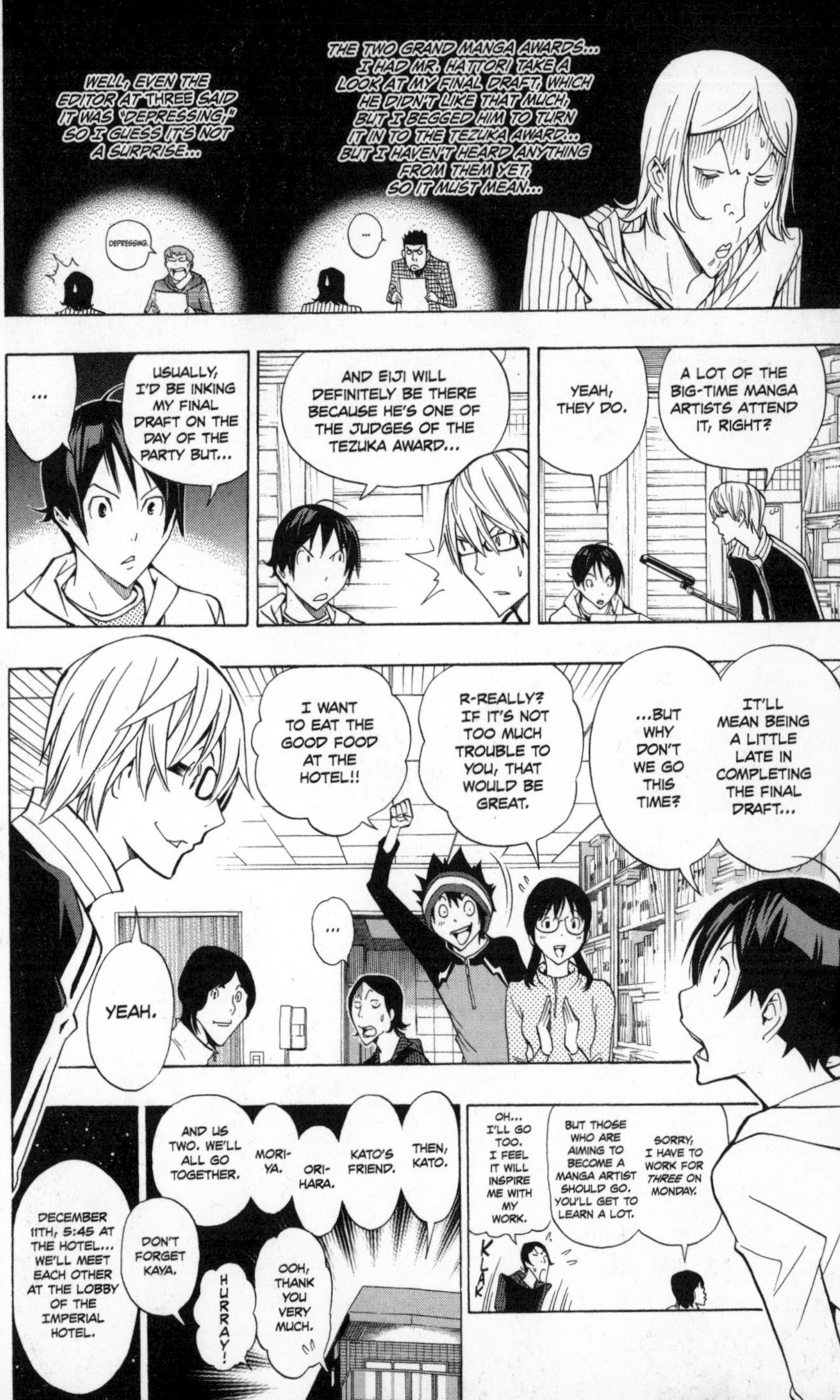
THE TWO GRAND MANGA AWARDS... I HAD MR. HATTORI TAKE A LOOK AT MY FINAL DRAFT, WHICH HE DIDN'T LIKE THAT MUCH, BUT I BEGGED HIM TO TURN IT IN TO THE TEZUKA AWARD... BUT I HAVEN'T HEARD ANYTHING FROM THEM YET, SO IT MUST MEAN...
...
WELL, EVEN THE EDITOR AT THREE SAID IT WAS "DEPRESSING," SO I GUESS IT'S NOT A SURPRISE...
DEPRESSING.
A LOT OF THE BIG-TIME MANGA ARTISTS ATTEND IT, RIGHT?
YEAH, THEY DO.
AND EIJI WILL DEFINITELY BE THERE BECAUSE HE'S ONE OF THE JUDGES OF THE TEZUKA AWARD...
USUALLY, I'D BE INKING MY FINAL DRAFT ON THE DAY OF THE PARTY BUT...
...
IT'LL MEAN BEING A LITTLE LATE IN COMPLETING THE FINAL DRAFT...
...BUT WHY DON'T WE GO THIS TIME?
R-REALLY? IF IT'S NOT TOO MUCH TROUBLE TO YOU, THAT WOULD BE GREAT.
I WANT TO EAT THE GOOD FOOD AT THE HOTEL!!
...
YEAH.
SORRY, I HAVE TO WORK FOR THREE ON MONDAY.
BUT THOSE WHO ARE AIMING TO BECOME A MANGA ARTIST SHOULD GO. YOU'LL GET TO LEARN A LOT.
OH... I'LL GO TOO. I FEEL IT WILL INSPIRE ME WITH MY WORK.
KLAK
THEN, KATO.
KATO'S FRIEND.
ORI-HARA.
MORI-YA.
AND US TWO. WE'LL ALL GO TOGETHER.
OOH, THANK YOU VERY MUCH.
HURRAY!
DON'T FORGET KAYA.
DECEMBER 11TH, 5:45 AT THE HOTEL... WE'LL MEET EACH OTHER AT THE LOBBY OF THE IMPERIAL HOTEL.

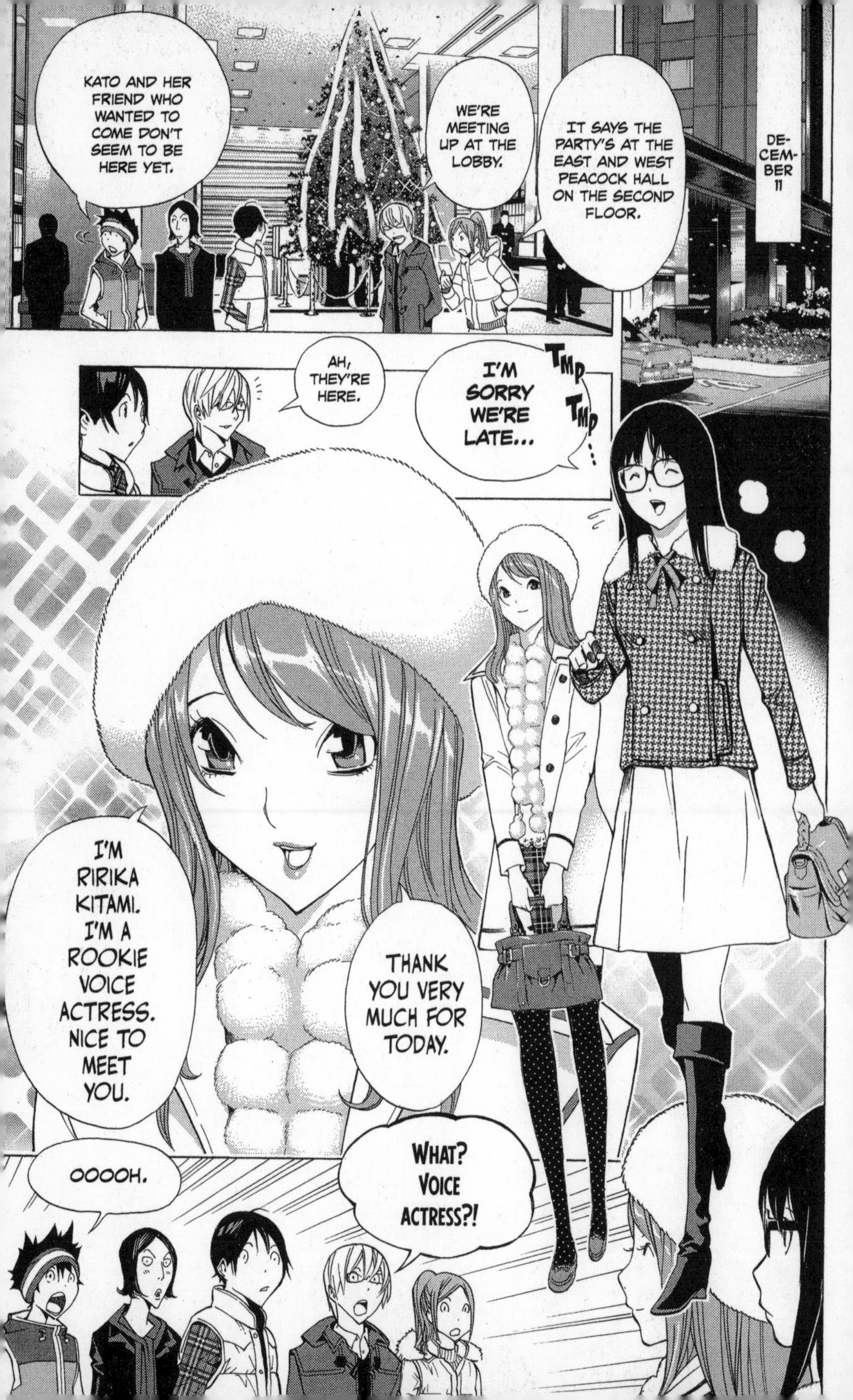
DE-CEM-BER 11
IT SAYS THE PARTY'S AT THE EAST AND WEST PEACOCK HALL ON THE SECOND FLOOR.
WE'RE MEETING UP AT THE LOBBY.
KATO AND HER FRIEND WHO WANTED TO COME DON'T SEEM TO BE HERE YET.
TMP TMP...
I'M SORRY WE'RE LATE...
AH, THEY'RE HERE.
THANK YOU VERY MUCH FOR TODAY.
I'M RIRIKA KITAMI. I'M A ROOKIE VOICE ACTRESS. NICE TO MEET YOU.
WHAT? VOICE ACTRESS?!
OOOOH.

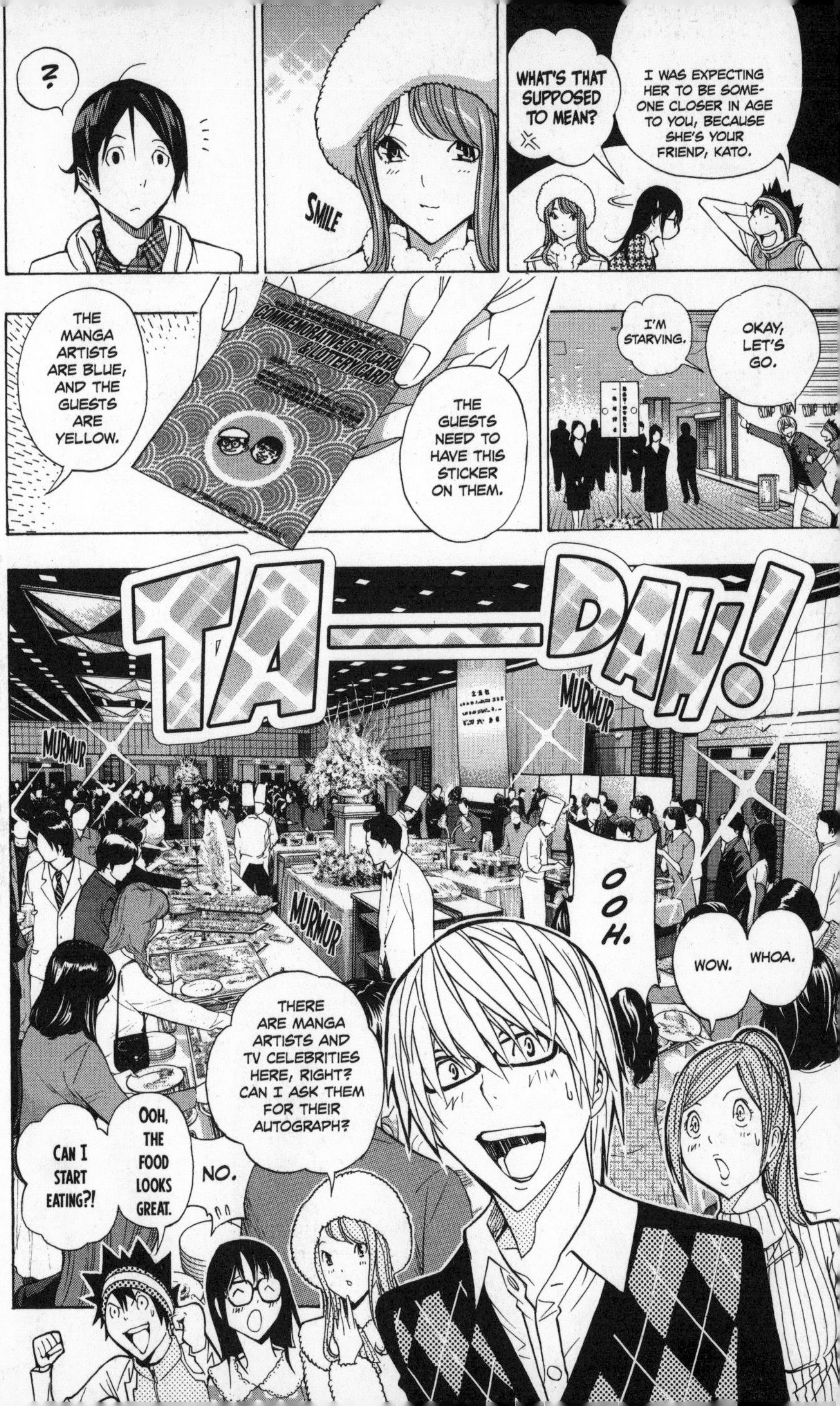
I WAS EXPECTING HER TO BE SOME-ONE CLOSER IN AGE TO YOU, BECAUSE SHE'S YOUR FRIEND, KATO.
WHAT'S THAT SUPPOSED TO MEAN?
SMILE
?
OKAY, LET'S GO.
I'M STARVING.
THE GUESTS NEED TO HAVE THIS STICKER ON THEM.
THE MANGA ARTISTS ARE BLUE, AND THE GUESTS ARE YELLOW.
COMMEMORATIVE GIFT CARD & LOTTERY CARD
TA——DAH!
MURMUR
MURMUR
MURMUR
OOH.
WOW.
WHOA.
THERE ARE MANGA ARTISTS AND TV CELEBRITIES HERE, RIGHT? CAN I ASK THEM FOR THEIR AUTOGRAPH?
NO.
OOH, THE FOOD LOOKS GREAT.
CAN I START EATING?!

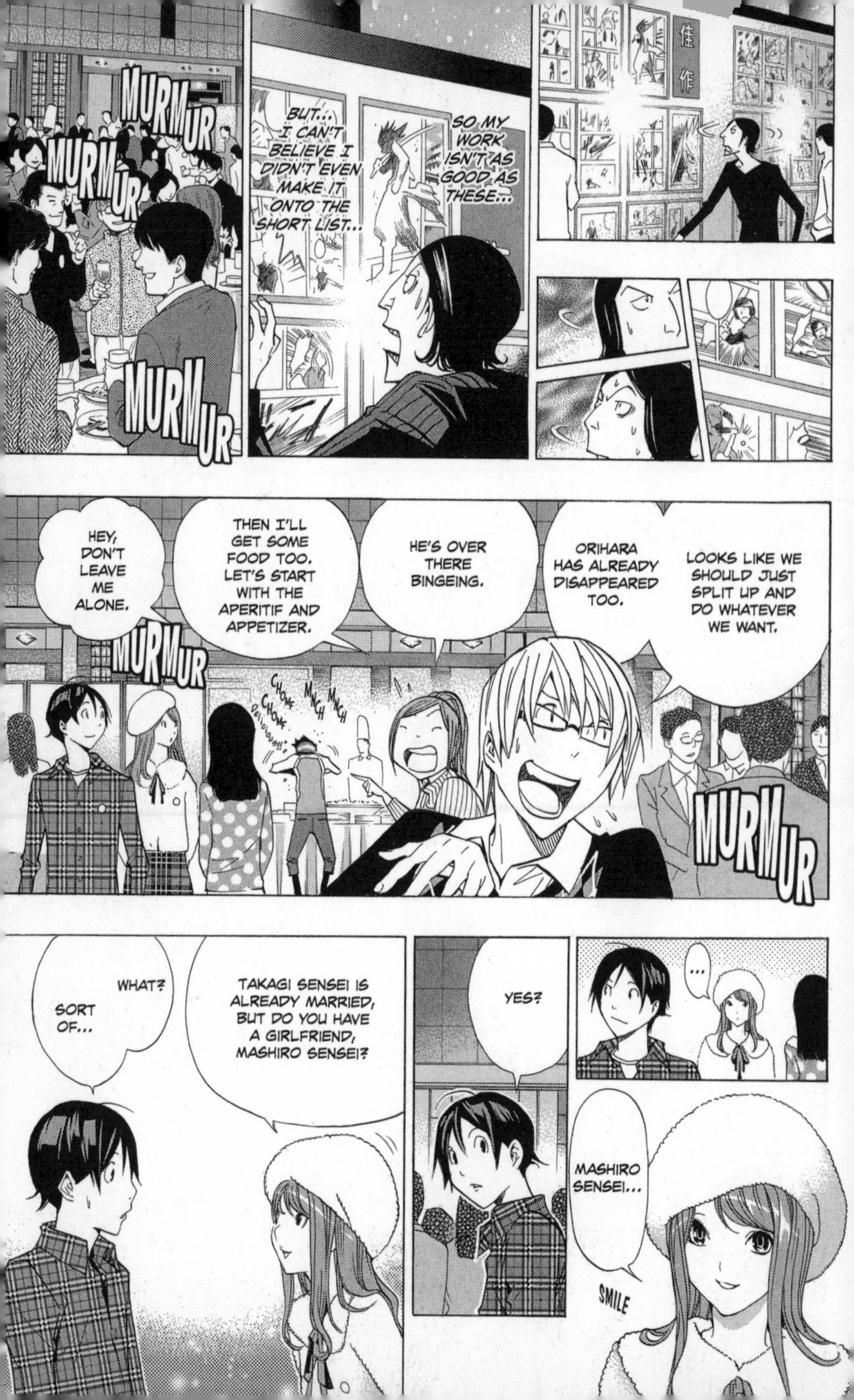
SO MY WORK ISN'T AS GOOD AS THESE...
BUT... I CAN'T BELIEVE I DIDN'T EVEN MAKE IT ONTO THE SHORT LIST...
MURMUR
MURMUR
MURMUR
LOOKS LIKE WE SHOULD JUST SPLIT UP AND DO WHATEVER WE WANT.
ORIHARA HAS ALREADY DISAPPEARED TOO.
HE'S OVER THERE BINGEING.
THEN I'LL GET SOME FOOD TOO. LET'S START WITH THE APERITIF AND APPETIZER.
HEY, DON'T LEAVE ME ALONE.
MURMUR
MNCH MNCH
CHOMF CHOMF
Delicious!!
MURMUR
...
YES?
TAKAGI SENSEI IS ALREADY MARRIED, BUT DO YOU HAVE A GIRLFRIEND, MASHIRO SENSEI?
WHAT?
SORT OF...
MASHIRO SENSEI...
SMILE

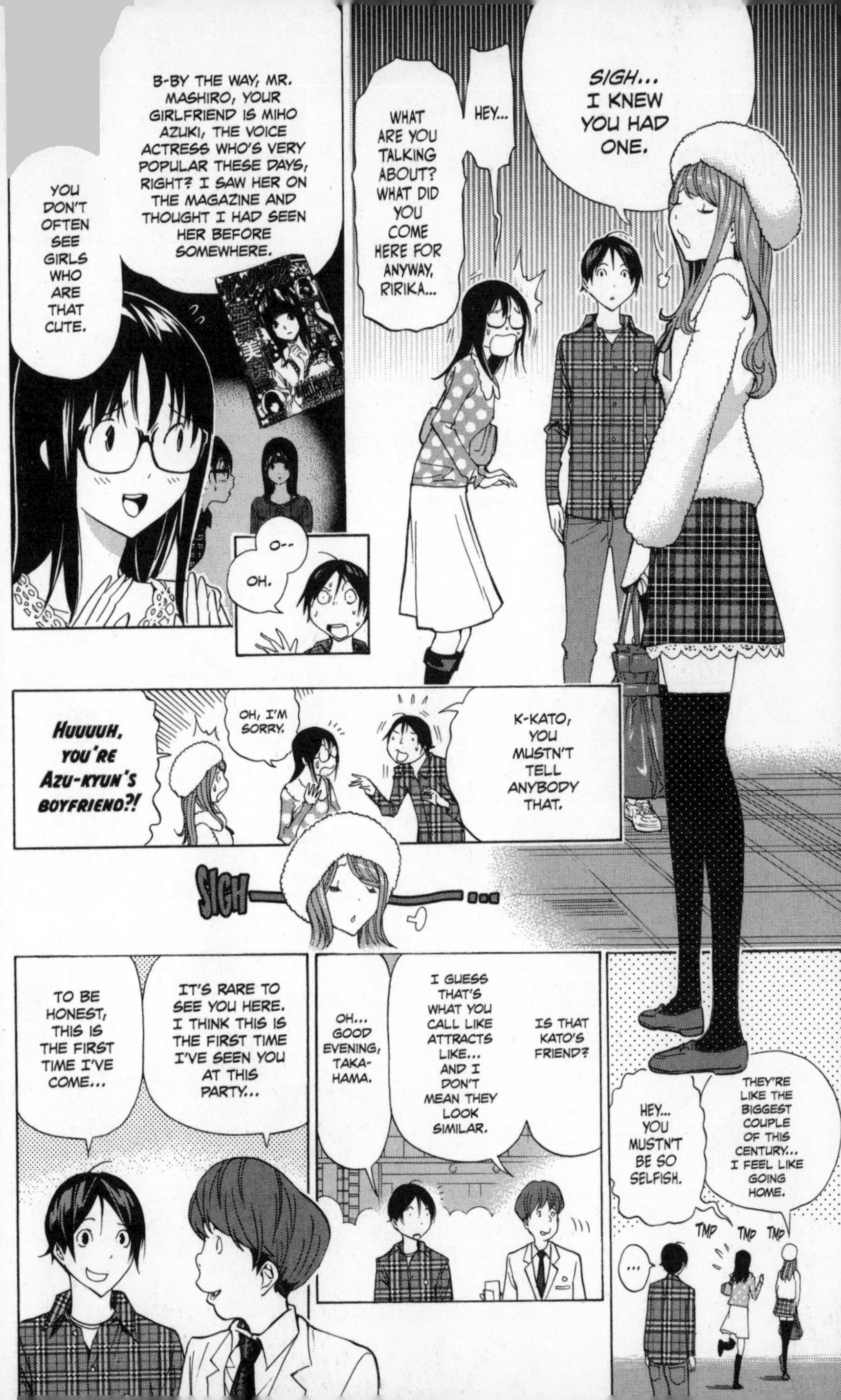
SIGH... I KNEW YOU HAD ONE.
HEY...
WHAT ARE YOU TALKING ABOUT? WHAT DID YOU COME HERE FOR ANYWAY, RIRIKA...
B-BY THE WAY, MR. MASHIRO, YOUR GIRLFRIEND IS MIHO AZUKI, THE VOICE ACTRESS WHO'S VERY POPULAR THESE DAYS, RIGHT? I SAW HER ON THE MAGAZINE AND THOUGHT I HAD SEEN HER BEFORE SOMEWHERE.
YOU DON'T OFTEN SEE GIRLS WHO ARE THAT CUTE.
O-- OH.
K-KATO, YOU MUSTN'T TELL ANYBODY THAT.
OH, I'M SORRY.
HUUUUH, YOU'RE AZU-KYUN'S BOYFRIEND?!
SIGH...
THEY'RE LIKE THE BIGGEST COUPLE OF THIS CENTURY... I FEEL LIKE GOING HOME.
HEY... YOU MUSTN'T BE SO SELFISH.
TMP TMP TMP
...
IS THAT KATO'S FRIEND?
I GUESS THAT'S WHAT YOU CALL LIKE ATTRACTS LIKE... AND I DON'T MEAN THEY LOOK SIMILAR.
OH... GOOD EVENING, TAKA-HAMA.
IT'S RARE TO SEE YOU HERE. I THINK THIS IS THE FIRST TIME I'VE SEEN YOU AT THIS PARTY...
TO BE HONEST, THIS IS THE FIRST TIME I'VE COME...

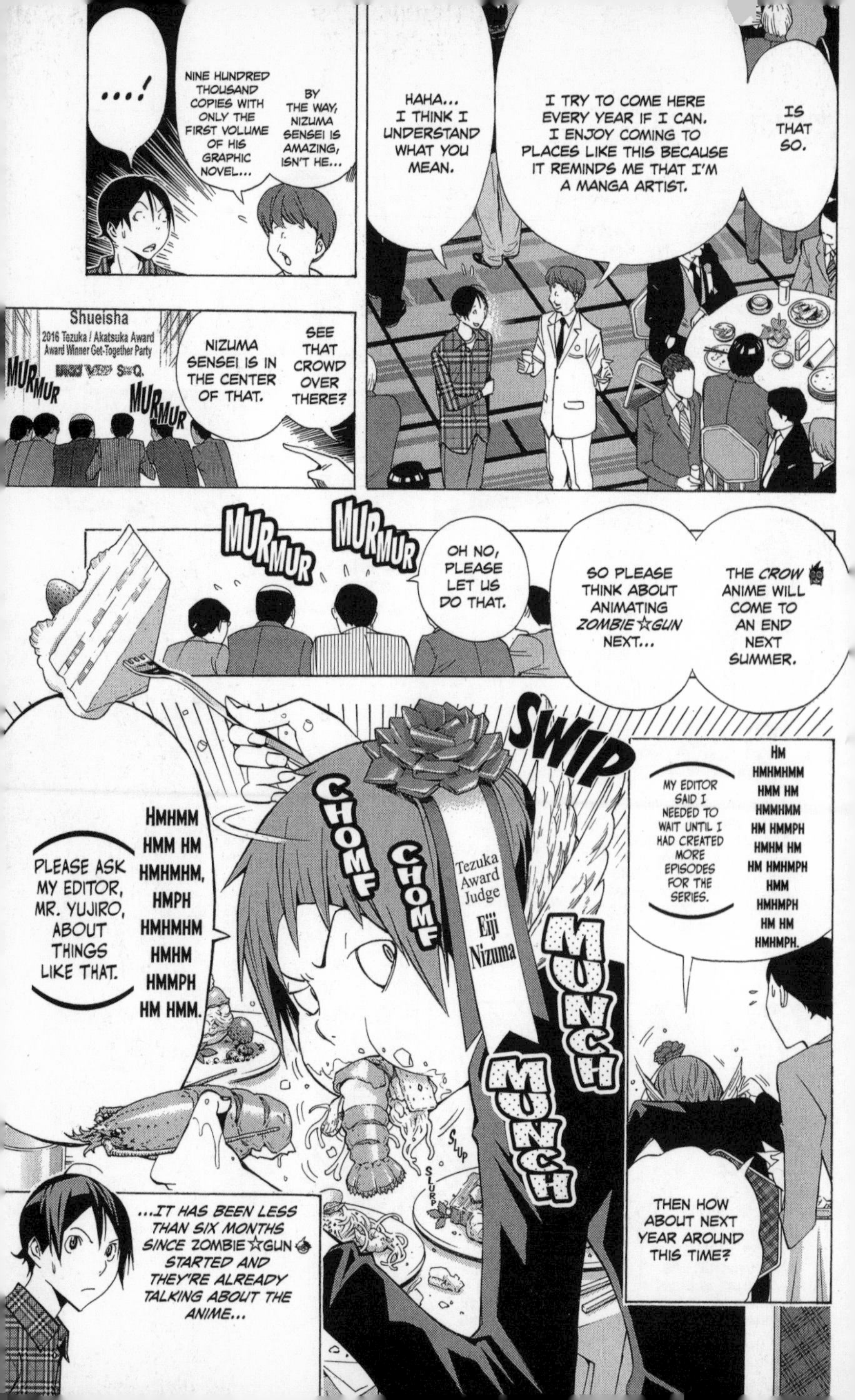
IS THAT SO.
I TRY TO COME HERE EVERY YEAR IF I CAN. I ENJOY COMING TO PLACES LIKE THIS BECAUSE IT REMINDS ME THAT I'M A MANGA ARTIST.
HAHA... I THINK I UNDERSTAND WHAT YOU MEAN.
BY THE WAY, NIZUMA SENSEI IS AMAZING, ISN'T HE...
NINE HUNDRED THOUSAND COPIES WITH ONLY THE FIRST VOLUME OF HIS GRAPHIC NOVEL...
...!
SEE THAT CROWD OVER THERE?
NIZUMA SENSEI IS IN THE CENTER OF THAT.
Shueisha
2016 Tezuka / Akatsuka Award
Award Winner Get-Together Party
MURMUR
MURMUR
THE CROW ANIME WILL COME TO AN END NEXT SUMMER.
SO PLEASE THINK ABOUT ANIMATING ZOMBIE☆GUN NEXT...
OH NO, PLEASE LET US DO THAT.
MURMUR
MURMUR
HM HMHMHMM HMM HM HMMHMM HM HMMPH HMHM HM HM HMHMPH HMM HMHMPH HM HM HMHMPH.
MY EDITOR SAID I NEEDED TO WAIT UNTIL I HAD CREATED MORE EPISODES FOR THE SERIES.
SWIP
CHOMF
CHOMF
Tezuka Award Judge Eiji Nizuma
HMHMM HMM HM HMHMHM, HMPH HMHMHM HMHM HMMPH HM HMM.
PLEASE ASK MY EDITOR, MR. YUJIRO, ABOUT THINGS LIKE THAT.
MUNCH
MUNCH
SLUP
SLURP
THEN HOW ABOUT NEXT YEAR AROUND THIS TIME?
...IT HAS BEEN LESS THAN SIX MONTHS SINCE ZOMBIE☆GUN STARTED AND THEY'RE ALREADY TALKING ABOUT THE ANIME...

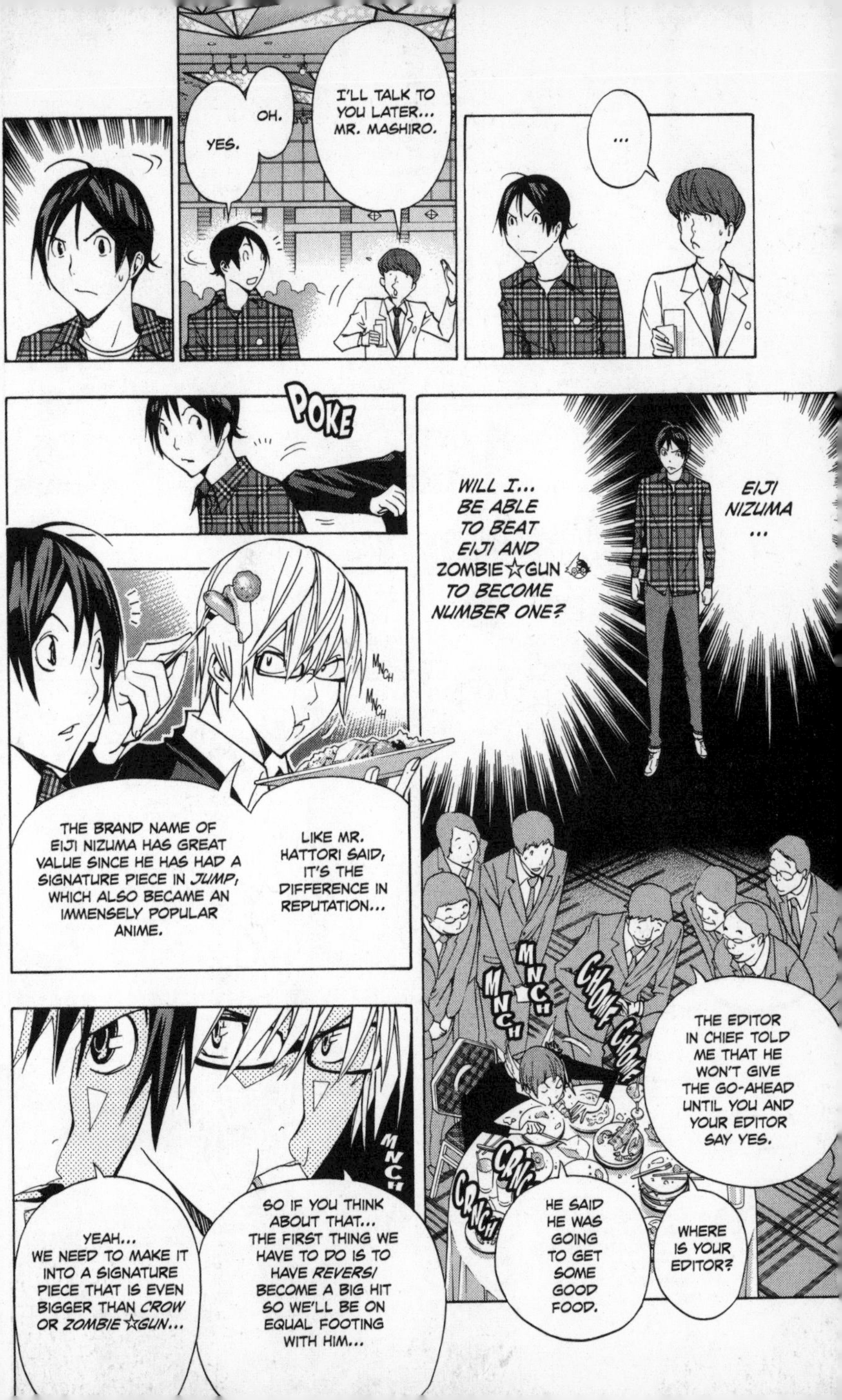
...
I'LL TALK TO YOU LATER... MR. MASHIRO.
OH.
YES.
EIJI NIZUMA ...
WILL I... BE ABLE TO BEAT EIJI AND ZOMBIE☆GUN TO BECOME NUMBER ONE?
THE EDITOR IN CHIEF TOLD ME THAT HE WON'T GIVE THE GO-AHEAD UNTIL YOU AND YOUR EDITOR SAY YES.
CHOMP CHOMP
MNCH
MNCH
WHERE IS YOUR EDITOR?
HE SAID HE WAS GOING TO GET SOME GOOD FOOD.
CRNCH
CRNCH
POKE
MNCH
MNCH
LIKE MR. HATTORI SAID, IT'S THE DIFFERENCE IN REPUTATION...
THE BRAND NAME OF EIJI NIZUMA HAS GREAT VALUE SINCE HE HAS HAD A SIGNATURE PIECE IN JUMP, WHICH ALSO BECAME AN IMMENSELY POPULAR ANIME.
MNCH
SO IF YOU THINK ABOUT THAT... THE FIRST THING WE HAVE TO DO IS TO HAVE REVERSI BECOME A BIG HIT SO WE'LL BE ON EQUAL FOOTING WITH HIM...
YEAH... WE NEED TO MAKE IT INTO A SIGNATURE PIECE THAT IS EVEN BIGGER THAN CROW OR ZOMBIE☆GUN...

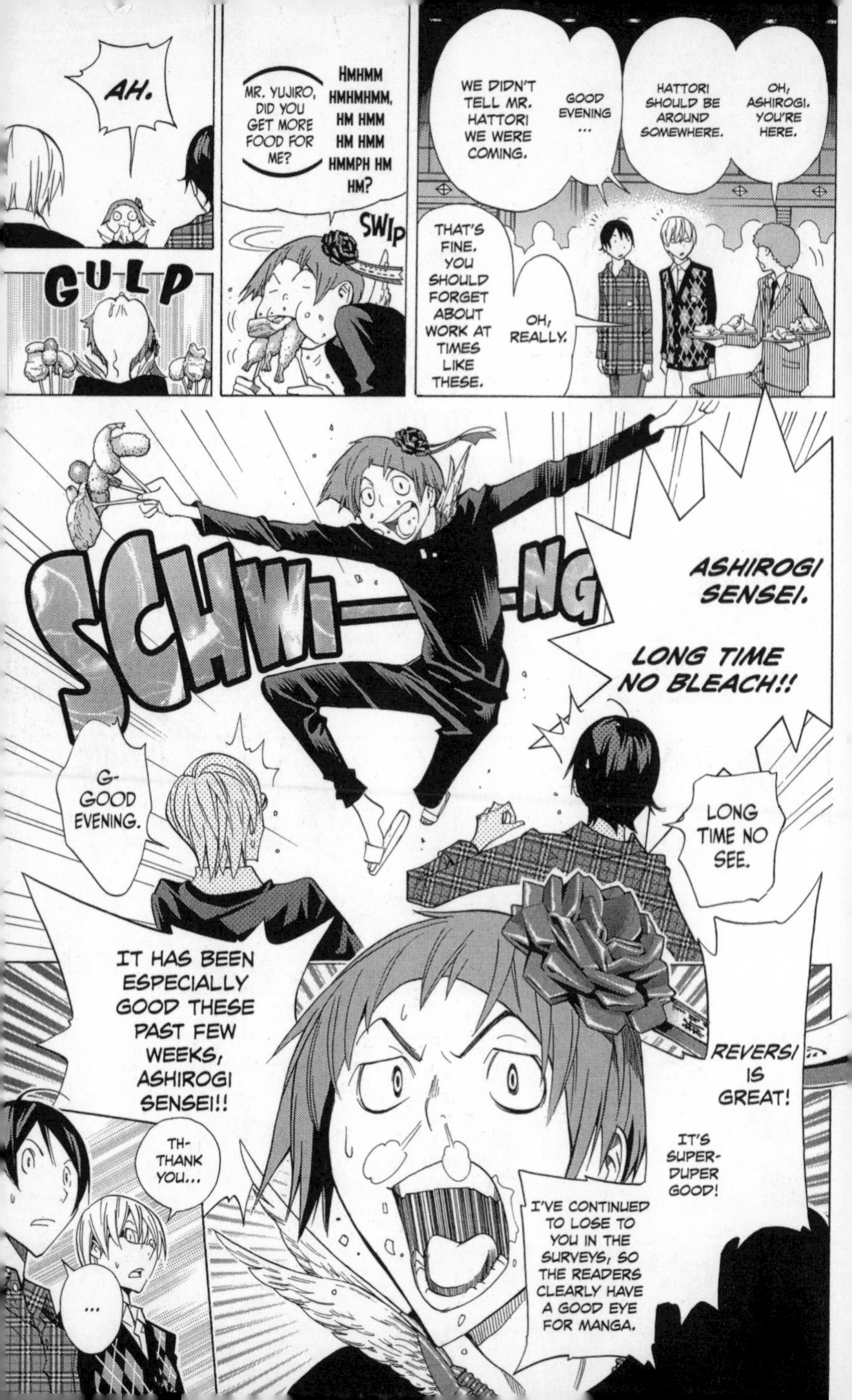
OH, ASHIROGI. YOU'RE HERE.
HATTORI SHOULD BE AROUND SOMEWHERE.
GOOD EVENING ...
WE DIDN'T TELL MR. HATTORI WE WERE COMING.
OH, REALLY.
THAT'S FINE. YOU SHOULD FORGET ABOUT WORK AT TIMES LIKE THESE.
HMHMM HMHMHMM, HM HMM HM HMM HMMPH HM HM?
MR. YUJIRO, DID YOU GET MORE FOOD FOR ME?
SWIP
AH.
GULP
ASHIROGI SENSEI.
LONG TIME NO BLEACH!!
SCHWI---NG
LONG TIME NO SEE.
G-GOOD EVENING.
REVERSI IS GREAT!
IT'S SUPER-DUPER GOOD!
I'VE CONTINUED TO LOSE TO YOU IN THE SURVEYS, SO THE READERS CLEARLY HAVE A GOOD EYE FOR MANGA.
IT HAS BEEN ESPECIALLY GOOD THESE PAST FEW WEEKS, ASHIROGI SENSEI!!
TH-THANK YOU...
...

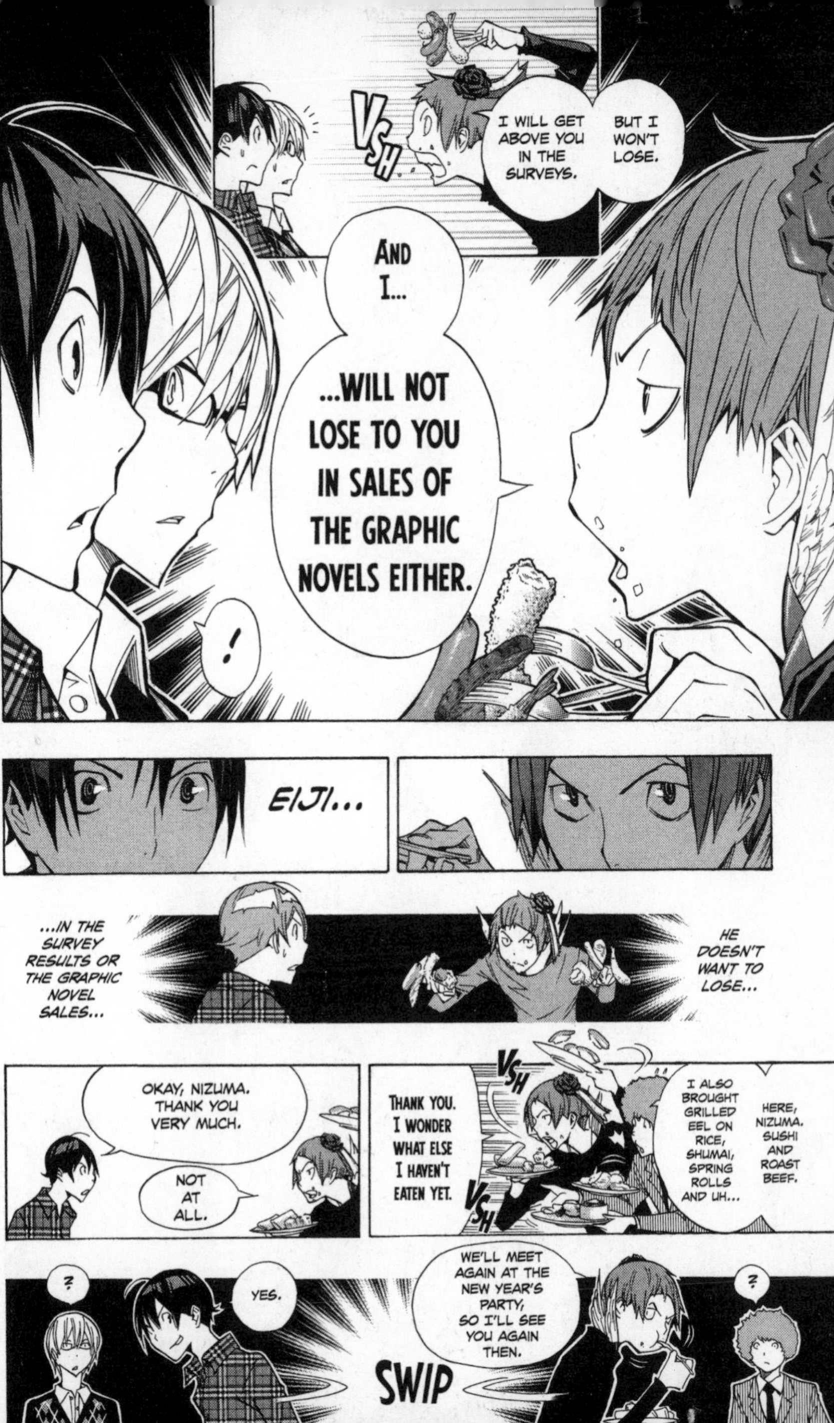
BUT I WON'T LOSE.
I WILL GET ABOVE YOU IN THE SURVEYS.
VSH
AND I...
...WILL NOT LOSE TO YOU IN SALES OF THE GRAPHIC NOVELS EITHER.
!
EIJI...
HE DOESN'T WANT TO LOSE...
...IN THE SURVEY RESULTS OR THE GRAPHIC NOVEL SALES...
HERE, NIZUMA. SUSHI AND ROAST BEEF.
I ALSO BROUGHT GRILLED EEL ON RICE, SHUMAI, SPRING ROLLS AND UH...
VSH
THANK YOU. I WONDER WHAT ELSE I HAVEN'T EATEN YET.
VSH
OKAY, NIZUMA. THANK YOU VERY MUCH.
NOT AT ALL.
?
WE'LL MEET AGAIN AT THE NEW YEAR'S PARTY, SO I'LL SEE YOU AGAIN THEN.
SWIP
YES.
?

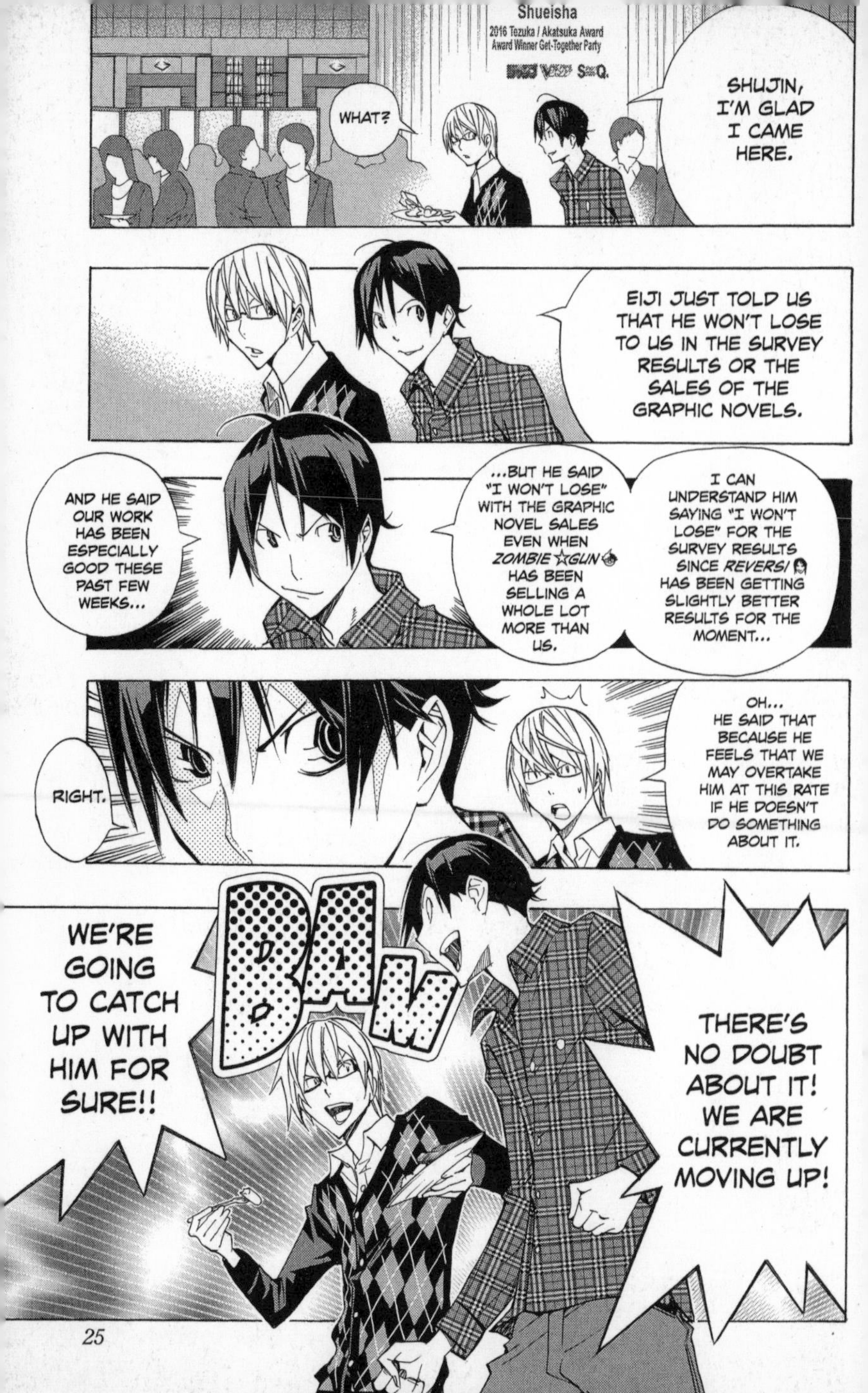
Shueisha
2016 Tezuka / Akatsuka Award
Award Winner Get-Together Party
SHUJIN, I'M GLAD I CAME HERE.
WHAT?
EIJI JUST TOLD US THAT HE WON'T LOSE TO US IN THE SURVEY RESULTS OR THE SALES OF THE GRAPHIC NOVELS.
I CAN UNDERSTAND HIM SAYING "I WON'T LOSE" FOR THE SURVEY RESULTS SINCE *REVERSI* HAS BEEN GETTING SLIGHTLY BETTER RESULTS FOR THE MOMENT...
...BUT HE SAID "I WON'T LOSE" WITH THE GRAPHIC NOVEL SALES EVEN WHEN *ZOMBIE☆GUN* HAS BEEN SELLING A WHOLE LOT MORE THAN US.
AND HE SAID OUR WORK HAS BEEN ESPECIALLY GOOD THESE PAST FEW WEEKS...
OH... HE SAID THAT BECAUSE HE FEELS THAT WE MAY OVERTAKE HIM AT THIS RATE IF HE DOESN'T DO SOMETHING ABOUT IT.
RIGHT.
THERE'S NO DOUBT ABOUT IT! WE ARE CURRENTLY MOVING UP!
DAM
WE'RE GOING TO CATCH UP WITH HIM FOR SURE!!

OHBA'S STORYBOARD

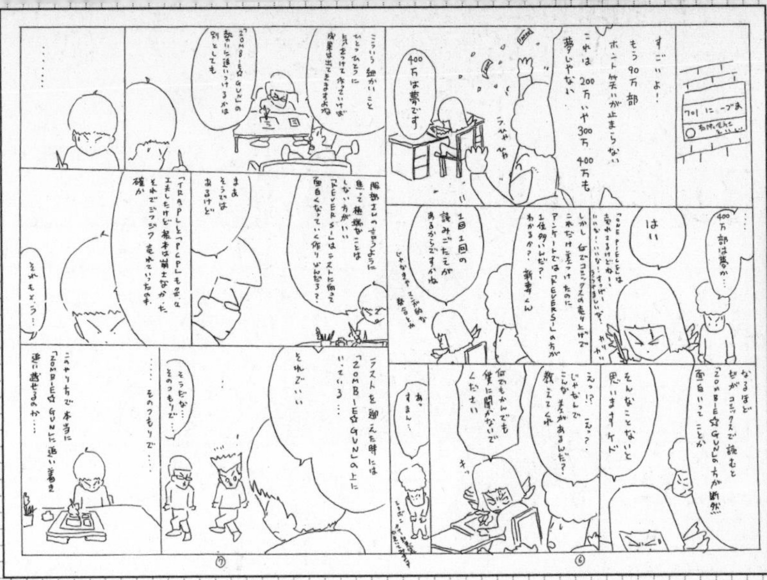
701 にーづま
すごいよ！ もう90万部 ホント笑いが止まらない これは200万 いや300万 400万も 夢じゃない
400万は夢です
400万部は夢か……
はい
「ONE PIECE」は凄いな…いいな…
しかし 台でコミックスの売り上げでこれだけ差つけたのにアンケートでは「REVERSI」の方が上位多いんだぜ？ わかるか？ 新妻くん
1回1回の読みごたえがあるからですかね
なるほど 甘がコミックスで読むと「ZOMBIE☆GUN」の方が断然面白いってことか
そんなことないと思いますケド
えっ！？ えっ？ じゃなんでこんな差があるんだ？ 教えてくれ
何でもかんでも僕に聞かないでください
あっ すまん…
こういう細かいこと ひとつひとつに気をつけて作っていけば成果は出てきますよね
「ZOMBIE☆GUN」の勢いに追いつけるかは別としても
……
服部さんの言うように焦って極端なことはしない方がいい 「REVERSI」はラストに向けて面白くなっていく作りじゃないか？
まぁ そうではあるけど
「TRAP」と「PCP」も発エましたけど根本は崩せなかった それでジワジワ売れていったのは確か
それもそう…
ラストを迎えた時には「ZOMBIE☆GUN」の上にいっている…
それでいい
そうだな… そのつもりで…
…そのつもりで…
このやり方で本当に「ZOMBIE☆GUN」に追い着き追い越せるのか…

OBATA'S STORYBOARD

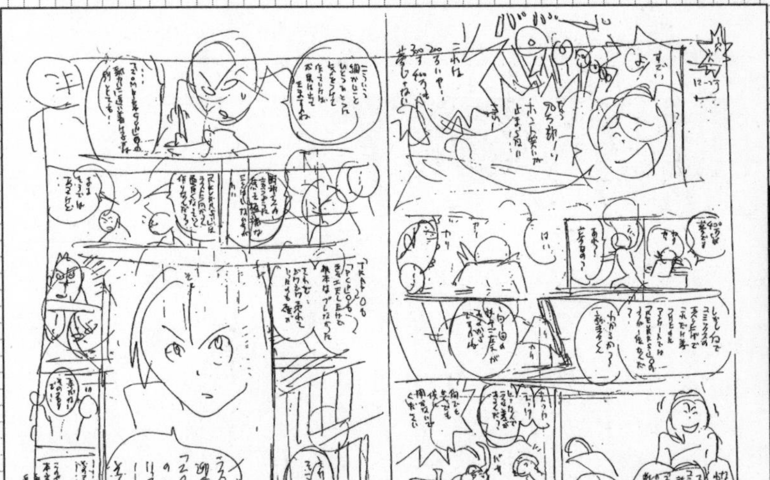

COMPLETE!

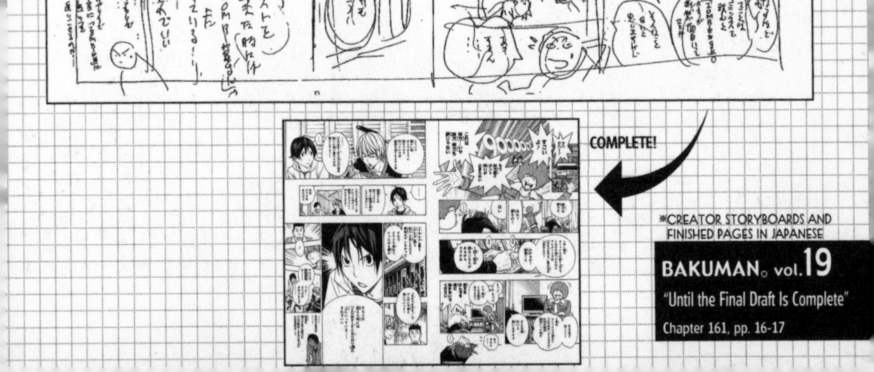

※CREATOR STORYBOARDS AND FINISHED PAGES IN JAPANESE

BAKUMAN。 vol.19

"Until the Final Draft Is Complete"

Chapter 161, pp. 16-17

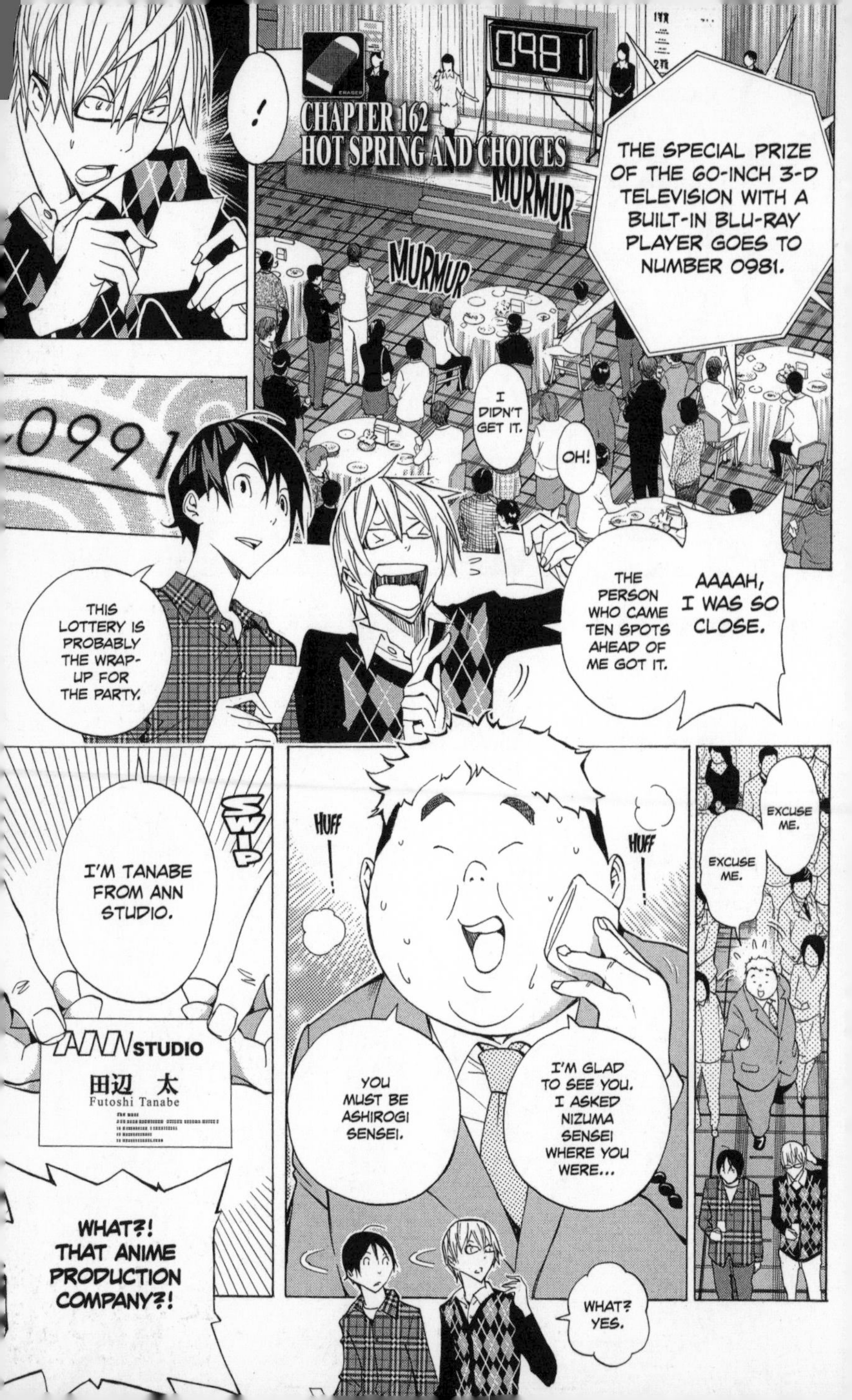
CHAPTER 162
HOT SPRING AND CHOICES
THE SPECIAL PRIZE OF THE 60-INCH 3-D TELEVISION WITH A BUILT-IN BLU-RAY PLAYER GOES TO NUMBER 0981.
MURMUR
MURMUR
I DIDN'T GET IT.
OH!
!
0991
AAAAH, I WAS SO CLOSE.
THE PERSON WHO CAME TEN SPOTS AHEAD OF ME GOT IT.
THIS LOTTERY IS PROBABLY THE WRAP-UP FOR THE PARTY.
EXCUSE ME.
EXCUSE ME.
HUFF
HUFF
I'M GLAD TO SEE YOU. I ASKED NIZUMA SENSEI WHERE YOU WERE...
YOU MUST BE ASHIROGI SENSEI.
WHAT? YES.
SWIP
I'M TANABE FROM ANN STUDIO.
ANN STUDIO
田辺 太
Futoshi Tanabe
WHAT?! THAT ANIME PRODUCTION COMPANY?!

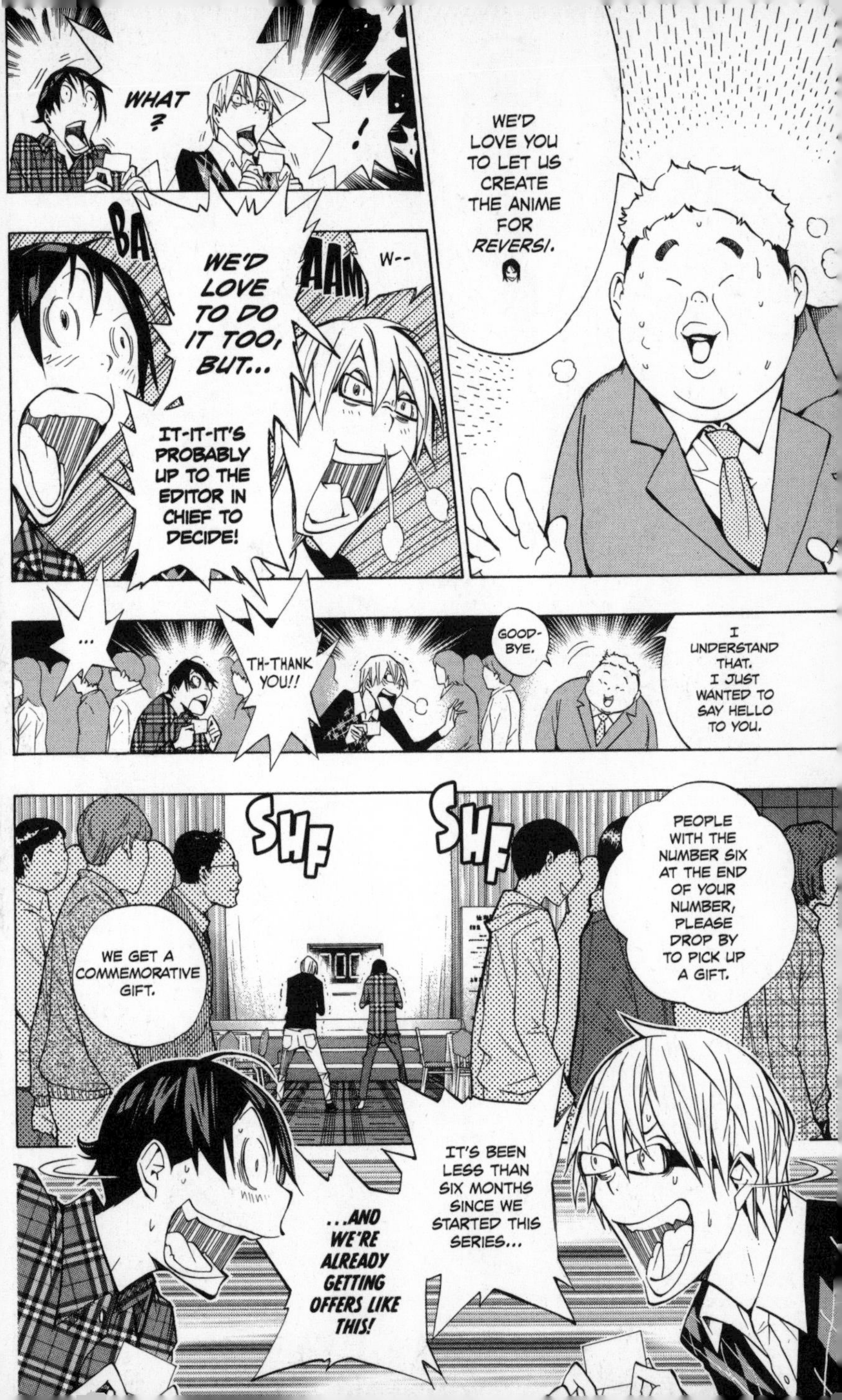
WE'D LOVE YOU TO LET US CREATE THE ANIME FOR REVERSI.
WHAT?
!
W--
BAAAM
WE'D LOVE TO DO IT TOO, BUT...
IT-IT-IT'S PROBABLY UP TO THE EDITOR IN CHIEF TO DECIDE!
I UNDERSTAND THAT. I JUST WANTED TO SAY HELLO TO YOU.
GOOD-BYE.
TH-THANK YOU!!
...
PEOPLE WITH THE NUMBER SIX AT THE END OF YOUR NUMBER, PLEASE DROP BY TO PICK UP A GIFT.
SHF
SHF
WE GET A COMMEMORATIVE GIFT.
IT'S BEEN LESS THAN SIX MONTHS SINCE WE STARTED THIS SERIES...
...AND WE'RE ALREADY GETTING OFFERS LIKE THIS!

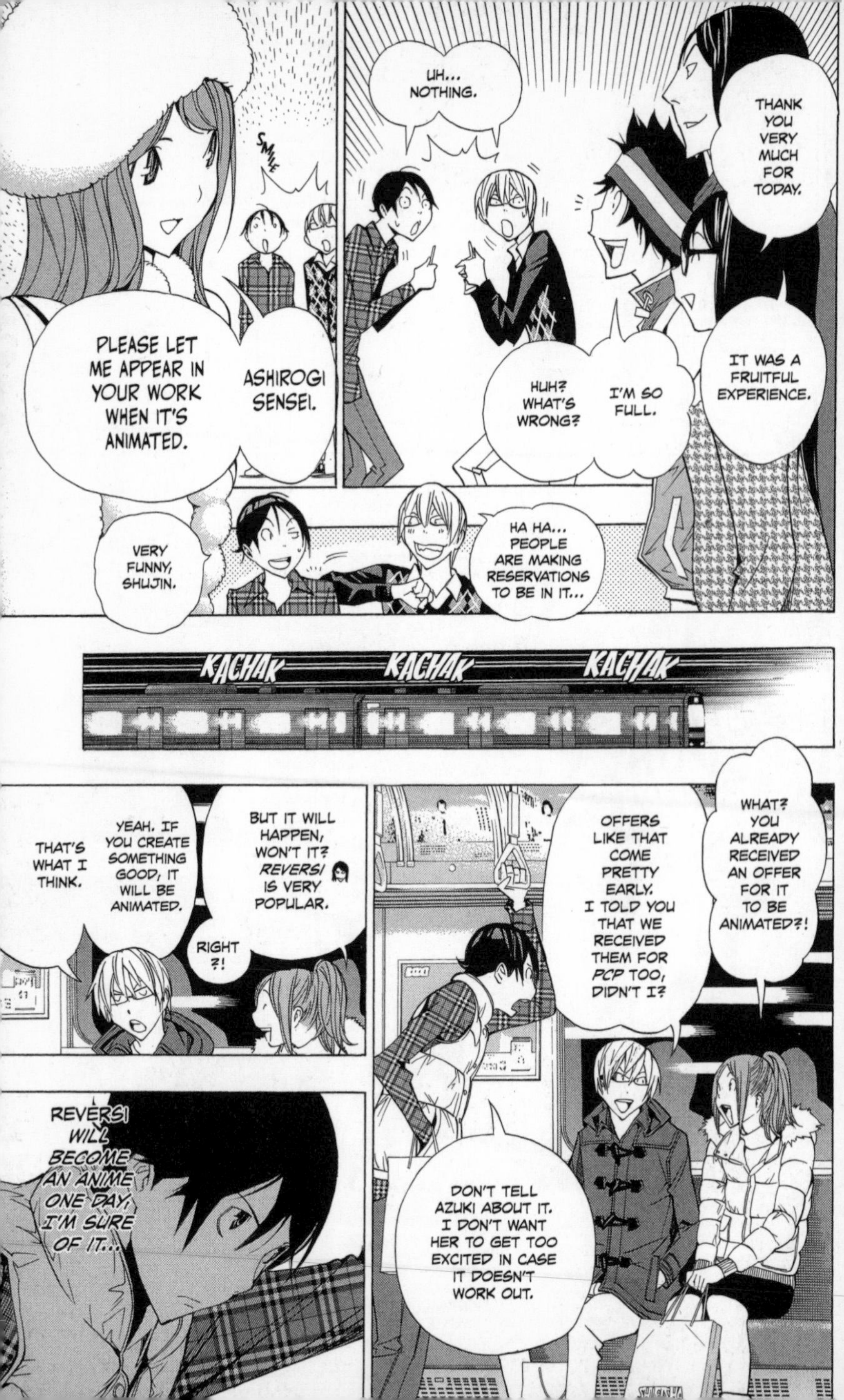
THANK YOU VERY MUCH FOR TODAY.
UH... NOTHING.
IT WAS A FRUITFUL EXPERIENCE.
I'M SO FULL.
HUH? WHAT'S WRONG?
SMILE
ASHIROGI SENSEI.
PLEASE LET ME APPEAR IN YOUR WORK WHEN IT'S ANIMATED.
HA HA... PEOPLE ARE MAKING RESERVATIONS TO BE IN IT...
VERY FUNNY, SHUJIN.
KACHAK
KACHAK
KACHAK
WHAT? YOU ALREADY RECEIVED AN OFFER FOR IT TO BE ANIMATED?!
OFFERS LIKE THAT COME PRETTY EARLY. I TOLD YOU THAT WE RECEIVED THEM FOR PCP TOO, DIDN'T I?
DON'T TELL AZUKI ABOUT IT. I DON'T WANT HER TO GET TOO EXCITED IN CASE IT DOESN'T WORK OUT.
BUT IT WILL HAPPEN, WON'T IT? REVERSI IS VERY POPULAR.
YEAH. IF YOU CREATE SOMETHING GOOD, IT WILL BE ANIMATED.
THAT'S WHAT I THINK.
RIGHT?!
REVERSI WILL BECOME AN ANIME ONE DAY, I'M SURE OF IT...

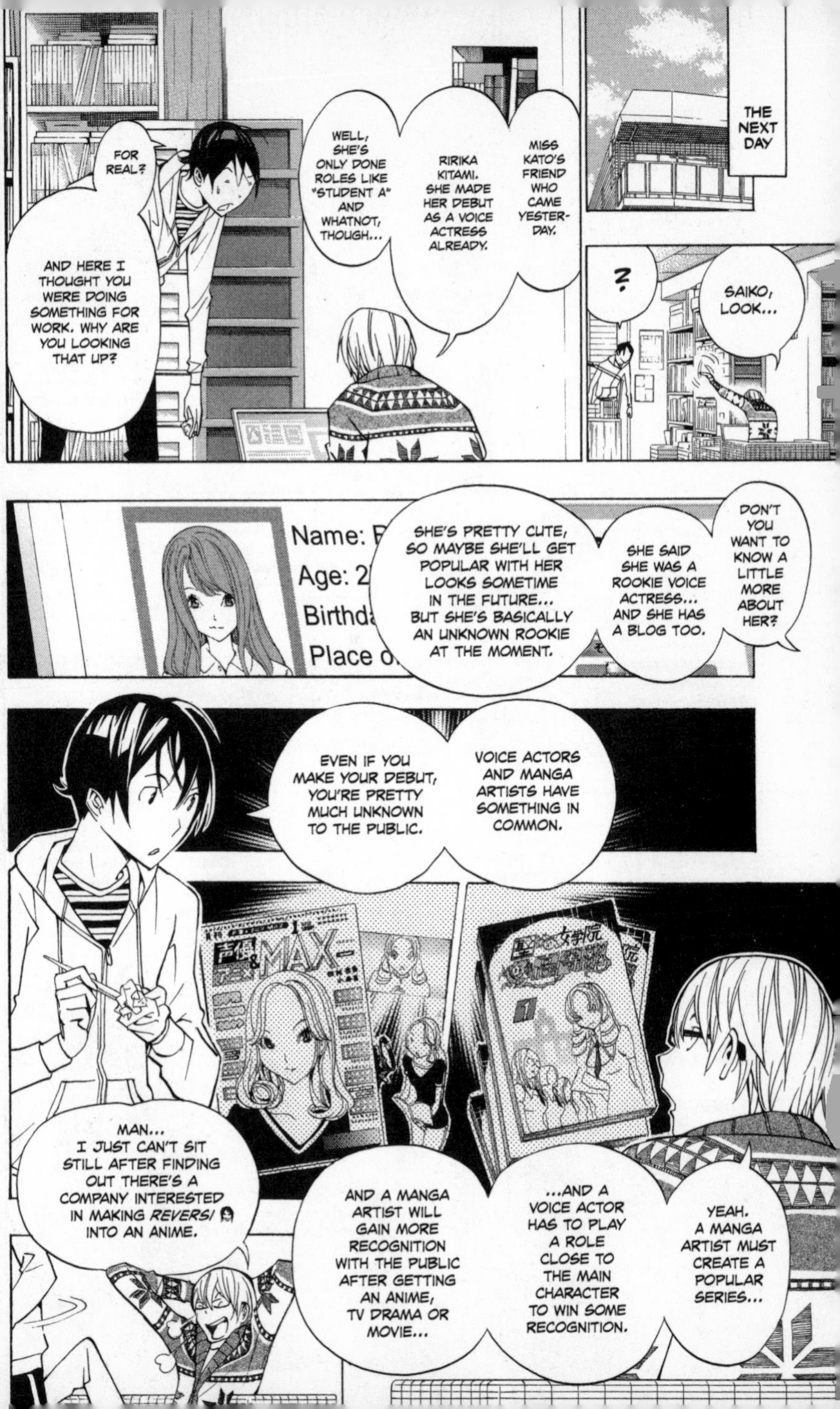
THE NEXT DAY
SAIKO, LOOK...
?
MISS KATO'S FRIEND WHO CAME YESTER-DAY.
RIRIKA KITAMI. SHE MADE HER DEBUT AS A VOICE ACTRESS ALREADY.
WELL, SHE'S ONLY DONE ROLES LIKE "STUDENT A" AND WHATNOT, THOUGH...
FOR REAL?
AND HERE I THOUGHT YOU WERE DOING SOMETHING FOR WORK. WHY ARE YOU LOOKING THAT UP?
DON'T YOU WANT TO KNOW A LITTLE MORE ABOUT HER?
SHE SAID SHE WAS A ROOKIE VOICE ACTRESS... AND SHE HAS A BLOG TOO.
SHE'S PRETTY CUTE, SO MAYBE SHE'LL GET POPULAR WITH HER LOOKS SOMETIME IN THE FUTURE... BUT SHE'S BASICALLY AN UNKNOWN ROOKIE AT THE MOMENT.
Name: R
Age: 2
Birthda
Place o
VOICE ACTORS AND MANGA ARTISTS HAVE SOMETHING IN COMMON.
EVEN IF YOU MAKE YOUR DEBUT, YOU'RE PRETTY MUCH UNKNOWN TO THE PUBLIC.
YEAH. A MANGA ARTIST MUST CREATE A POPULAR SERIES...
...AND A VOICE ACTOR HAS TO PLAY A ROLE CLOSE TO THE MAIN CHARACTER TO WIN SOME RECOGNITION.
AND A MANGA ARTIST WILL GAIN MORE RECOGNITION WITH THE PUBLIC AFTER GETTING AN ANIME, TV DRAMA OR MOVIE...
MAN... I JUST CAN'T SIT STILL AFTER FINDING OUT THERE'S A COMPANY INTERESTED IN MAKING *REVERSI* INTO AN ANIME.

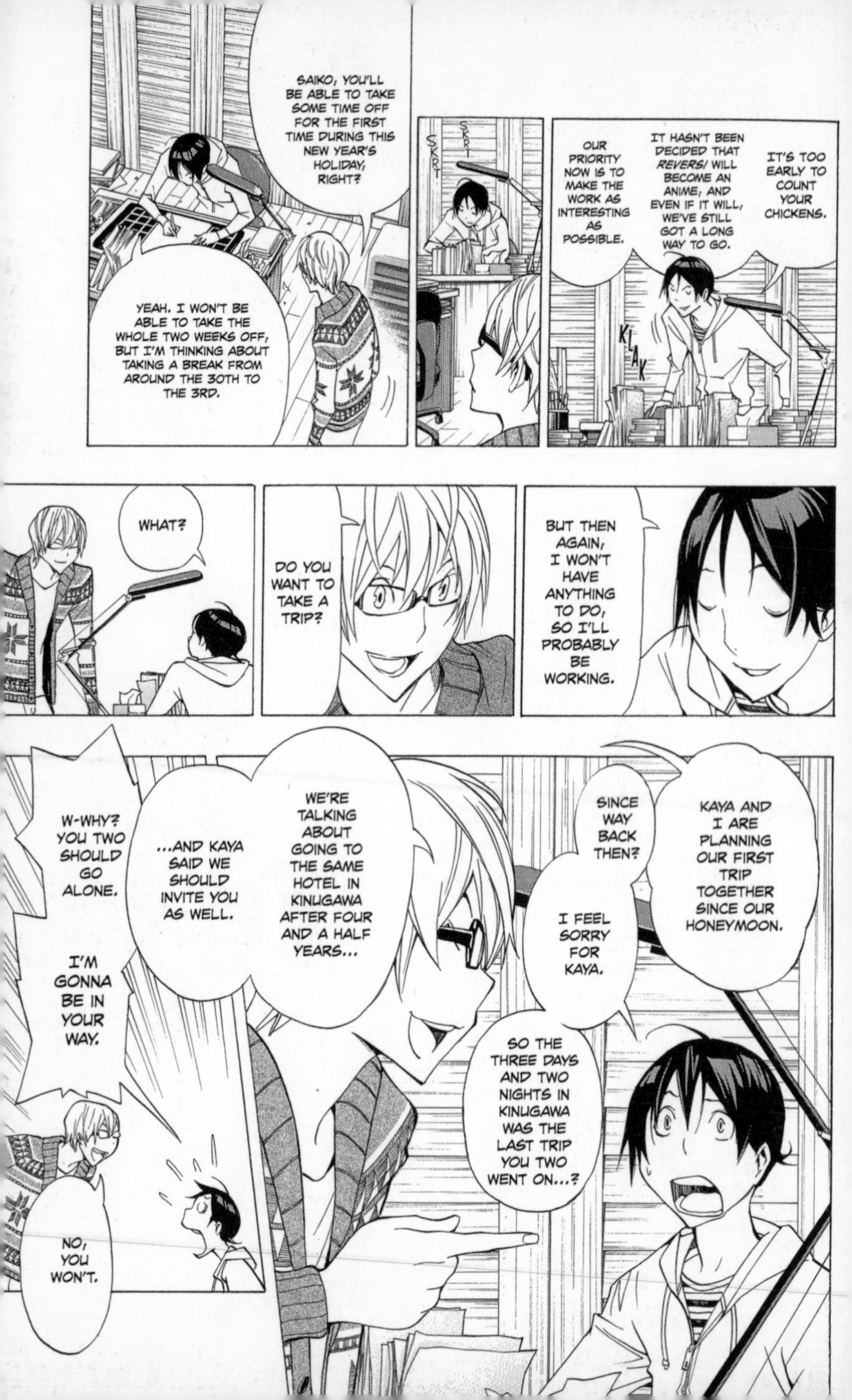
IT'S TOO EARLY TO COUNT YOUR CHICKENS.
IT HASN'T BEEN DECIDED THAT *REVERS!* WILL BECOME AN ANIME, AND EVEN IF IT WILL, WE'VE STILL GOT A LONG WAY TO GO.
OUR PRIORITY NOW IS TO MAKE THE WORK AS INTERESTING AS POSSIBLE.
KLAK
SKRT SKRT
SAIKO, YOU'LL BE ABLE TO TAKE SOME TIME OFF FOR THE FIRST TIME DURING THIS NEW YEAR'S HOLIDAY, RIGHT?
YEAH. I WON'T BE ABLE TO TAKE THE WHOLE TWO WEEKS OFF, BUT I'M THINKING ABOUT TAKING A BREAK FROM AROUND THE 30TH TO THE 3RD.
BUT THEN AGAIN, I WON'T HAVE ANYTHING TO DO, SO I'LL PROBABLY BE WORKING.
DO YOU WANT TO TAKE A TRIP?
WHAT?
KAYA AND I ARE PLANNING OUR FIRST TRIP TOGETHER SINCE OUR HONEYMOON.
SINCE WAY BACK THEN?
I FEEL SORRY FOR KAYA.
SO THE THREE DAYS AND TWO NIGHTS IN KINUGAWA WAS THE LAST TRIP YOU TWO WENT ON...?
WE'RE TALKING ABOUT GOING TO THE SAME HOTEL IN KINUGAWA AFTER FOUR AND A HALF YEARS...
...AND KAYA SAID WE SHOULD INVITE YOU AS WELL.
W-WHY? YOU TWO SHOULD GO ALONE.
I'M GONNA BE IN YOUR WAY.
NO, YOU WON'T.

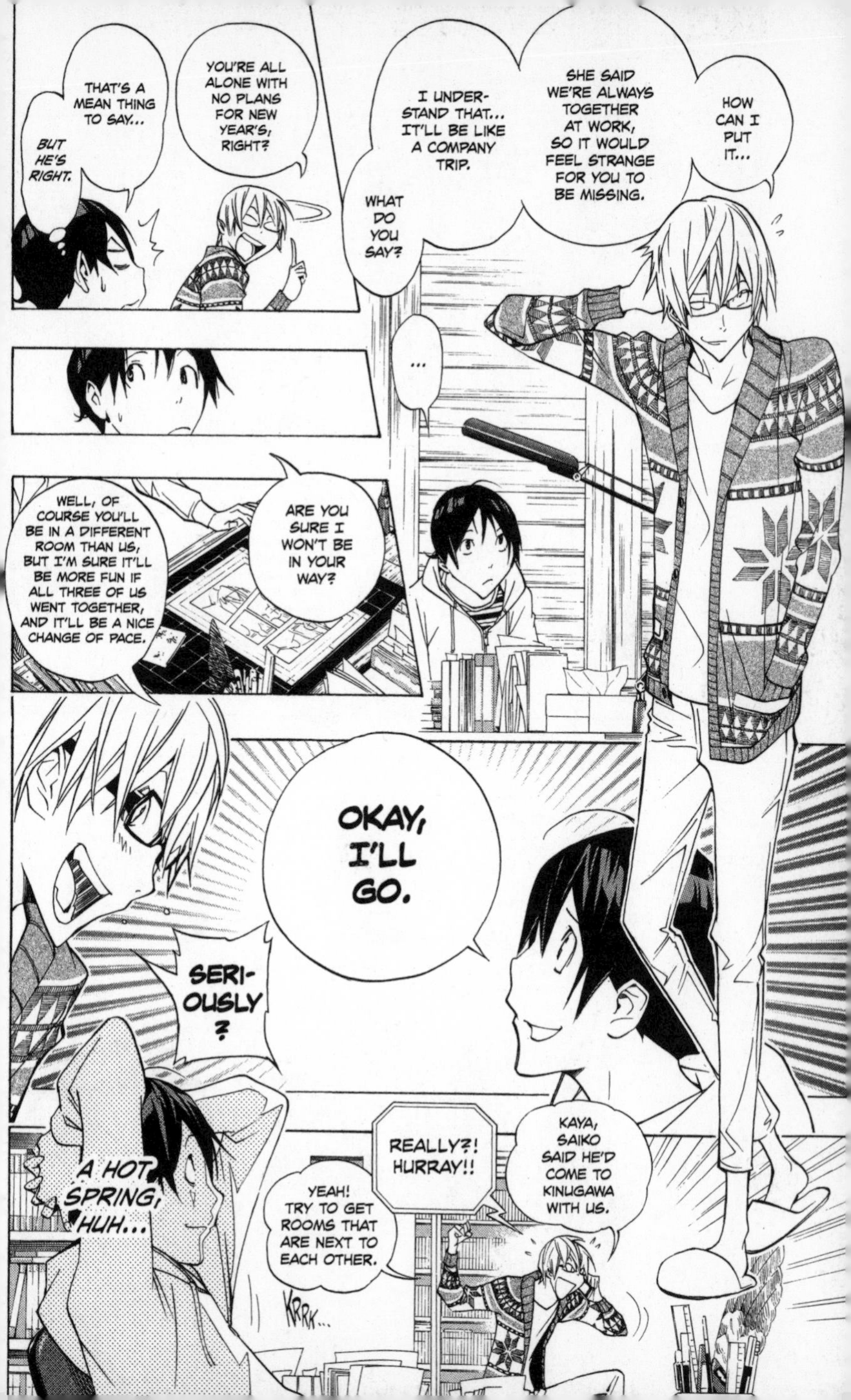
HOW CAN I PUT IT...
SHE SAID WE'RE ALWAYS TOGETHER AT WORK, SO IT WOULD FEEL STRANGE FOR YOU TO BE MISSING.
I UNDER-STAND THAT... IT'LL BE LIKE A COMPANY TRIP.
WHAT DO YOU SAY?
...
YOU'RE ALL ALONE WITH NO PLANS FOR NEW YEAR'S, RIGHT?
THAT'S A MEAN THING TO SAY...
BUT HE'S RIGHT.
ARE YOU SURE I WON'T BE IN YOUR WAY?
WELL, OF COURSE YOU'LL BE IN A DIFFERENT ROOM THAN US, BUT I'M SURE IT'LL BE MORE FUN IF ALL THREE OF US WENT TOGETHER, AND IT'LL BE A NICE CHANGE OF PACE.
OKAY, I'LL GO.
SERI-OUSLY?
KAYA, SAIKO SAID HE'D COME TO KINUGAWA WITH US.
REALLY?! HURRAY!!
YEAH! TRY TO GET ROOMS THAT ARE NEXT TO EACH OTHER.
KRRK...
A HOT SPRING, HUH...

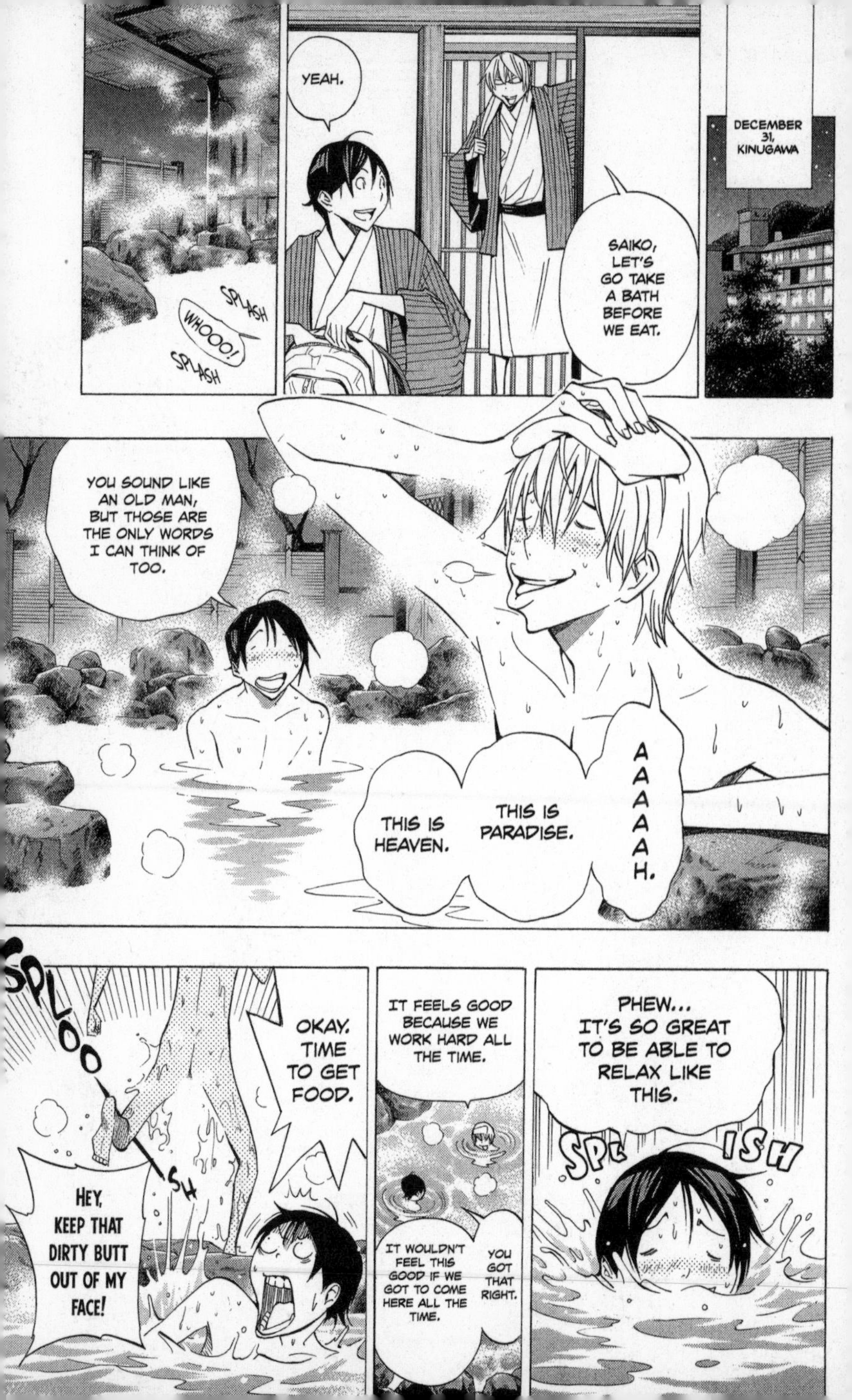
DECEMBER 31, KINUGAWA
SAIKO, LET'S GO TAKE A BATH BEFORE WE EAT.
YEAH.
SPLASH
WHOOO!
SPLASH
AAAAAAH.
THIS IS PARADISE.
THIS IS HEAVEN.
YOU SOUND LIKE AN OLD MAN, BUT THOSE ARE THE ONLY WORDS I CAN THINK OF TOO.
PHEW... IT'S SO GREAT TO BE ABLE TO RELAX LIKE THIS.
SPLISH
IT FEELS GOOD BECAUSE WE WORK HARD ALL THE TIME.
YOU GOT THAT RIGHT.
IT WOULDN'T FEEL THIS GOOD IF WE GOT TO COME HERE ALL THE TIME.
OKAY. TIME TO GET FOOD.
SPLOOSH
HEY, KEEP THAT DIRTY BUTT OUT OF MY FACE!

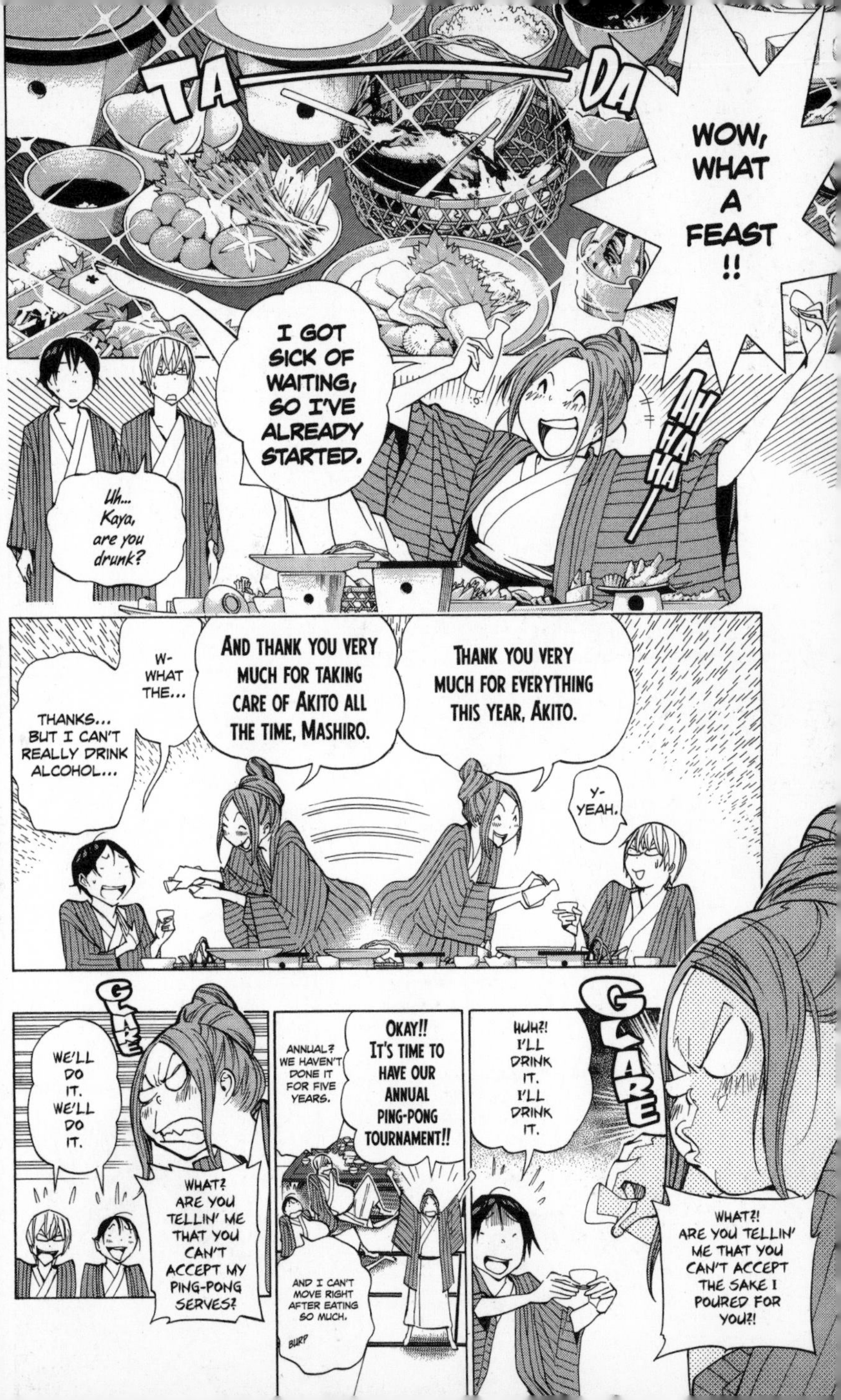
TA
DA
WOW, WHAT A FEAST!!
AHAHAHA
I GOT SICK OF WAITING, SO I'VE ALREADY STARTED.
Uh... Kaya, are you drunk?
THANK YOU VERY MUCH FOR EVERYTHING THIS YEAR, AKITO.
Y-YEAH.
AND THANK YOU VERY MUCH FOR TAKING CARE OF AKITO ALL THE TIME, MASHIRO.
W-WHAT THE...
THANKS... BUT I CAN'T REALLY DRINK ALCOHOL...
WHAT?! ARE YOU TELLIN' ME THAT YOU CAN'T ACCEPT THE SAKE I POURED FOR YOU?!
GLARE
HUH?! I'LL DRINK IT. I'LL DRINK IT.
OKAY!! IT'S TIME TO HAVE OUR ANNUAL PING-PONG TOURNAMENT!!
ANNUAL? WE HAVEN'T DONE IT FOR FIVE YEARS.
AND I CAN'T MOVE RIGHT AFTER EATING SO MUCH.
BURP
GLARE
WHAT? ARE YOU TELLIN' ME THAT YOU CAN'T ACCEPT MY PING-PONG SERVES?
WE'LL DO IT. WE'LL DO IT.

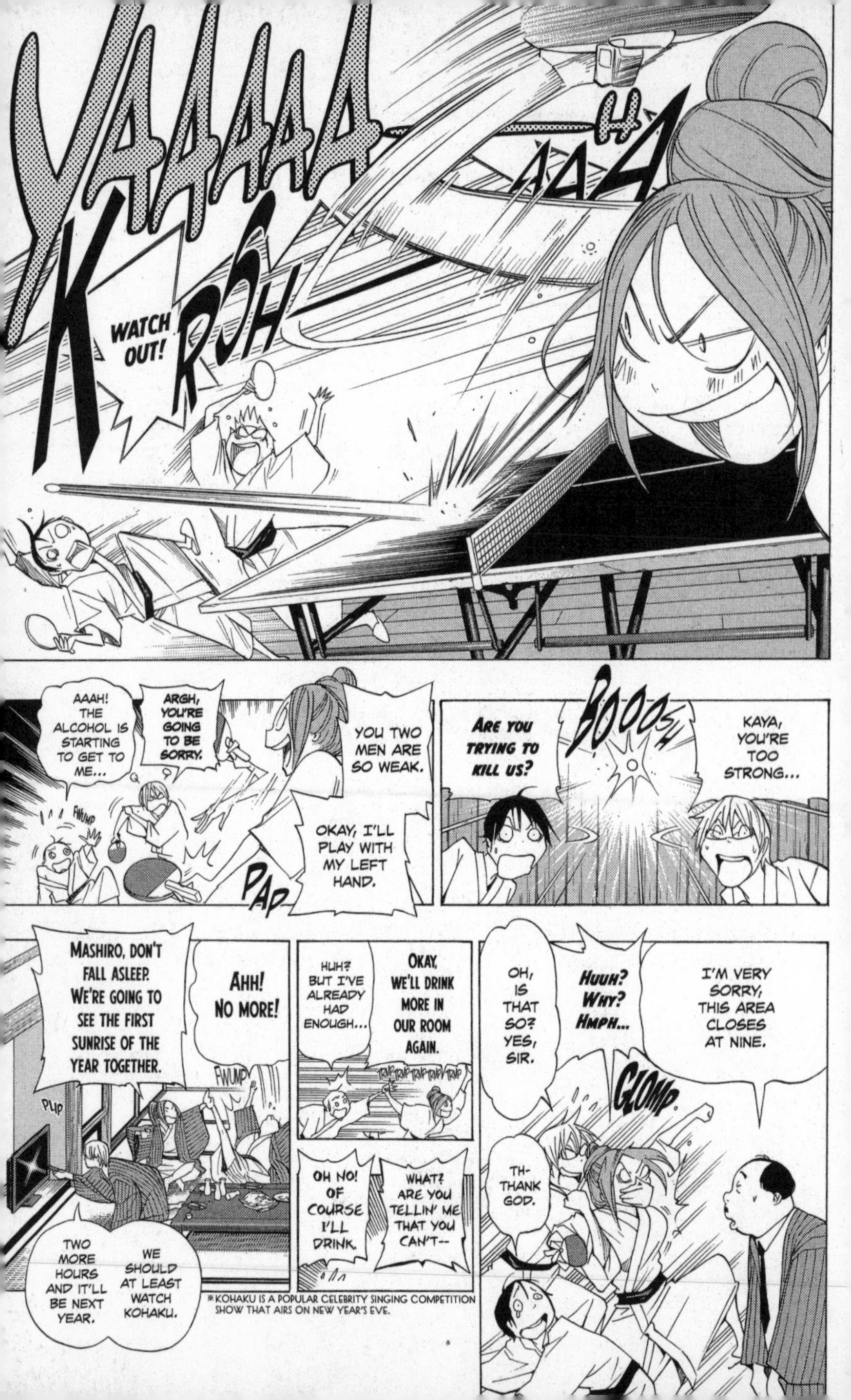
YAAAAAAAAH
KRSH
WATCH OUT!
KAYA, YOU'RE TOO STRONG...
BOOOSH
ARE YOU TRYING TO KILL US?
YOU TWO MEN ARE SO WEAK.
ARGH, YOU'RE GOING TO BE SORRY.
AAAH! THE ALCOHOL IS STARTING TO GET TO ME...
FWUMP
OKAY, I'LL PLAY WITH MY LEFT HAND.
PAP
I'M VERY SORRY, THIS AREA CLOSES AT NINE.
HUUH? WHY? HMPH...
OH, IS THAT SO? YES, SIR.
GLOMP
TH-THANK GOD.
OKAY, WE'LL DRINK MORE IN OUR ROOM AGAIN.
HUH? BUT I'VE ALREADY HAD ENOUGH...
TRMP TRMP TRMP TRMP TRMP
WHAT? ARE YOU TELLIN' ME THAT YOU CAN'T--
OH NO! OF COURSE I'LL DRINK.
MASHIRO, DON'T FALL ASLEEP. WE'RE GOING TO SEE THE FIRST SUNRISE OF THE YEAR TOGETHER.
AHH! NO MORE!
FWUMP
PLIP
WE SHOULD AT LEAST WATCH KOHAKU.
TWO MORE HOURS AND IT'LL BE NEXT YEAR.
* KOHAKU IS A POPULAR CELEBRITY SINGING COMPETITION SHOW THAT AIRS ON NEW YEAR'S EVE.

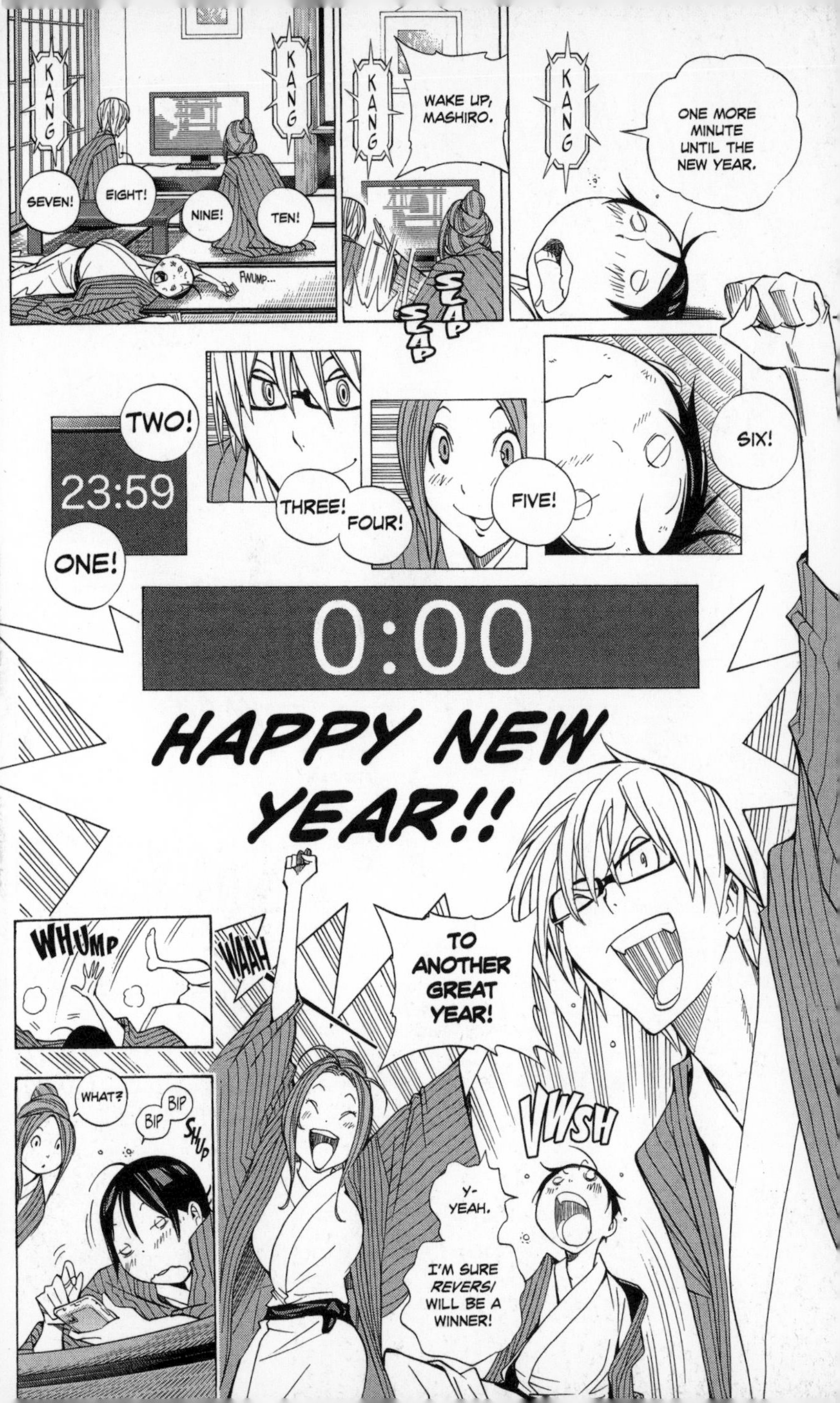
KANG
ONE MORE MINUTE UNTIL THE NEW YEAR.
KANG
WAKE UP, MASHIRO.
SLAP SLAP
KANG
KANG
SEVEN!
EIGHT!
NINE!
TEN!
FWUMP...
SIX!
FIVE!
FOUR!
THREE!
TWO!
23:59
ONE!
0:00
HAPPY NEW YEAR!!
TO ANOTHER GREAT YEAR!
WAAH
WHUMP
VWSH
Y- YEAH.
I'M SURE REVERSI WILL BE A WINNER!
WHAT?
BIP BIP
SHUP

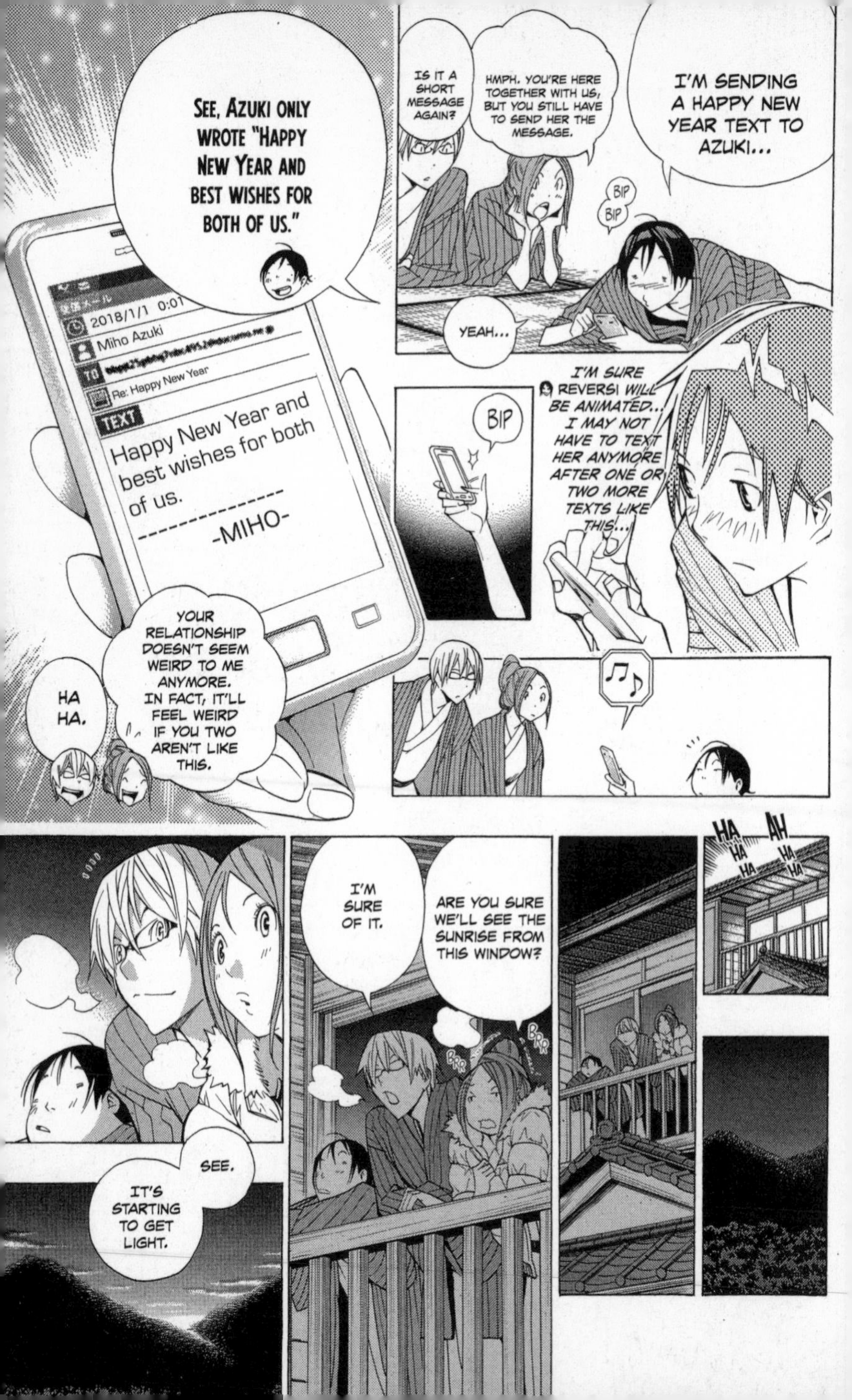
I'M SENDING A HAPPY NEW YEAR TEXT TO AZUKI...
HMPH. YOU'RE HERE TOGETHER WITH US, BUT YOU STILL HAVE TO SEND HER THE MESSAGE.
IS IT A SHORT MESSAGE AGAIN?
BIP
BIP
YEAH...
I'M SURE REVERSI WILL BE ANIMATED... I MAY NOT HAVE TO TEXT HER ANYMORE AFTER ONE OR TWO MORE TEXTS LIKE THIS...
BIP
♫♪
SEE, AZUKI ONLY WROTE "HAPPY NEW YEAR AND BEST WISHES FOR BOTH OF US."
2018/1/1 0:01
Miho Azuki
Re: Happy New Year
TEXT
Happy New Year and best wishes for both of us.

-MIHO-
YOUR RELATIONSHIP DOESN'T SEEM WEIRD TO ME ANYMORE. IN FACT, IT'LL FEEL WEIRD IF YOU TWO AREN'T LIKE THIS.
HA HA.
HA HA HA
AH HA HA
ARE YOU SURE WE'LL SEE THE SUNRISE FROM THIS WINDOW?
I'M SURE OF IT.
BRR
BRR
SEE.
IT'S STARTING TO GET LIGHT.

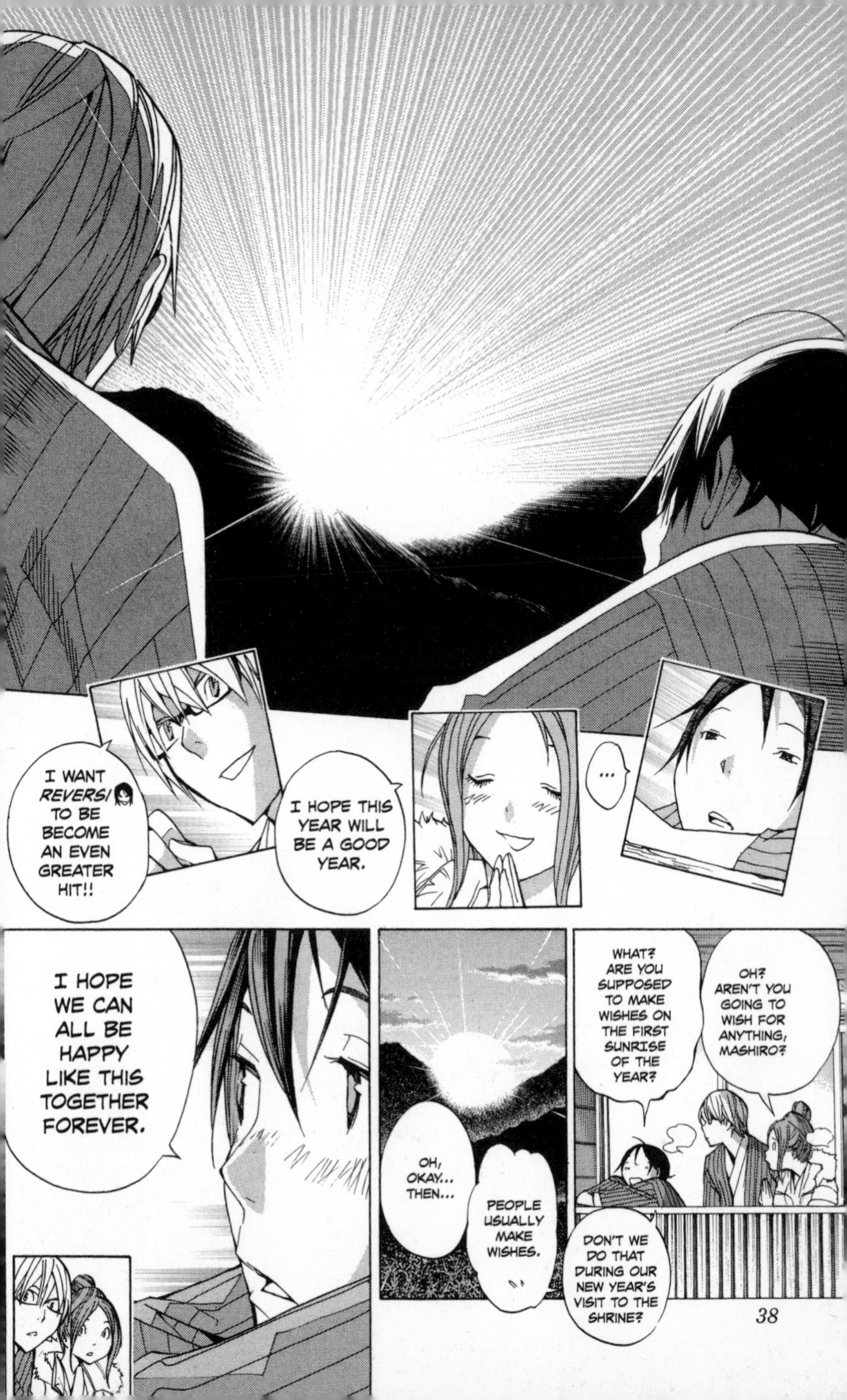
...
I HOPE THIS YEAR WILL BE A GOOD YEAR.
I WANT REVERSI TO BE BECOME AN EVEN GREATER HIT!!
OH? AREN'T YOU GOING TO WISH FOR ANYTHING, MASHIRO?
WHAT? ARE YOU SUPPOSED TO MAKE WISHES ON THE FIRST SUNRISE OF THE YEAR?
DON'T WE DO THAT DURING OUR NEW YEAR'S VISIT TO THE SHRINE?
PEOPLE USUALLY MAKE WISHES.
OH, OKAY... THEN...
I HOPE WE CAN ALL BE HAPPY LIKE THIS TOGETHER FOREVER.

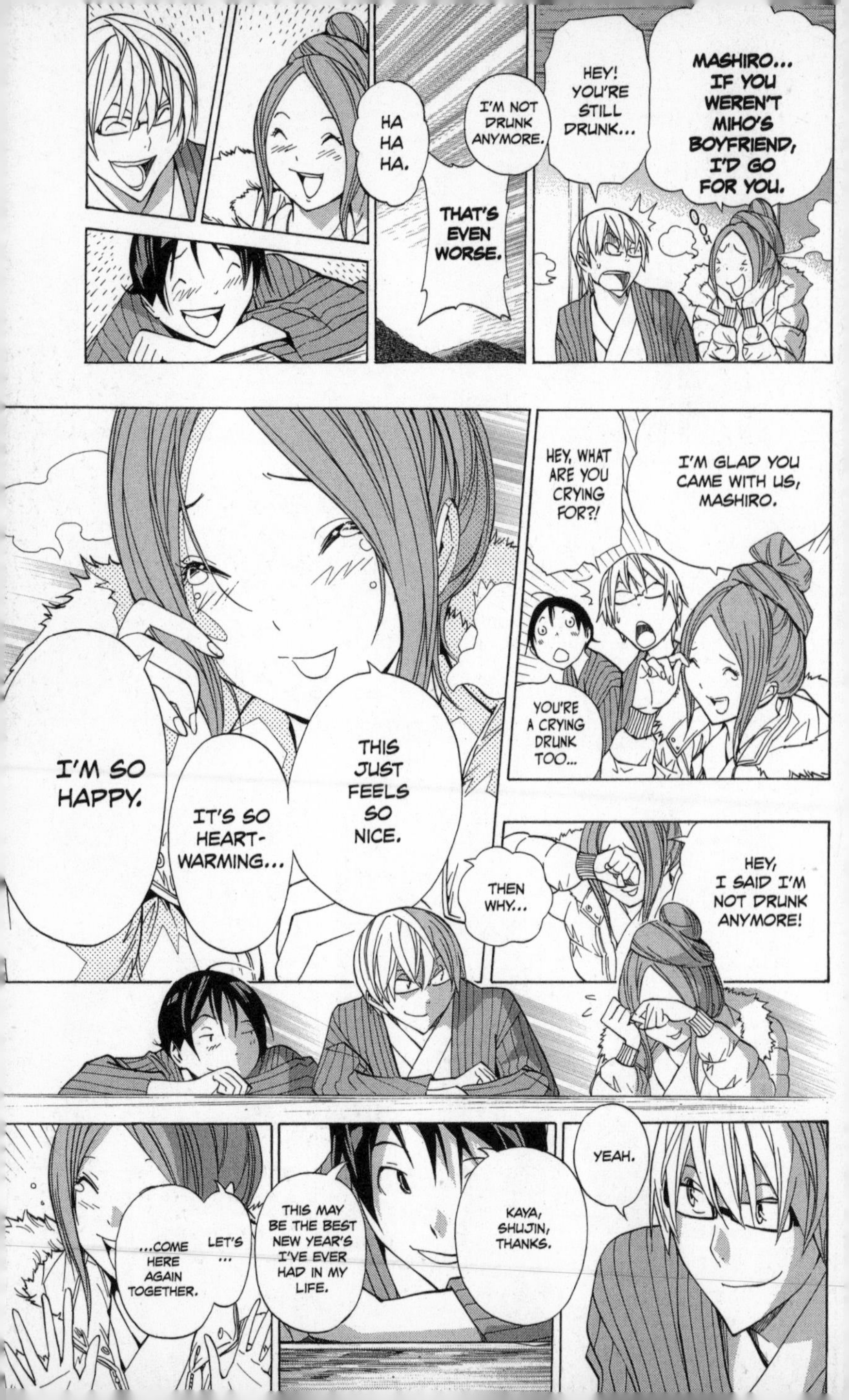
MASHIRO... IF YOU WEREN'T MIHO'S BOYFRIEND, I'D GO FOR YOU.
HEY! YOU'RE STILL DRUNK...
I'M NOT DRUNK ANYMORE.
THAT'S EVEN WORSE.
HA HA HA.
I'M GLAD YOU CAME WITH US, MASHIRO.
HEY, WHAT ARE YOU CRYING FOR?!
YOU'RE A CRYING DRUNK TOO...
HEY, I SAID I'M NOT DRUNK ANYMORE!
THEN WHY...
THIS JUST FEELS SO NICE.
IT'S SO HEART-WARMING...
I'M SO HAPPY.
YEAH.
KAYA, SHUJIN, THANKS.
THIS MAY BE THE BEST NEW YEAR'S I'VE EVER HAD IN MY LIFE.
LET'S ...
...COME HERE AGAIN TOGETHER.

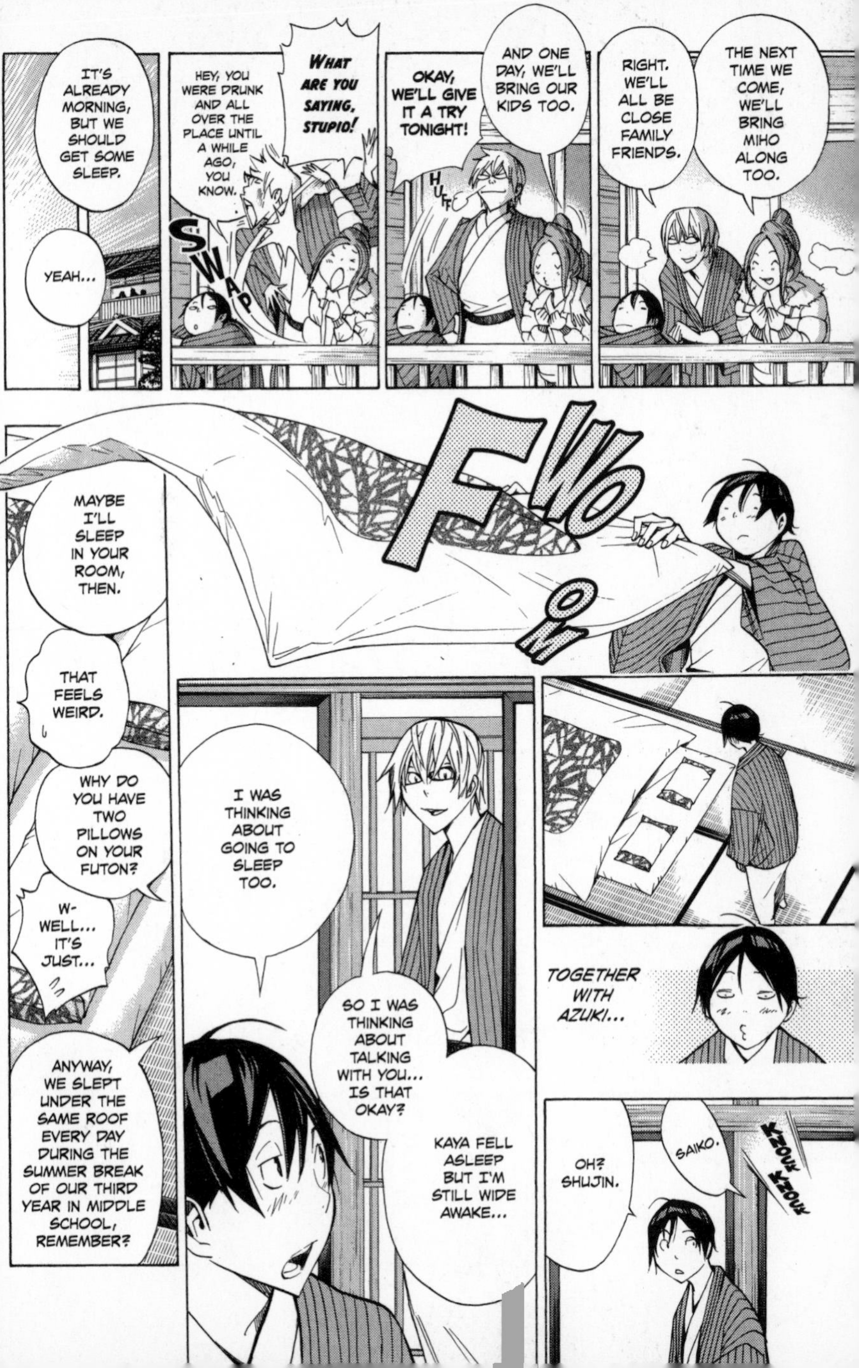
THE NEXT TIME WE COME, WE'LL BRING MIHO ALONG TOO.
RIGHT. WE'LL ALL BE CLOSE FAMILY FRIENDS.
AND ONE DAY, WE'LL BRING OUR KIDS TOO.
OKAY, WE'LL GIVE IT A TRY TONIGHT!
HUFF
WHAT ARE YOU SAYING, STUPID!
HEY, YOU WERE DRUNK AND ALL OVER THE PLACE UNTIL A WHILE AGO, YOU KNOW.
SWAP
IT'S ALREADY MORNING, BUT WE SHOULD GET SOME SLEEP.
YEAH...
FWOOM
TOGETHER WITH AZUKI...
KNOCK KNOCK
SAIKO.
OH? SHUJIN.
I WAS THINKING ABOUT GOING TO SLEEP TOO.
SO I WAS THINKING ABOUT TALKING WITH YOU... IS THAT OKAY?
KAYA FELL ASLEEP BUT I'M STILL WIDE AWAKE...
MAYBE I'LL SLEEP IN YOUR ROOM, THEN.
THAT FEELS WEIRD.
WHY DO YOU HAVE TWO PILLOWS ON YOUR FUTON?
W- WELL... IT'S JUST...
ANYWAY, WE SLEPT UNDER THE SAME ROOF EVERY DAY DURING THE SUMMER BREAK OF OUR THIRD YEAR IN MIDDLE SCHOOL, REMEMBER?

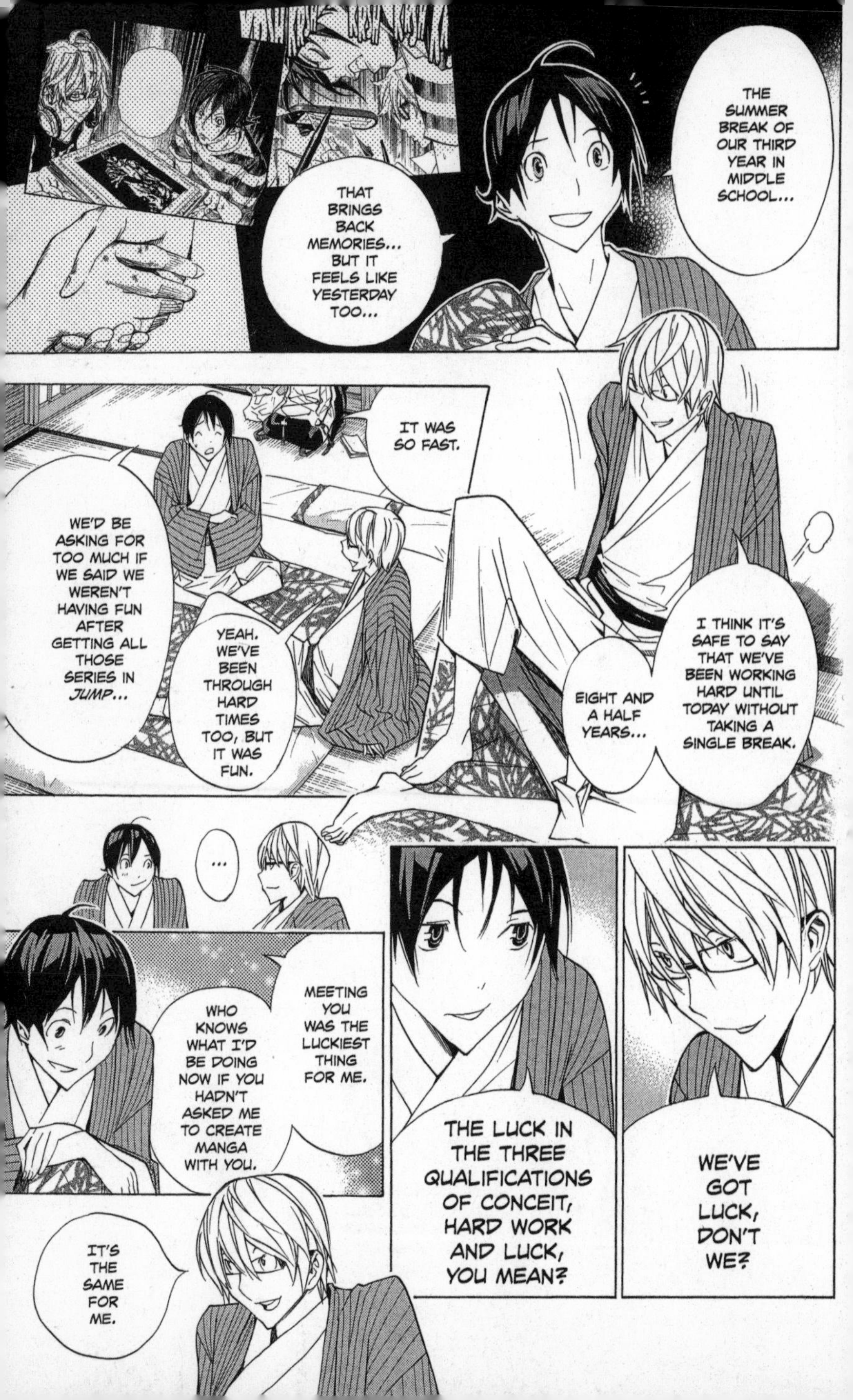
THE SUMMER BREAK OF OUR THIRD YEAR IN MIDDLE SCHOOL...
THAT BRINGS BACK MEMORIES... BUT IT FEELS LIKE YESTERDAY TOO...
I THINK IT'S SAFE TO SAY THAT WE'VE BEEN WORKING HARD UNTIL TODAY WITHOUT TAKING A SINGLE BREAK.
EIGHT AND A HALF YEARS...
IT WAS SO FAST.
YEAH. WE'VE BEEN THROUGH HARD TIMES TOO, BUT IT WAS FUN.
WE'D BE ASKING FOR TOO MUCH IF WE SAID WE WEREN'T HAVING FUN AFTER GETTING ALL THOSE SERIES IN *JUMP*...
...
MEETING YOU WAS THE LUCKIEST THING FOR ME.
WHO KNOWS WHAT I'D BE DOING NOW IF YOU HADN'T ASKED ME TO CREATE MANGA WITH YOU.
IT'S THE SAME FOR ME.
WE'VE GOT LUCK, DON'T WE?
THE LUCK IN THE THREE QUALIFICATIONS OF CONCEIT, HARD WORK AND LUCK, YOU MEAN?

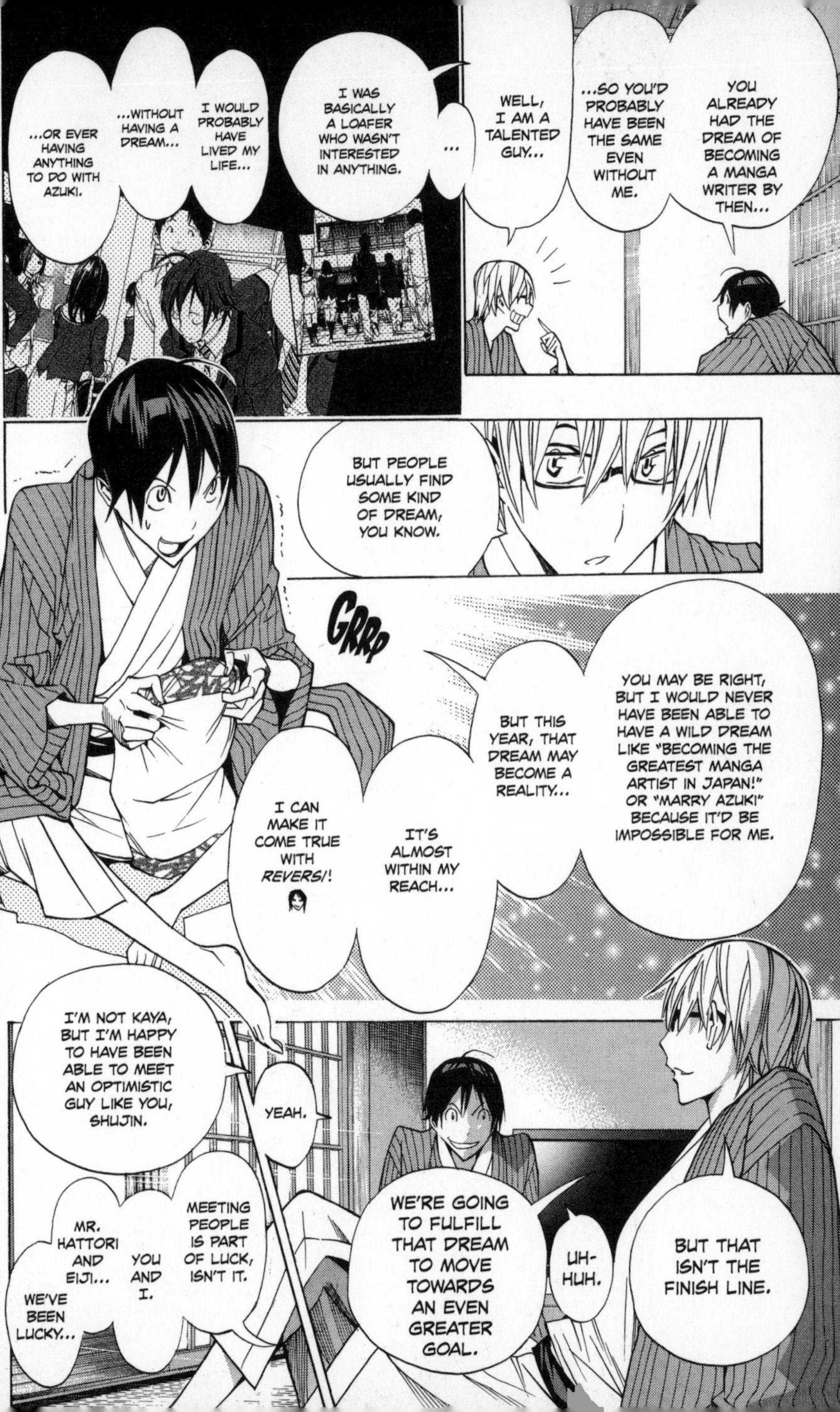
YOU ALREADY HAD THE DREAM OF BECOMING A MANGA WRITER BY THEN...
...SO YOU'D PROBABLY HAVE BEEN THE SAME EVEN WITHOUT ME.
WELL, I AM A TALENTED GUY...
...
I WAS BASICALLY A LOAFER WHO WASN'T INTERESTED IN ANYTHING.
I WOULD PROBABLY HAVE LIVED MY LIFE...
...WITHOUT HAVING A DREAM...
...OR EVER HAVING ANYTHING TO DO WITH AZUKI.
BUT PEOPLE USUALLY FIND SOME KIND OF DREAM, YOU KNOW.
GRRR
YOU MAY BE RIGHT, BUT I WOULD NEVER HAVE BEEN ABLE TO HAVE A WILD DREAM LIKE "BECOMING THE GREATEST MANGA ARTIST IN JAPAN!" OR "MARRY AZUKI" BECAUSE IT'D BE IMPOSSIBLE FOR ME.
BUT THIS YEAR, THAT DREAM MAY BECOME A REALITY...
IT'S ALMOST WITHIN MY REACH...
I CAN MAKE IT COME TRUE WITH REVERSI!
BUT THAT ISN'T THE FINISH LINE.
UH-HUH.
WE'RE GOING TO FULFILL THAT DREAM TO MOVE TOWARDS AN EVEN GREATER GOAL.
YEAH.
I'M NOT KAYA, BUT I'M HAPPY TO HAVE BEEN ABLE TO MEET AN OPTIMISTIC GUY LIKE YOU, SHUJIN.
MEETING PEOPLE IS PART OF LUCK, ISN'T IT.
YOU AND I.
MR. HATTORI AND EIJI...
WE'VE BEEN LUCKY...

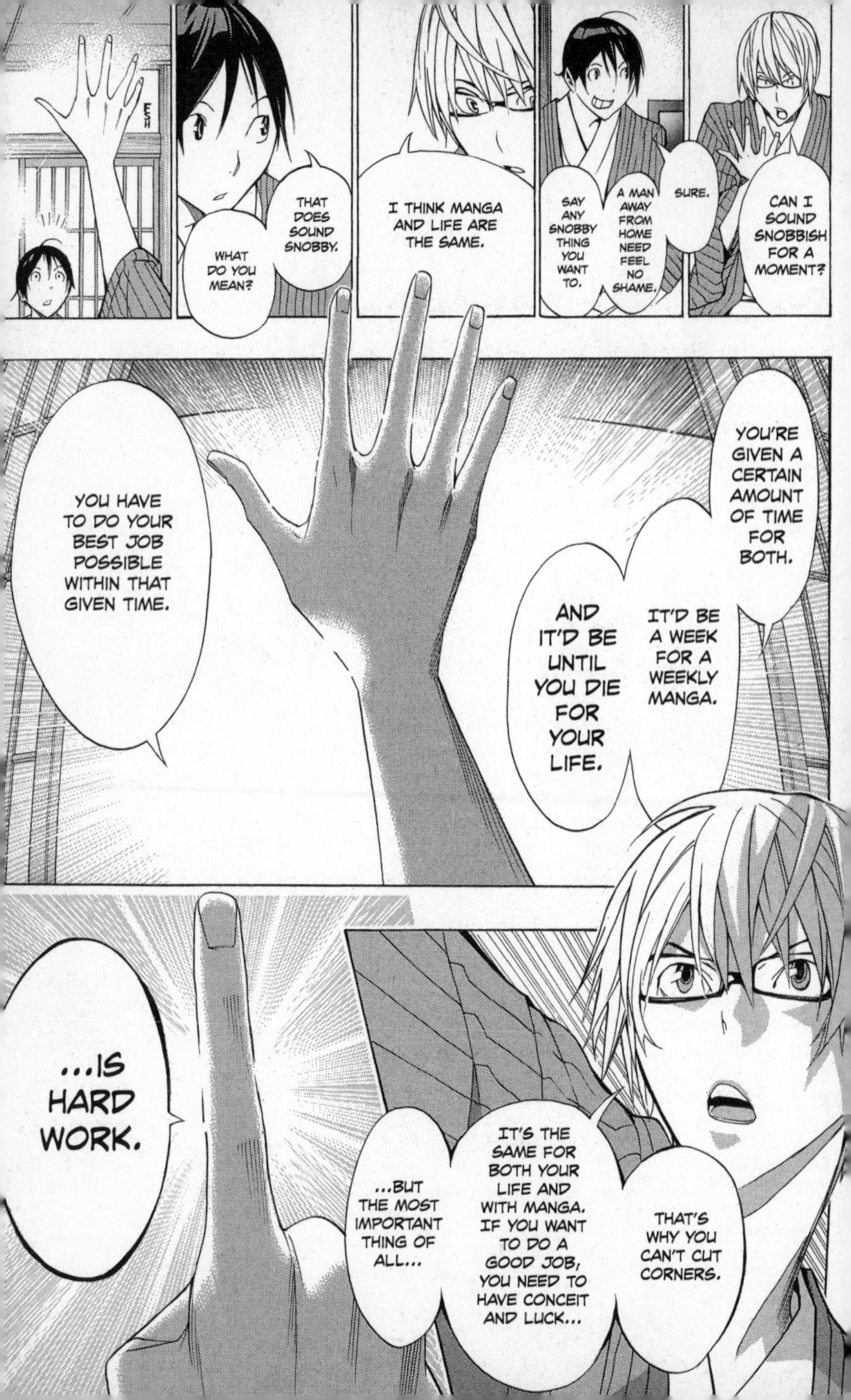
CAN I SOUND SNOBBISH FOR A MOMENT?
SURE.
A MAN AWAY FROM HOME NEED FEEL NO SHAME.
SAY ANY SNOBBY THING YOU WANT TO.
I THINK MANGA AND LIFE ARE THE SAME.
THAT DOES SOUND SNOBBY.
WHAT DO YOU MEAN?
ESH
YOU'RE GIVEN A CERTAIN AMOUNT OF TIME FOR BOTH.
IT'D BE A WEEK FOR A WEEKLY MANGA.
AND IT'D BE UNTIL YOU DIE FOR YOUR LIFE.
YOU HAVE TO DO YOUR BEST JOB POSSIBLE WITHIN THAT GIVEN TIME.
THAT'S WHY YOU CAN'T CUT CORNERS.
IT'S THE SAME FOR BOTH YOUR LIFE AND WITH MANGA. IF YOU WANT TO DO A GOOD JOB, YOU NEED TO HAVE CONCEIT AND LUCK...
...BUT THE MOST IMPORTANT THING OF ALL...
...IS HARD WORK.

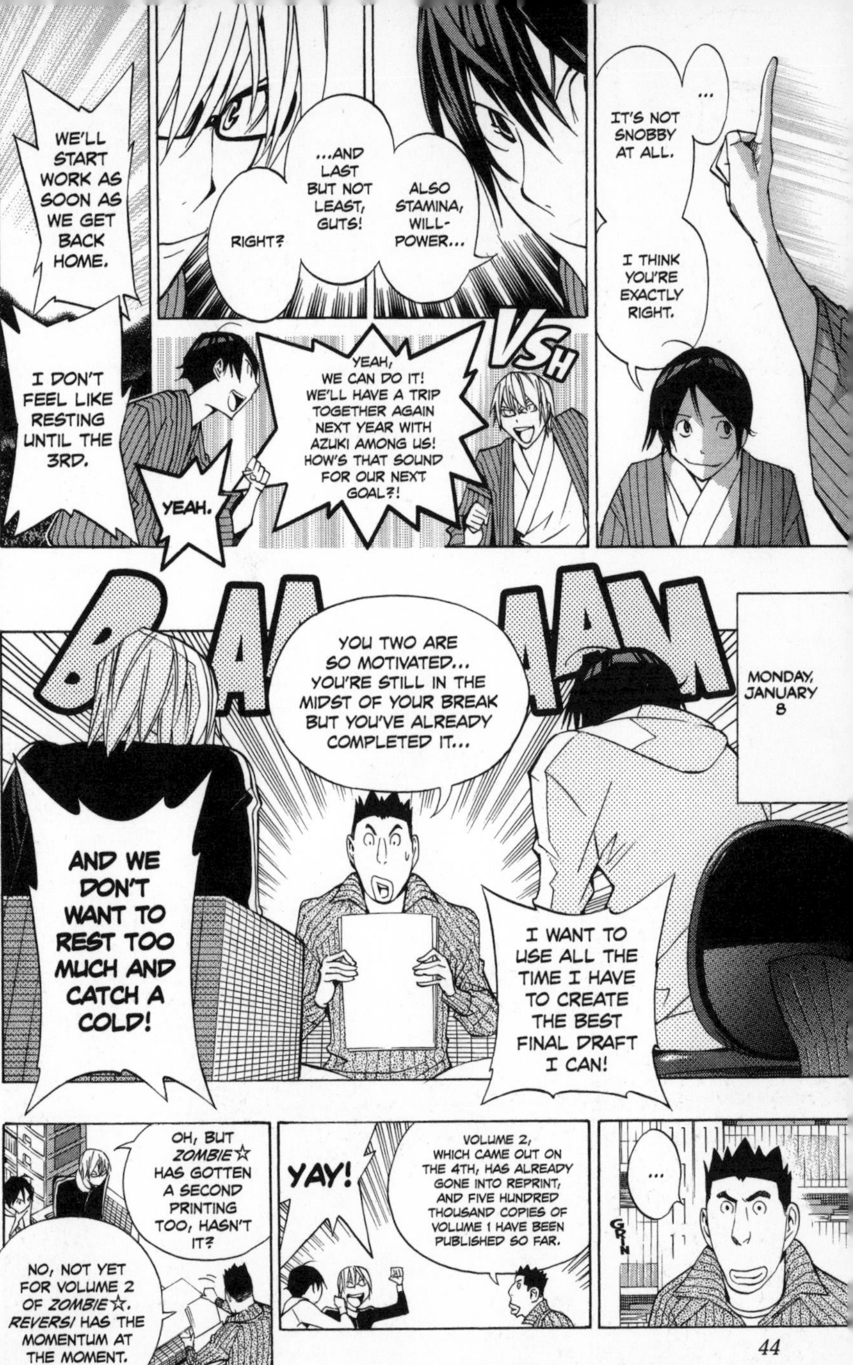
...
IT'S NOT SNOBBY AT ALL.
I THINK YOU'RE EXACTLY RIGHT.
ALSO STAMINA, WILL-POWER...
...AND LAST BUT NOT LEAST, GUTS!
RIGHT?
VSH
YEAH, WE CAN DO IT! WE'LL HAVE A TRIP TOGETHER AGAIN NEXT YEAR WITH AZUKI AMONG US! HOW'S THAT SOUND FOR OUR NEXT GOAL?!
YEAH.
WE'LL START WORK AS SOON AS WE GET BACK HOME.
I DON'T FEEL LIKE RESTING UNTIL THE 3RD.
MONDAY, JANUARY 8
YOU TWO ARE SO MOTIVATED... YOU'RE STILL IN THE MIDST OF YOUR BREAK BUT YOU'VE ALREADY COMPLETED IT...
I WANT TO USE ALL THE TIME I HAVE TO CREATE THE BEST FINAL DRAFT I CAN!
AND WE DON'T WANT TO REST TOO MUCH AND CATCH A COLD!
...
GRIN
VOLUME 2, WHICH CAME OUT ON THE 4TH, HAS ALREADY GONE INTO REPRINT, AND FIVE HUNDRED THOUSAND COPIES OF VOLUME 1 HAVE BEEN PUBLISHED SO FAR.
YAY!
OH, BUT ZOMBIE☆ HAS GOTTEN A SECOND PRINTING TOO, HASN'T IT?
NO, NOT YET FOR VOLUME 2 OF ZOMBIE☆. REVERSI HAS THE MOMENTUM AT THE MOMENT.

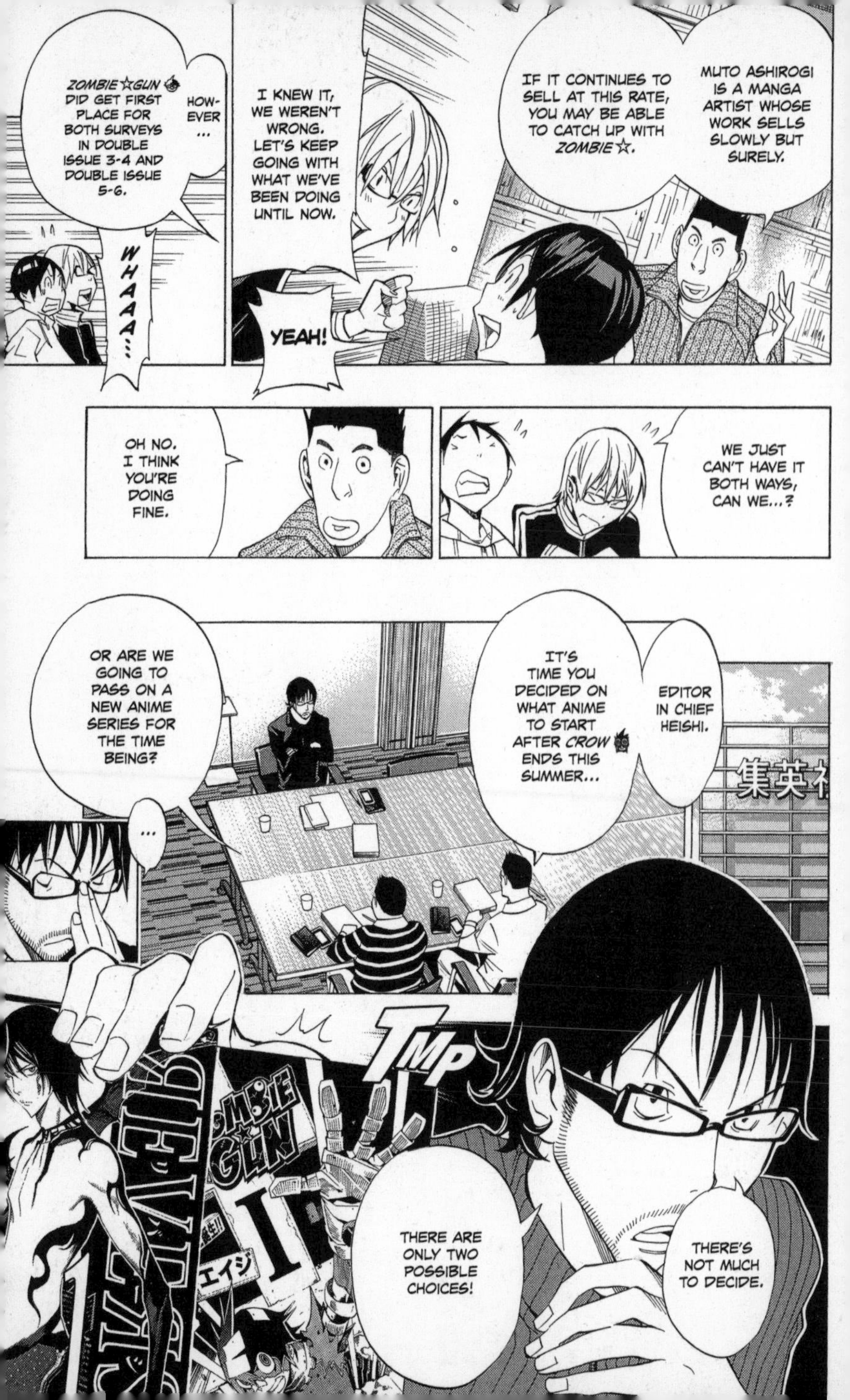
MUTO ASHIROGI IS A MANGA ARTIST WHOSE WORK SELLS SLOWLY BUT SURELY.
IF IT CONTINUES TO SELL AT THIS RATE, YOU MAY BE ABLE TO CATCH UP WITH ZOMBIE☆.
YEAH!
I KNEW IT, WE WEREN'T WRONG. LET'S KEEP GOING WITH WHAT WE'VE BEEN DOING UNTIL NOW.
HOW-EVER ...
ZOMBIE☆GUN DID GET FIRST PLACE FOR BOTH SURVEYS IN DOUBLE ISSUE 3-4 AND DOUBLE ISSUE 5-6.
WHAAAA...
WE JUST CAN'T HAVE IT BOTH WAYS, CAN WE...?
OH NO. I THINK YOU'RE DOING FINE.
EDITOR IN CHIEF HEISHI.
IT'S TIME YOU DECIDED ON WHAT ANIME TO START AFTER CROW ENDS THIS SUMMER...
OR ARE WE GOING TO PASS ON A NEW ANIME SERIES FOR THE TIME BEING?
...
TMP
THERE'S NOT MUCH TO DECIDE.
THERE ARE ONLY TWO POSSIBLE CHOICES!

※CREATOR STORYBOARDS AND FINISHED PAGES IN JAPANESE

BAKUMAN。vol.19

"Until the Final Draft Is Complete"

Chapter 162, pp. 40-41

COMPLETE!

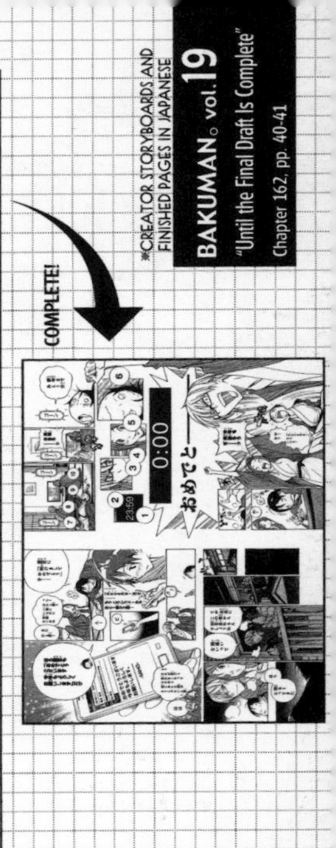

OBATA'S STORYBOARD

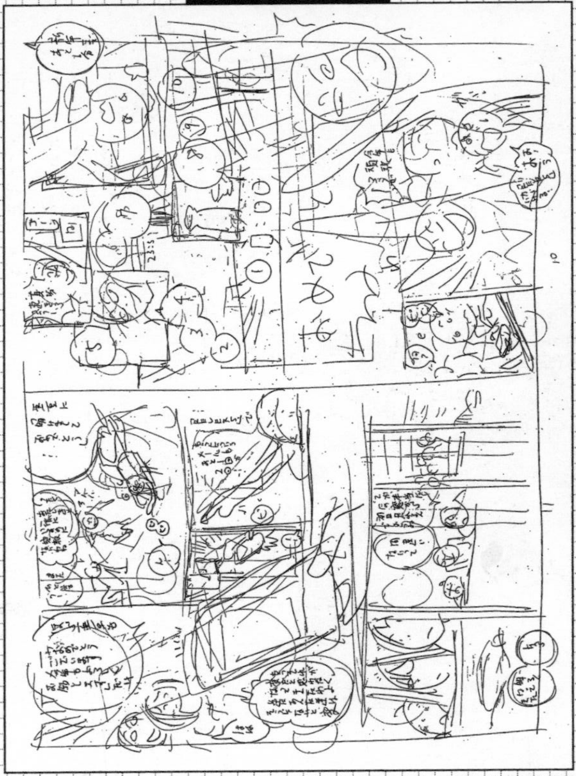

OHBA'S STORYBOARD

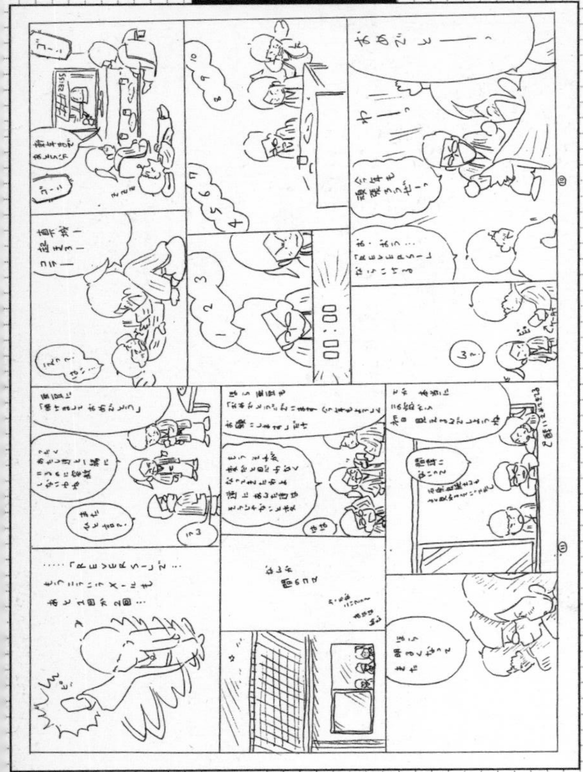

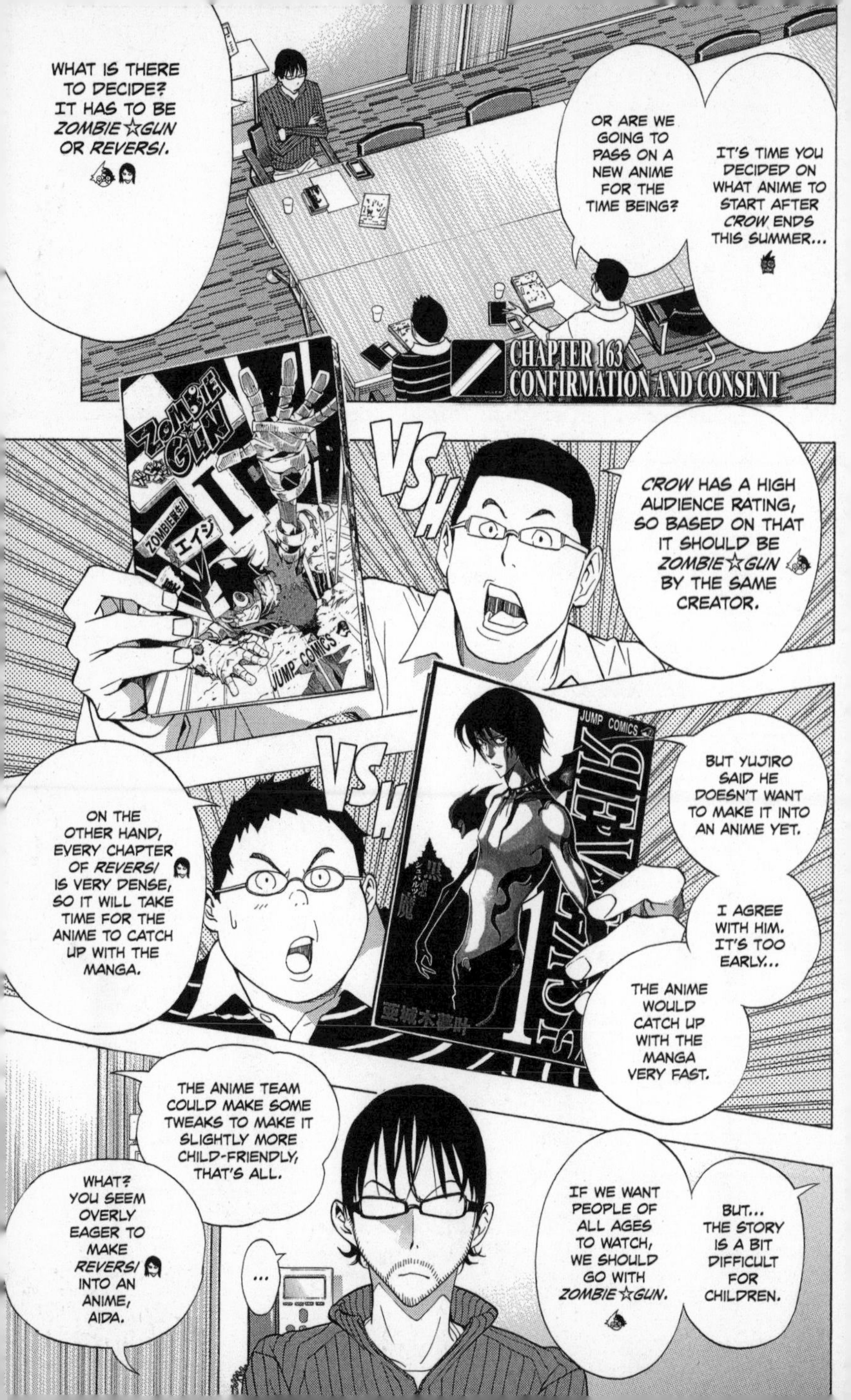

IT'S TIME YOU DECIDED ON WHAT ANIME TO START AFTER *CROW* ENDS THIS SUMMER...
OR ARE WE GOING TO PASS ON A NEW ANIME FOR THE TIME BEING?
WHAT IS THERE TO DECIDE? IT HAS TO BE *ZOMBIE☆GUN* OR *REVERSI*.
CHAPTER 163 CONFIRMATION AND CONSENT
CROW HAS A HIGH AUDIENCE RATING, SO BASED ON THAT IT SHOULD BE *ZOMBIE☆GUN* BY THE SAME CREATOR.
ZOMBIE☆GUN
JUMP COMICS
VSH
BUT YUJIRO SAID HE DOESN'T WANT TO MAKE IT INTO AN ANIME YET.
I AGREE WITH HIM. IT'S TOO EARLY...
THE ANIME WOULD CATCH UP WITH THE MANGA VERY FAST.
ON THE OTHER HAND, EVERY CHAPTER OF *REVERSI* IS VERY DENSE, SO IT WILL TAKE TIME FOR THE ANIME TO CATCH UP WITH THE MANGA.
VSH
JUMP COMICS
BUT... THE STORY IS A BIT DIFFICULT FOR CHILDREN.
IF WE WANT PEOPLE OF ALL AGES TO WATCH, WE SHOULD GO WITH *ZOMBIE☆GUN*.
THE ANIME TEAM COULD MAKE SOME TWEAKS TO MAKE IT SLIGHTLY MORE CHILD-FRIENDLY, THAT'S ALL.
WHAT? YOU SEEM OVERLY EAGER TO MAKE *REVERSI* INTO AN ANIME, AIDA.
...

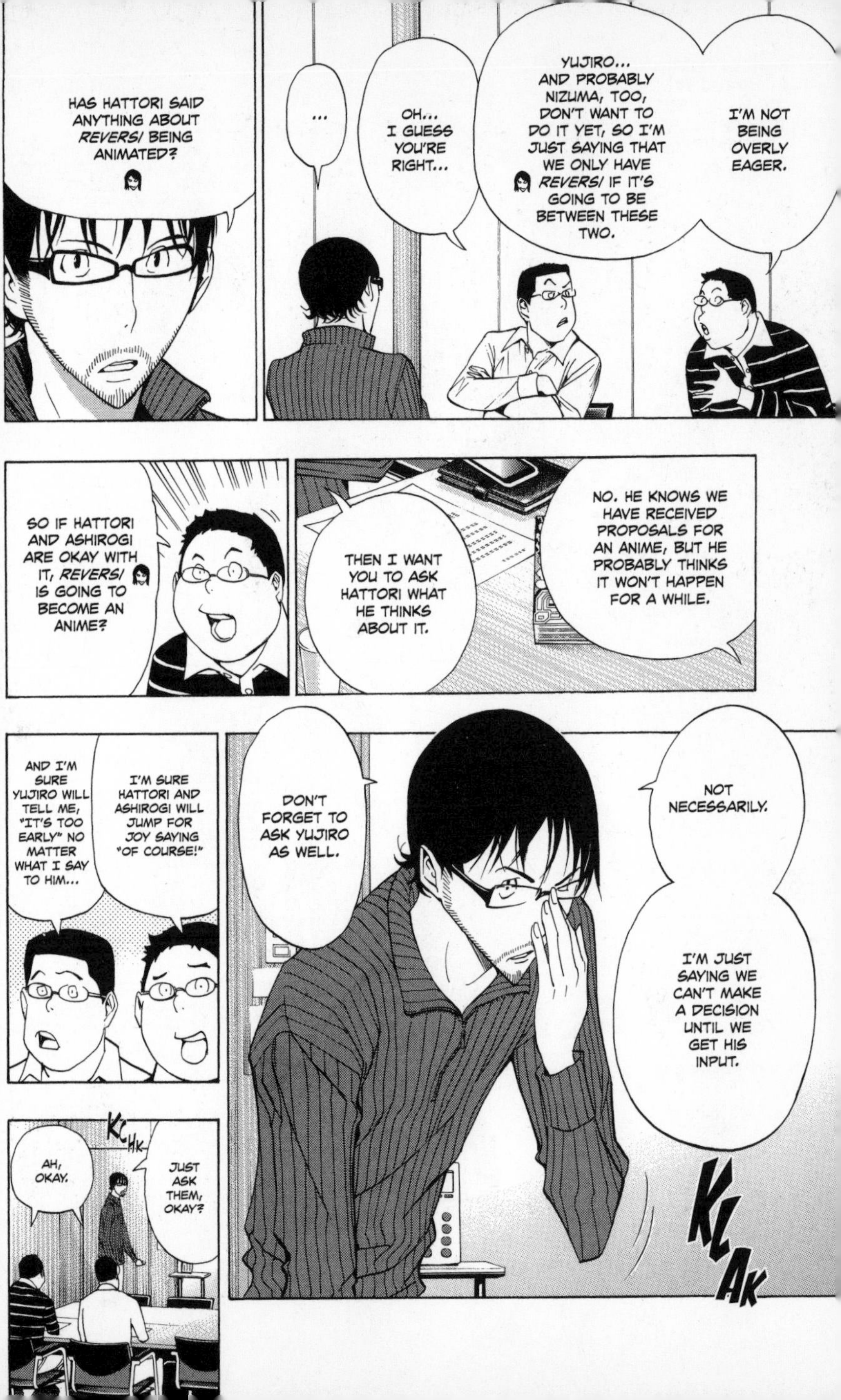
I'M NOT BEING OVERLY EAGER.
YUJIRO... AND PROBABLY NIZUMA, TOO, DON'T WANT TO DO IT YET, SO I'M JUST SAYING THAT WE ONLY HAVE REVERSI IF IT'S GOING TO BE BETWEEN THESE TWO.
OH... I GUESS YOU'RE RIGHT...
...
HAS HATTORI SAID ANYTHING ABOUT REVERSI BEING ANIMATED?
NO. HE KNOWS WE HAVE RECEIVED PROPOSALS FOR AN ANIME, BUT HE PROBABLY THINKS IT WON'T HAPPEN FOR A WHILE.
THEN I WANT YOU TO ASK HATTORI WHAT HE THINKS ABOUT IT.
SO IF HATTORI AND ASHIROGI ARE OKAY WITH IT, REVERSI IS GOING TO BECOME AN ANIME?
NOT NECESSARILY.
I'M JUST SAYING WE CAN'T MAKE A DECISION UNTIL WE GET HIS INPUT.
DON'T FORGET TO ASK YUJIRO AS WELL.
KLAK
I'M SURE HATTORI AND ASHIROGI WILL JUMP FOR JOY SAYING "OF COURSE!"
AND I'M SURE YUJIRO WILL TELL ME, "IT'S TOO EARLY" NO MATTER WHAT I SAY TO HIM...
K'CHK
JUST ASK THEM, OKAY?
AH, OKAY.

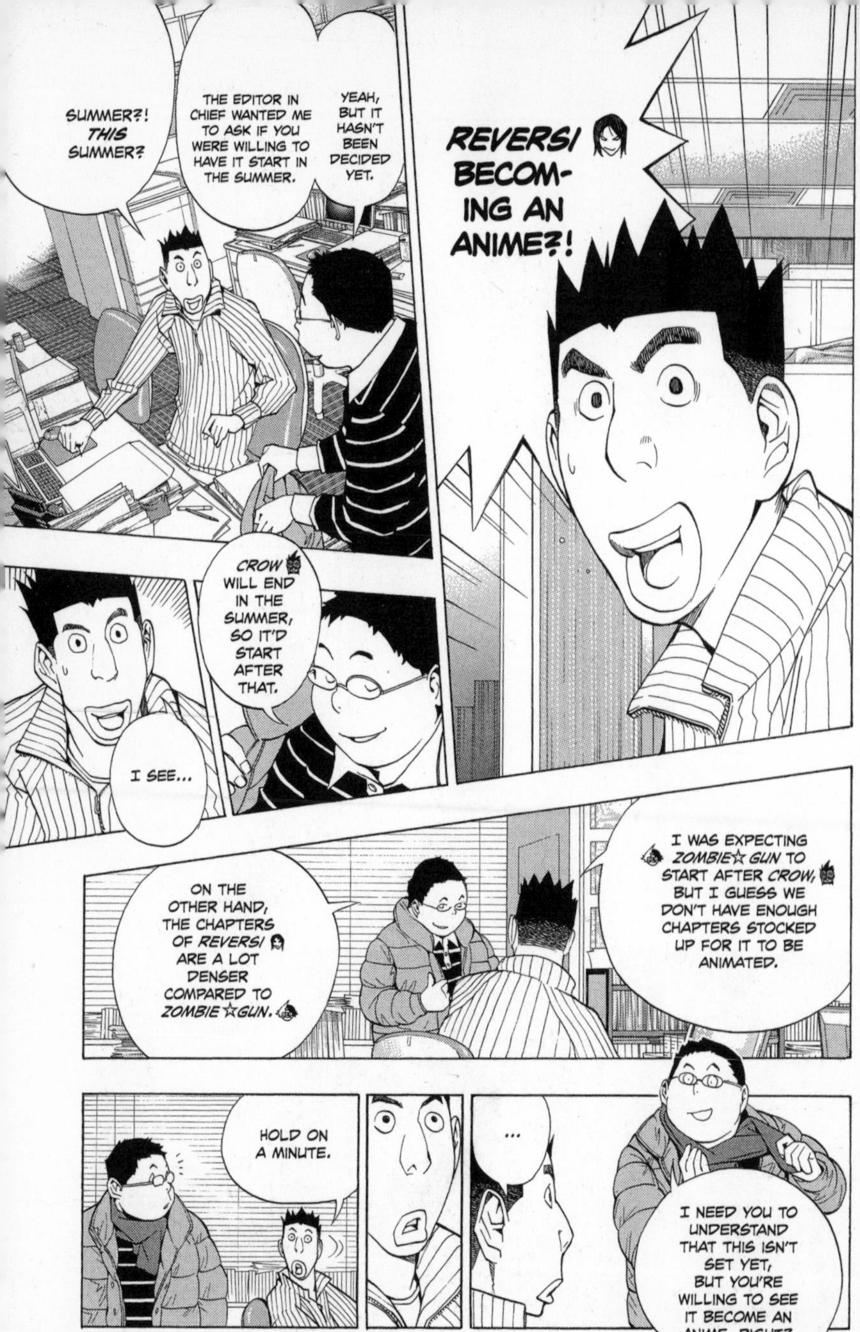
REVERSI BECOMING AN ANIME?!
YEAH, BUT IT HASN'T BEEN DECIDED YET.
THE EDITOR IN CHIEF WANTED ME TO ASK IF YOU WERE WILLING TO HAVE IT START IN THE SUMMER.
SUMMER?! THIS SUMMER?
CROW WILL END IN THE SUMMER, SO IT'D START AFTER THAT.
I SEE...
I WAS EXPECTING ZOMBIE☆GUN TO START AFTER CROW, BUT I GUESS WE DON'T HAVE ENOUGH CHAPTERS STOCKED UP FOR IT TO BE ANIMATED.
ON THE OTHER HAND, THE CHAPTERS OF REVERSI ARE A LOT DENSER COMPARED TO ZOMBIE☆GUN.
I NEED YOU TO UNDERSTAND THAT THIS ISN'T SET YET, BUT YOU'RE WILLING TO SEE IT BECOME AN ANIME, RIGHT?
...
HOLD ON A MINUTE.

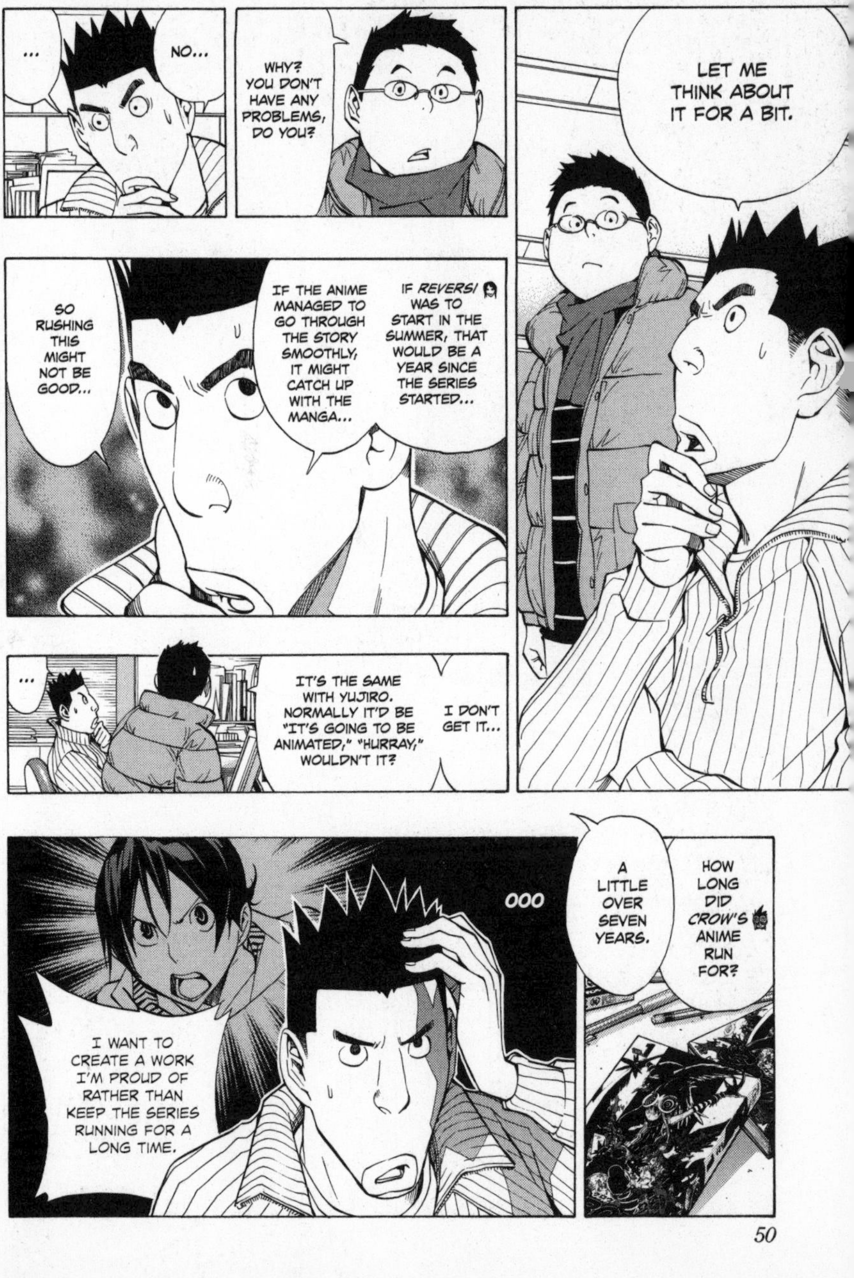
LET ME THINK ABOUT IT FOR A BIT.
WHY? YOU DON'T HAVE ANY PROBLEMS, DO YOU?
NO...
...
IF REVERSI WAS TO START IN THE SUMMER, THAT WOULD BE A YEAR SINCE THE SERIES STARTED...
IF THE ANIME MANAGED TO GO THROUGH THE STORY SMOOTHLY, IT MIGHT CATCH UP WITH THE MANGA...
SO RUSHING THIS MIGHT NOT BE GOOD...
I DON'T GET IT...
IT'S THE SAME WITH YUJIRO. NORMALLY IT'D BE "IT'S GOING TO BE ANIMATED," "HURRAY," WOULDN'T IT?
...
HOW LONG DID CROW'S ANIME RUN FOR?
A LITTLE OVER SEVEN YEARS.
OOO
I WANT TO CREATE A WORK I'M PROUD OF RATHER THAN KEEP THE SERIES RUNNING FOR A LONG TIME.

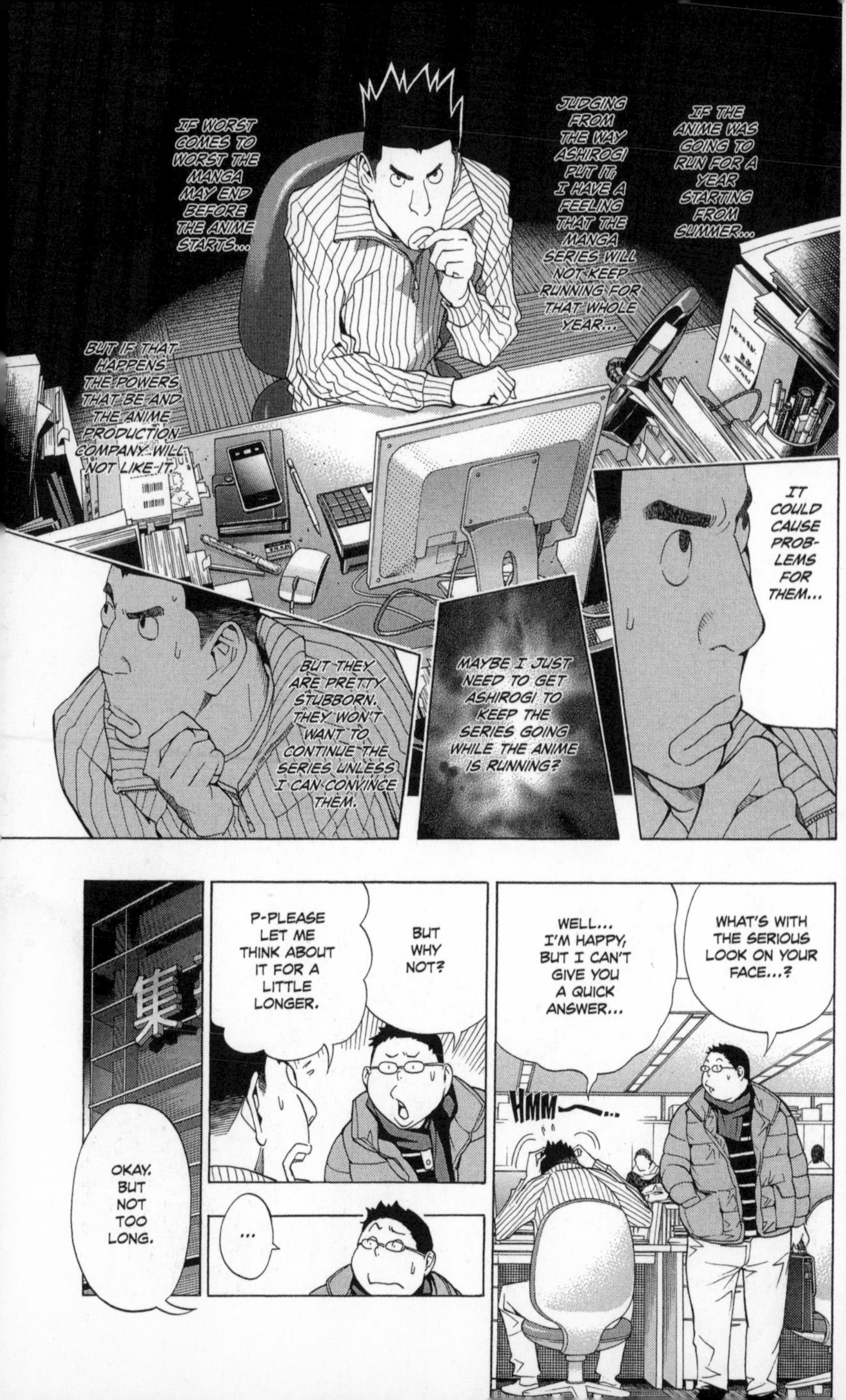
IF THE ANIME WAS GOING TO RUN FOR A YEAR STARTING FROM SUMMER...
JUDGING FROM THE WAY ASHIROGI PUT IT, I HAVE A FEELING THAT THE MANGA SERIES WILL NOT KEEP RUNNING FOR THAT WHOLE YEAR...
IF WORST COMES TO WORST THE MANGA MAY END BEFORE THE ANIME STARTS...
BUT IF THAT HAPPENS THE POWERS THAT BE AND THE ANIME PRODUCTION COMPANY WILL NOT LIKE IT.
IT COULD CAUSE PROB-LEMS FOR THEM...
MAYBE I JUST NEED TO GET ASHIROGI TO KEEP THE SERIES GOING WHILE THE ANIME IS RUNNING?
BUT THEY ARE PRETTY STUBBORN. THEY WON'T WANT TO CONTINUE THE SERIES UNLESS I CAN CONVINCE THEM.
WHAT'S WITH THE SERIOUS LOOK ON YOUR FACE...?
WELL... I'M HAPPY, BUT I CAN'T GIVE YOU A QUICK ANSWER...
HMM~...
BUT WHY NOT?
P-PLEASE LET ME THINK ABOUT IT FOR A LITTLE LONGER.
...
OKAY. BUT NOT TOO LONG.

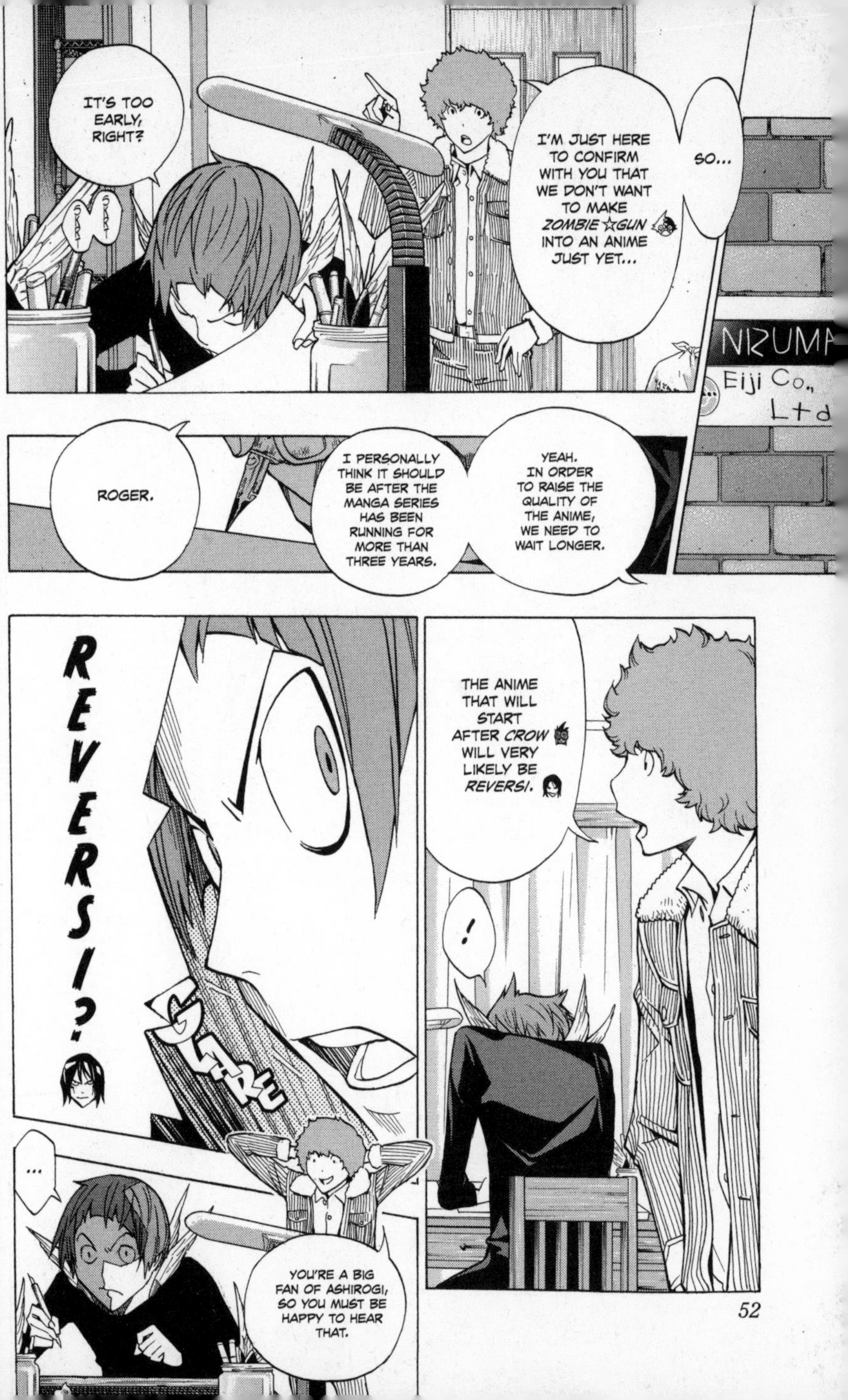
SO...
I'M JUST HERE TO CONFIRM WITH YOU THAT WE DON'T WANT TO MAKE ZOMBIE☆GUN INTO AN ANIME JUST YET...
IT'S TOO EARLY, RIGHT?
SKRT
SKRT
NIZUMA
Eiji Co., Ltd
YEAH. IN ORDER TO RAISE THE QUALITY OF THE ANIME, WE NEED TO WAIT LONGER.
I PERSONALLY THINK IT SHOULD BE AFTER THE MANGA SERIES HAS BEEN RUNNING FOR MORE THAN THREE YEARS.
ROGER.
THE ANIME THAT WILL START AFTER CROW WILL VERY LIKELY BE REVERSI.
!
REVERSI?!
GLARE
YOU'RE A BIG FAN OF ASHIROGI, SO YOU MUST BE HAPPY TO HEAR THAT.
...

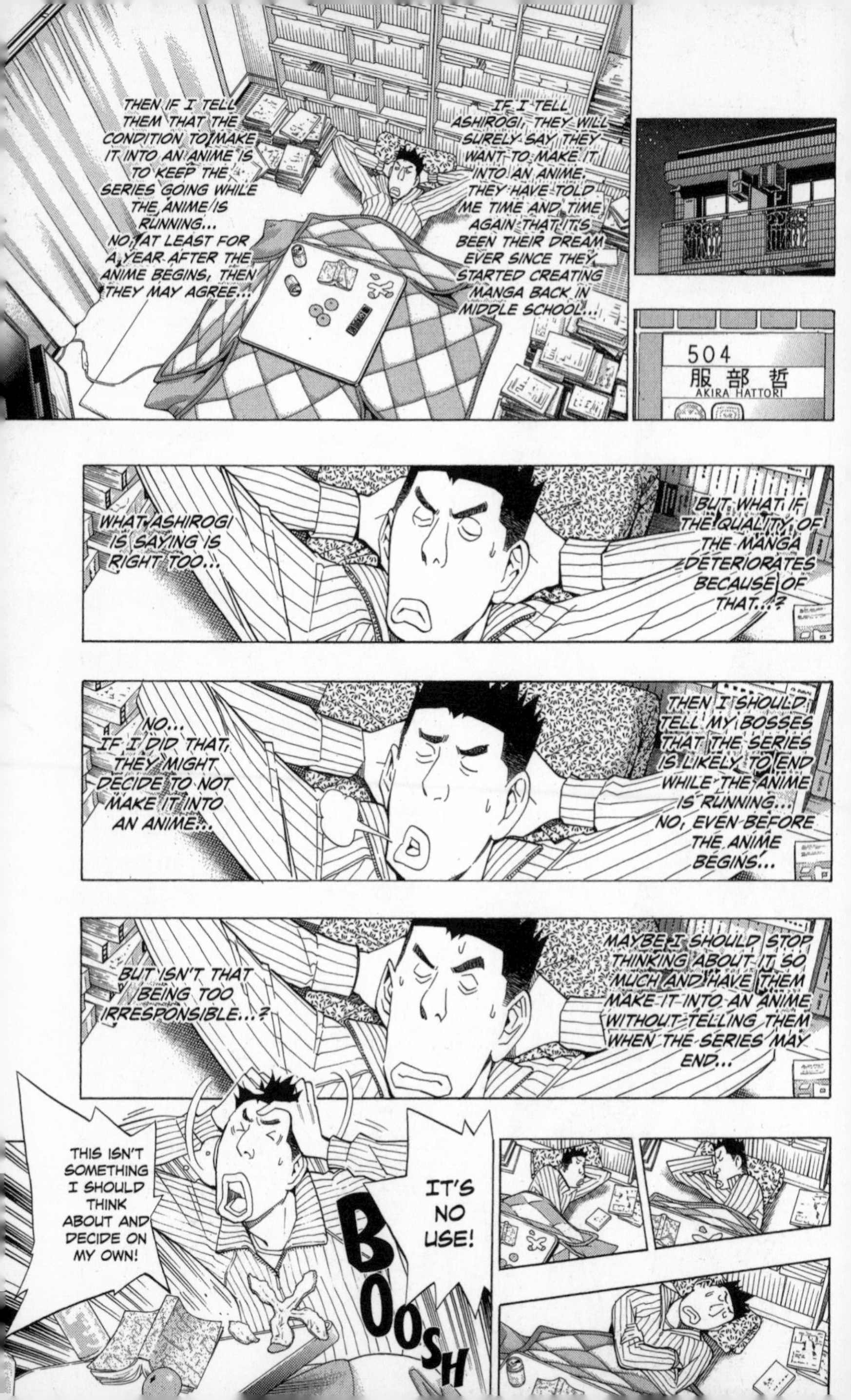
504
服部 哲
AKIRA HATTORI
IF I TELL ASHIROGI, THEY WILL SURELY SAY THEY WANT TO MAKE IT INTO AN ANIME. THEY HAVE TOLD ME TIME AND TIME AGAIN THAT IT'S BEEN THEIR DREAM EVER SINCE THEY STARTED CREATING MANGA BACK IN MIDDLE SCHOOL...
THEN IF I TELL THEM THAT THE CONDITION TO MAKE IT INTO AN ANIME IS TO KEEP THE SERIES GOING WHILE THE ANIME IS RUNNING...
NO, AT LEAST FOR A YEAR AFTER THE ANIME BEGINS, THEN THEY MAY AGREE...
BUT WHAT IF THE QUALITY OF THE MANGA DETERIORATES BECAUSE OF THAT...?
WHAT ASHIROGI IS SAYING IS RIGHT TOO...
THEN I SHOULD TELL MY BOSSES THAT THE SERIES IS LIKELY TO END WHILE THE ANIME IS RUNNING... NO, EVEN BEFORE THE ANIME BEGINS...
NO... IF I DID THAT, THEY MIGHT DECIDE TO NOT MAKE IT INTO AN ANIME...
MAYBE I SHOULD STOP THINKING ABOUT IT SO MUCH AND HAVE THEM MAKE IT INTO AN ANIME WITHOUT TELLING THEM WHEN THE SERIES MAY END...
BUT ISN'T THAT BEING TOO IRRESPONSIBLE...?
IT'S NO USE!
THIS ISN'T SOMETHING I SHOULD THINK ABOUT AND DECIDE ON MY OWN!
BOOSH

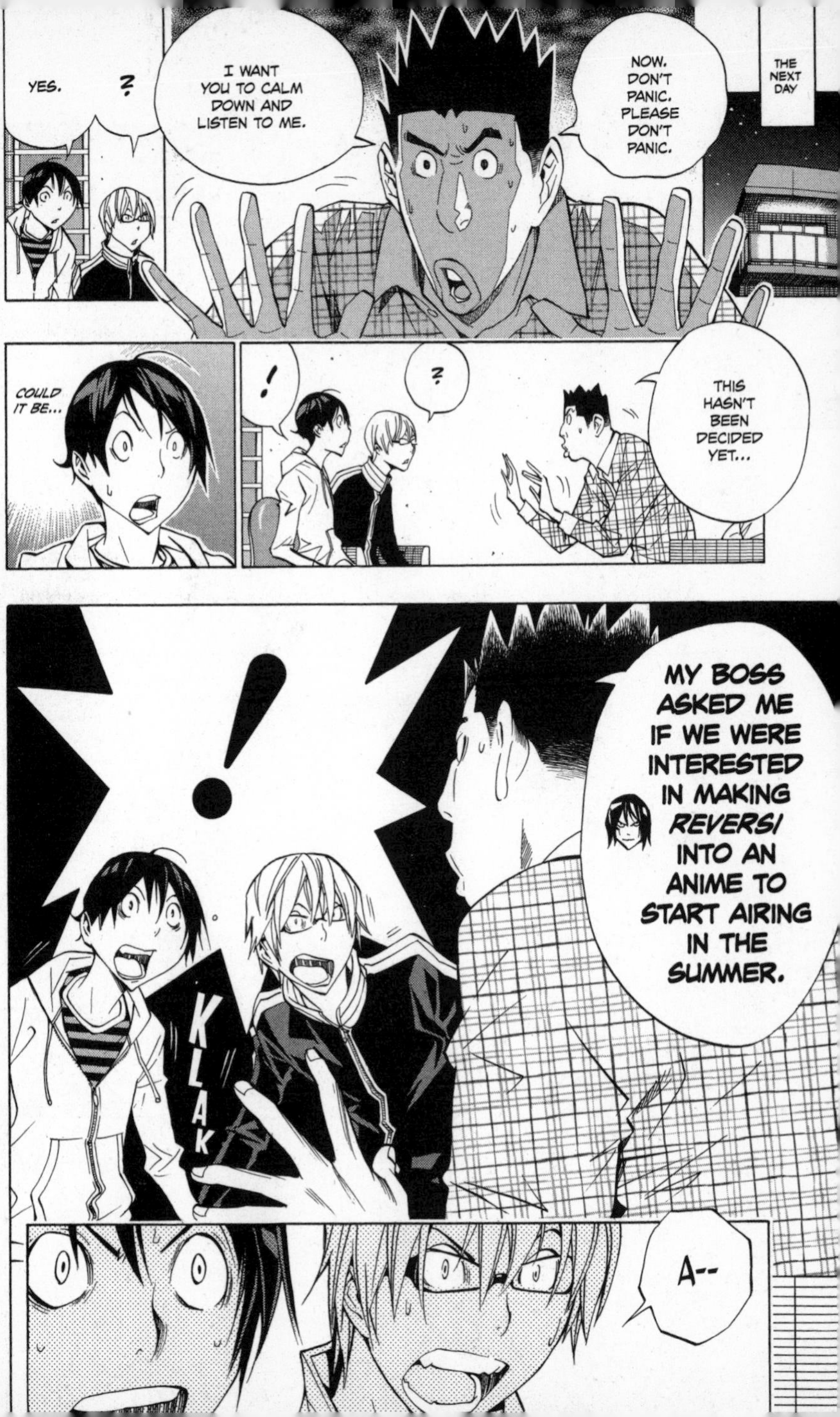
THE NEXT DAY
NOW. DON'T PANIC. PLEASE DON'T PANIC.
I WANT YOU TO CALM DOWN AND LISTEN TO ME.
?
YES.
THIS HASN'T BEEN DECIDED YET...
?
!
COULD IT BE...
MY BOSS ASKED ME IF WE WERE INTERESTED IN MAKING *REVERSI* INTO AN ANIME TO START AIRING IN THE SUMMER.
!
KLAK
A--

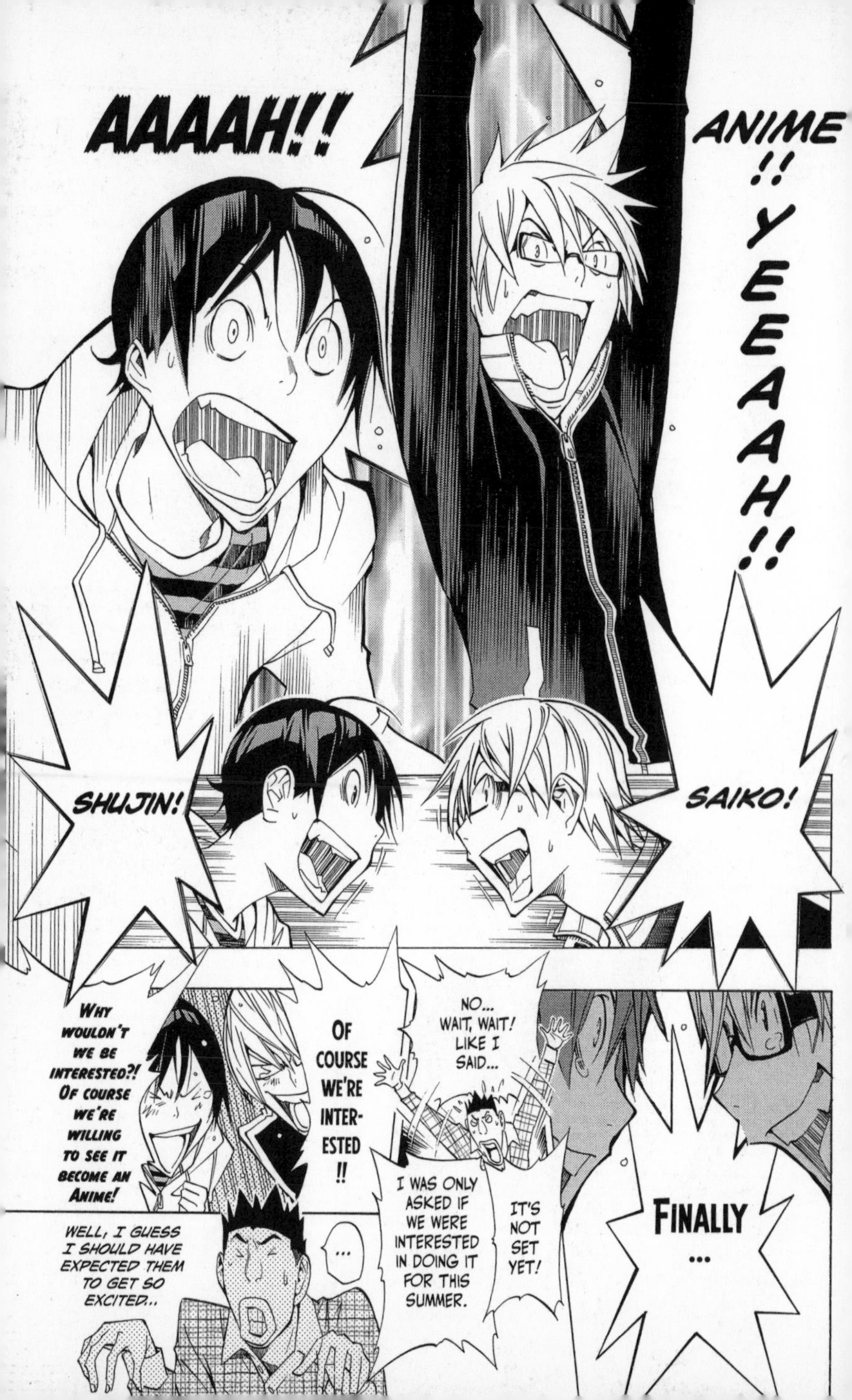
ANIME!! YEEAAAH!!
AAAAH!!
SAIKO!
SHUJIN!
FINALLY...
NO... WAIT, WAIT! LIKE I SAID...
OF COURSE WE'RE INTER-ESTED!!
WHY WOULDN'T WE BE INTERESTED?! OF COURSE WE'RE WILLING TO SEE IT BECOME AN ANIME!
IT'S NOT SET YET!
I WAS ONLY ASKED IF WE WERE INTERESTED IN DOING IT FOR THIS SUMMER.
...
WELL, I GUESS I SHOULD HAVE EXPECTED THEM TO GET SO EXCITED...

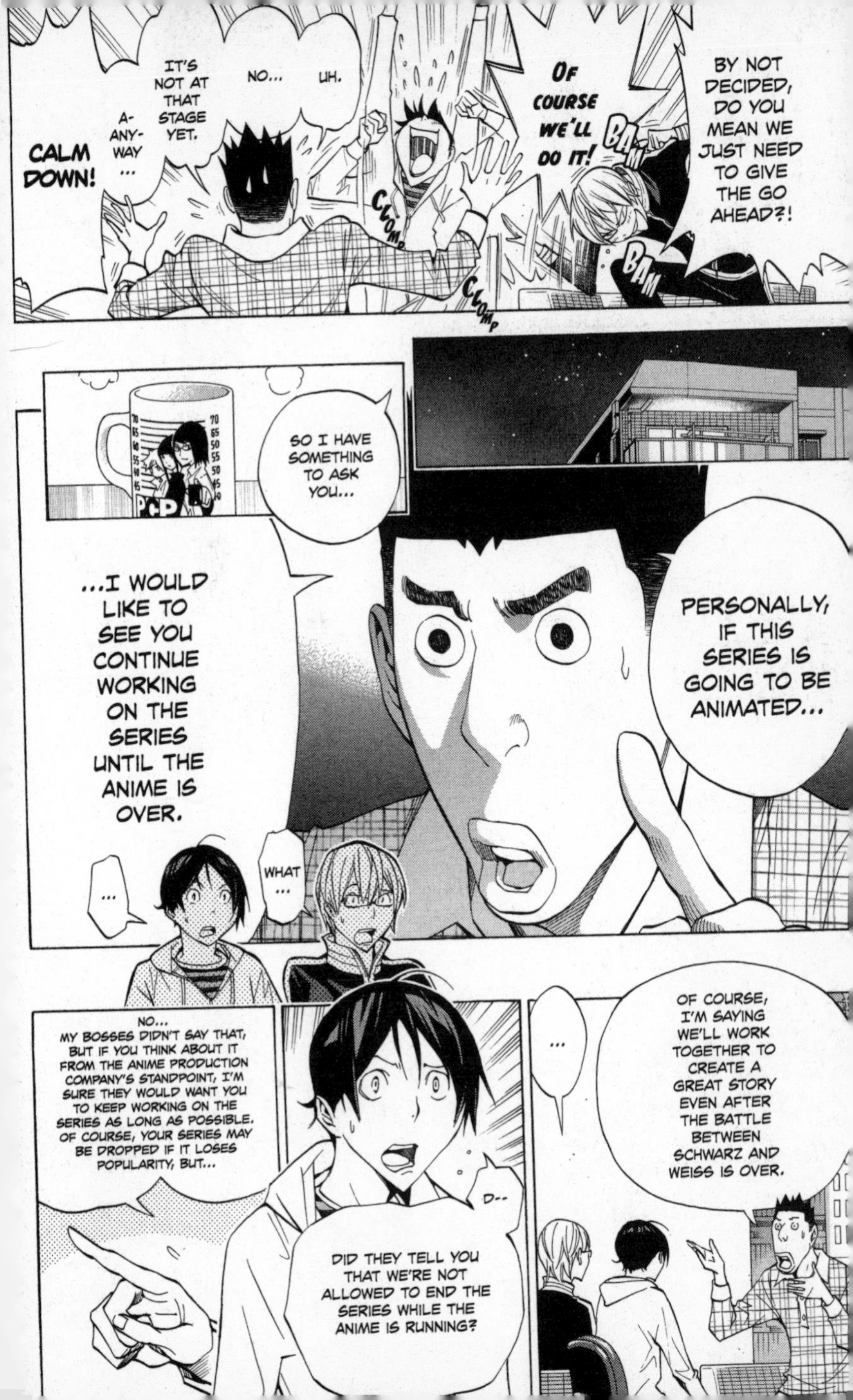
BY NOT DECIDED, DO YOU MEAN WE JUST NEED TO GIVE THE GO AHEAD?!
BAM
BAM
OF COURSE WE'LL DO IT!
CLOMP
CLOMP
UH.
NO...
IT'S NOT AT THAT STAGE YET.
A- ANY- WAY ...
CALM DOWN!
SO I HAVE SOMETHING TO ASK YOU...
PERSONALLY, IF THIS SERIES IS GOING TO BE ANIMATED...
...I WOULD LIKE TO SEE YOU CONTINUE WORKING ON THE SERIES UNTIL THE ANIME IS OVER.
WHAT ...
...
OF COURSE, I'M SAYING WE'LL WORK TOGETHER TO CREATE A GREAT STORY EVEN AFTER THE BATTLE BETWEEN SCHWARZ AND WEISS IS OVER.
...
D--
DID THEY TELL YOU THAT WE'RE NOT ALLOWED TO END THE SERIES WHILE THE ANIME IS RUNNING?
NO... MY BOSSES DIDN'T SAY THAT, BUT IF YOU THINK ABOUT IT FROM THE ANIME PRODUCTION COMPANY'S STANDPOINT, I'M SURE THEY WOULD WANT YOU TO KEEP WORKING ON THE SERIES AS LONG AS POSSIBLE. OF COURSE, YOUR SERIES MAY BE DROPPED IF IT LOSES POPULARITY, BUT...

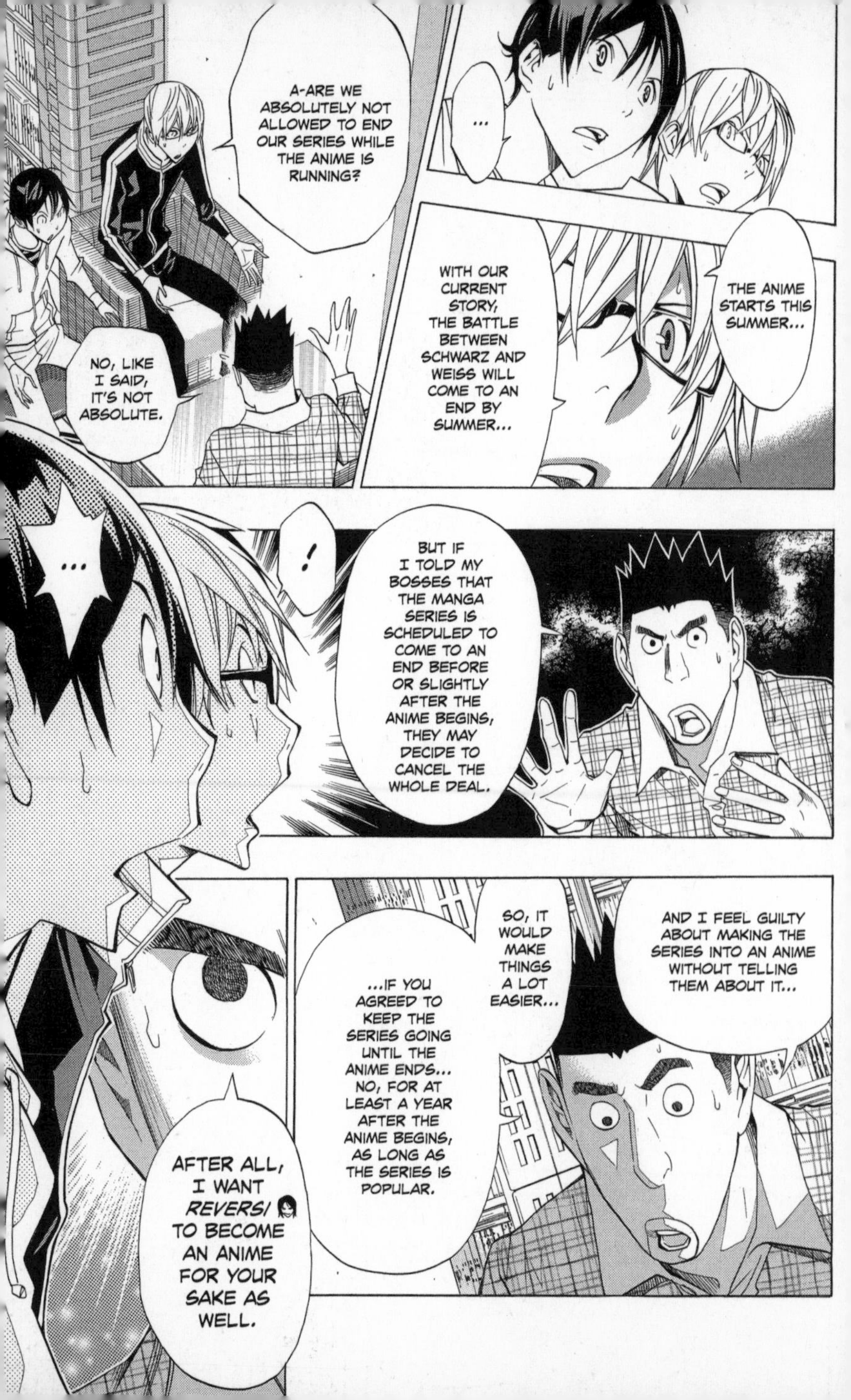
...
THE ANIME STARTS THIS SUMMER...
WITH OUR CURRENT STORY, THE BATTLE BETWEEN SCHWARZ AND WEISS WILL COME TO AN END BY SUMMER...
A-ARE WE ABSOLUTELY NOT ALLOWED TO END OUR SERIES WHILE THE ANIME IS RUNNING?
NO, LIKE I SAID, IT'S NOT ABSOLUTE.
BUT IF I TOLD MY BOSSES THAT THE MANGA SERIES IS SCHEDULED TO COME TO AN END BEFORE OR SLIGHTLY AFTER THE ANIME BEGINS, THEY MAY DECIDE TO CANCEL THE WHOLE DEAL.
!
...
AND I FEEL GUILTY ABOUT MAKING THE SERIES INTO AN ANIME WITHOUT TELLING THEM ABOUT IT...
SO, IT WOULD MAKE THINGS A LOT EASIER...
...IF YOU AGREED TO KEEP THE SERIES GOING UNTIL THE ANIME ENDS... NO, FOR AT LEAST A YEAR AFTER THE ANIME BEGINS, AS LONG AS THE SERIES IS POPULAR.
AFTER ALL, I WANT *REVERSI* TO BECOME AN ANIME FOR YOUR SAKE AS WELL.

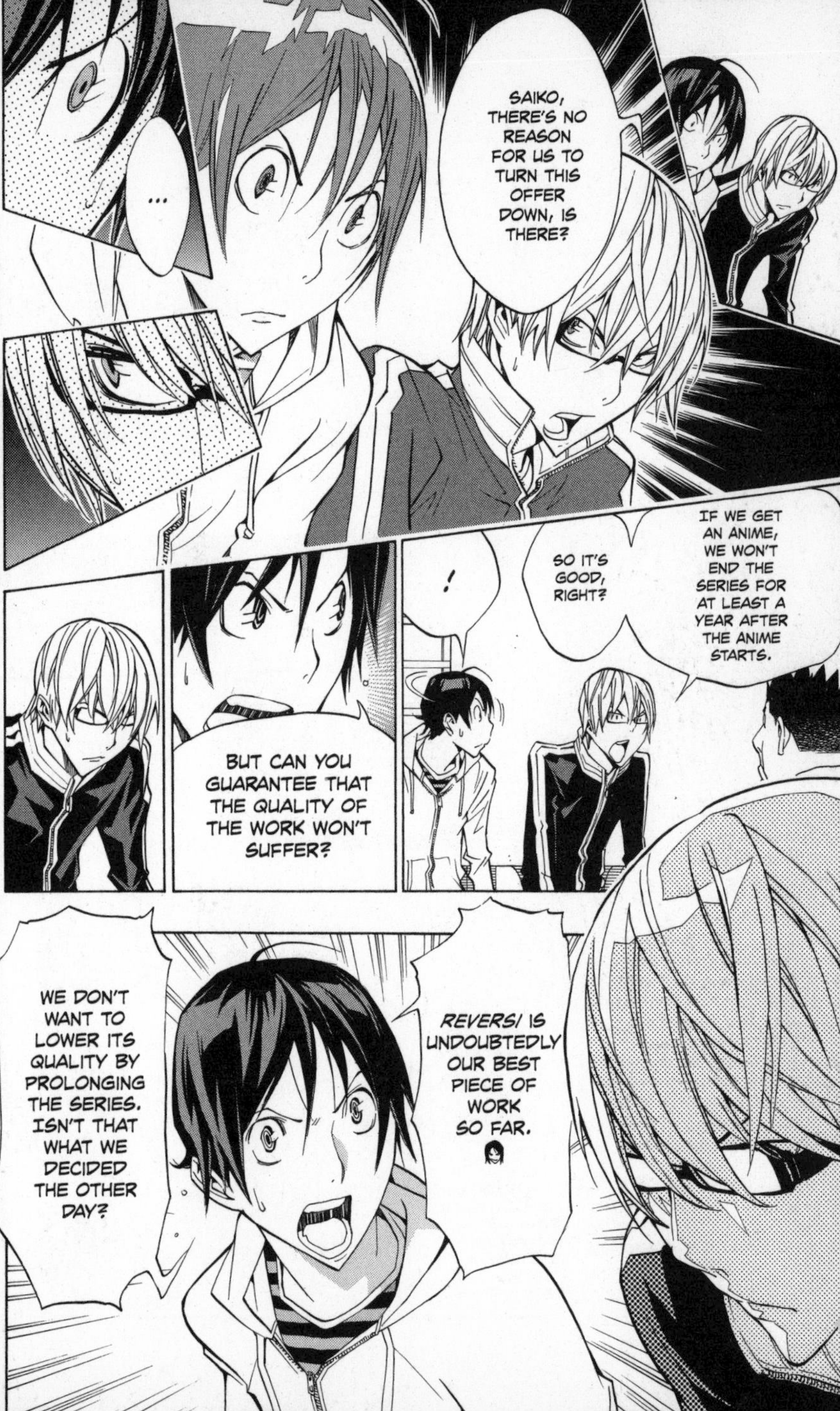
SAIKO, THERE'S NO REASON FOR US TO TURN THIS OFFER DOWN, IS THERE?
...
IF WE GET AN ANIME, WE WON'T END THE SERIES FOR AT LEAST A YEAR AFTER THE ANIME STARTS.
SO IT'S GOOD, RIGHT?
!
BUT CAN YOU GUARANTEE THAT THE QUALITY OF THE WORK WON'T SUFFER?
REVERSI IS UNDOUBTEDLY OUR BEST PIECE OF WORK SO FAR.
WE DON'T WANT TO LOWER ITS QUALITY BY PROLONGING THE SERIES. ISN'T THAT WHAT WE DECIDED THE OTHER DAY?

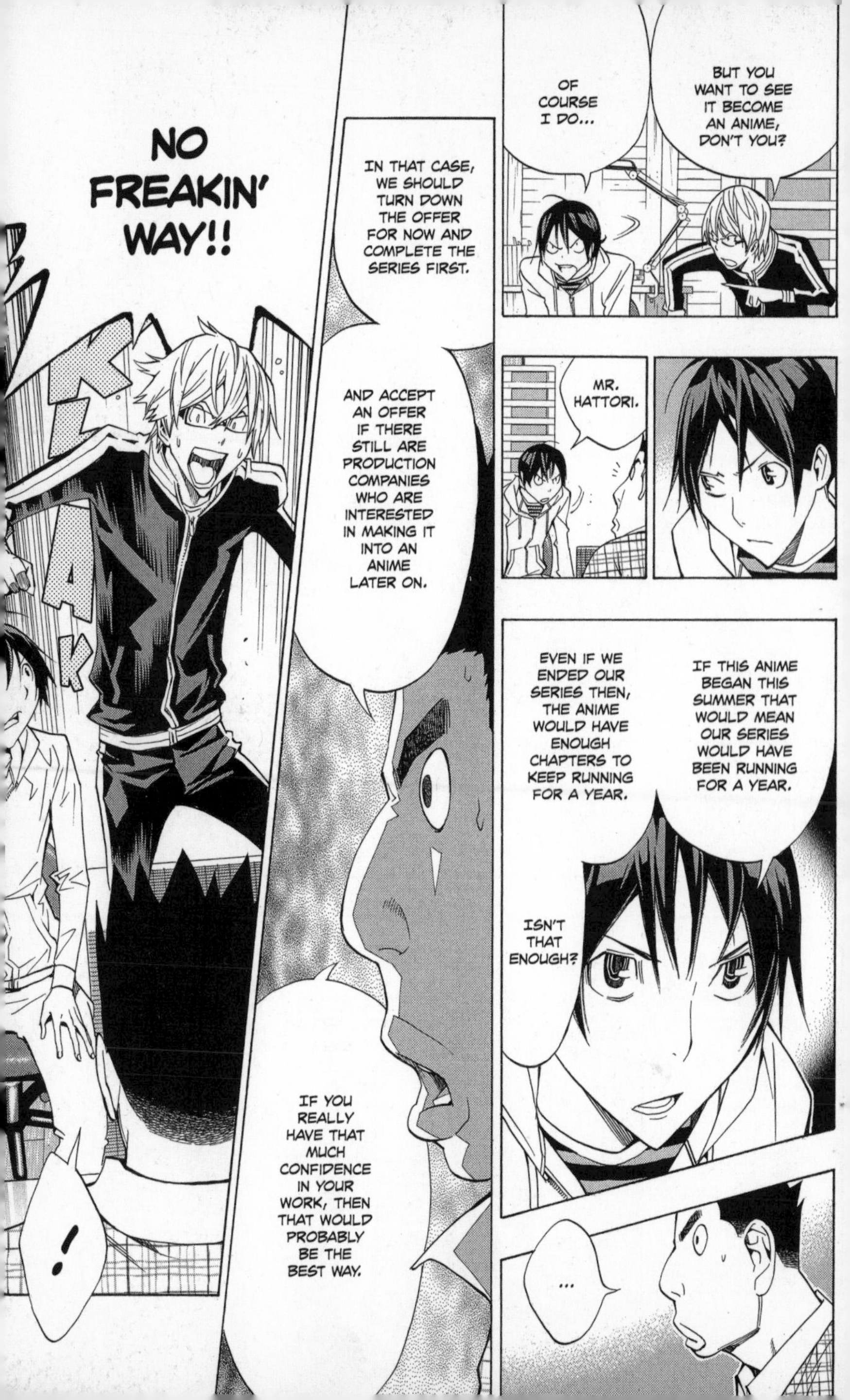
BUT YOU WANT TO SEE IT BECOME AN ANIME, DON'T YOU?
OF COURSE I DO...
MR. HATTORI.
IF THIS ANIME BEGAN THIS SUMMER THAT WOULD MEAN OUR SERIES WOULD HAVE BEEN RUNNING FOR A YEAR.
EVEN IF WE ENDED OUR SERIES THEN, THE ANIME WOULD HAVE ENOUGH CHAPTERS TO KEEP RUNNING FOR A YEAR.
ISN'T THAT ENOUGH?
...
IN THAT CASE, WE SHOULD TURN DOWN THE OFFER FOR NOW AND COMPLETE THE SERIES FIRST.
AND ACCEPT AN OFFER IF THERE STILL ARE PRODUCTION COMPANIES WHO ARE INTERESTED IN MAKING IT INTO AN ANIME LATER ON.
IF YOU REALLY HAVE THAT MUCH CONFIDENCE IN YOUR WORK, THEN THAT WOULD PROBABLY BE THE BEST WAY.
NO FREAKIN' WAY!!
!

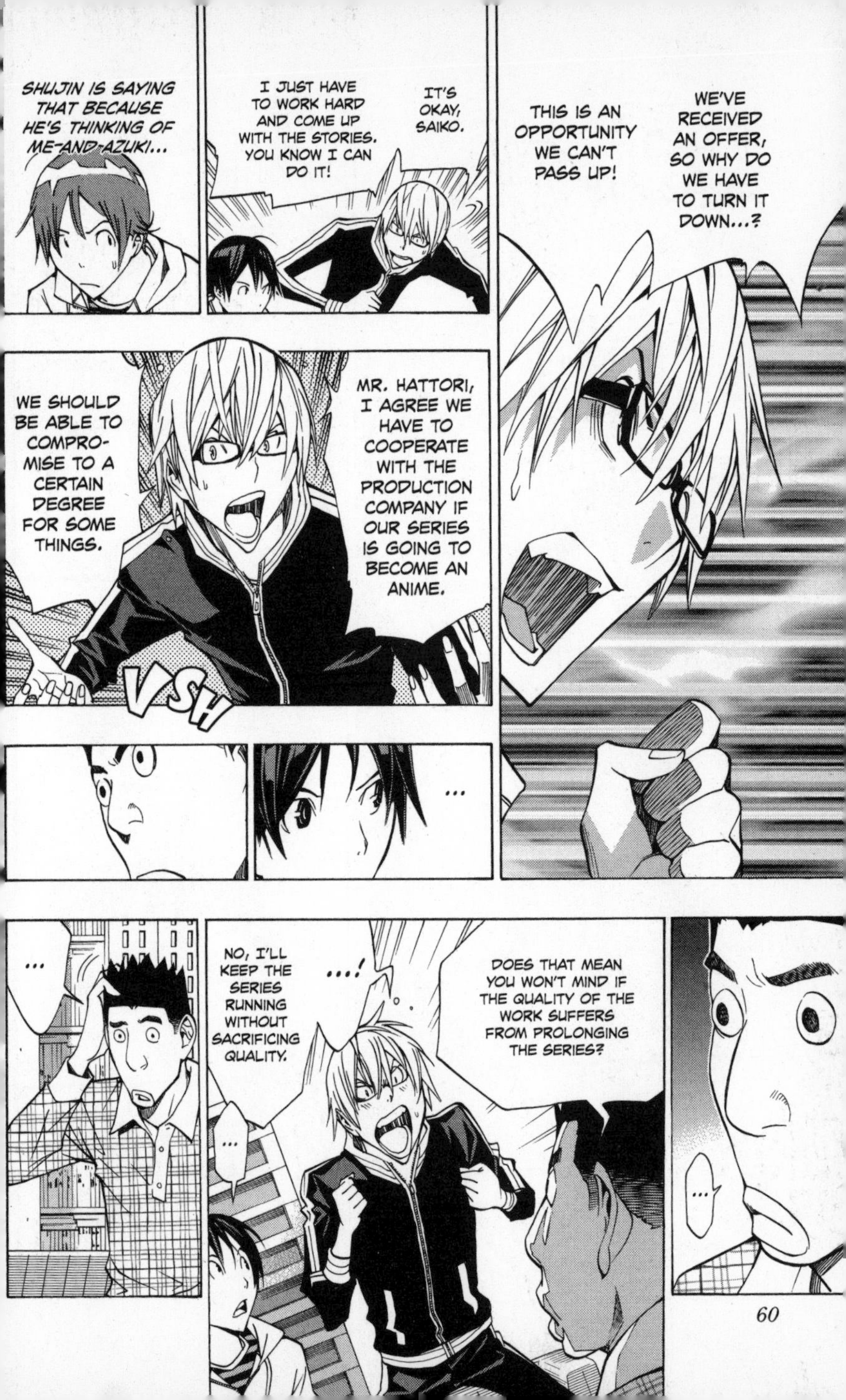
WE'VE RECEIVED AN OFFER, SO WHY DO WE HAVE TO TURN IT DOWN...?
THIS IS AN OPPORTUNITY WE CAN'T PASS UP!
IT'S OKAY, SAIKO.
I JUST HAVE TO WORK HARD AND COME UP WITH THE STORIES. YOU KNOW I CAN DO IT!
SHUJIN IS SAYING THAT BECAUSE HE'S THINKING OF ME-AND-AZUKI...
MR. HATTORI, I AGREE WE HAVE TO COOPERATE WITH THE PRODUCTION COMPANY IF OUR SERIES IS GOING TO BECOME AN ANIME.
WE SHOULD BE ABLE TO COMPROMISE TO A CERTAIN DEGREE FOR SOME THINGS.
VSH
...
...
DOES THAT MEAN YOU WON'T MIND IF THE QUALITY OF THE WORK SUFFERS FROM PROLONGING THE SERIES?
...!
NO, I'LL KEEP THE SERIES RUNNING WITHOUT SACRIFICING QUALITY.
...
...

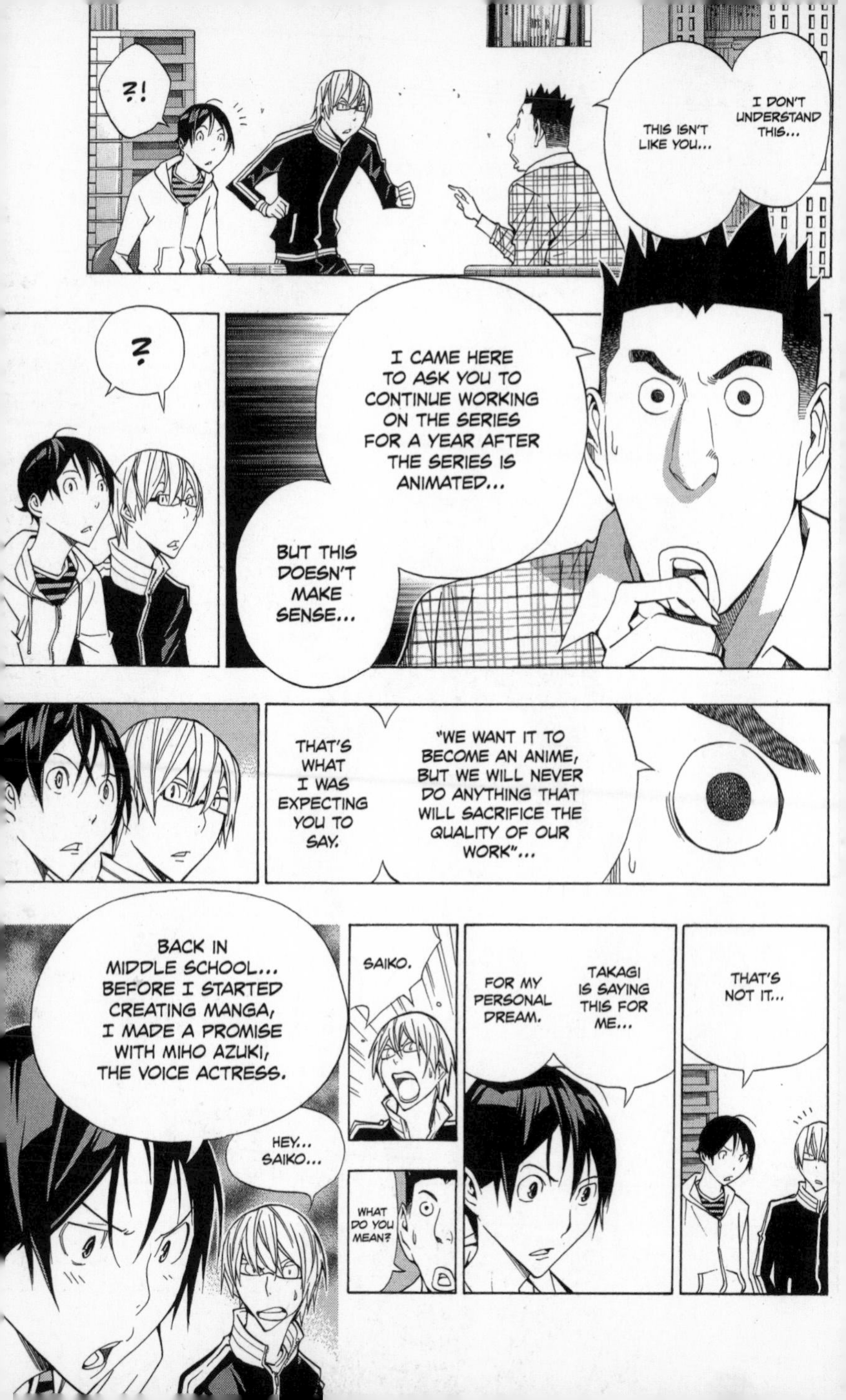
I DON'T UNDERSTAND THIS...
THIS ISN'T LIKE YOU...
?!
I CAME HERE TO ASK YOU TO CONTINUE WORKING ON THE SERIES FOR A YEAR AFTER THE SERIES IS ANIMATED...
BUT THIS DOESN'T MAKE SENSE...
?
"WE WANT IT TO BECOME AN ANIME, BUT WE WILL NEVER DO ANYTHING THAT WILL SACRIFICE THE QUALITY OF OUR WORK"...
THAT'S WHAT I WAS EXPECTING YOU TO SAY.
THAT'S NOT IT...
TAKAGI IS SAYING THIS FOR ME...
FOR MY PERSONAL DREAM.
WHAT DO YOU MEAN?
SAIKO.
BACK IN MIDDLE SCHOOL... BEFORE I STARTED CREATING MANGA, I MADE A PROMISE WITH MIHO AZUKI, THE VOICE ACTRESS.
HEY... SAIKO...

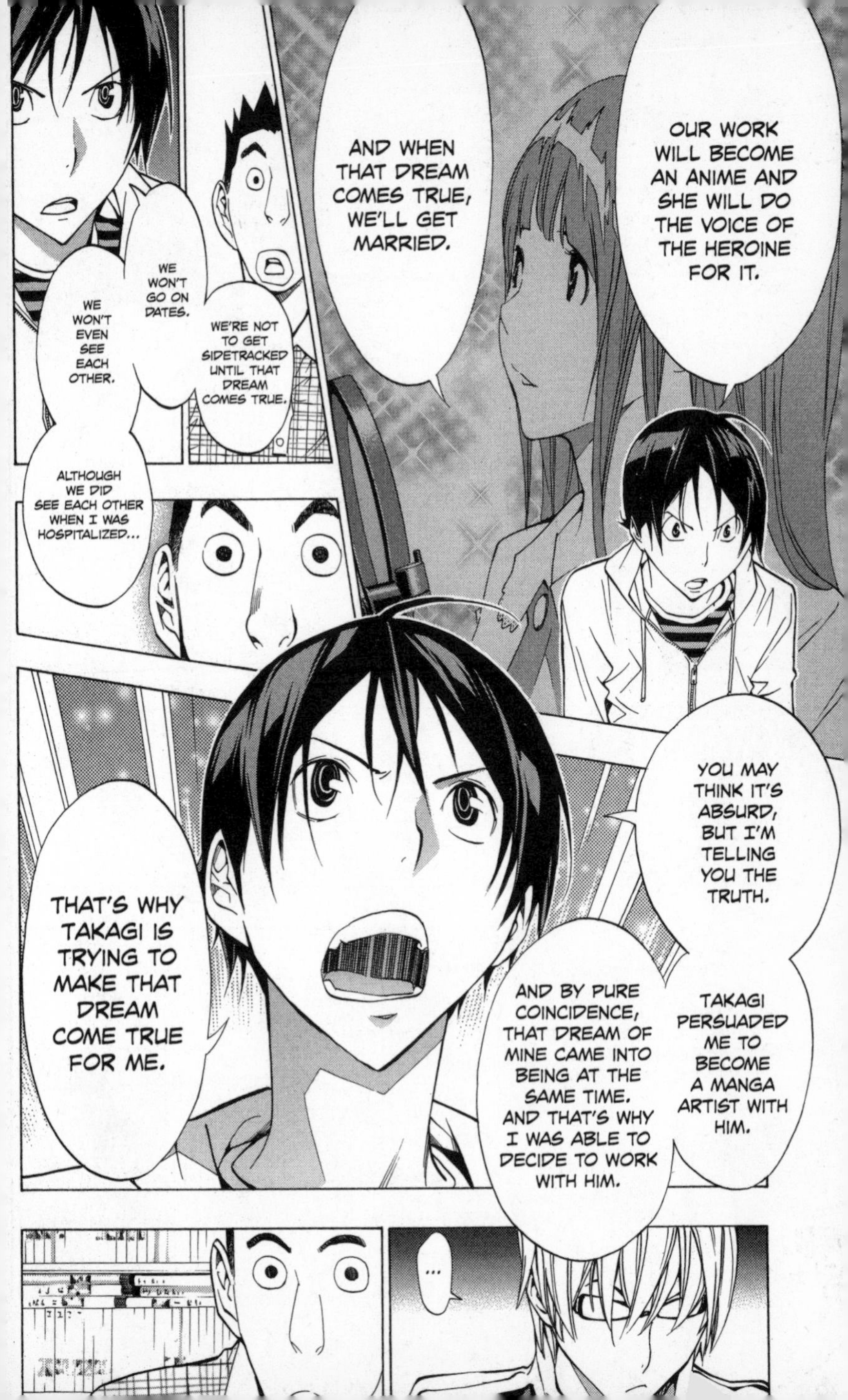
OUR WORK WILL BECOME AN ANIME AND SHE WILL DO THE VOICE OF THE HEROINE FOR IT.
AND WHEN THAT DREAM COMES TRUE, WE'LL GET MARRIED.
WE'RE NOT TO GET SIDETRACKED UNTIL THAT DREAM COMES TRUE.
WE WON'T GO ON DATES.
WE WON'T EVEN SEE EACH OTHER.
ALTHOUGH WE DID SEE EACH OTHER WHEN I WAS HOSPITALIZED...
YOU MAY THINK IT'S ABSURD, BUT I'M TELLING YOU THE TRUTH.
TAKAGI PERSUADED ME TO BECOME A MANGA ARTIST WITH HIM.
AND BY PURE COINCIDENCE, THAT DREAM OF MINE CAME INTO BEING AT THE SAME TIME. AND THAT'S WHY I WAS ABLE TO DECIDE TO WORK WITH HIM.
THAT'S WHY TAKAGI IS TRYING TO MAKE THAT DREAM COME TRUE FOR ME.
...

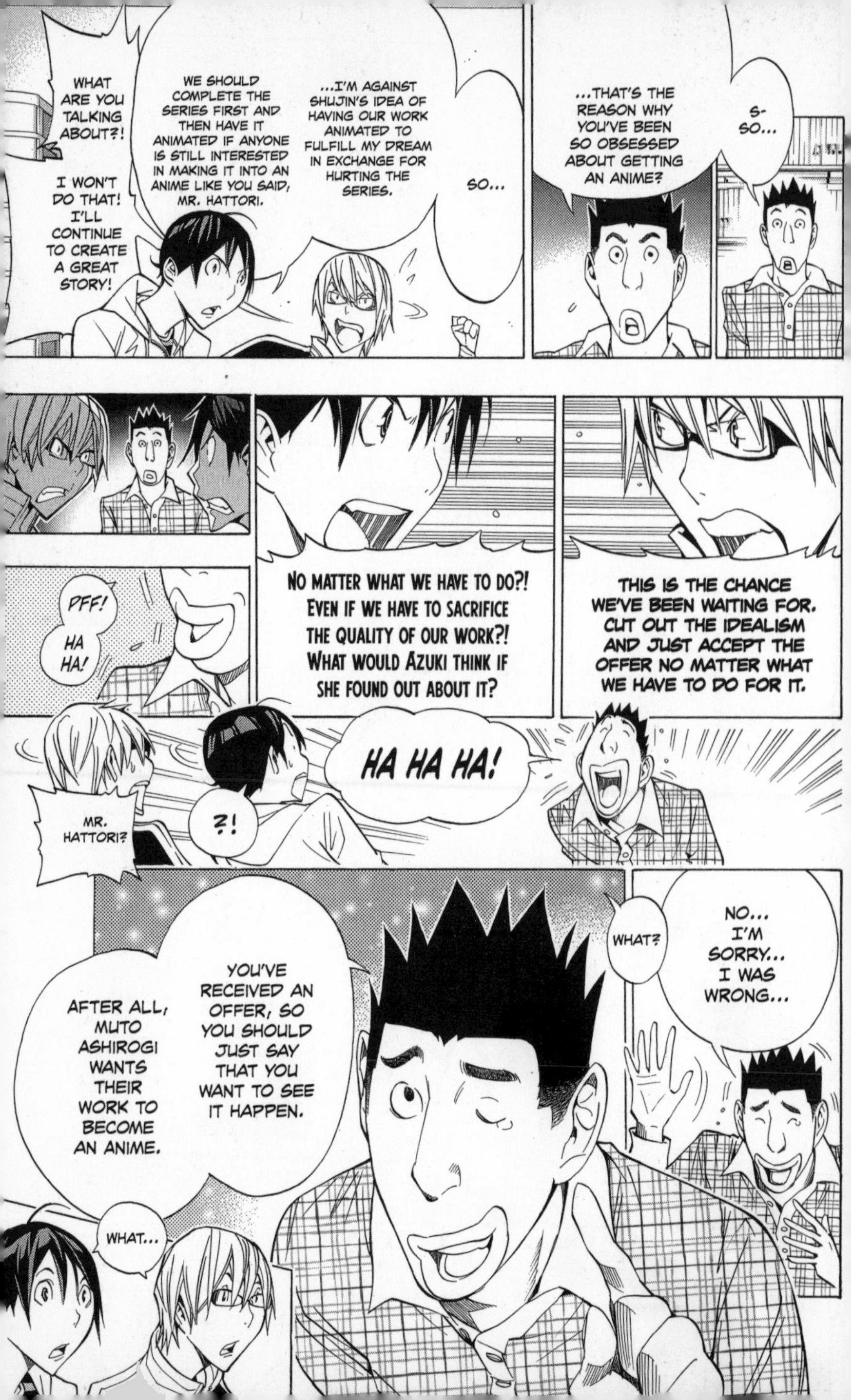
S-
SO...
...THAT'S THE REASON WHY YOU'VE BEEN SO OBSESSED ABOUT GETTING AN ANIME?
SO...
...I'M AGAINST SHUJIN'S IDEA OF HAVING OUR WORK ANIMATED TO FULFILL MY DREAM IN EXCHANGE FOR HURTING THE SERIES.
WE SHOULD COMPLETE THE SERIES FIRST AND THEN HAVE IT ANIMATED IF ANYONE IS STILL INTERESTED IN MAKING IT INTO AN ANIME LIKE YOU SAID, MR. HATTORI.
WHAT ARE YOU TALKING ABOUT?!
I WON'T DO THAT! I'LL CONTINUE TO CREATE A GREAT STORY!
THIS IS THE CHANCE WE'VE BEEN WAITING FOR. CUT OUT THE IDEALISM AND JUST ACCEPT THE OFFER NO MATTER WHAT WE HAVE TO DO FOR IT.
NO MATTER WHAT WE HAVE TO DO?! EVEN IF WE HAVE TO SACRIFICE THE QUALITY OF OUR WORK?! WHAT WOULD AZUKI THINK IF SHE FOUND OUT ABOUT IT?
PFF!
HA HA!
HA HA HA!
?!
MR. HATTORI?
NO... I'M SORRY... I WAS WRONG...
WHAT?
YOU'VE RECEIVED AN OFFER, SO YOU SHOULD JUST SAY THAT YOU WANT TO SEE IT HAPPEN.
AFTER ALL, MUTO ASHIROGI WANTS THEIR WORK TO BECOME AN ANIME.
WHAT...

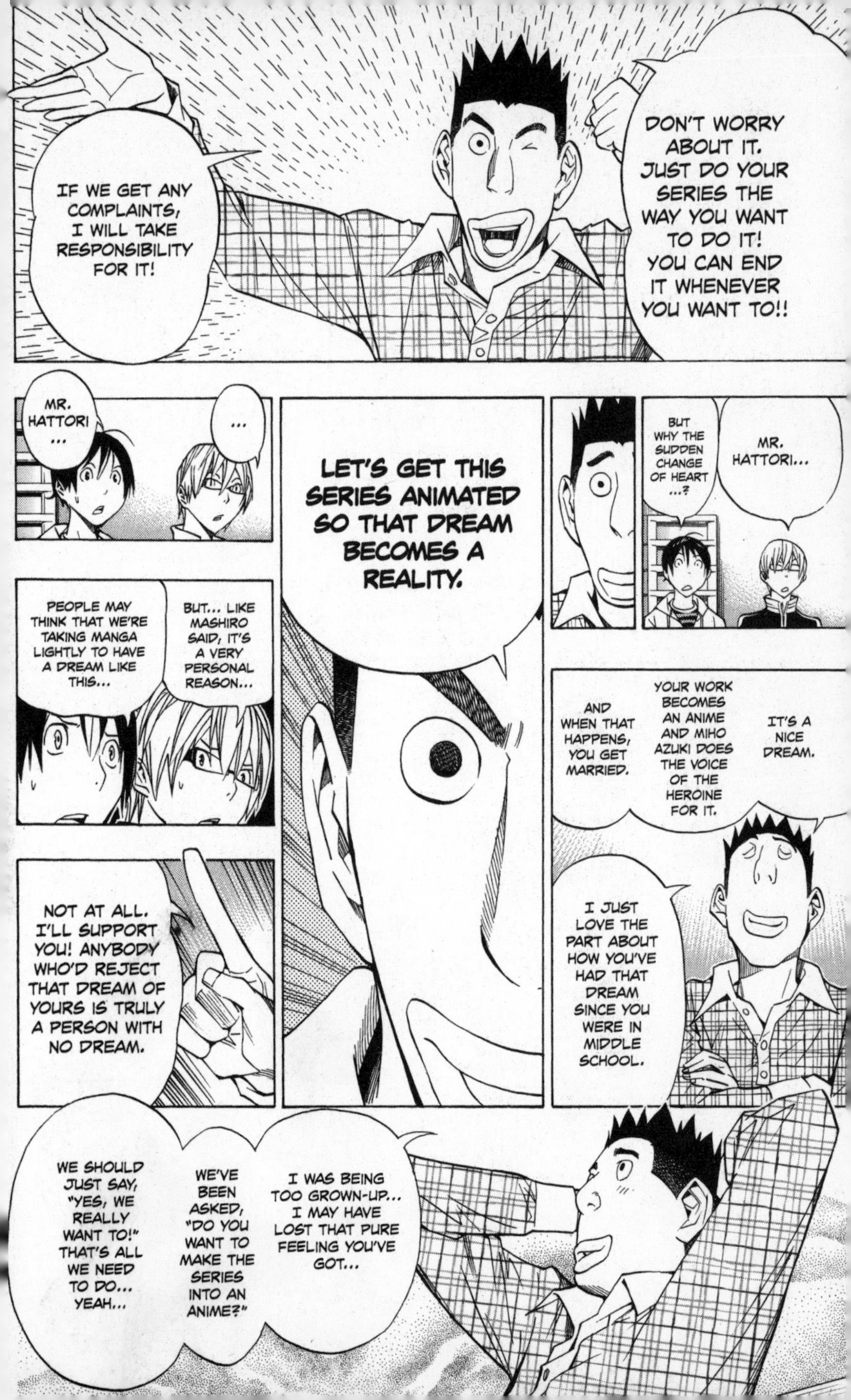
DON'T WORRY ABOUT IT. JUST DO YOUR SERIES THE WAY YOU WANT TO DO IT! YOU CAN END IT WHENEVER YOU WANT TO!!
IF WE GET ANY COMPLAINTS, I WILL TAKE RESPONSIBILITY FOR IT!
MR. HATTORI...
BUT WHY THE SUDDEN CHANGE OF HEART ...?
IT'S A NICE DREAM.
YOUR WORK BECOMES AN ANIME AND MIHO AZUKI DOES THE VOICE OF THE HEROINE FOR IT.
AND WHEN THAT HAPPENS, YOU GET MARRIED.
I JUST LOVE THE PART ABOUT HOW YOU'VE HAD THAT DREAM SINCE YOU WERE IN MIDDLE SCHOOL.
LET'S GET THIS SERIES ANIMATED SO THAT DREAM BECOMES A REALITY.
MR. HATTORI ...
...
BUT... LIKE MASHIRO SAID, IT'S A VERY PERSONAL REASON...
PEOPLE MAY THINK THAT WE'RE TAKING MANGA LIGHTLY TO HAVE A DREAM LIKE THIS...
NOT AT ALL. I'LL SUPPORT YOU! ANYBODY WHO'D REJECT THAT DREAM OF YOURS IS TRULY A PERSON WITH NO DREAM.
I WAS BEING TOO GROWN-UP... I MAY HAVE LOST THAT PURE FEELING YOU'VE GOT...
WE'VE BEEN ASKED, "DO YOU WANT TO MAKE THE SERIES INTO AN ANIME?"
WE SHOULD JUST SAY, "YES, WE REALLY WANT TO!" THAT'S ALL WE NEED TO DO... YEAH...

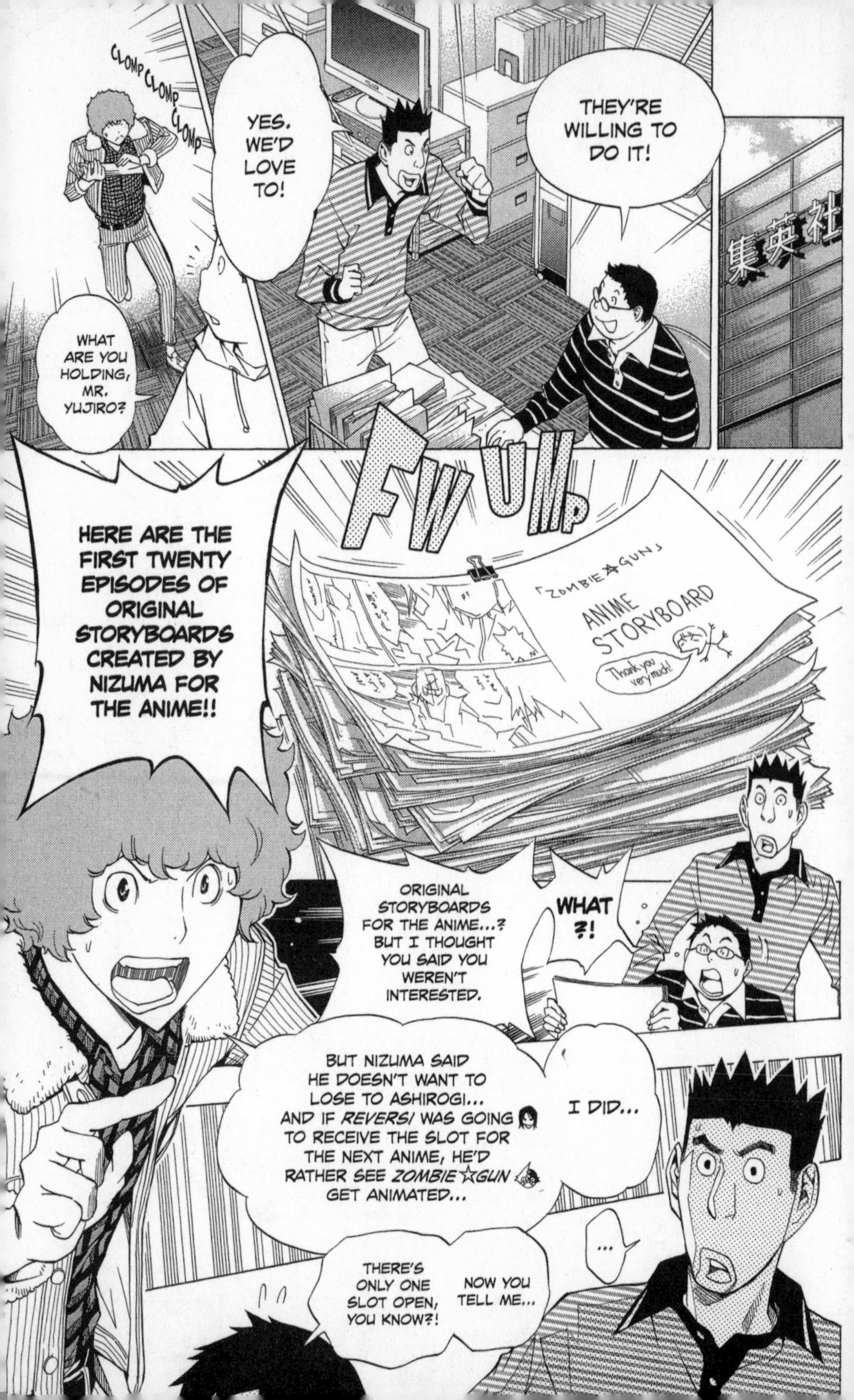
集英社
THEY'RE WILLING TO DO IT!
YES. WE'D LOVE TO!
CLOMP CLOMP CLOMP
WHAT ARE YOU HOLDING, MR. YUJIRO?
FWUMP
HERE ARE THE FIRST TWENTY EPISODES OF ORIGINAL STORYBOARDS CREATED BY NIZUMA FOR THE ANIME!!
「ZOMBIE☆GUN」 ANIME STORYBOARD
Thank you very much!
WHAT?!
ORIGINAL STORYBOARDS FOR THE ANIME...? BUT I THOUGHT YOU SAID YOU WEREN'T INTERESTED.
I DID...
BUT NIZUMA SAID HE DOESN'T WANT TO LOSE TO ASHIROGI... AND IF *REVERSI* WAS GOING TO RECEIVE THE SLOT FOR THE NEXT ANIME, HE'D RATHER SEE *ZOMBIE☆GUN* GET ANIMATED...
...
NOW YOU TELL ME...
THERE'S ONLY ONE SLOT OPEN, YOU KNOW?!

※CREATOR STORYBOARDS AND FINISHED PAGES IN JAPANESE

BAKUMAN。vol. 19

"Until the Final Draft Is Complete"

Chapter 163, pp. 52-53

COMPLETE!

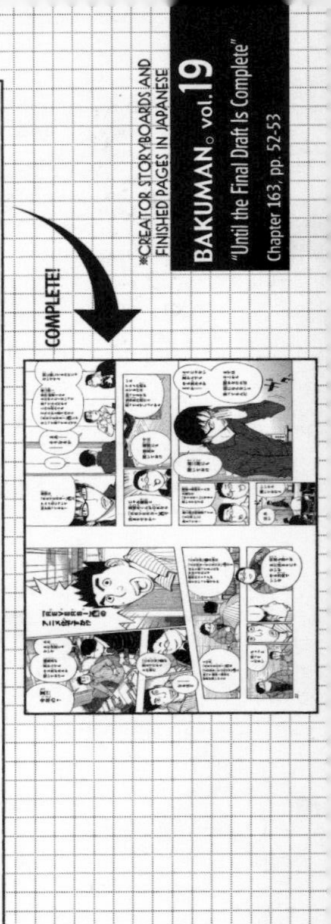

OBATA'S STORYBOARD

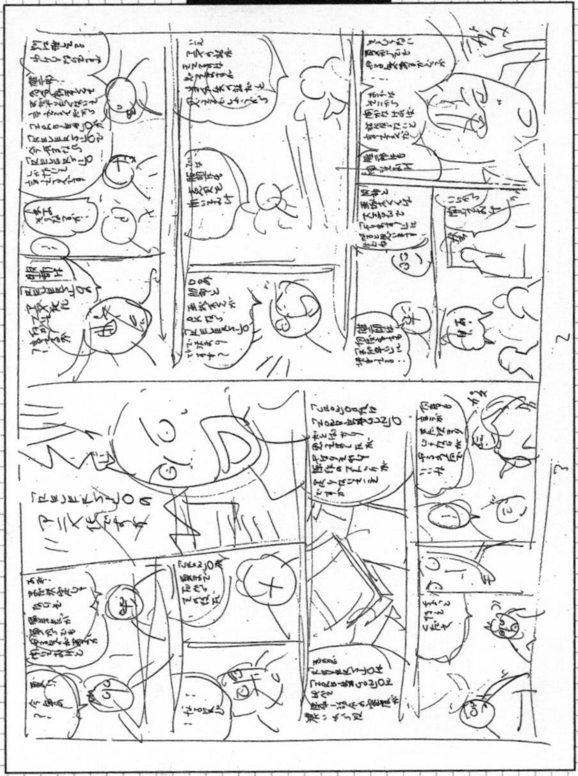

OHBA'S STORYBOARD

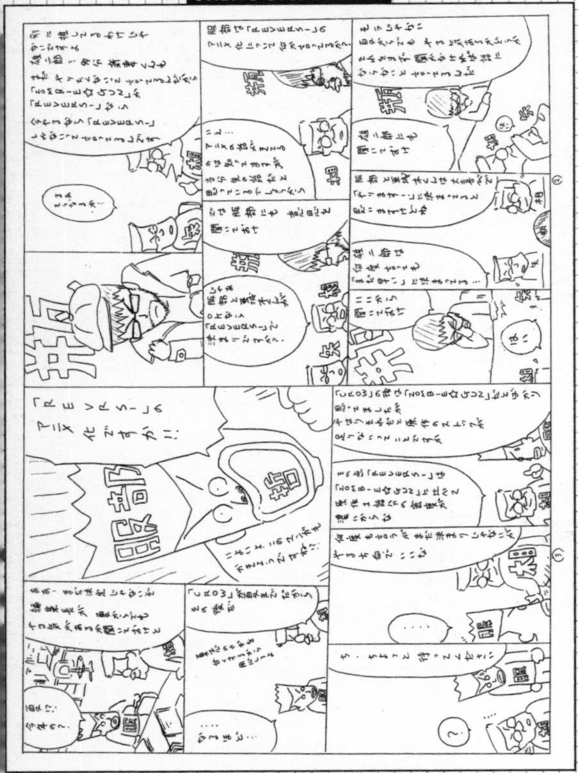

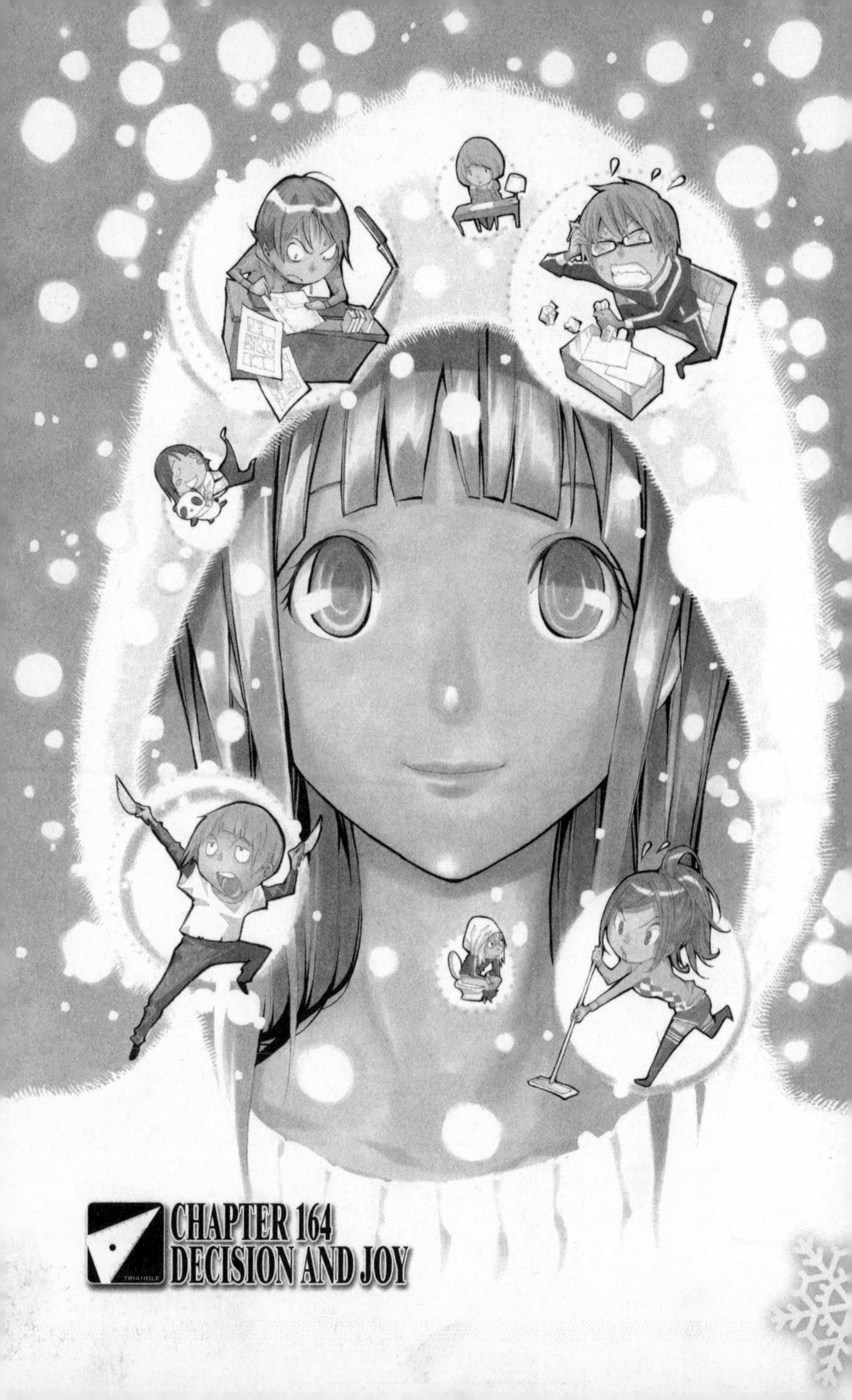

CHAPTER 164
DECISION AND JOY

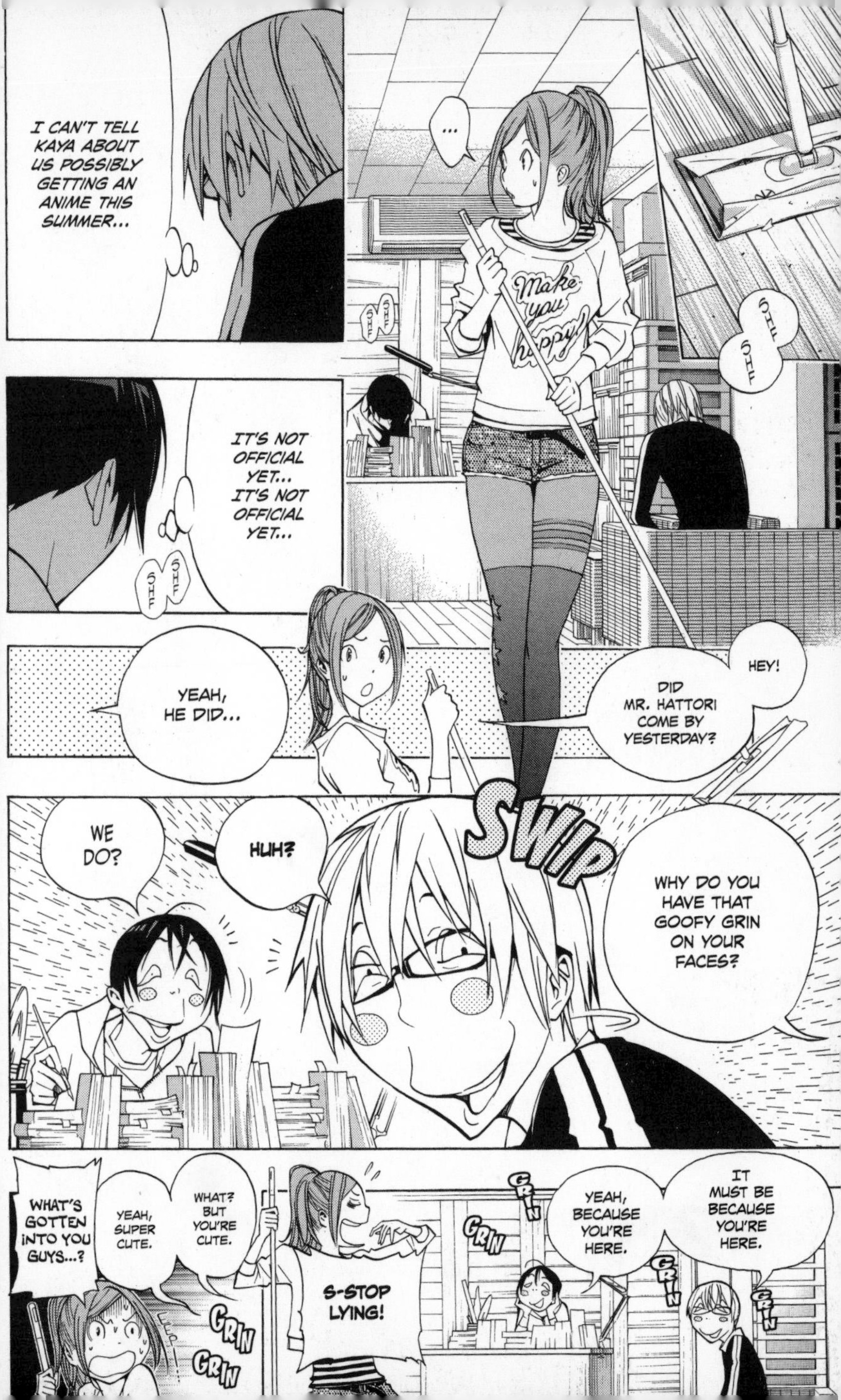
SHF SHF
...
I CAN'T TELL KAYA ABOUT US POSSIBLY GETTING AN ANIME THIS SUMMER...
SHF SHF
HEY!
DID MR. HATTORI COME BY YESTERDAY?
IT'S NOT OFFICIAL YET... IT'S NOT OFFICIAL YET...
SHF SHF
YEAH, HE DID...
SWIP
WHY DO YOU HAVE THAT GOOFY GRIN ON YOUR FACES?
HUH?
WE DO?
IT MUST BE BECAUSE YOU'RE HERE.
GRIN
YEAH, BECAUSE YOU'RE HERE.
GRIN
GRIN
S-STOP LYING!
WHAT? BUT YOU'RE CUTE.
YEAH, SUPER CUTE.
GRIN GRIN
WHAT'S GOTTEN INTO YOU GUYS...?

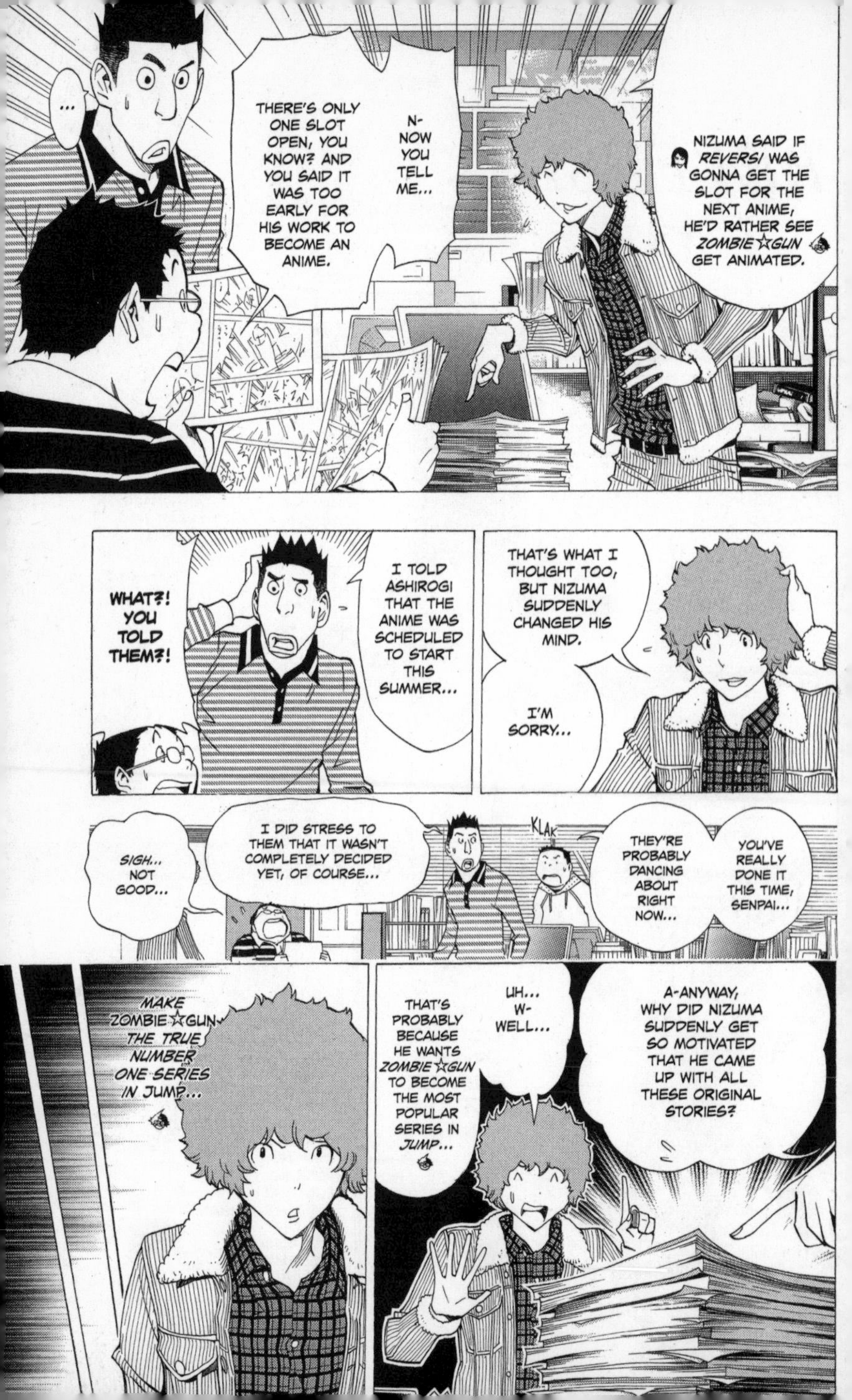
NIZUMA SAID IF REVERSI WAS GONNA GET THE SLOT FOR THE NEXT ANIME, HE'D RATHER SEE ZOMBIE☆GUN GET ANIMATED.
N-NOW YOU TELL ME...
THERE'S ONLY ONE SLOT OPEN, YOU KNOW? AND YOU SAID IT WAS TOO EARLY FOR HIS WORK TO BECOME AN ANIME.
...
THAT'S WHAT I THOUGHT TOO, BUT NIZUMA SUDDENLY CHANGED HIS MIND.
I'M SORRY...
I TOLD ASHIROGI THAT THE ANIME WAS SCHEDULED TO START THIS SUMMER...
WHAT?! YOU TOLD THEM?!
YOU'VE REALLY DONE IT THIS TIME, SENPAI...
THEY'RE PROBABLY DANCING ABOUT RIGHT NOW...
KLAK
I DID STRESS TO THEM THAT IT WASN'T COMPLETELY DECIDED YET, OF COURSE...
SIGH... NOT GOOD...
A-ANYWAY, WHY DID NIZUMA SUDDENLY GET SO MOTIVATED THAT HE CAME UP WITH ALL THESE ORIGINAL STORIES?
UH... W-WELL...
THAT'S PROBABLY BECAUSE HE WANTS ZOMBIE☆GUN TO BECOME THE MOST POPULAR SERIES IN JUMP...
MAKE ZOMBIE☆GUN THE TRUE NUMBER ONE SERIES IN JUMP...

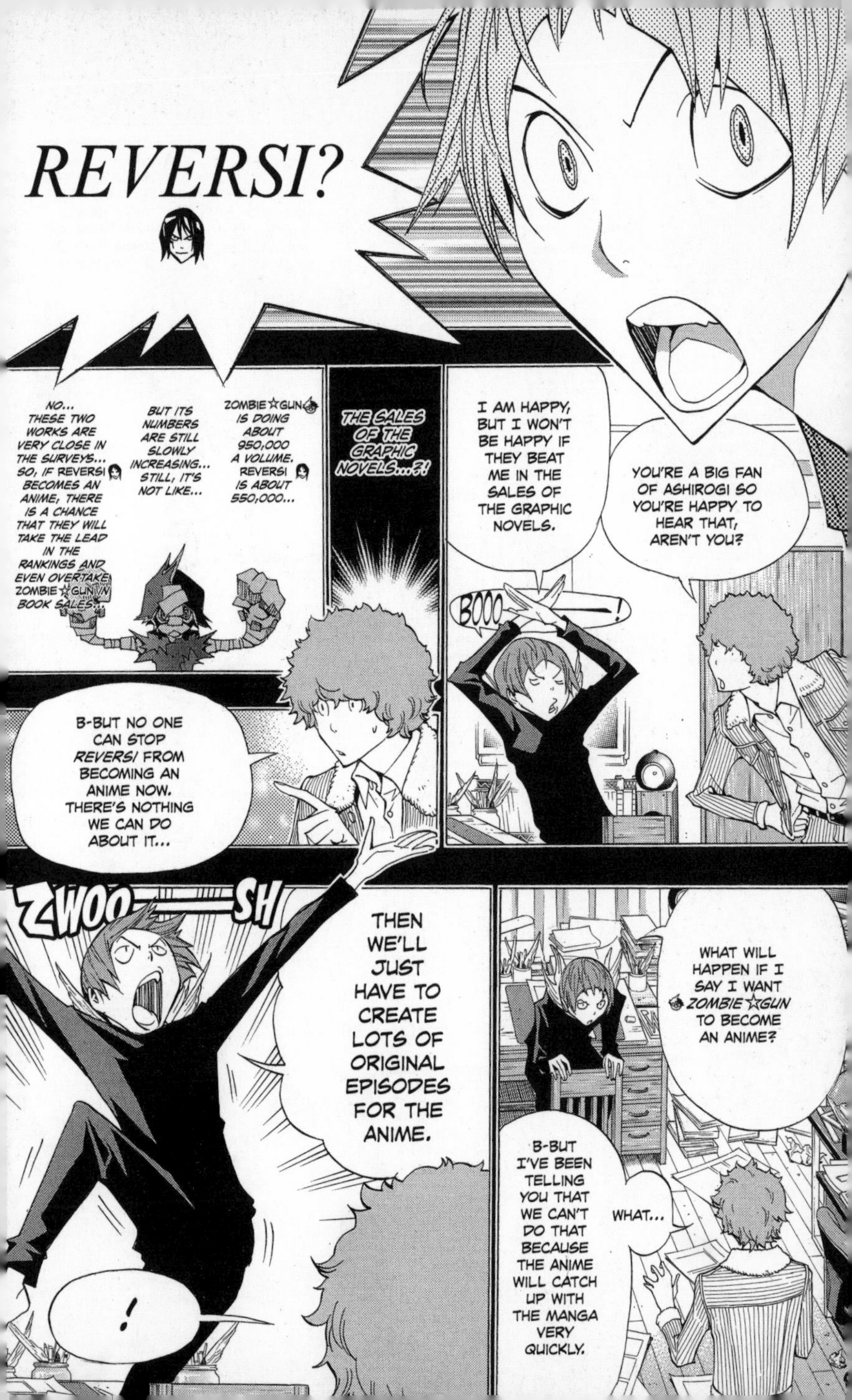
REVERSI?
YOU'RE A BIG FAN OF ASHIROGI SO YOU'RE HAPPY TO HEAR THAT, AREN'T YOU?
I AM HAPPY, BUT I WON'T BE HAPPY IF THEY BEAT ME IN THE SALES OF THE GRAPHIC NOVELS.
BOOO—!
THE SALES OF THE GRAPHIC NOVELS...?!
ZOMBIE☆GUN IS DOING ABOUT 950,000 A VOLUME. REVERSI IS ABOUT 550,000...
BUT ITS NUMBERS ARE STILL SLOWLY INCREASING... STILL, IT'S NOT LIKE...
NO... THESE TWO WORKS ARE VERY CLOSE IN THE SURVEYS... SO, IF REVERSI BECOMES AN ANIME, THERE IS A CHANCE THAT THEY WILL TAKE THE LEAD IN THE RANKINGS AND EVEN OVERTAKE ZOMBIE☆GUN IN BOOK SALES...
B-BUT NO ONE CAN STOP REVERSI FROM BECOMING AN ANIME NOW. THERE'S NOTHING WE CAN DO ABOUT IT...
WHAT WILL HAPPEN IF I SAY I WANT ZOMBIE☆GUN TO BECOME AN ANIME?
WHAT...
B-BUT I'VE BEEN TELLING YOU THAT WE CAN'T DO THAT BECAUSE THE ANIME WILL CATCH UP WITH THE MANGA VERY QUICKLY.
ZWOO—SH
THEN WE'LL JUST HAVE TO CREATE LOTS OF ORIGINAL EPISODES FOR THE ANIME.
!

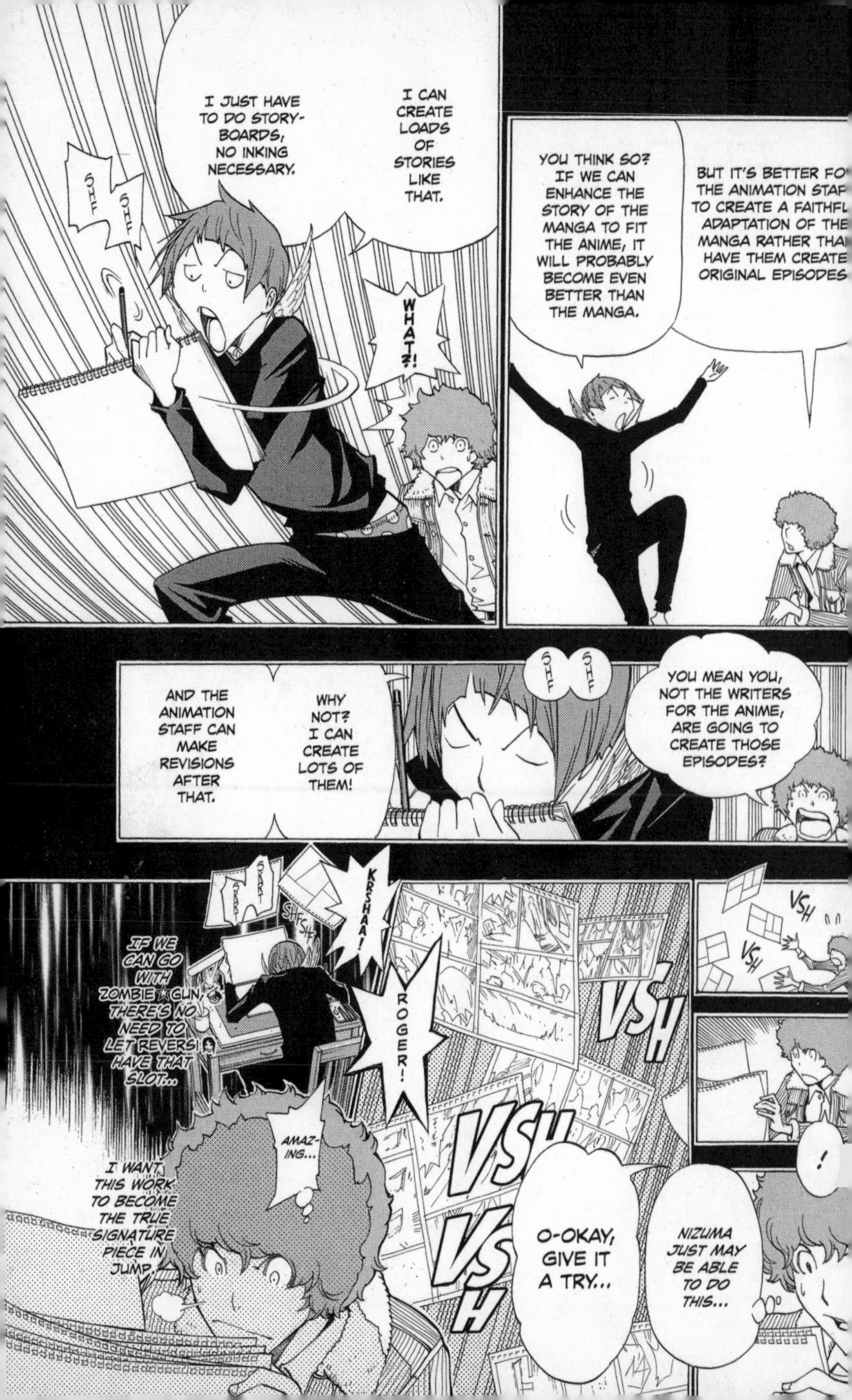

BUT IT'S BETTER FO THE ANIMATION STAF TO CREATE A FAITHFL ADAPTATION OF THE MANGA RATHER THA HAVE THEM CREATE ORIGINAL EPISODES
YOU THINK SO? IF WE CAN ENHANCE THE STORY OF THE MANGA TO FIT THE ANIME, IT WILL PROBABLY BECOME EVEN BETTER THAN THE MANGA.
WHAT?!
I CAN CREATE LOADS OF STORIES LIKE THAT.
I JUST HAVE TO DO STORY-BOARDS, NO INKING NECESSARY.
SHF
SHF
YOU MEAN YOU, NOT THE WRITERS FOR THE ANIME, ARE GOING TO CREATE THOSE EPISODES?
SHF
SHF
WHY NOT? I CAN CREATE LOTS OF THEM!
AND THE ANIMATION STAFF CAN MAKE REVISIONS AFTER THAT.
VSH
VSH
VSH
!
NIZUMA JUST MAY BE ABLE TO DO THIS...
O-OKAY, GIVE IT A TRY...
VSH
VSH
KRSHAA!
SKRT
SKRT
SHFSH
ROGER!
IF WE CAN GO WITH ZOMBIE☆GUN, THERE'S NO NEED TO LET REVERSI HAVE THAT SLOT...
AMAZ-ING...
I WANT THIS WORK TO BECOME THE TRUE SIGNATURE PIECE IN JUMP.

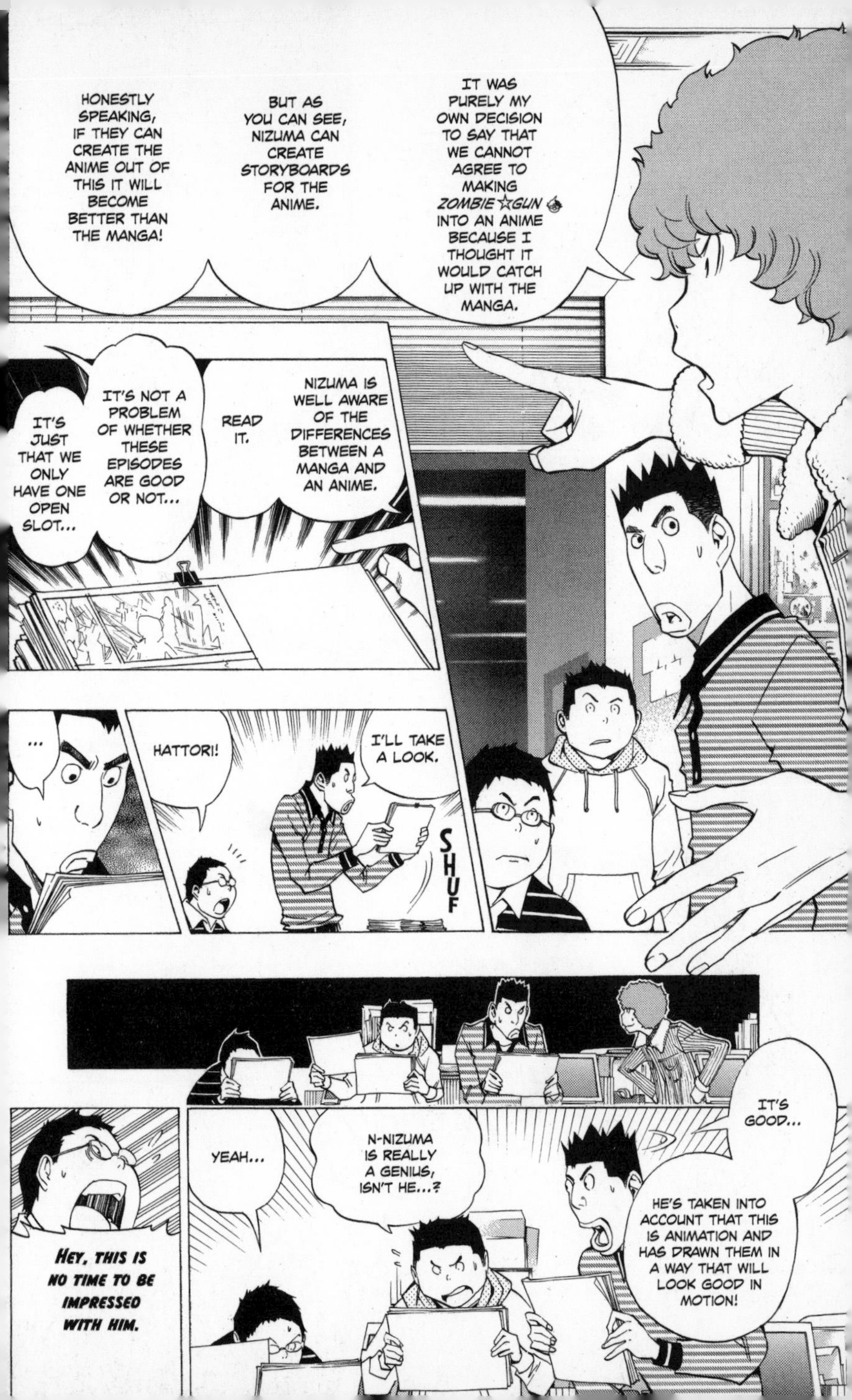
IT WAS PURELY MY OWN DECISION TO SAY THAT WE CANNOT AGREE TO MAKING *ZOMBIE☆GUN* INTO AN ANIME BECAUSE I THOUGHT IT WOULD CATCH UP WITH THE MANGA.
BUT AS YOU CAN SEE, NIZUMA CAN CREATE STORYBOARDS FOR THE ANIME.
HONESTLY SPEAKING, IF THEY CAN CREATE THE ANIME OUT OF THIS IT WILL BECOME BETTER THAN THE MANGA!
NIZUMA IS WELL AWARE OF THE DIFFERENCES BETWEEN A MANGA AND AN ANIME.
READ IT.
IT'S NOT A PROBLEM OF WHETHER THESE EPISODES ARE GOOD OR NOT...
IT'S JUST THAT WE ONLY HAVE ONE OPEN SLOT...
I'LL TAKE A LOOK.
SHUF
HATTORI!
...
IT'S GOOD...
HE'S TAKEN INTO ACCOUNT THAT THIS IS ANIMATION AND HAS DRAWN THEM IN A WAY THAT WILL LOOK GOOD IN MOTION!
N-NIZUMA IS REALLY A GENIUS, ISN'T HE...?
YEAH...
HEY, THIS IS NO TIME TO BE IMPRESSED WITH HIM.

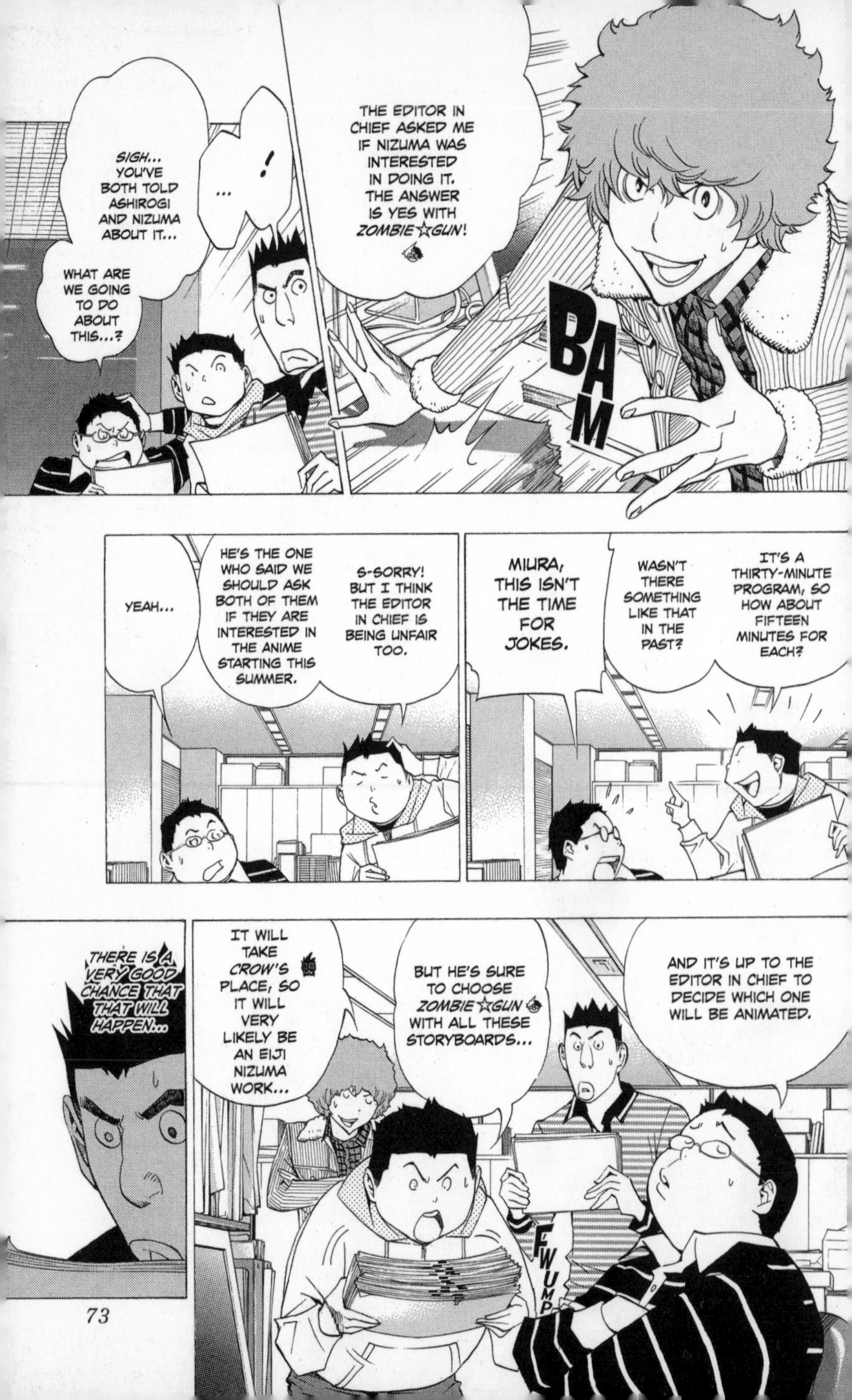
THE EDITOR IN CHIEF ASKED ME IF NIZUMA WAS INTERESTED IN DOING IT. THE ANSWER IS YES WITH ZOMBIE☆GUN!
BAM
!
...
SIGH... YOU'VE BOTH TOLD ASHIROGI AND NIZUMA ABOUT IT...
WHAT ARE WE GOING TO DO ABOUT THIS...?
IT'S A THIRTY-MINUTE PROGRAM, SO HOW ABOUT FIFTEEN MINUTES FOR EACH?
WASN'T THERE SOMETHING LIKE THAT IN THE PAST?
MIURA, THIS ISN'T THE TIME FOR JOKES.
S-SORRY! BUT I THINK THE EDITOR IN CHIEF IS BEING UNFAIR TOO.
HE'S THE ONE WHO SAID WE SHOULD ASK BOTH OF THEM IF THEY ARE INTERESTED IN THE ANIME STARTING THIS SUMMER.
YEAH...
AND IT'S UP TO THE EDITOR IN CHIEF TO DECIDE WHICH ONE WILL BE ANIMATED.
BUT HE'S SURE TO CHOOSE ZOMBIE☆GUN WITH ALL THESE STORYBOARDS...
FWUMP
IT WILL TAKE CROW'S PLACE, SO IT WILL VERY LIKELY BE AN EIJI NIZUMA WORK...
THERE IS A VERY GOOD CHANCE THAT THAT WILL HAPPEN...

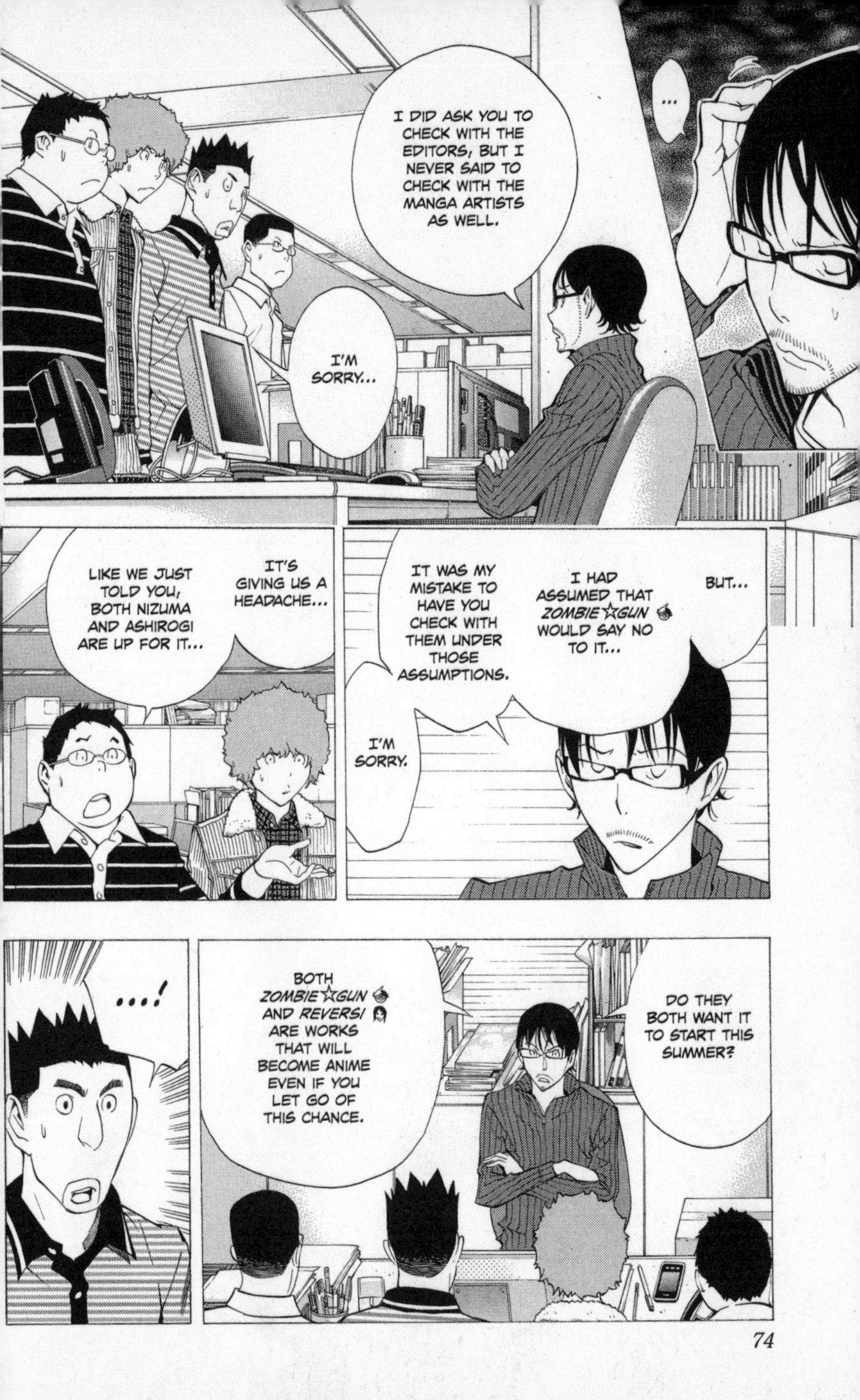
...
I DID ASK YOU TO CHECK WITH THE EDITORS, BUT I NEVER SAID TO CHECK WITH THE MANGA ARTISTS AS WELL.
I'M SORRY...
BUT...
I HAD ASSUMED THAT ZOMBIE☆GUN WOULD SAY NO TO IT...
IT WAS MY MISTAKE TO HAVE YOU CHECK WITH THEM UNDER THOSE ASSUMPTIONS.
I'M SORRY.
IT'S GIVING US A HEADACHE...
LIKE WE JUST TOLD YOU, BOTH NIZUMA AND ASHIROGI ARE UP FOR IT...
DO THEY BOTH WANT IT TO START THIS SUMMER?
BOTH ZOMBIE☆GUN AND REVERSI ARE WORKS THAT WILL BECOME ANIME EVEN IF YOU LET GO OF THIS CHANCE.
...!

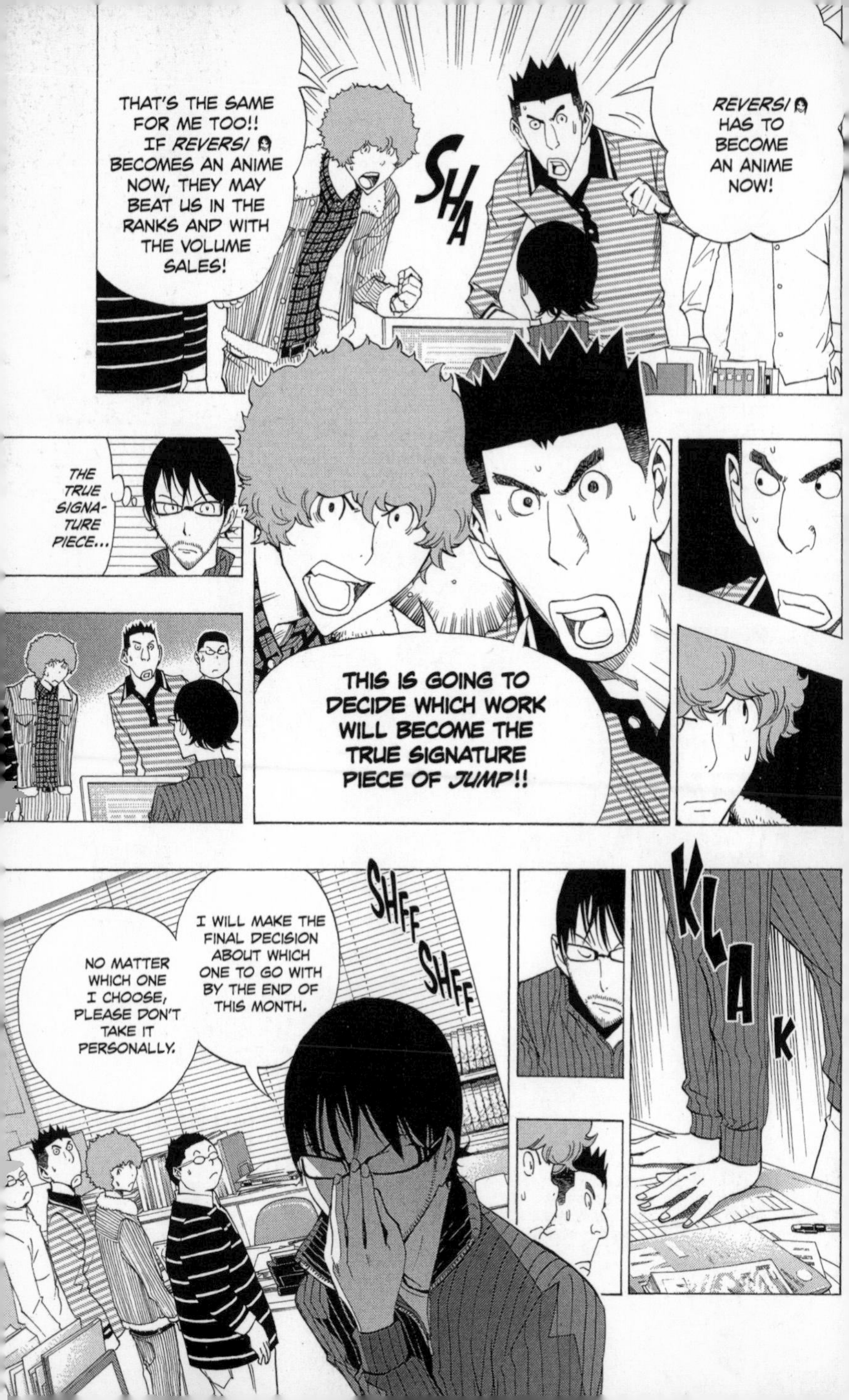
REVERSI HAS TO BECOME AN ANIME NOW!
SHA
THAT'S THE SAME FOR ME TOO!! IF REVERSI BECOMES AN ANIME NOW, THEY MAY BEAT US IN THE RANKS AND WITH THE VOLUME SALES!
THIS IS GOING TO DECIDE WHICH WORK WILL BECOME THE TRUE SIGNATURE PIECE OF JUMP!!
THE TRUE SIGNATURE PIECE...
KLAK
SHFF SHFF
I WILL MAKE THE FINAL DECISION ABOUT WHICH ONE TO GO WITH BY THE END OF THIS MONTH.
NO MATTER WHICH ONE I CHOOSE, PLEASE DON'T TAKE IT PERSONALLY.

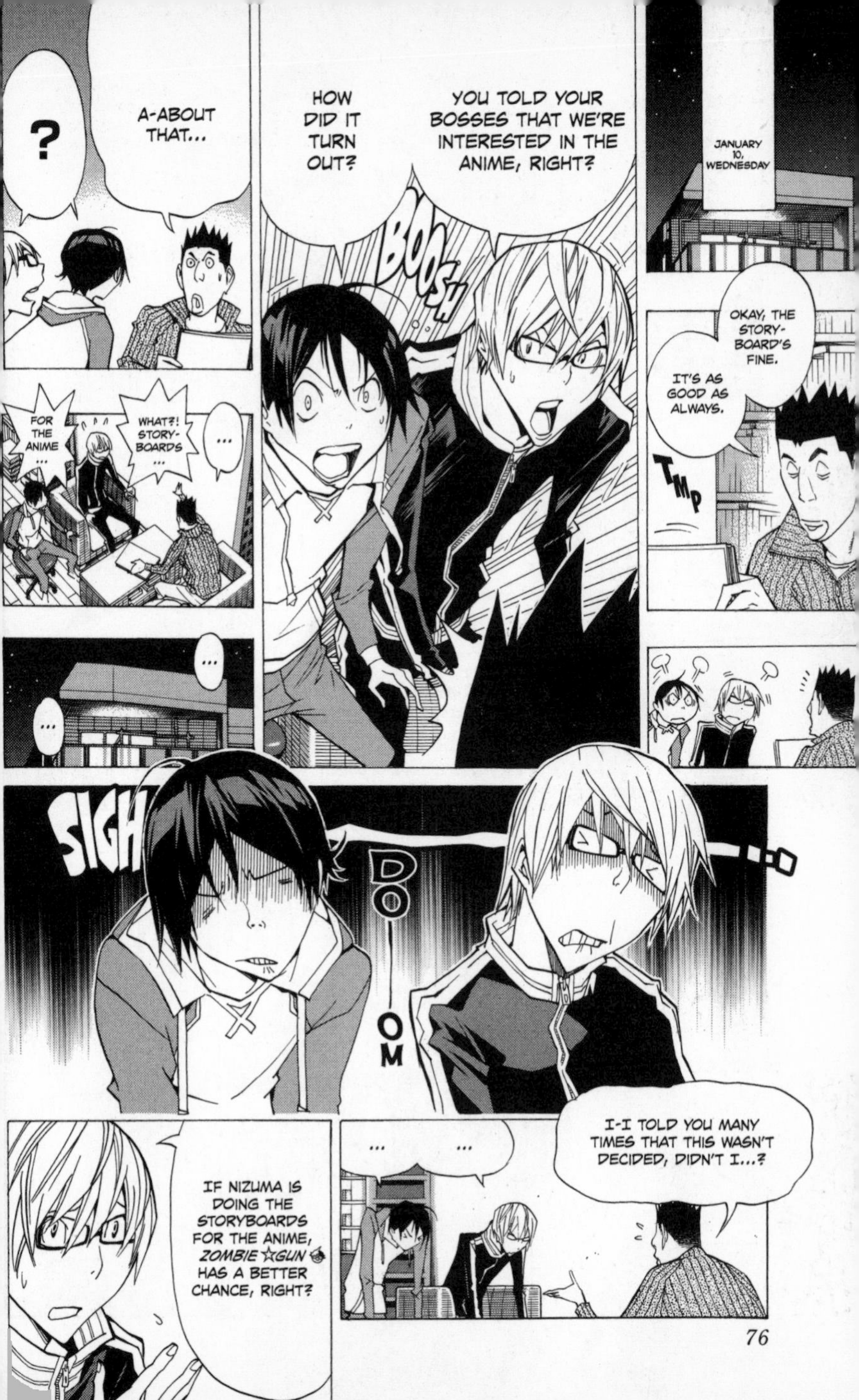
JANUARY 10, WEDNESDAY
OKAY, THE STORYBOARD'S FINE.
IT'S AS GOOD AS ALWAYS.
TMP
YOU TOLD YOUR BOSSES THAT WE'RE INTERESTED IN THE ANIME, RIGHT?
HOW DID IT TURN OUT?
BOOSH
A-ABOUT THAT...
?
WHAT?! STORYBOARDS...
FOR THE ANIME...
...
...
...
SIGH
DO—OM
I-I TOLD YOU MANY TIMES THAT THIS WASN'T DECIDED, DIDN'T I...?
... ...
IF NIZUMA IS DOING THE STORYBOARDS FOR THE ANIME, ZOMBIE☆GUN HAS A BETTER CHANCE, RIGHT?

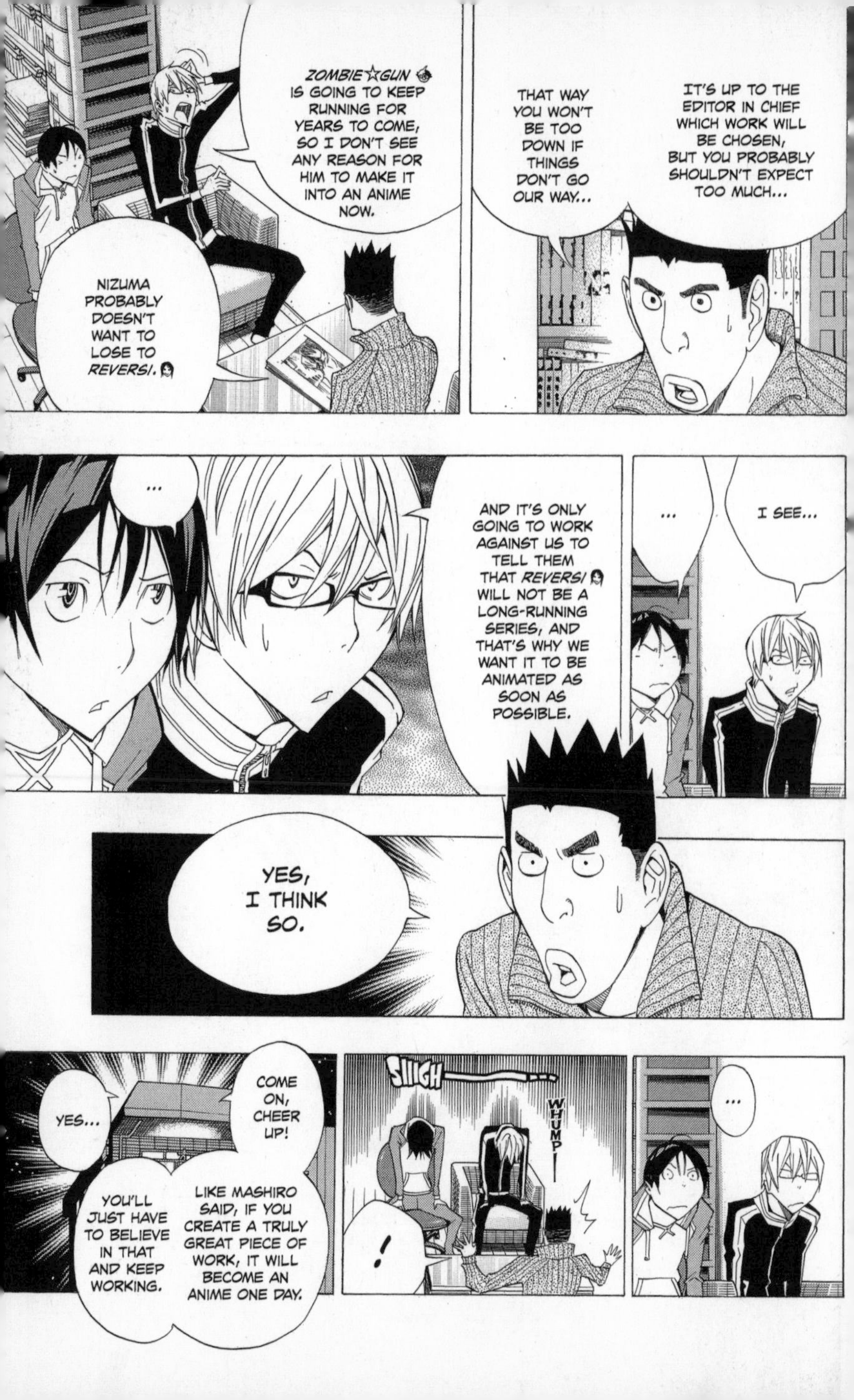
IT'S UP TO THE EDITOR IN CHIEF WHICH WORK WILL BE CHOSEN, BUT YOU PROBABLY SHOULDN'T EXPECT TOO MUCH...
THAT WAY YOU WON'T BE TOO DOWN IF THINGS DON'T GO OUR WAY...
ZOMBIE☆GUN IS GOING TO KEEP RUNNING FOR YEARS TO COME, SO I DON'T SEE ANY REASON FOR HIM TO MAKE IT INTO AN ANIME NOW.
NIZUMA PROBABLY DOESN'T WANT TO LOSE TO REVERSI.
I SEE...
...
AND IT'S ONLY GOING TO WORK AGAINST US TO TELL THEM THAT REVERSI WILL NOT BE A LONG-RUNNING SERIES, AND THAT'S WHY WE WANT IT TO BE ANIMATED AS SOON AS POSSIBLE.
...
YES, I THINK SO.
...
SIIGH
WHUMP!
!
COME ON, CHEER UP!
LIKE MASHIRO SAID, IF YOU CREATE A TRULY GREAT PIECE OF WORK, IT WILL BECOME AN ANIME ONE DAY.
YOU'LL JUST HAVE TO BELIEVE IN THAT AND KEEP WORKING.
YES...

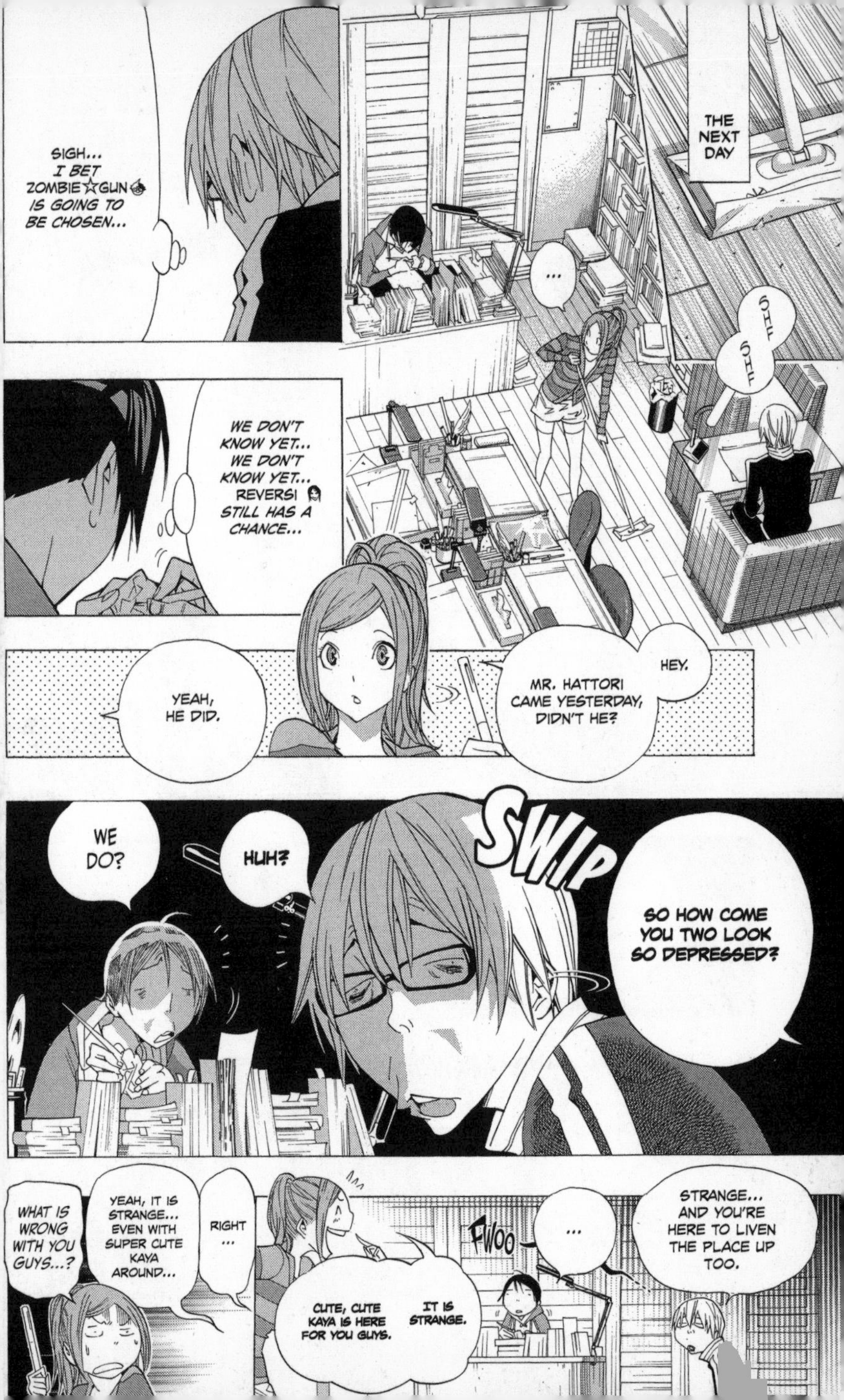
THE NEXT DAY
SHF SHF
...
SIGH... I BET ZOMBIE☆GUN IS GOING TO BE CHOSEN...
WE DON'T KNOW YET... WE DON'T KNOW YET... REVERSI STILL HAS A CHANCE...
HEY.
MR. HATTORI CAME YESTERDAY, DIDN'T HE?
YEAH, HE DID.
SWIP
SO HOW COME YOU TWO LOOK SO DEPRESSED?
HUH?
WE DO?
STRANGE... AND YOU'RE HERE TO LIVEN THE PLACE UP TOO.
FWOO
...
IT IS STRANGE.
CUTE, CUTE KAYA IS HERE FOR YOU GUYS.
RIGHT ...
YEAH, IT IS STRANGE... EVEN WITH SUPER CUTE KAYA AROUND...
WHAT IS WRONG WITH YOU GUYS...?

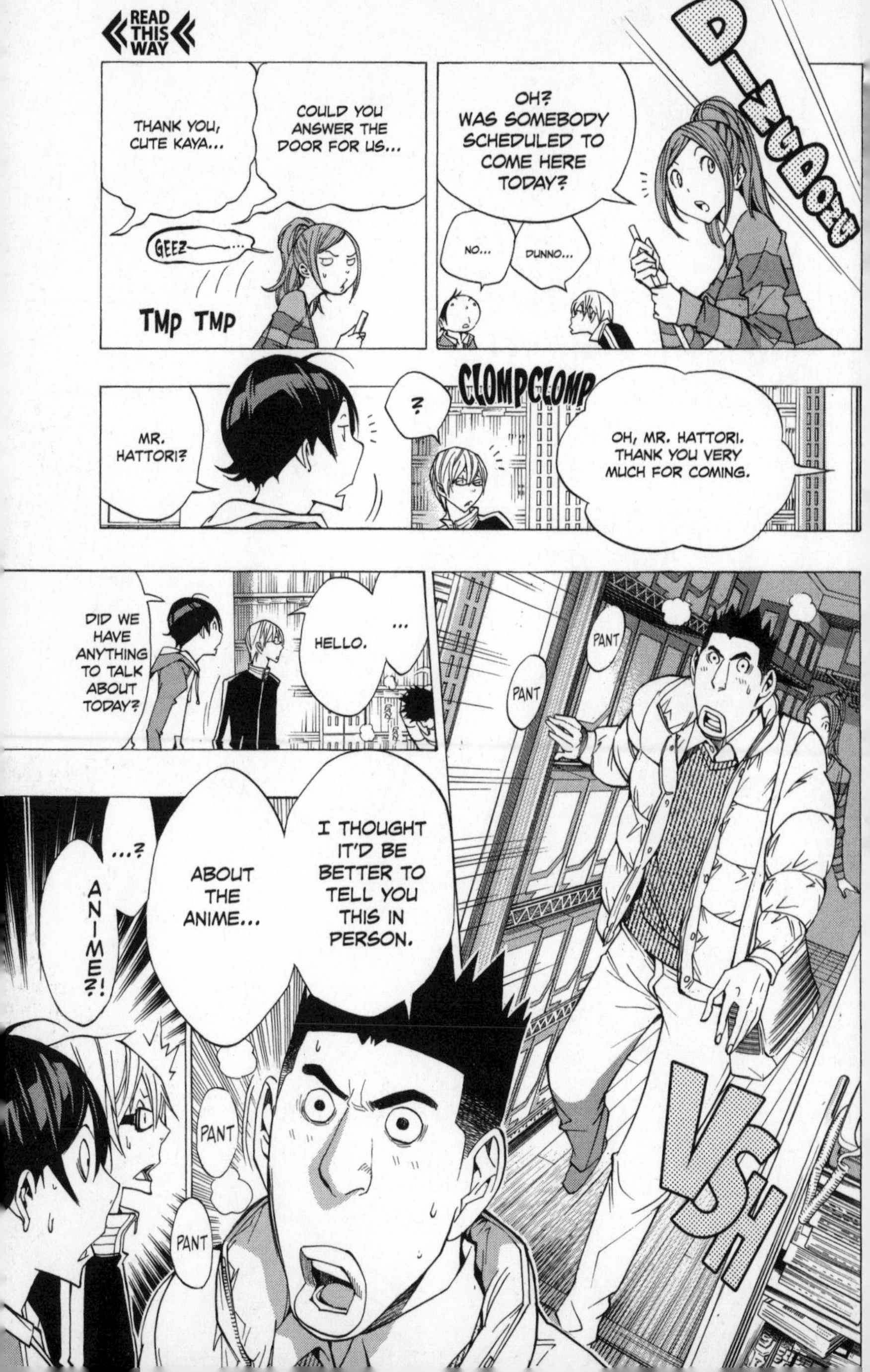
READ THIS WAY
DINGDONG
OH? WAS SOMEBODY SCHEDULED TO COME HERE TODAY?
DUNNO...
NO...
COULD YOU ANSWER THE DOOR FOR US...
THANK YOU, CUTE KAYA...
GEEZ......
TMP TMP
OH, MR. HATTORI. THANK YOU VERY MUCH FOR COMING.
CLOMPCLOMP
?
MR. HATTORI?
PANT
PANT
...
HELLO.
DID WE HAVE ANYTHING TO TALK ABOUT TODAY?
VSH
I THOUGHT IT'D BE BETTER TO TELL YOU THIS IN PERSON.
ABOUT THE ANIME...
...?
ANIME?!
PANT
PANT

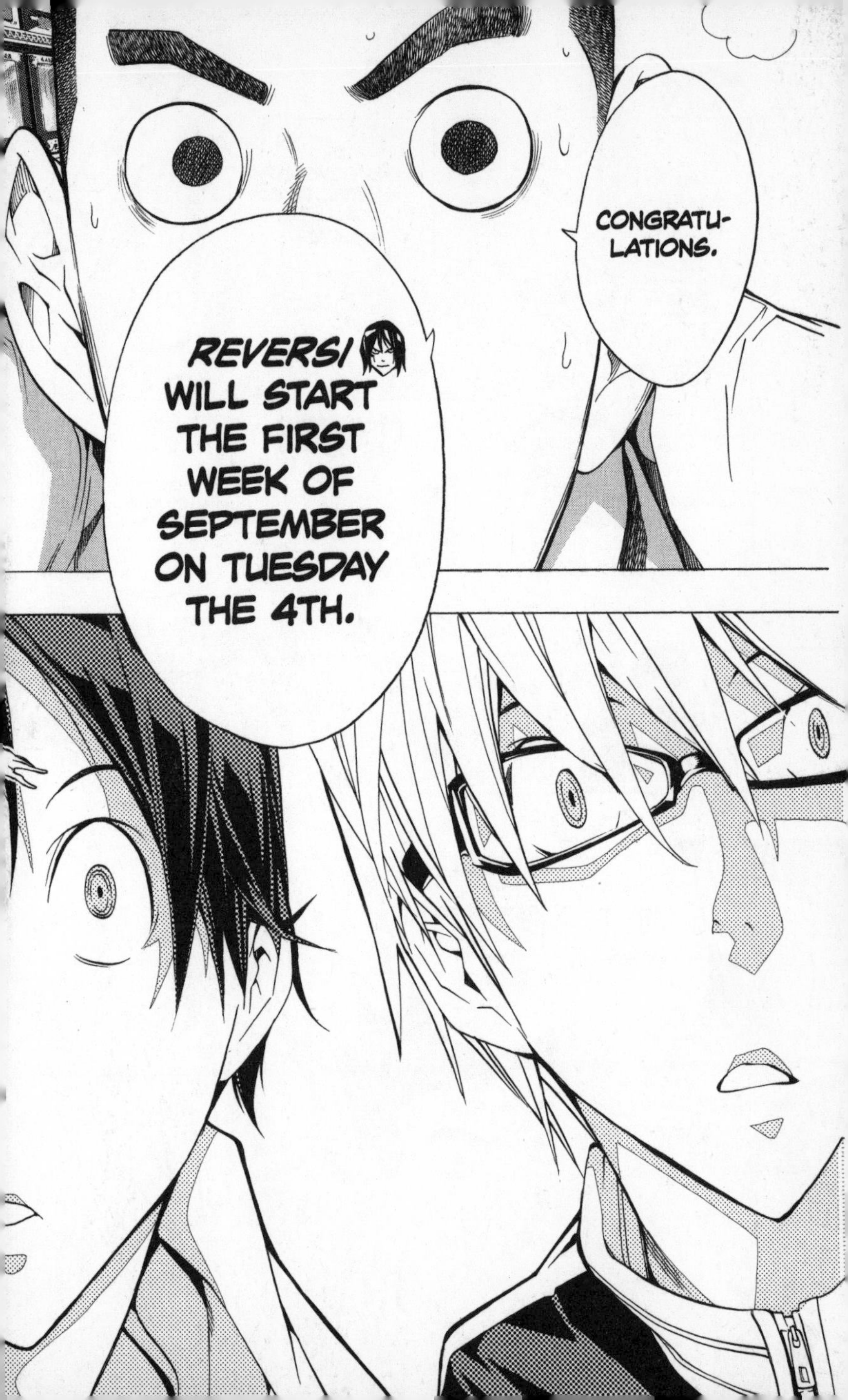
CONGRATU-LATIONS.
REVERSI WILL START THE FIRST WEEK OF SEPTEMBER ON TUESDAY THE 4TH.

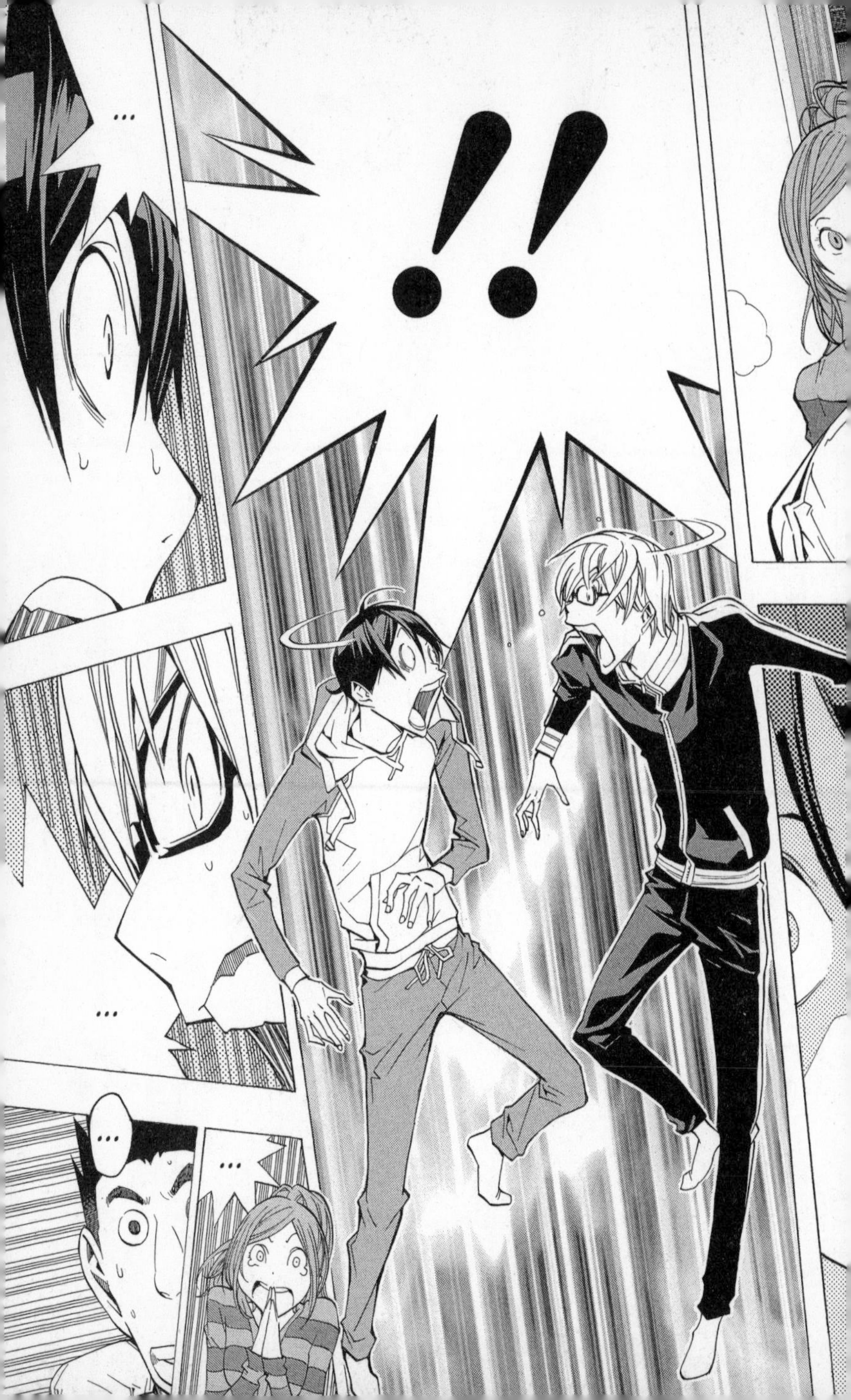
!!
...
...
...
...

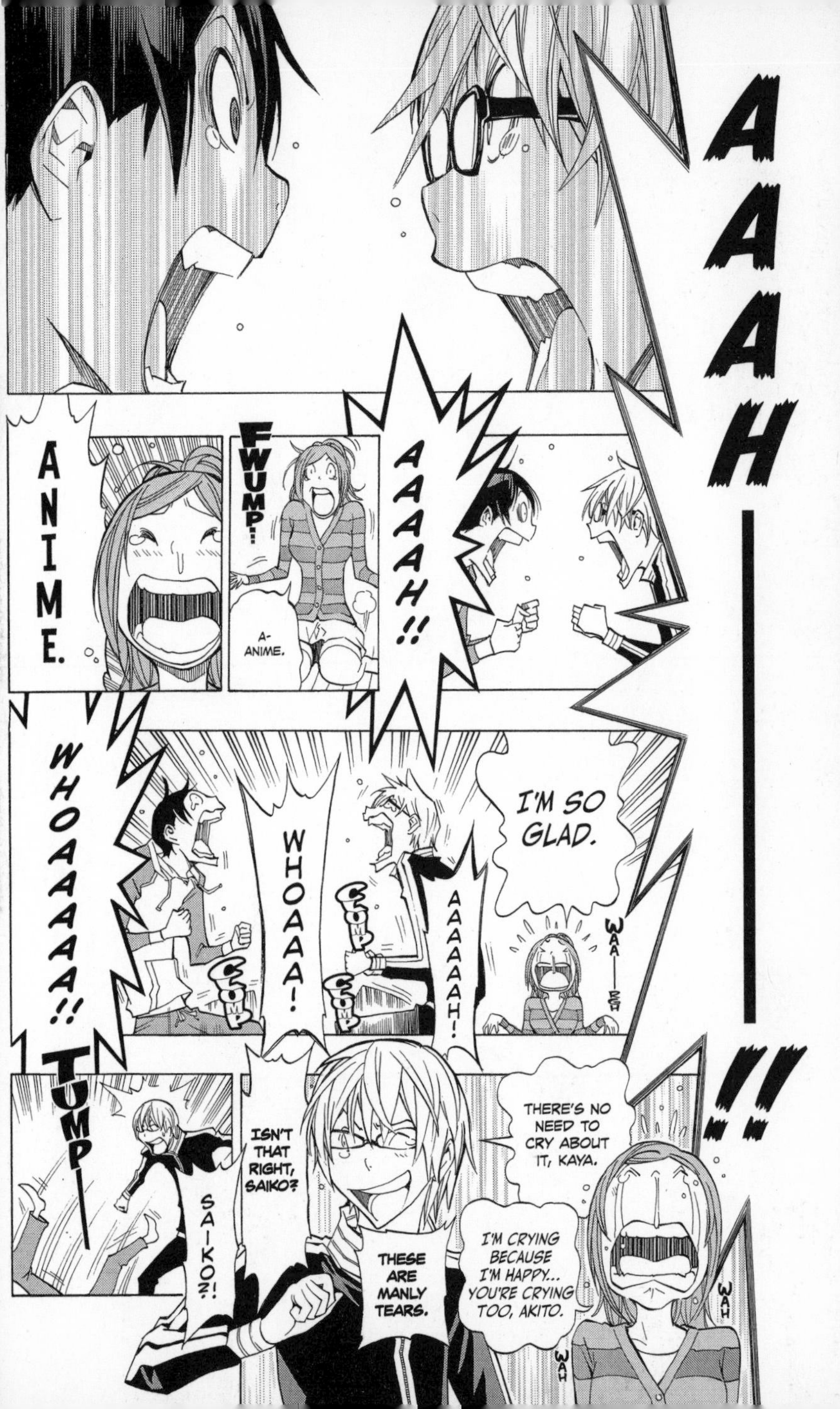
AAAAH—!!
AAAAH!!
FWUMP!
A- ANIME.
ANIME.
I'M SO GLAD.
WAA—EGH
AAAAAAH!
WHOAAA!
CLOMP
CLOMP
CLOMP
CLOMP
WHOAAAAAAA!!
THERE'S NO NEED TO CRY ABOUT IT, KAYA.
I'M CRYING BECAUSE I'M HAPPY... YOU'RE CRYING TOO, AKITO.
WAH
WAH
THESE ARE MANLY TEARS.
ISN'T THAT RIGHT, SAIKO?
TUMP—
SAIKO?!

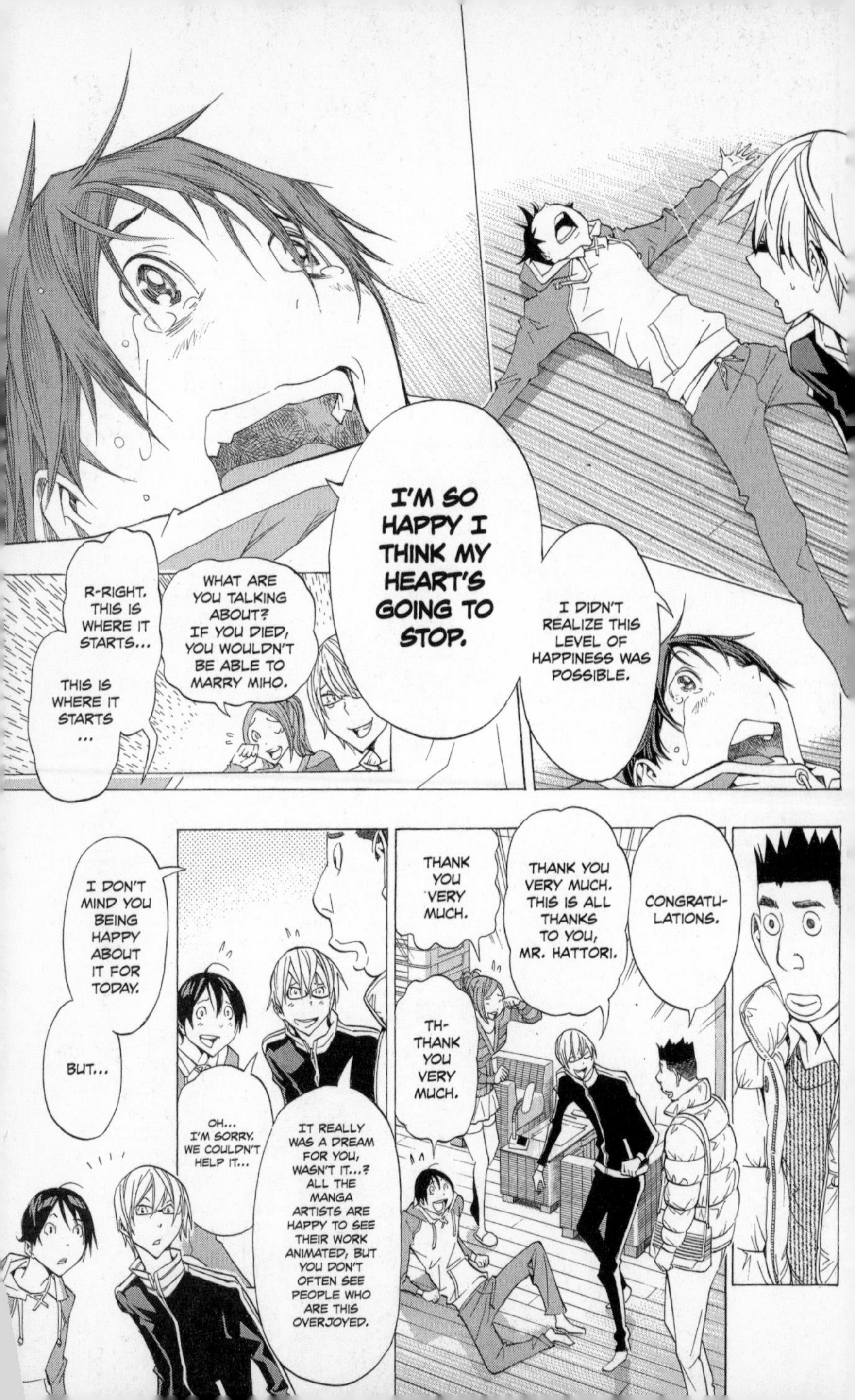
I DIDN'T REALIZE THIS LEVEL OF HAPPINESS WAS POSSIBLE.
I'M SO HAPPY I THINK MY HEART'S GOING TO STOP.
WHAT ARE YOU TALKING ABOUT? IF YOU DIED, YOU WOULDN'T BE ABLE TO MARRY MIHO.
R-RIGHT. THIS IS WHERE IT STARTS...
THIS IS WHERE IT STARTS ...
CONGRATU-LATIONS.
THANK YOU VERY MUCH. THIS IS ALL THANKS TO YOU, MR. HATTORI.
THANK YOU VERY MUCH.
TH-THANK YOU VERY MUCH.
IT REALLY WAS A DREAM FOR YOU, WASN'T IT...? ALL THE MANGA ARTISTS ARE HAPPY TO SEE THEIR WORK ANIMATED, BUT YOU DON'T OFTEN SEE PEOPLE WHO ARE THIS OVERJOYED.
OH... I'M SORRY. WE COULDN'T HELP IT...
I DON'T MIND YOU BEING HAPPY ABOUT IT FOR TODAY.
BUT...

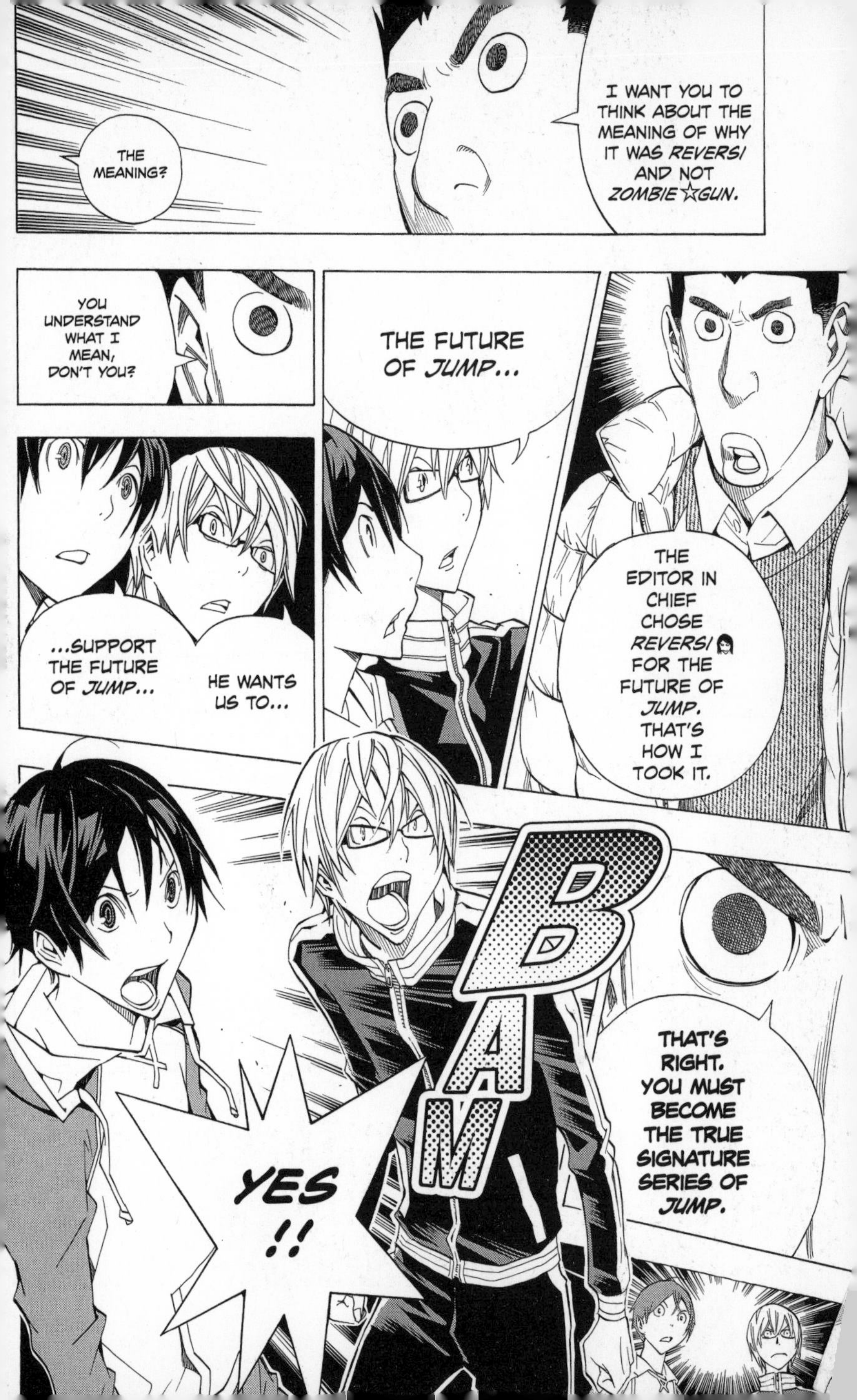
I WANT YOU TO THINK ABOUT THE MEANING OF WHY IT WAS *REVERSI* AND NOT *ZOMBIE☆GUN*.
THE MEANING?
THE EDITOR IN CHIEF CHOSE *REVERSI* FOR THE FUTURE OF *JUMP*. THAT'S HOW I TOOK IT.
THE FUTURE OF *JUMP*...
YOU UNDERSTAND WHAT I MEAN, DON'T YOU?
HE WANTS US TO...
...SUPPORT THE FUTURE OF *JUMP*...
THAT'S RIGHT. YOU MUST BECOME THE TRUE SIGNATURE SERIES OF *JUMP*.
BAM
YES!!

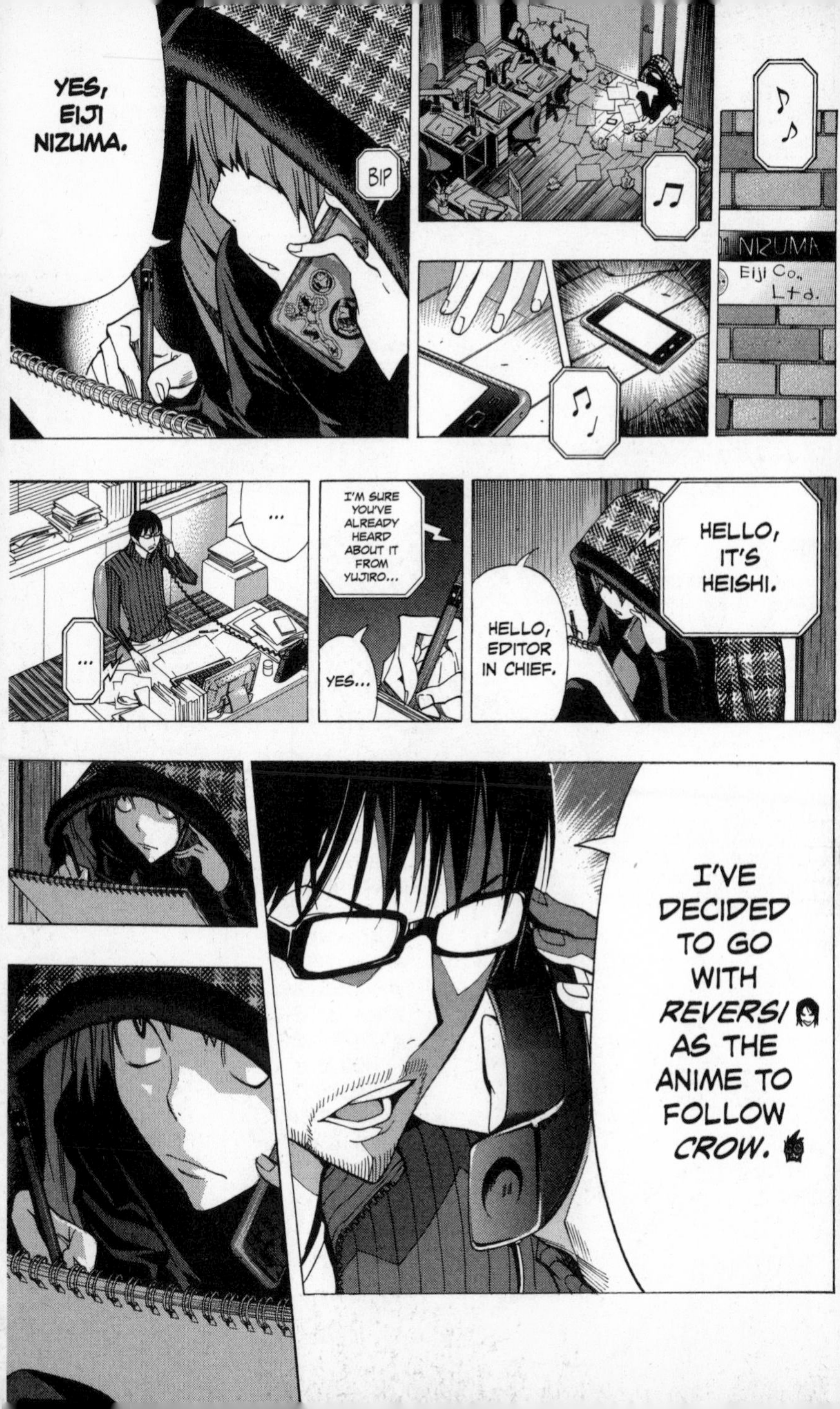
♪ ♪
NIZUMA
Eiji Co., Ltd.
♫
♪
BIP
YES, EIJI NIZUMA.
HELLO, IT'S HEISHI.
HELLO, EDITOR IN CHIEF.
I'M SURE YOU'VE ALREADY HEARD ABOUT IT FROM YUJIRO...
YES...
...
...
I'VE DECIDED TO GO WITH REVERSI AS THE ANIME TO FOLLOW CROW.

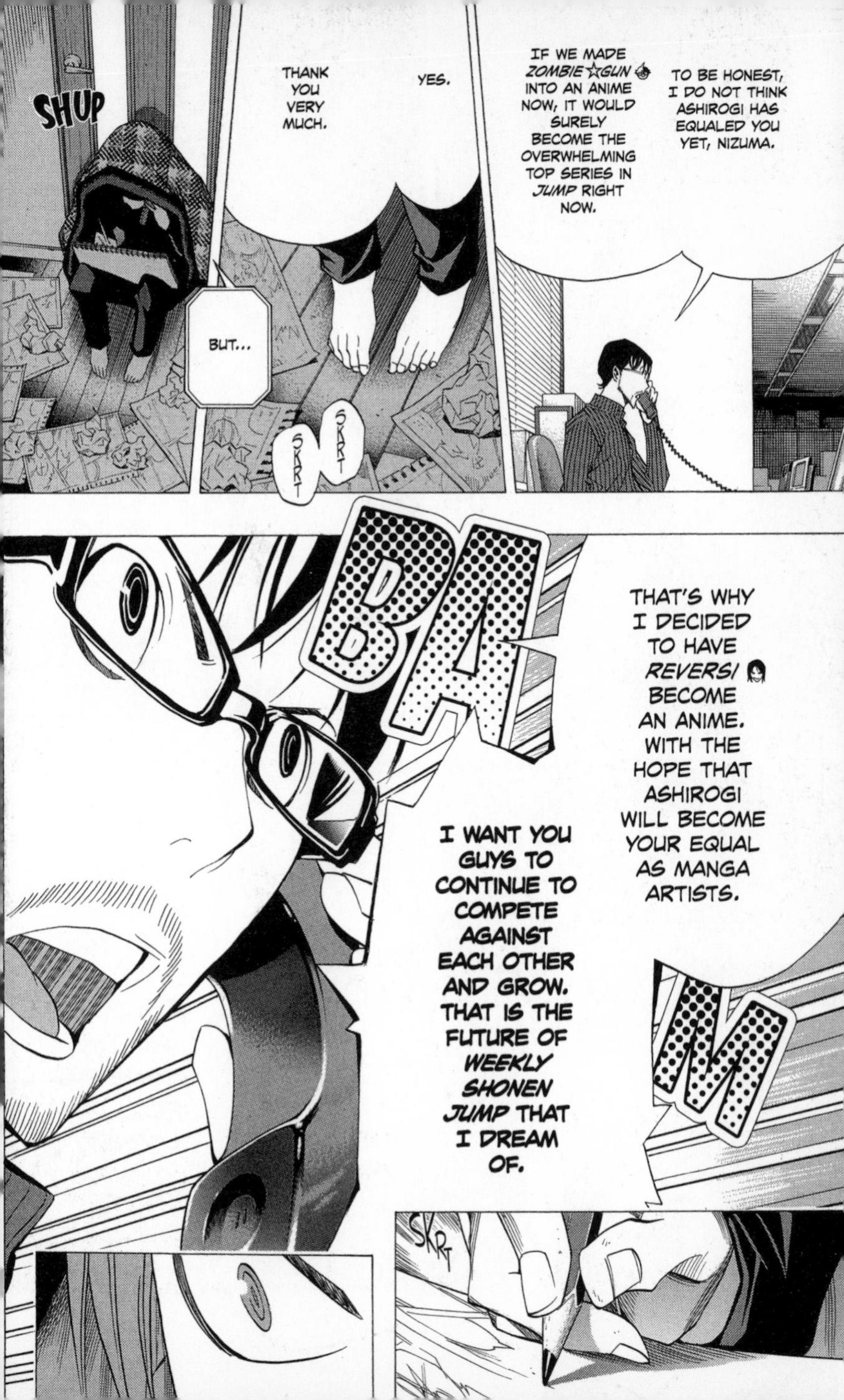
TO BE HONEST, I DO NOT THINK ASHIROGI HAS EQUALED YOU YET, NIZUMA.
IF WE MADE ZOMBIE☆GUN INTO AN ANIME NOW, IT WOULD SURELY BECOME THE OVERWHELMING TOP SERIES IN JUMP RIGHT NOW.
YES.
THANK YOU VERY MUCH.
SHUP
BUT...
SKRT
SKRT
THAT'S WHY I DECIDED TO HAVE REVERSI BECOME AN ANIME. WITH THE HOPE THAT ASHIROGI WILL BECOME YOUR EQUAL AS MANGA ARTISTS.
BAM
I WANT YOU GUYS TO CONTINUE TO COMPETE AGAINST EACH OTHER AND GROW. THAT IS THE FUTURE OF WEEKLY SHONEN JUMP THAT I DREAM OF.
SKRT

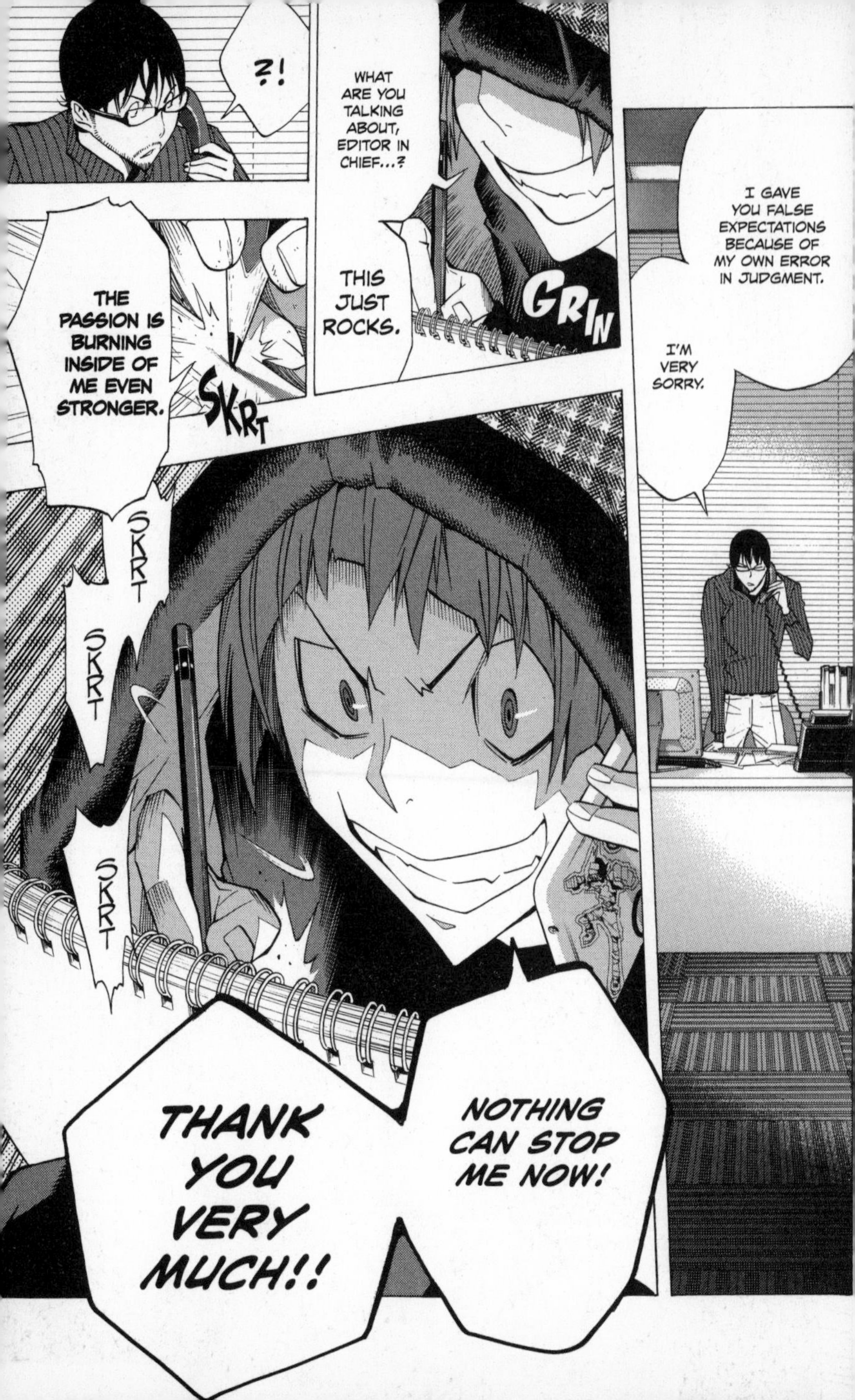
I GAVE YOU FALSE EXPECTATIONS BECAUSE OF MY OWN ERROR IN JUDGMENT.
I'M VERY SORRY.
WHAT ARE YOU TALKING ABOUT, EDITOR IN CHIEF...?
THIS JUST ROCKS.
GRIN
?!
THE PASSION IS BURNING INSIDE OF ME EVEN STRONGER.
SKRT
SKRT
SKRT
SKRT
NOTHING CAN STOP ME NOW!
THANK YOU VERY MUCH!!

OHBA'S STORYBOARD

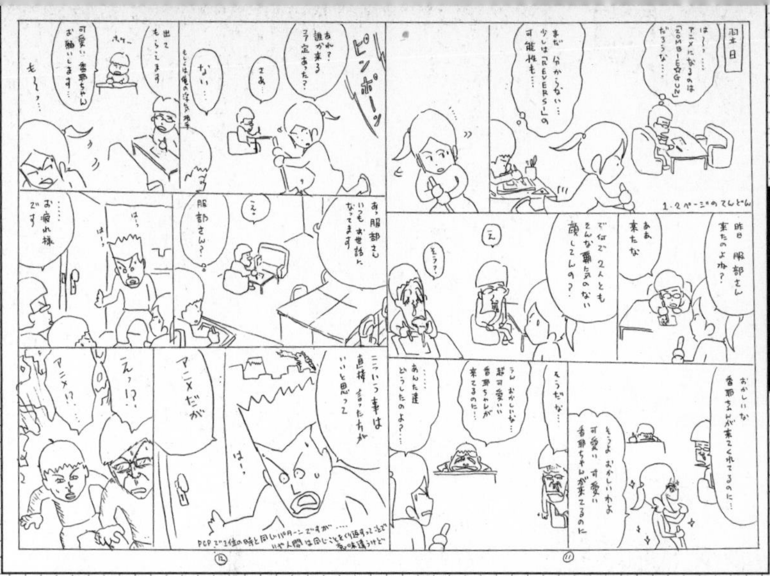
翌日
は～っ……アニメになるのは『ZOMBIE☆GUN』だろうな……
まだ分からない…少しは『REVERSI』の可能性も…
昨日服部さん来たのよね？
ああ来たな
で何で2人ともそんな覇気のない顔してんの？
え
そう？
おかしいな香耶ちゃんが来てくれてるのに…
そうよおかしいわよ可愛い可愛い香耶ちゃんが来てるのに
そうだな…
うん おかしいな… 超可愛い香耶ちゃんが来てるのに…
……あんた達どうしたのよ…？
ピンポーン
あれ？誰か来る予定あった？
さあ…
ない…
出てもらえます
可愛い香耶ちゃんお願いします…
も～っ…
あっ服部さんいつもお世話になってます
え
服部さん？
は…
…お疲れ様です
こういう事は直接言った方がいいと思って
は…
アニメだが
え…!?
アニメ!?…

OBATA'S STORYBOARD

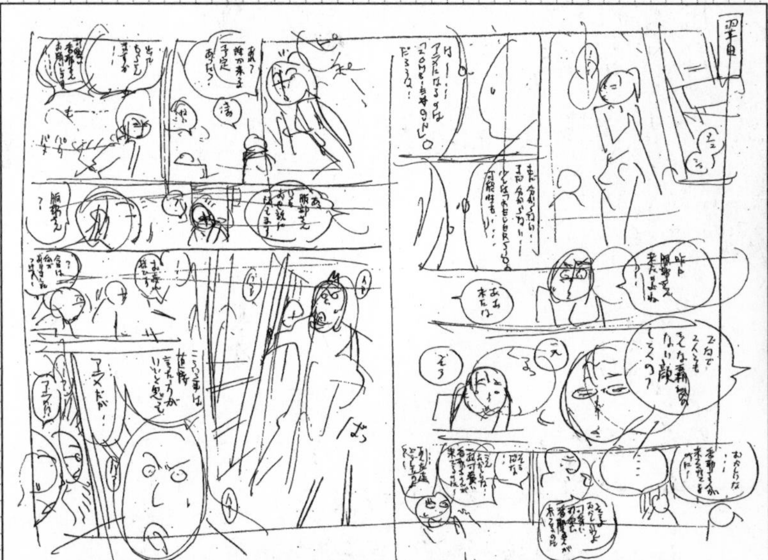

COMPLETE!

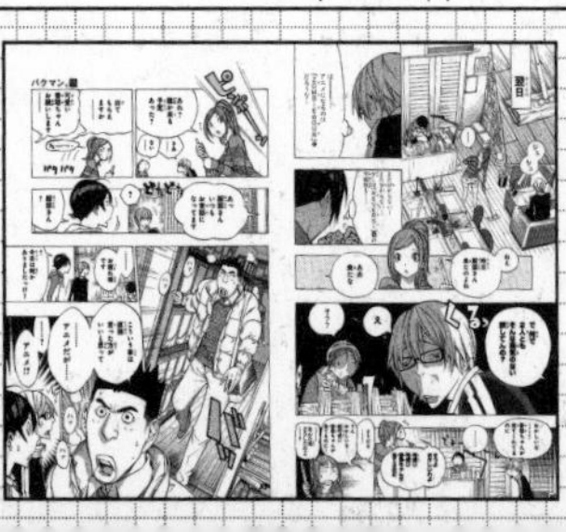

※CREATOR STORYBOARDS AND FINISHED PAGES IN JAPANESE

BAKUMAN。 vol.19

"Until the Final Draft Is Complete"

Chapter 164, pp. 82-83

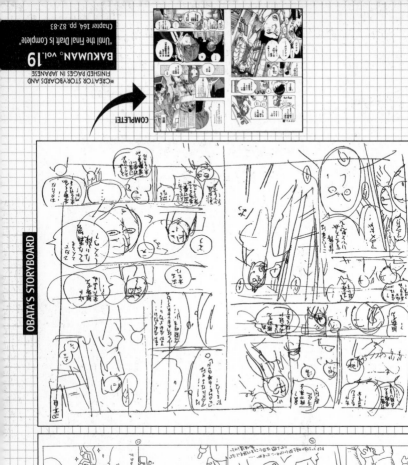

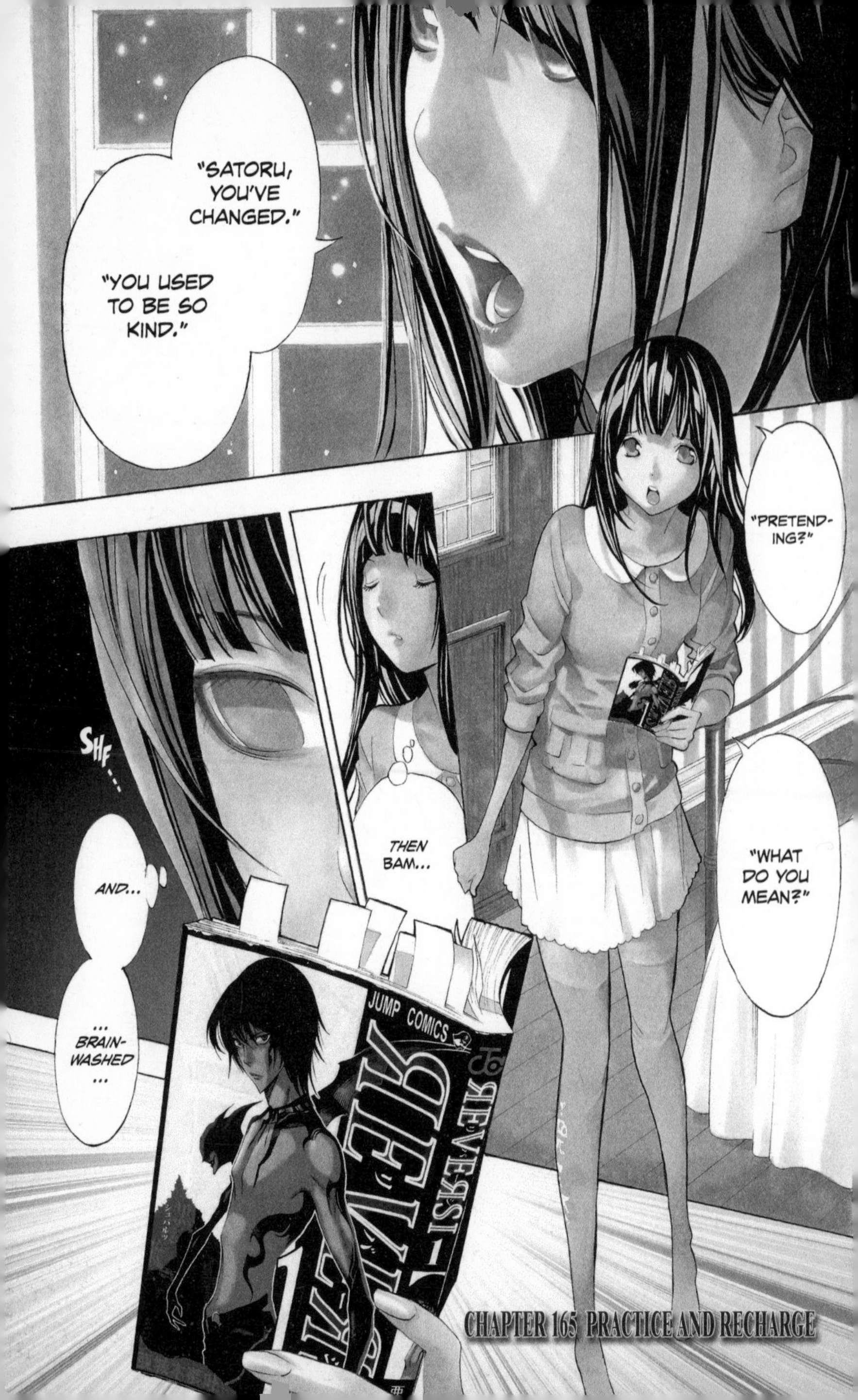
"SATORU, YOU'VE CHANGED."
"YOU USED TO BE SO KIND."
"PRETEND-ING?"
"WHAT DO YOU MEAN?"
THEN BAM...
SHF...
AND...
...BRAIN-WASHED...
JUMP COMICS

CHAPTER 165 PRACTICE AND RECHARGE

CHAPTER 165
PRACTICE AND RECHARGE

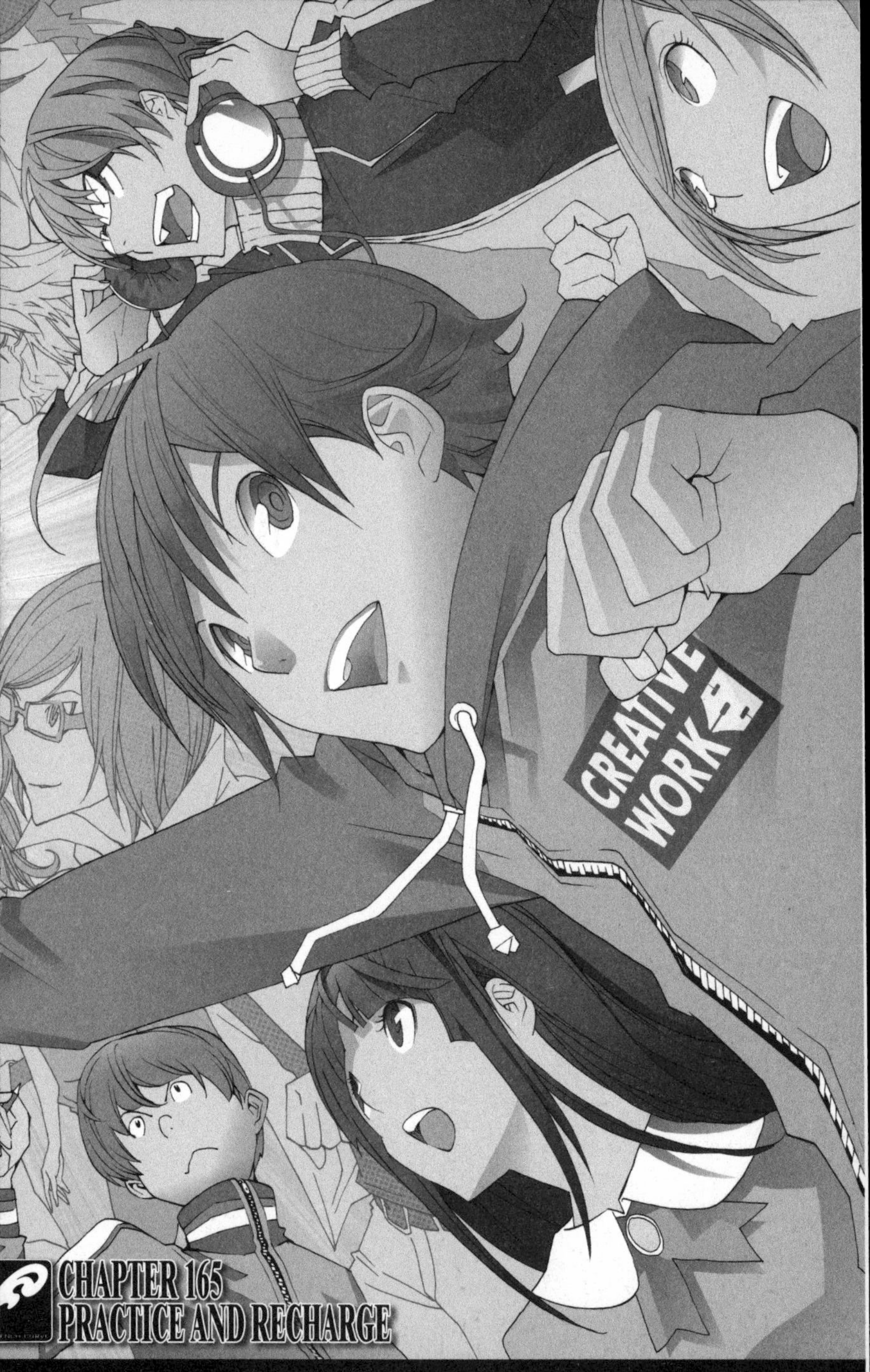
CREATIVE WORK

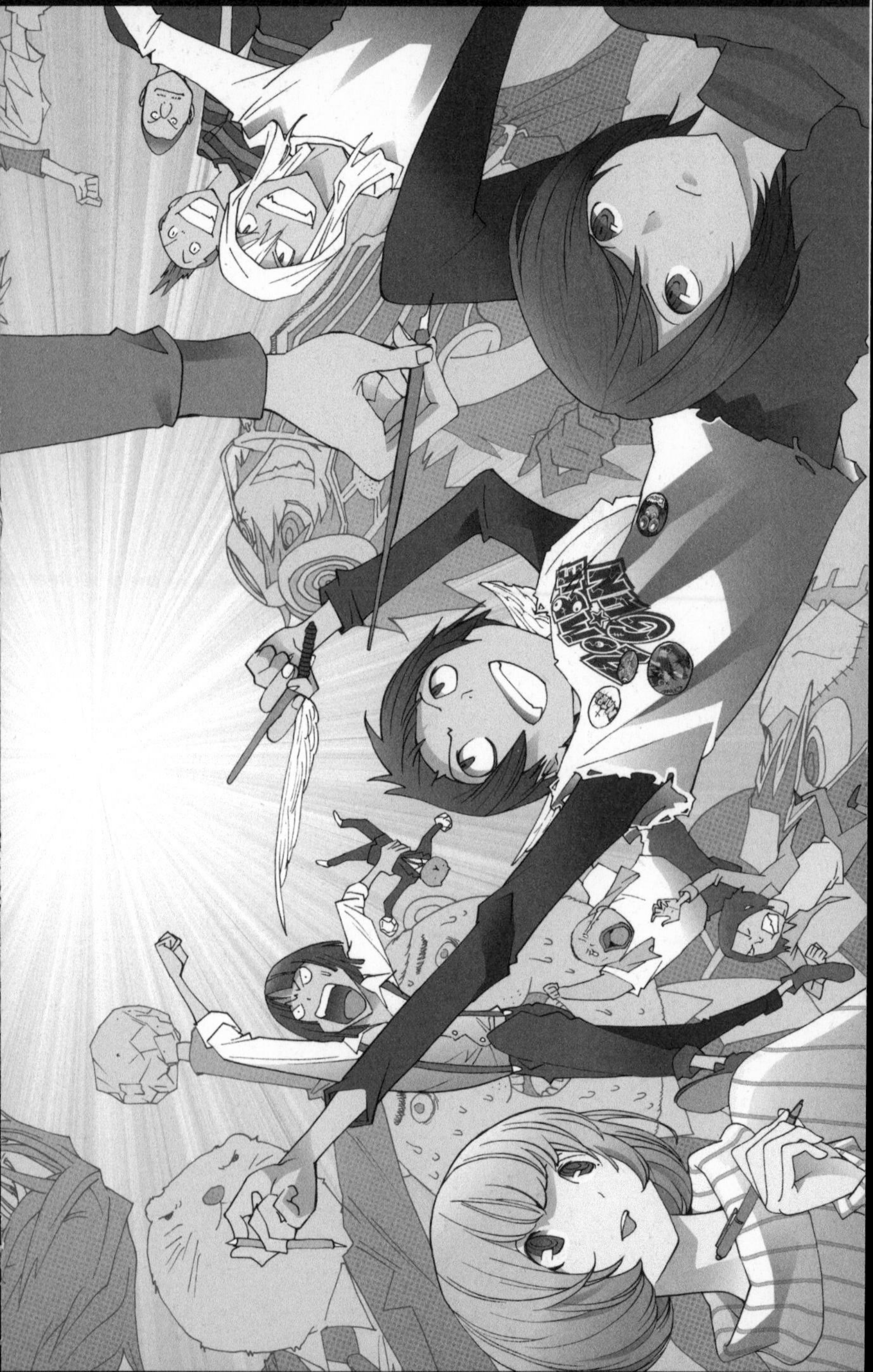

BAKUMAN

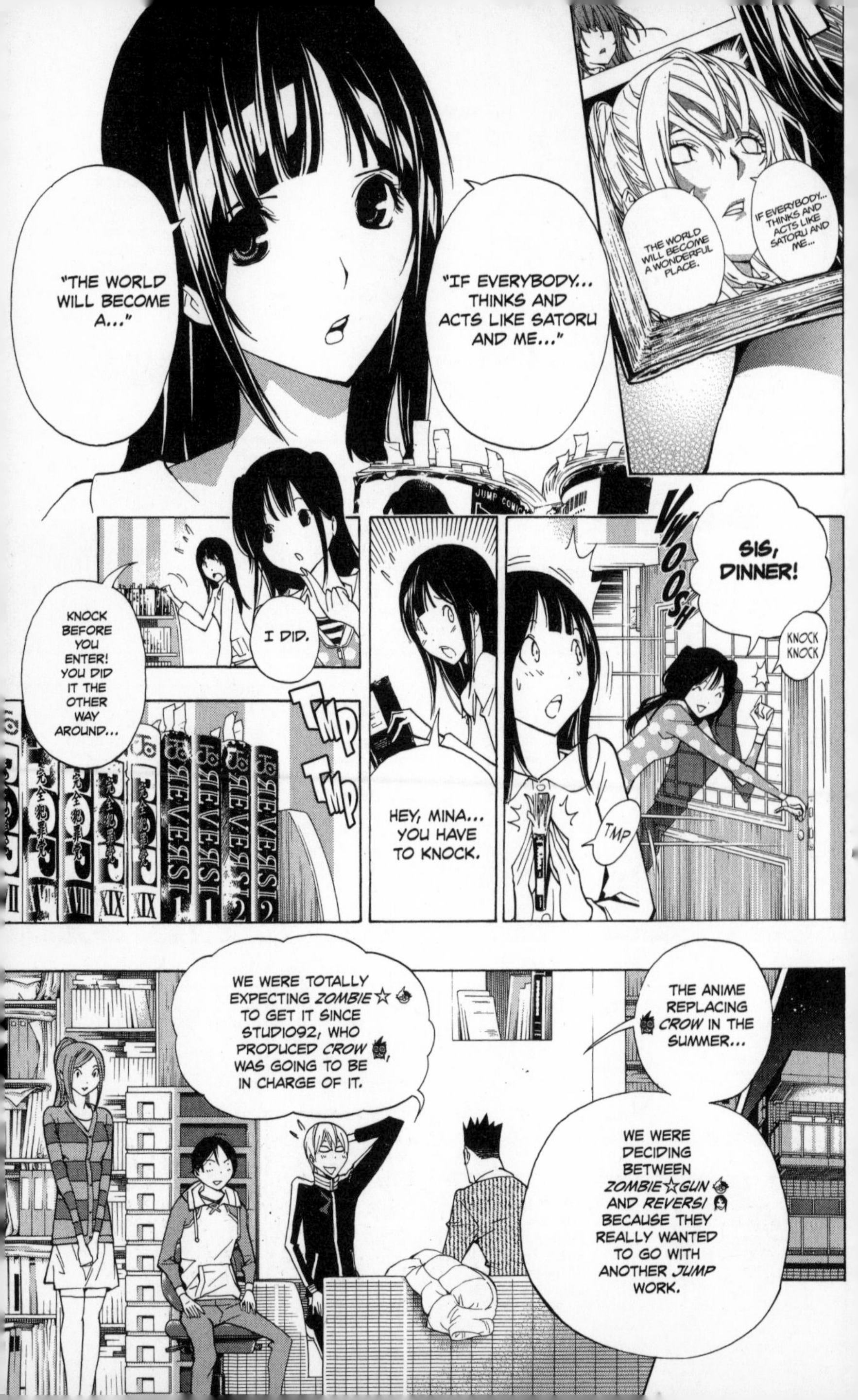
IF EVERYBODY... THINKS AND ACTS LIKE SATORU AND ME...
THE WORLD WILL BECOME A WONDERFUL PLACE.
"IF EVERYBODY... THINKS AND ACTS LIKE SATORU AND ME..."
"THE WORLD WILL BECOME A..."
VWOOSH
SIS, DINNER!
KNOCK KNOCK
TMP
HEY, MINA... YOU HAVE TO KNOCK.
I DID.
KNOCK BEFORE YOU ENTER! YOU DID IT THE OTHER WAY AROUND...
TMP
TMP
THE ANIME REPLACING CROW IN THE SUMMER...
WE WERE DECIDING BETWEEN ZOMBIE☆GUN AND REVERSI BECAUSE THEY REALLY WANTED TO GO WITH ANOTHER JUMP WORK.
WE WERE TOTALLY EXPECTING ZOMBIE☆ TO GET IT SINCE STUDIO92, WHO PRODUCED CROW, WAS GOING TO BE IN CHARGE OF IT.

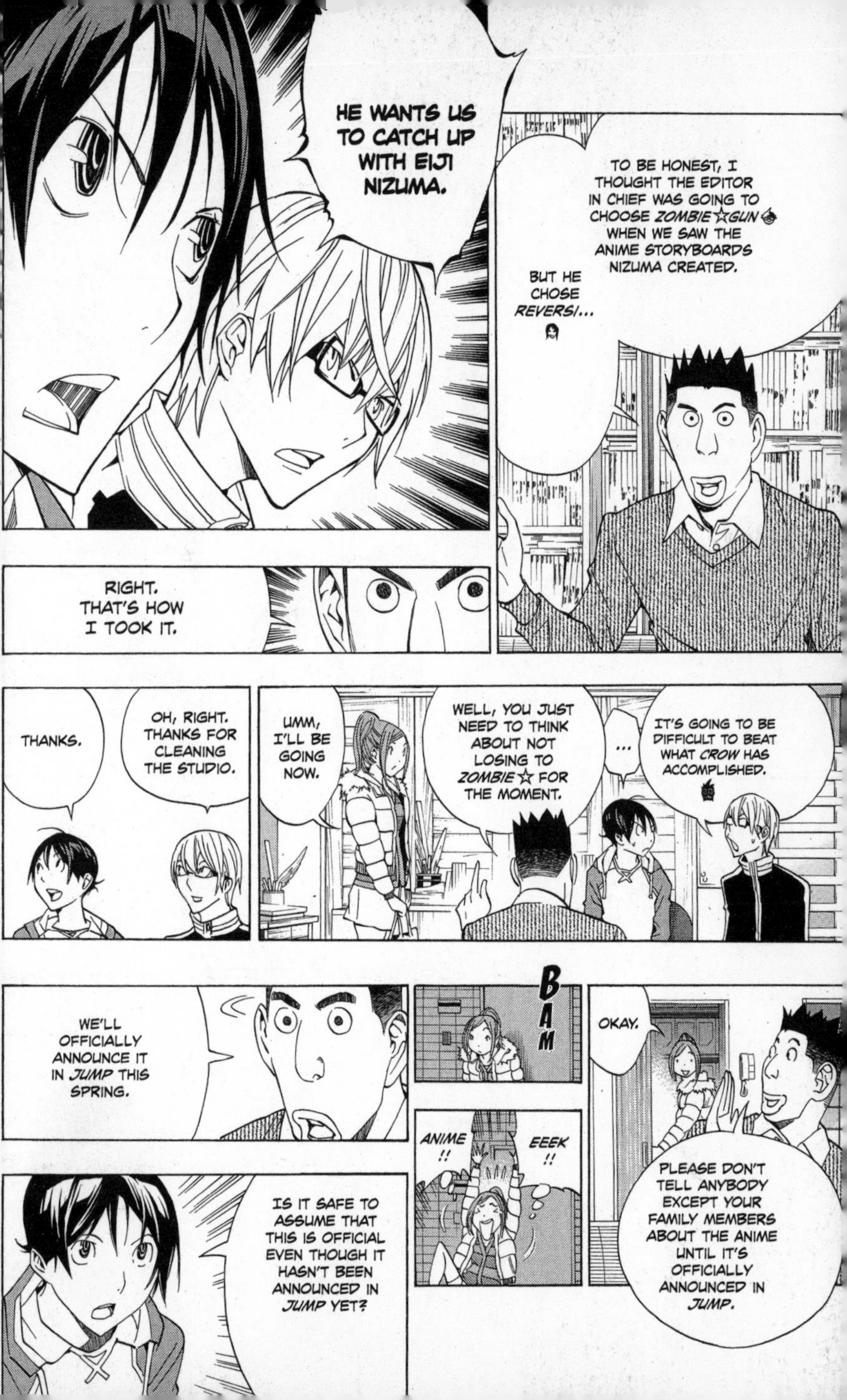
TO BE HONEST, I THOUGHT THE EDITOR IN CHIEF WAS GOING TO CHOOSE *ZOMBIE☆GUN* WHEN WE SAW THE ANIME STORYBOARDS NIZUMA CREATED.
BUT HE CHOSE *REVERSI*...
HE WANTS US TO CATCH UP WITH EIJI NIZUMA.
RIGHT. THAT'S HOW I TOOK IT.
IT'S GOING TO BE DIFFICULT TO BEAT WHAT *CROW* HAS ACCOMPLISHED.
...
WELL, YOU JUST NEED TO THINK ABOUT NOT LOSING TO *ZOMBIE☆* FOR THE MOMENT.
UMM, I'LL BE GOING NOW.
OH, RIGHT. THANKS FOR CLEANING THE STUDIO.
THANKS.
OKAY.
PLEASE DON'T TELL ANYBODY EXCEPT YOUR FAMILY MEMBERS ABOUT THE ANIME UNTIL IT'S OFFICIALLY ANNOUNCED IN *JUMP*.
BAM
EEEK !!
ANIME !!
WE'LL OFFICIALLY ANNOUNCE IT IN *JUMP* THIS SPRING.
IS IT SAFE TO ASSUME THAT THIS IS OFFICIAL EVEN THOUGH IT HASN'T BEEN ANNOUNCED IN *JUMP* YET?

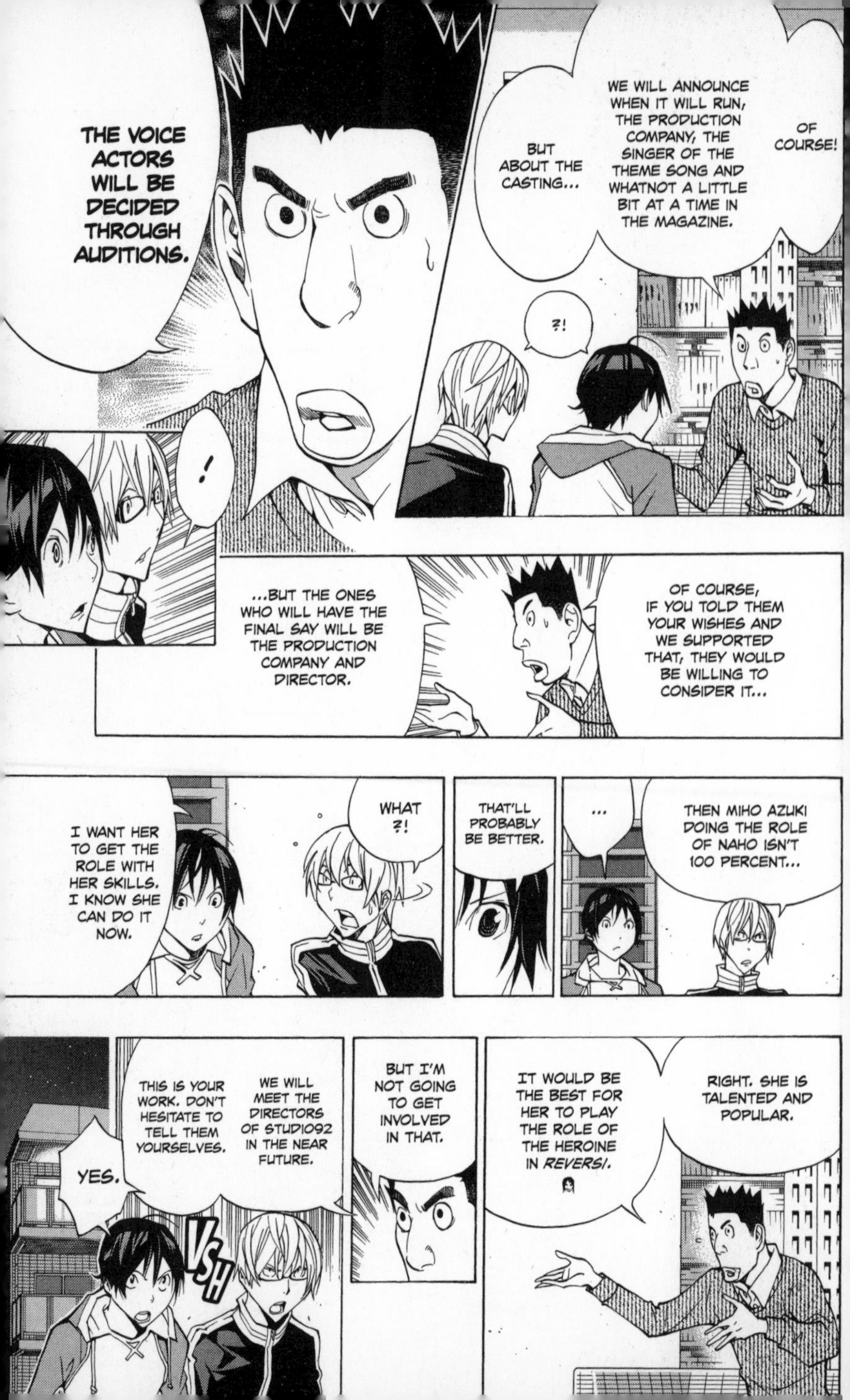
OF COURSE!
WE WILL ANNOUNCE WHEN IT WILL RUN, THE PRODUCTION COMPANY, THE SINGER OF THE THEME SONG AND WHATNOT A LITTLE BIT AT A TIME IN THE MAGAZINE.
BUT ABOUT THE CASTING...
?!
THE VOICE ACTORS WILL BE DECIDED THROUGH AUDITIONS.
!
OF COURSE, IF YOU TOLD THEM YOUR WISHES AND WE SUPPORTED THAT, THEY WOULD BE WILLING TO CONSIDER IT...
...BUT THE ONES WHO WILL HAVE THE FINAL SAY WILL BE THE PRODUCTION COMPANY AND DIRECTOR.
THEN MIHO AZUKI DOING THE ROLE OF NAHO ISN'T 100 PERCENT...
...
THAT'LL PROBABLY BE BETTER.
WHAT ?!
I WANT HER TO GET THE ROLE WITH HER SKILLS. I KNOW SHE CAN DO IT NOW.
RIGHT. SHE IS TALENTED AND POPULAR.
IT WOULD BE THE BEST FOR HER TO PLAY THE ROLE OF THE HEROINE IN REVERSI.
BUT I'M NOT GOING TO GET INVOLVED IN THAT.
WE WILL MEET THE DIRECTORS OF STUDIO92 IN THE NEAR FUTURE.
THIS IS YOUR WORK. DON'T HESITATE TO TELL THEM YOURSELVES.
YES.
VSH

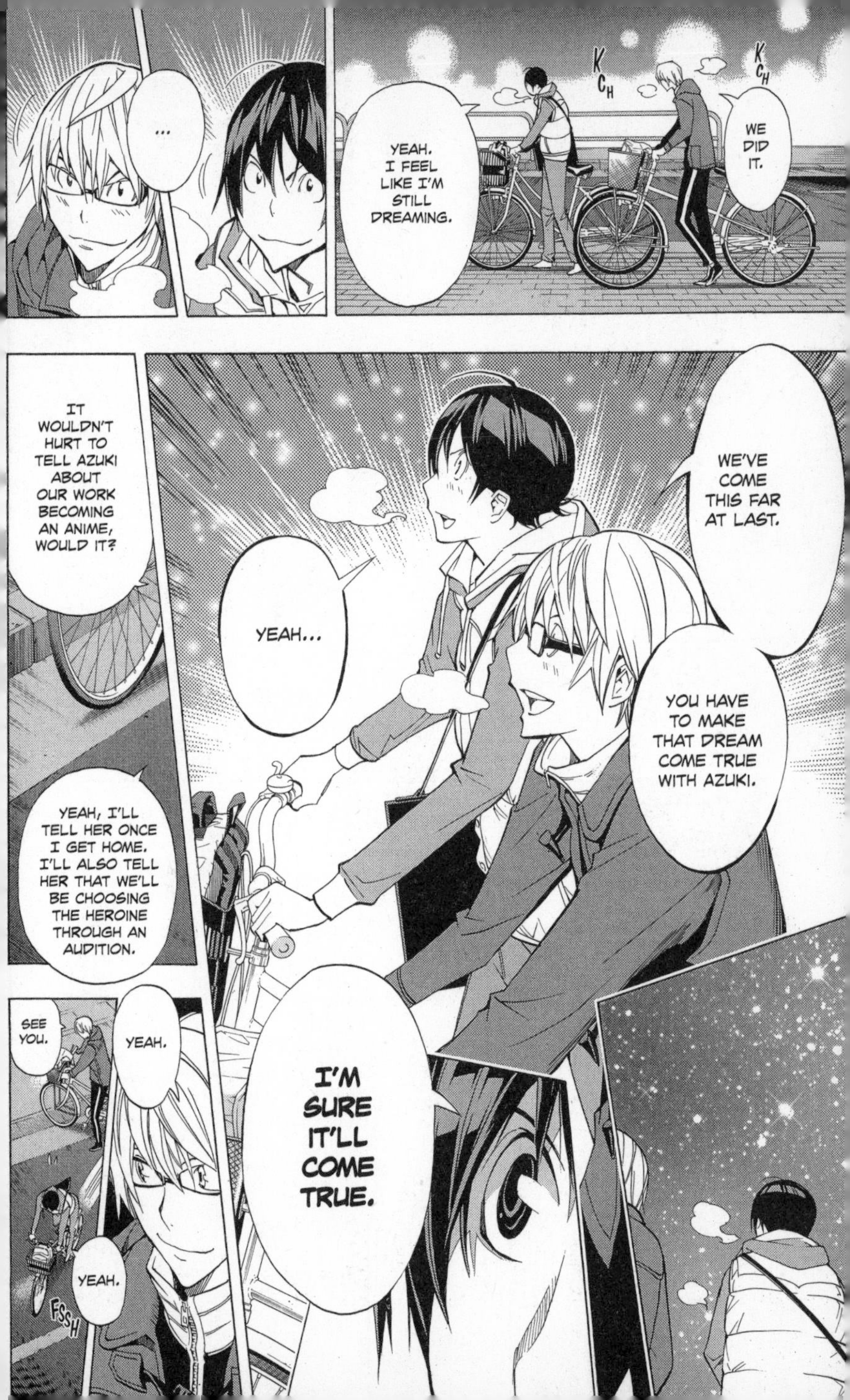
KCH
WE DID IT.
KCH
YEAH. I FEEL LIKE I'M STILL DREAMING.
...
WE'VE COME THIS FAR AT LAST.
YOU HAVE TO MAKE THAT DREAM COME TRUE WITH AZUKI.
YEAH...
IT WOULDN'T HURT TO TELL AZUKI ABOUT OUR WORK BECOMING AN ANIME, WOULD IT?
YEAH, I'LL TELL HER ONCE I GET HOME. I'LL ALSO TELL HER THAT WE'LL BE CHOOSING THE HEROINE THROUGH AN AUDITION.
I'M SURE IT'LL COME TRUE.
YEAH.
SEE YOU.
YEAH.
FSSH

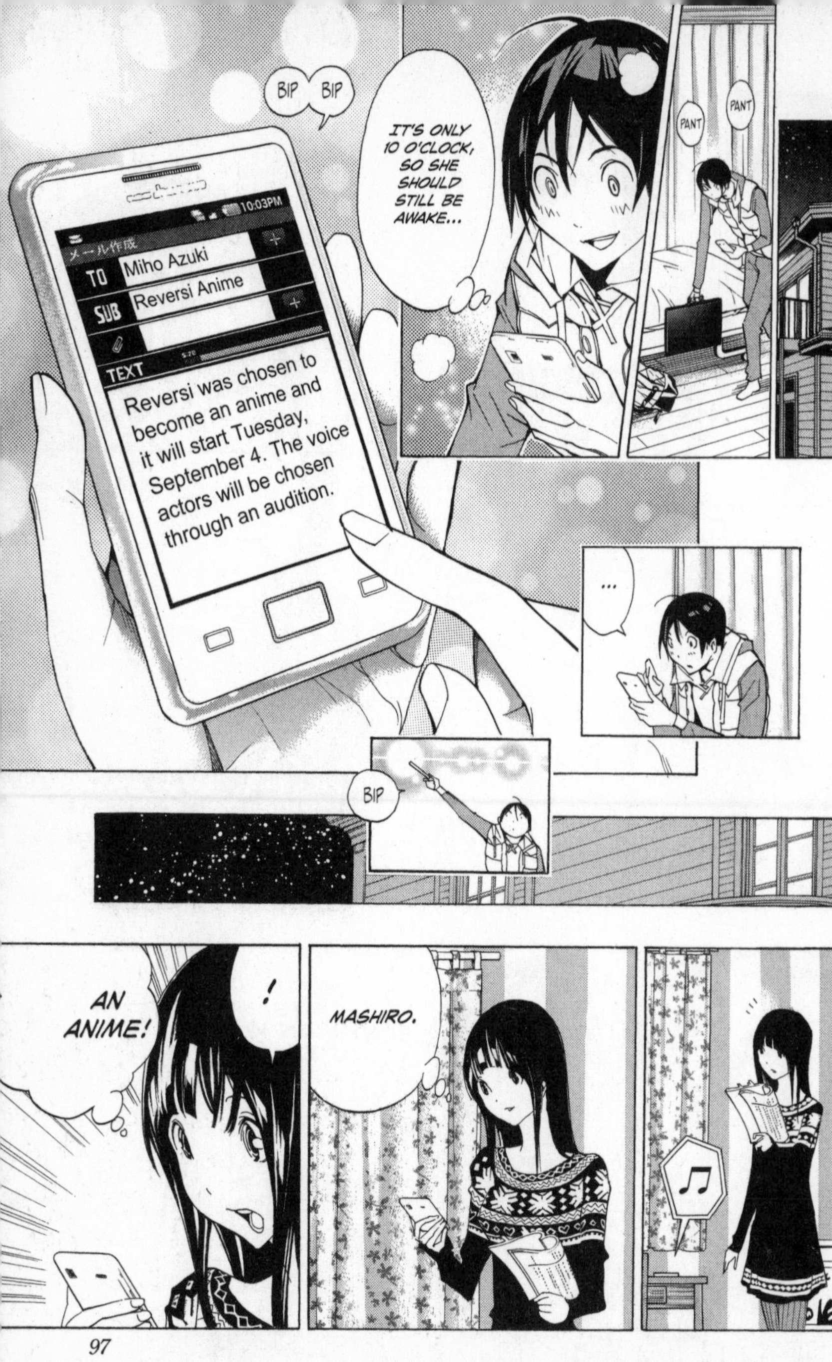
PANT
PANT
IT'S ONLY 10 O'CLOCK, SO SHE SHOULD STILL BE AWAKE...
BIP
BIP
10:03PM
メール作成
TO
Miho Azuki
SUB
Reversi Anime
TEXT
Reversi was chosen to become an anime and it will start Tuesday, September 4. The voice actors will be chosen through an audition.
...
BIP
MASHIRO.
!
AN ANIME!

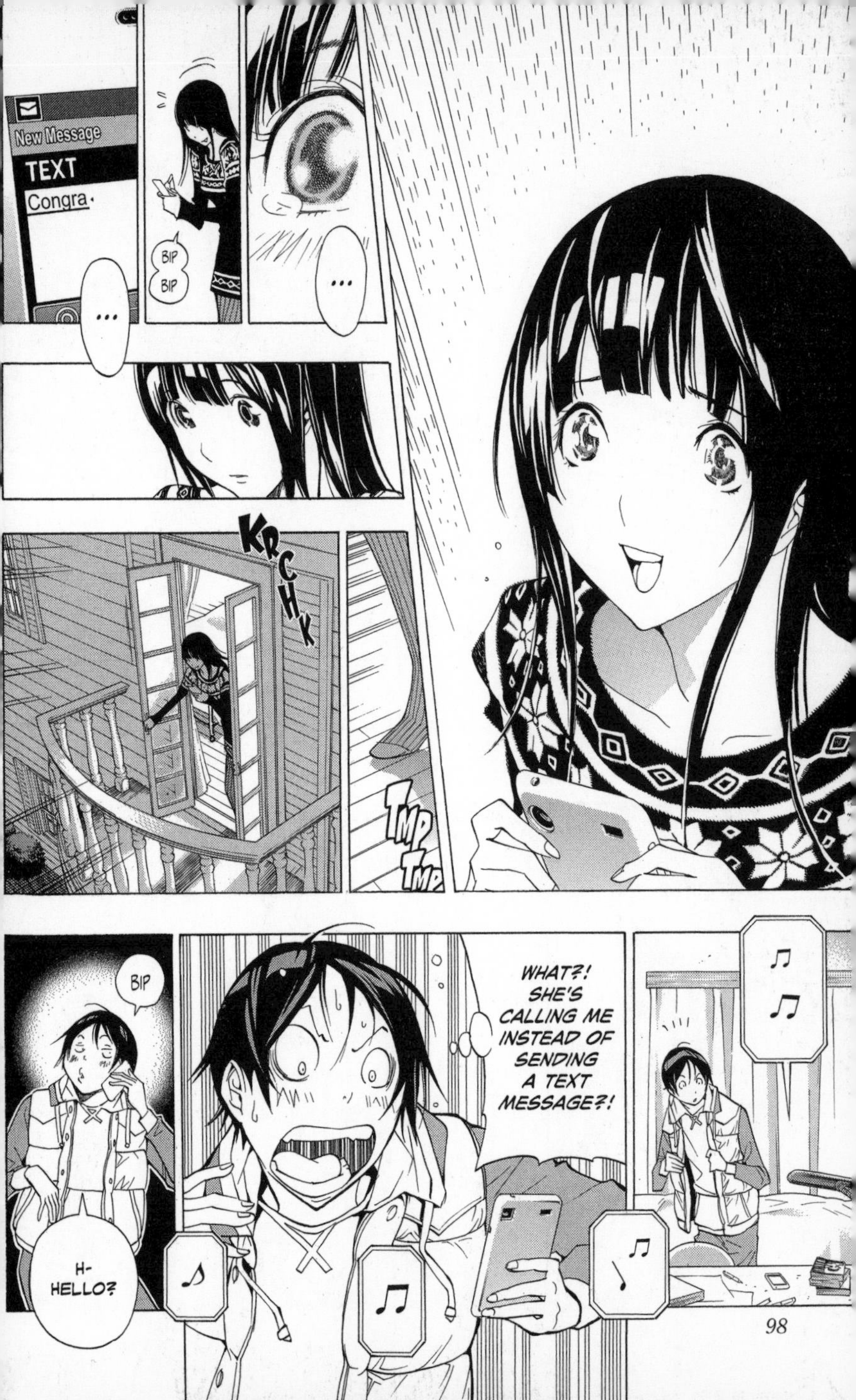
...
BIP
BIP
New Message
TEXT
Congra
...
KRCHK
TMP
TMP
♫
WHAT?! SHE'S CALLING ME INSTEAD OF SENDING A TEXT MESSAGE?!
BIP
H- HELLO?

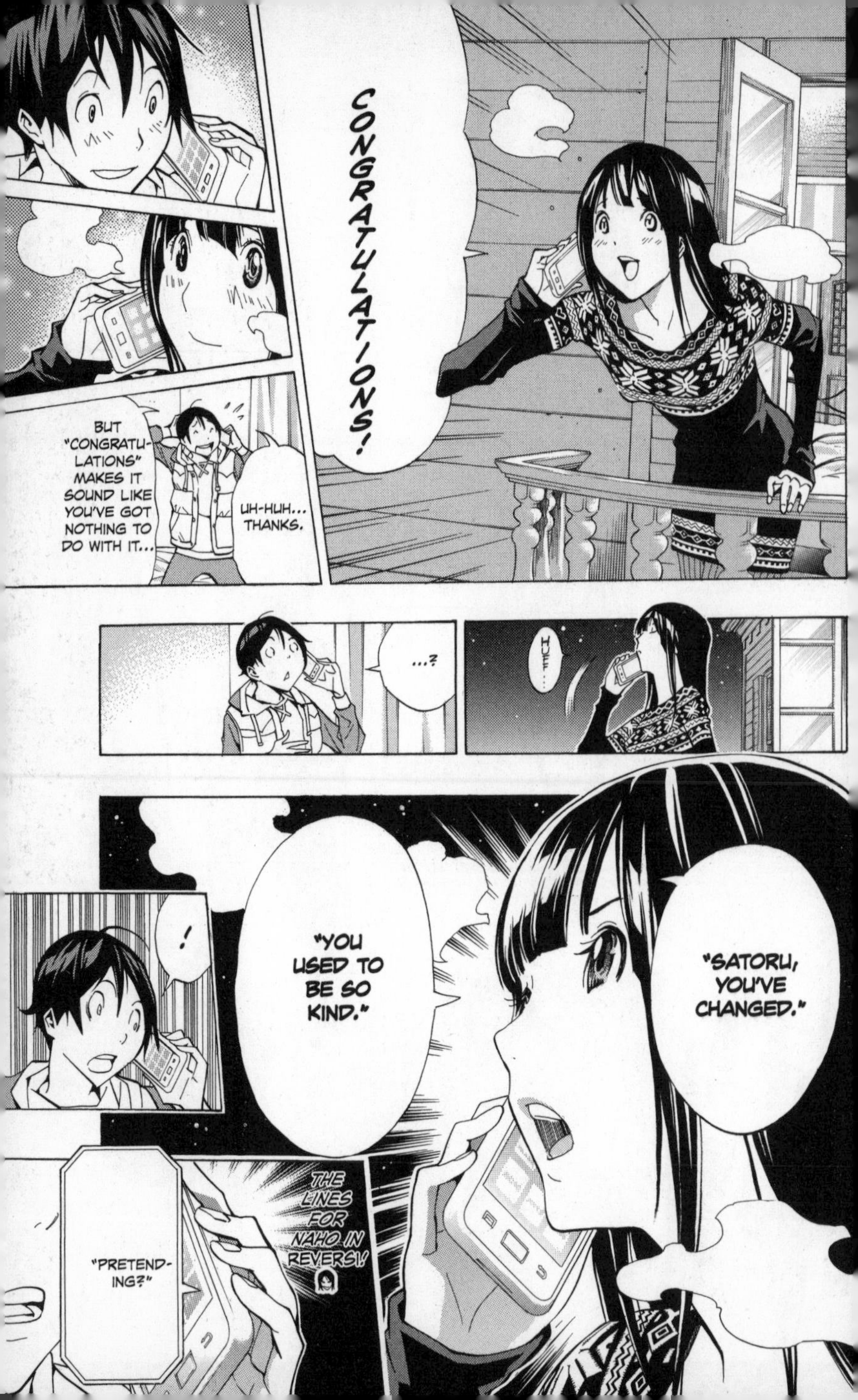
CONGRATULATIONS!
UH-HUH... THANKS.
BUT "CONGRATULATIONS" MAKES IT SOUND LIKE YOU'VE GOT NOTHING TO DO WITH IT...
HUF...
...?
"SATORU, YOU'VE CHANGED."
"YOU USED TO BE SO KIND."
!
THE LINES FOR NAHO IN REVERSI!
"PRETENDING?"

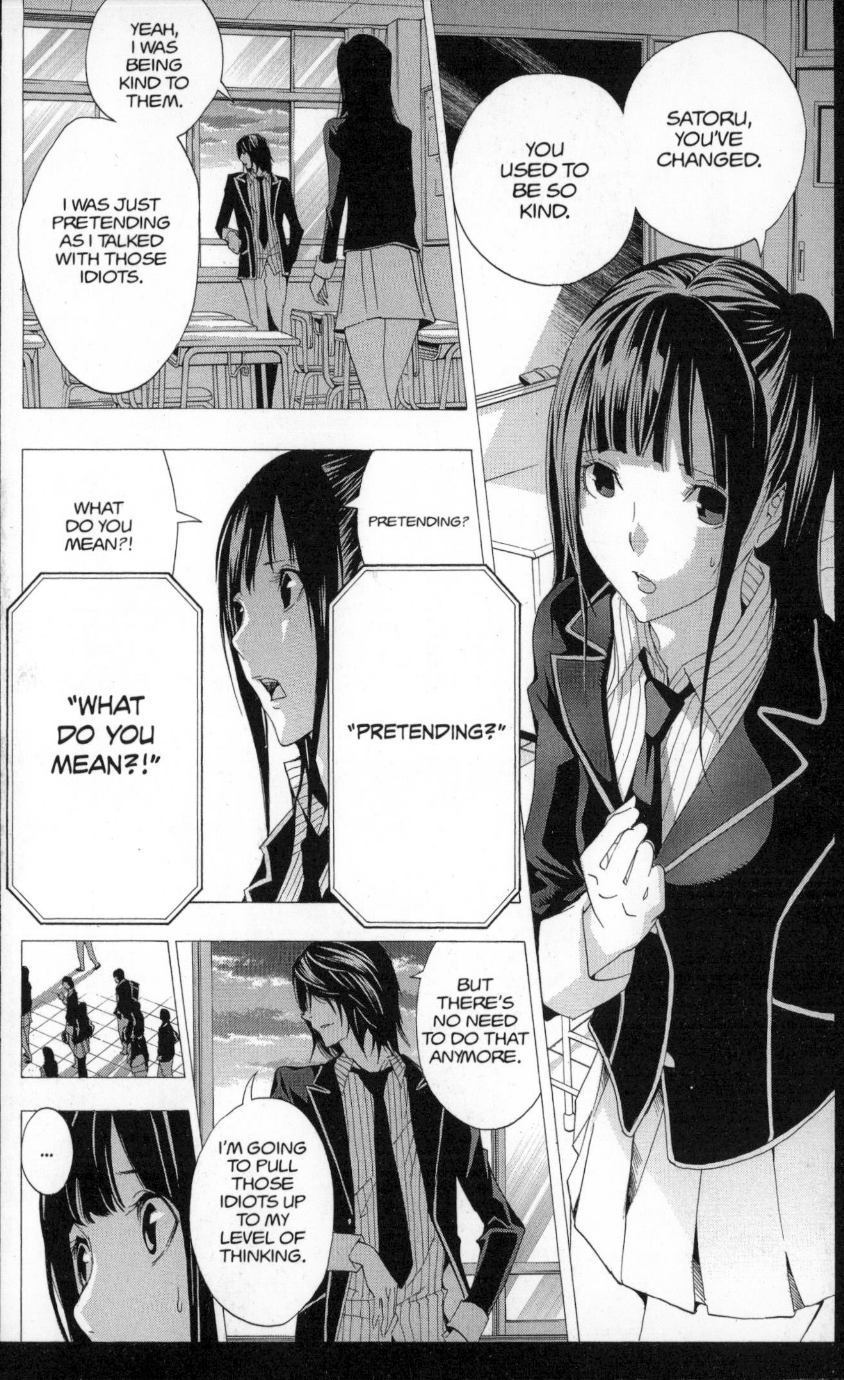
SATORU, YOU'VE CHANGED.
YOU USED TO BE SO KIND.
YEAH, I WAS BEING KIND TO THEM.
I WAS JUST PRETENDING AS I TALKED WITH THOSE IDIOTS.
PRETENDING?
"PRETENDING?"
WHAT DO YOU MEAN?!
"WHAT DO YOU MEAN?!"
BUT THERE'S NO NEED TO DO THAT ANYMORE.
I'M GOING TO PULL THOSE IDIOTS UP TO MY LEVEL OF THINKING.
...

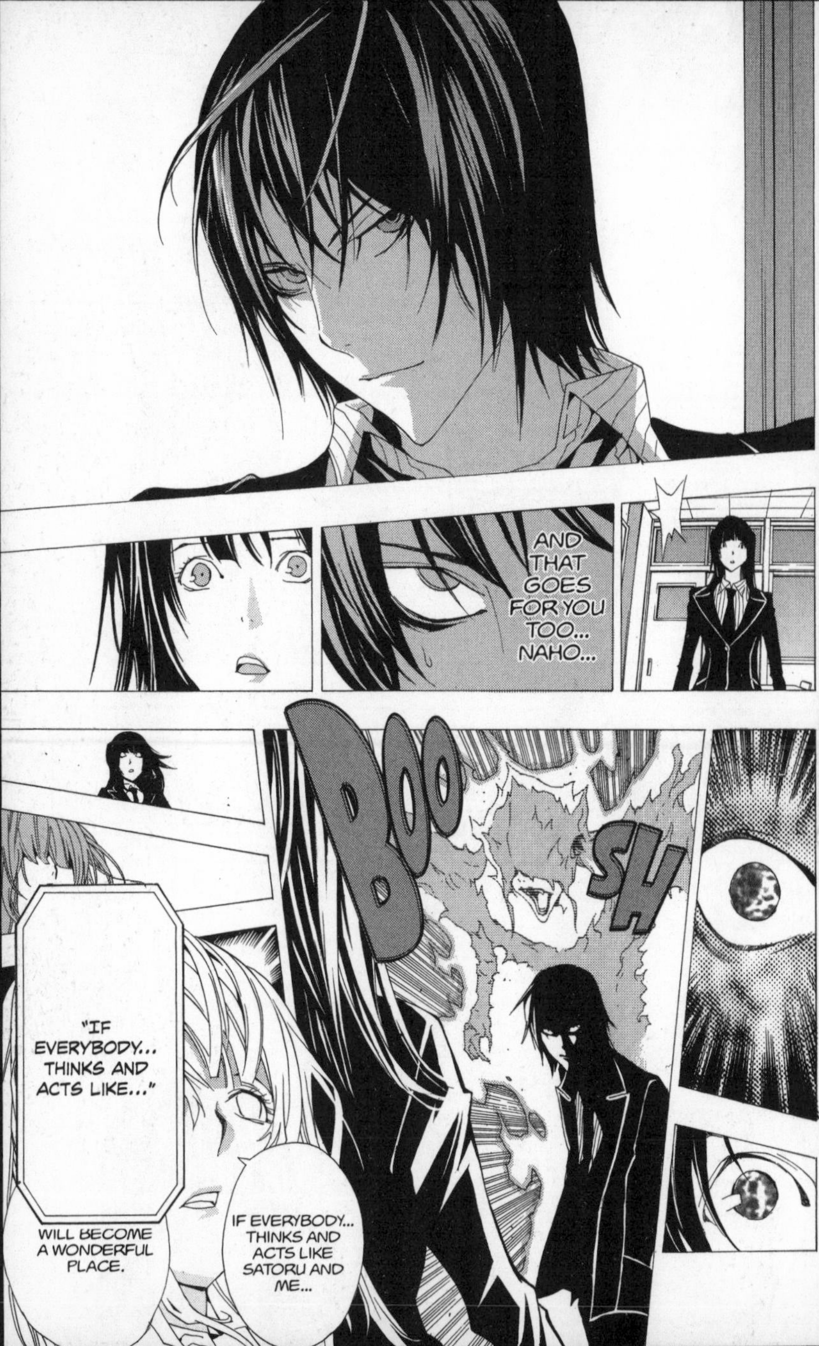
AND THAT GOES FOR YOU TOO... NAHO...
BOOSH
IF EVERYBODY... THINKS AND ACTS LIKE SATORU AND ME...
"IF EVERYBODY... THINKS AND ACTS LIKE..."
WILL BECOME A WONDERFUL PLACE.

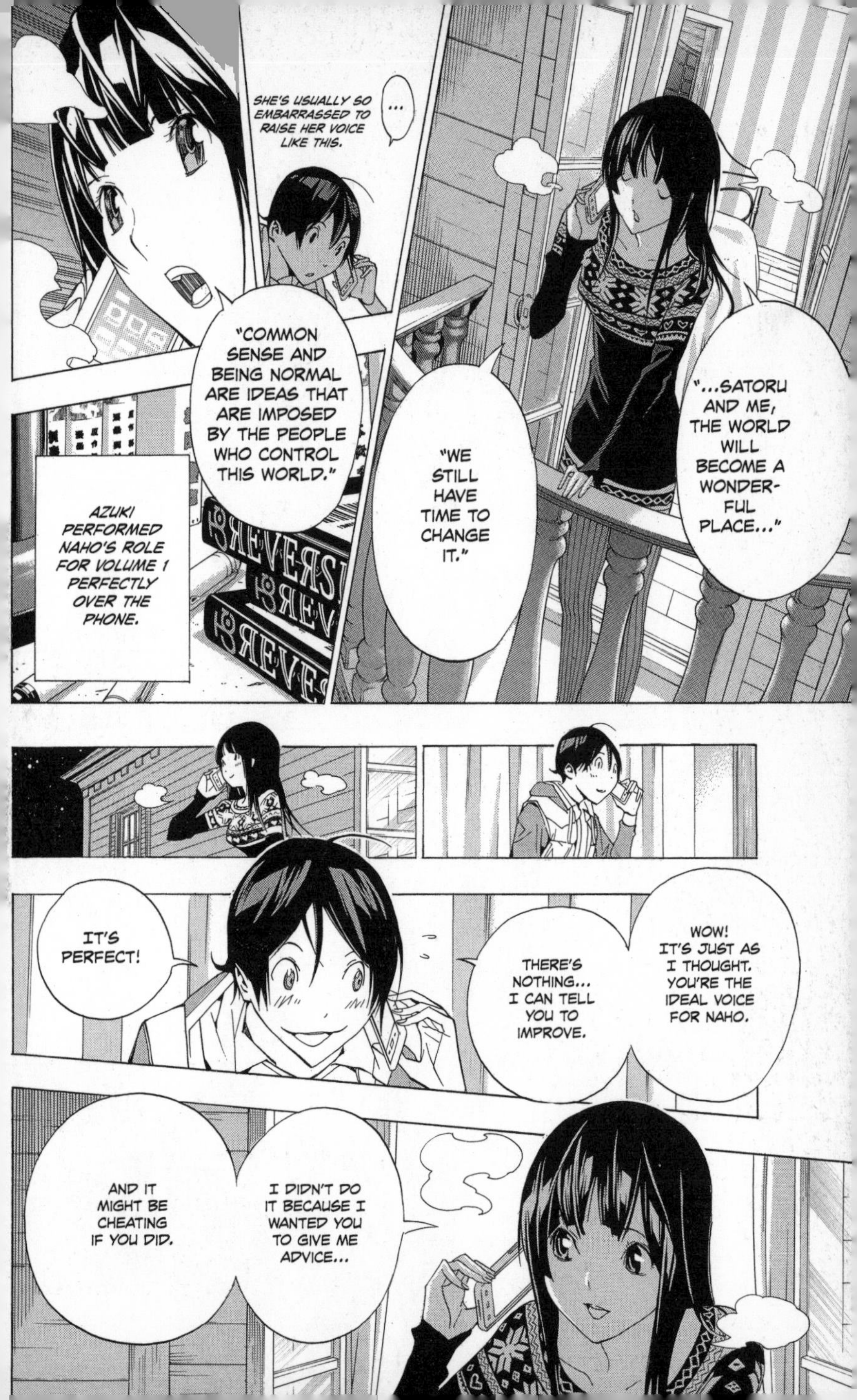

"...SATORU AND ME, THE WORLD WILL BECOME A WONDER-FUL PLACE..."
"WE STILL HAVE TIME TO CHANGE IT."
...
SHE'S USUALLY SO EMBARRASSED TO RAISE HER VOICE LIKE THIS.
"COMMON SENSE AND BEING NORMAL ARE IDEAS THAT ARE IMPOSED BY THE PEOPLE WHO CONTROL THIS WORLD."
AZUKI PERFORMED NAHO'S ROLE FOR VOLUME 1 PERFECTLY OVER THE PHONE.
WOW! IT'S JUST AS I THOUGHT. YOU'RE THE IDEAL VOICE FOR NAHO.
THERE'S NOTHING... I CAN TELL YOU TO IMPROVE.
IT'S PERFECT!
I DIDN'T DO IT BECAUSE I WANTED YOU TO GIVE ME ADVICE...
AND IT MIGHT BE CHEATING IF YOU DID.

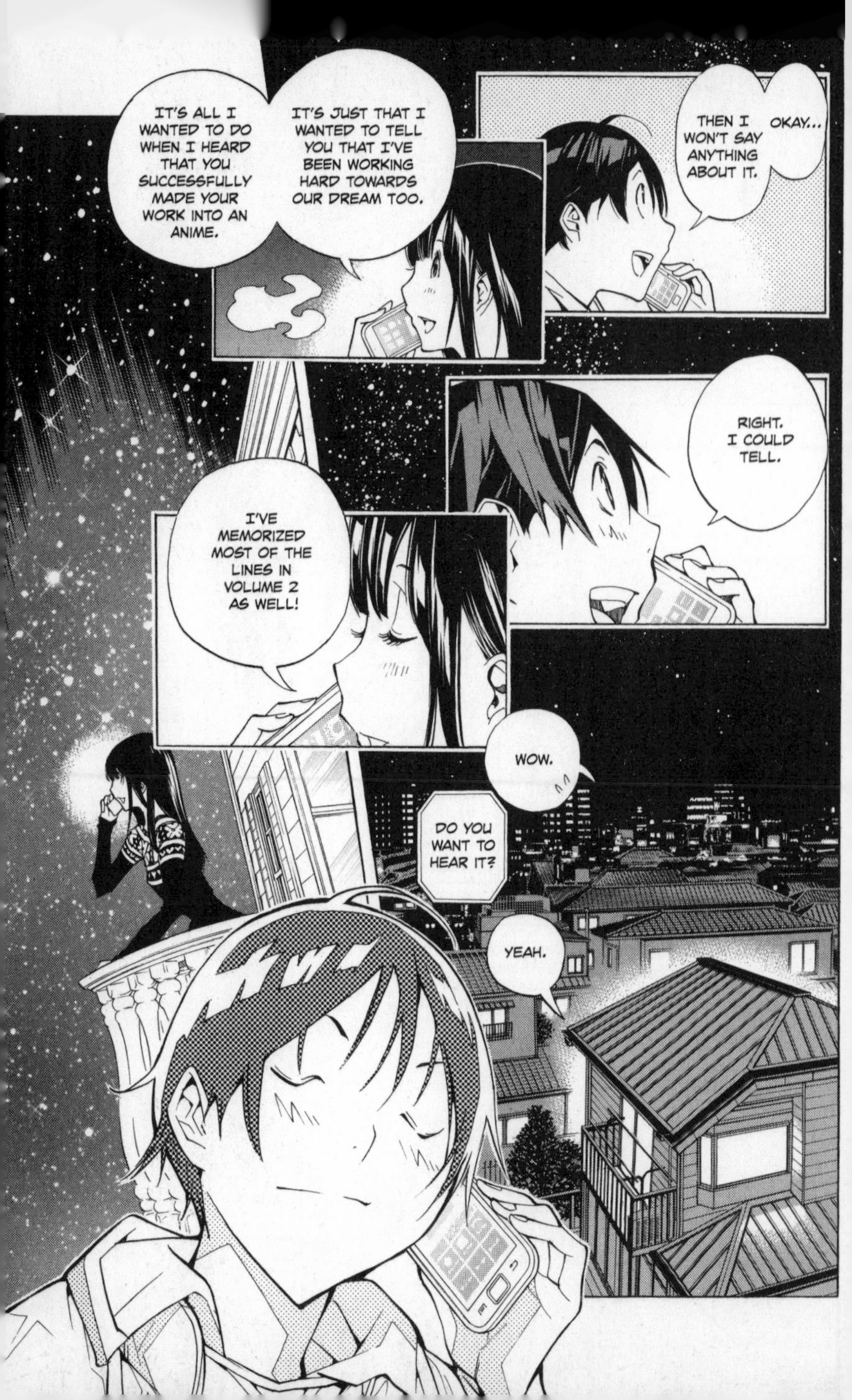
OKAY...
THEN I WON'T SAY ANYTHING ABOUT IT.
IT'S JUST THAT I WANTED TO TELL YOU THAT I'VE BEEN WORKING HARD TOWARDS OUR DREAM TOO.
IT'S ALL I WANTED TO DO WHEN I HEARD THAT YOU SUCCESSFULLY MADE YOUR WORK INTO AN ANIME.
RIGHT. I COULD TELL.
I'VE MEMORIZED MOST OF THE LINES IN VOLUME 2 AS WELL!
WOW.
DO YOU WANT TO HEAR IT?
YEAH.

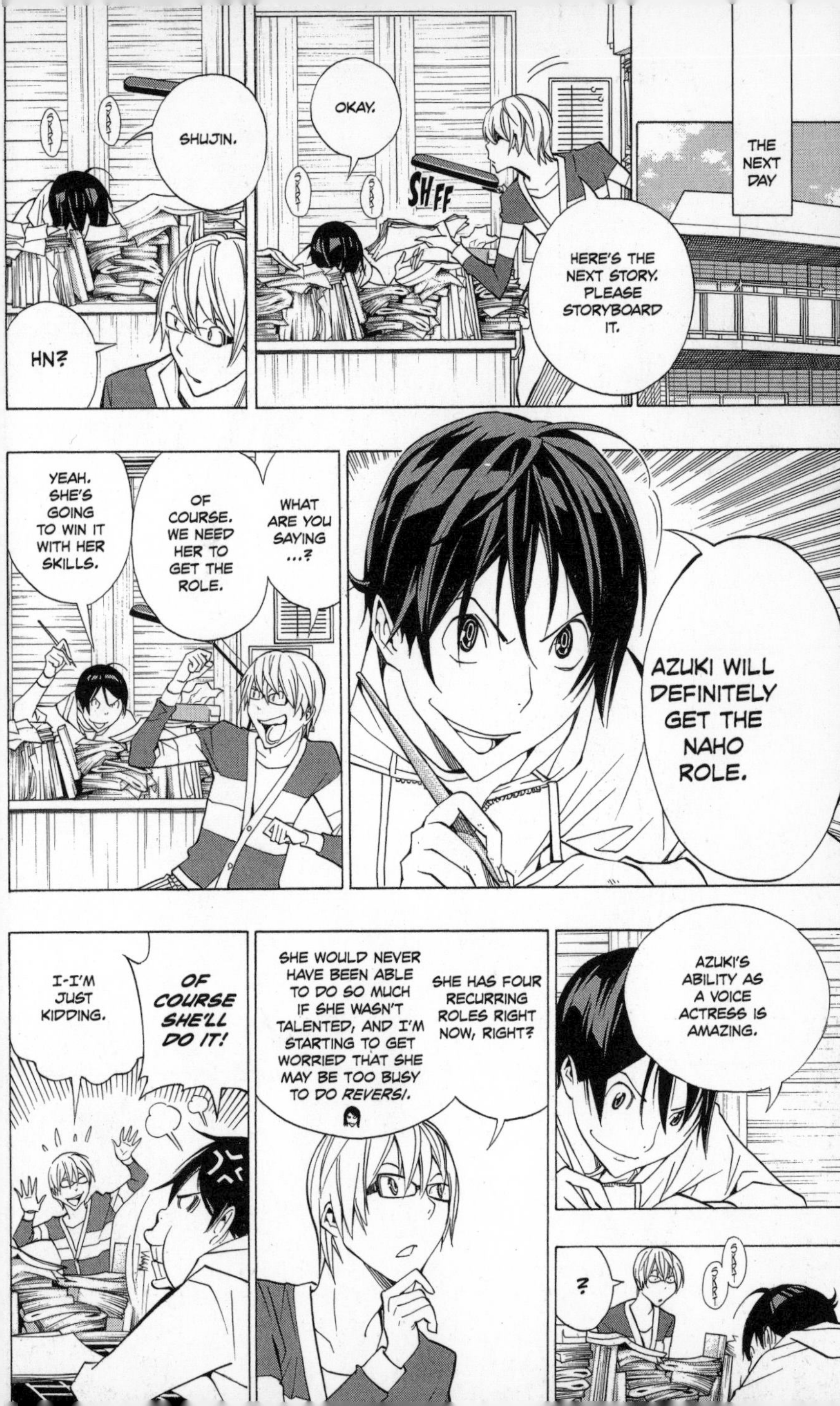
THE NEXT DAY
HERE'S THE NEXT STORY. PLEASE STORYBOARD IT.
SHFF
OKAY.
SKRT
SKRT
SHUJIN.
SKRT
SKRT
HN?
AZUKI WILL DEFINITELY GET THE NAHO ROLE.
WHAT ARE YOU SAYING ...?
OF COURSE. WE NEED HER TO GET THE ROLE.
YEAH. SHE'S GOING TO WIN IT WITH HER SKILLS.
AZUKI'S ABILITY AS A VOICE ACTRESS IS AMAZING.
SKRT
SKRT
?
SHE HAS FOUR RECURRING ROLES RIGHT NOW, RIGHT?
SHE WOULD NEVER HAVE BEEN ABLE TO DO SO MUCH IF SHE WASN'T TALENTED, AND I'M STARTING TO GET WORRIED THAT SHE MAY BE TOO BUSY TO DO REVERSI.
OF COURSE SHE'LL DO IT!
I-I'M JUST KIDDING.

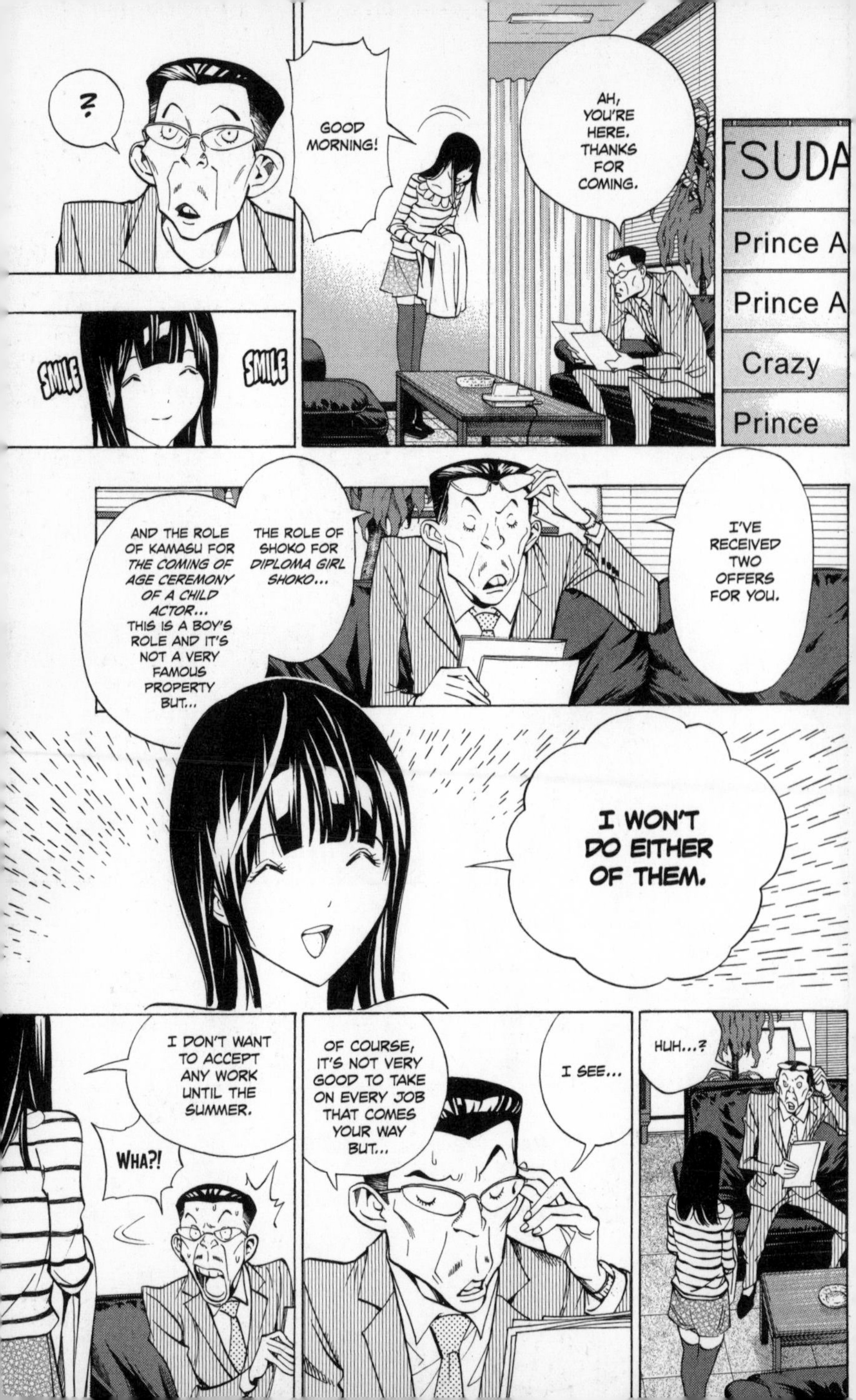
TSUDA
Prince A
Prince A
Crazy
Prince
AH, YOU'RE HERE. THANKS FOR COMING.
GOOD MORNING!
?
SMILE
SMILE
I'VE RECEIVED TWO OFFERS FOR YOU.
THE ROLE OF SHOKO FOR *DIPLOMA GIRL SHOKO*...
AND THE ROLE OF KAMASU FOR *THE COMING OF AGE CEREMONY OF A CHILD ACTOR*... THIS IS A BOY'S ROLE AND IT'S NOT A VERY FAMOUS PROPERTY BUT...
I WON'T DO EITHER OF THEM.
HUH...?
I SEE...
OF COURSE, IT'S NOT VERY GOOD TO TAKE ON EVERY JOB THAT COMES YOUR WAY BUT...
I DON'T WANT TO ACCEPT ANY WORK UNTIL THE SUMMER.
WHA?!

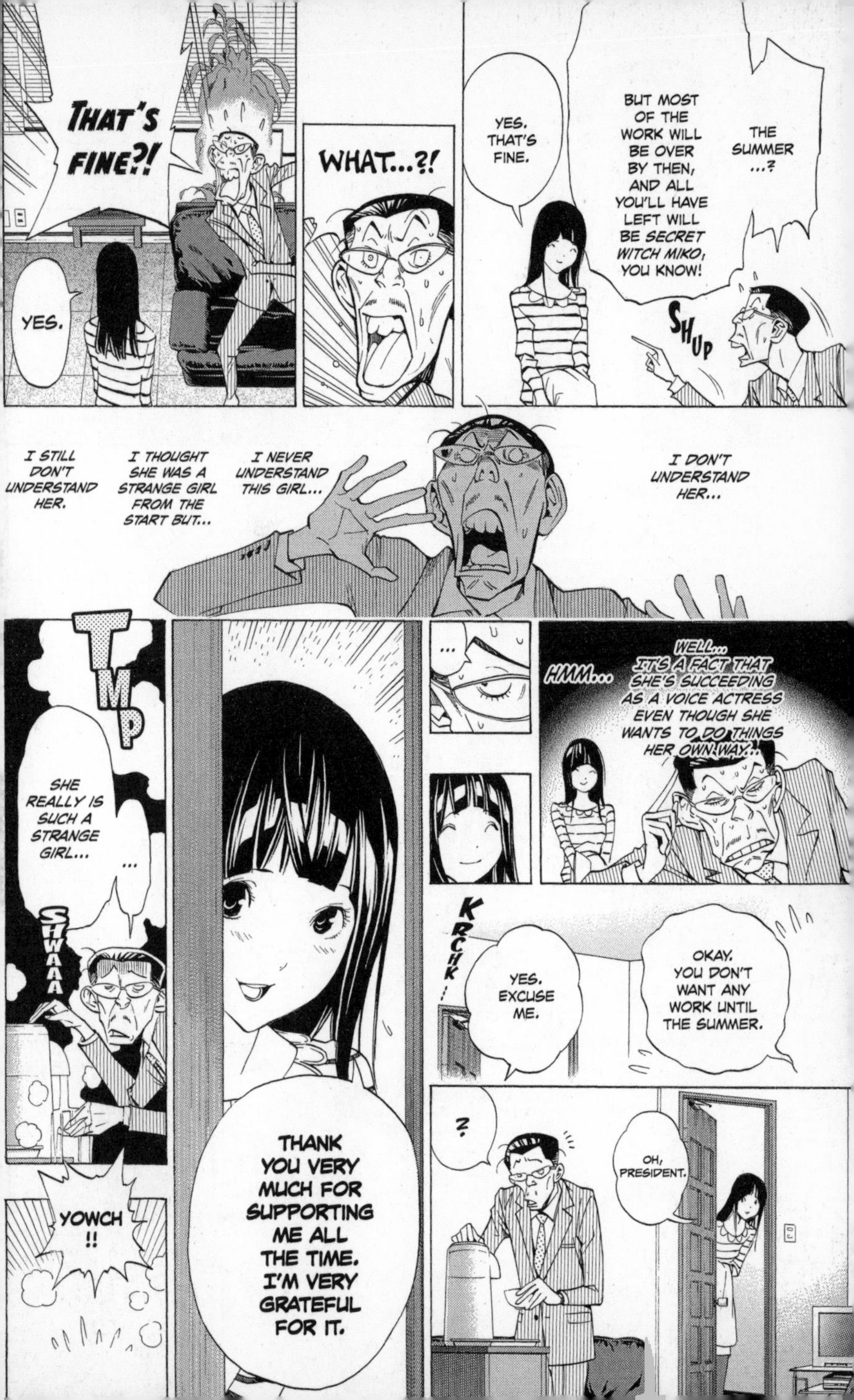
THE SUMMER ...?
BUT MOST OF THE WORK WILL BE OVER BY THEN, AND ALL YOU'LL HAVE LEFT WILL BE *SECRET WITCH MIKO*, YOU KNOW!
SHUP
YES. THAT'S FINE.
WHAT...?!
THAT'S FINE?!
YES.
I DON'T UNDERSTAND HER...
I NEVER UNDERSTAND THIS GIRL...
I THOUGHT SHE WAS A STRANGE GIRL FROM THE START BUT...
I STILL DON'T UNDERSTAND HER.
HMM...
WELL... IT'S A FACT THAT SHE'S SUCCEEDING AS A VOICE ACTRESS EVEN THOUGH SHE WANTS TO DO THINGS HER OWN WAY...
...
OKAY. YOU DON'T WANT ANY WORK UNTIL THE SUMMER.
YES. EXCUSE ME.
KRCHK...
OH, PRESIDENT.
?
THANK YOU VERY MUCH FOR SUPPORTING ME ALL THE TIME. I'M VERY GRATEFUL FOR IT.
TMP
SHE REALLY IS SUCH A STRANGE GIRL...
...
SHWAAA
YOWCH !!

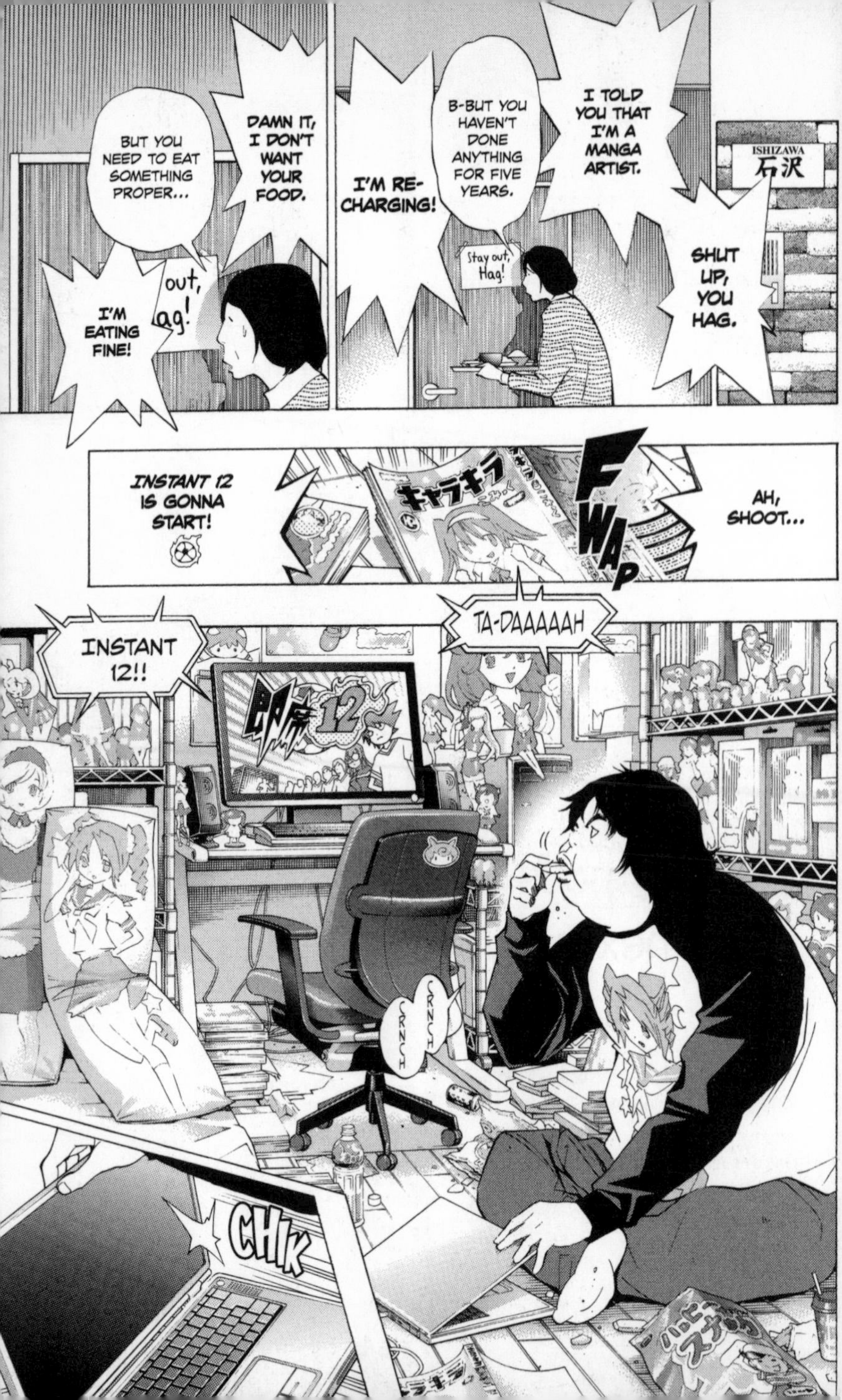
ISHIZAWA
石沢
I TOLD YOU THAT I'M A MANGA ARTIST.
SHUT UP, YOU HAG.
B-BUT YOU HAVEN'T DONE ANYTHING FOR FIVE YEARS.
Stay out, Hag!
I'M RE-CHARGING!
DAMN IT, I DON'T WANT YOUR FOOD.
BUT YOU NEED TO EAT SOMETHING PROPER...
out, ag!
I'M EATING FINE!
AH, SHOOT...
FWAP
キャラキラ
INSTANT 12 IS GONNA START!
TA-DAAAAAH
INSTANT 12!!
12
CRNCH CRNCH
CHIK

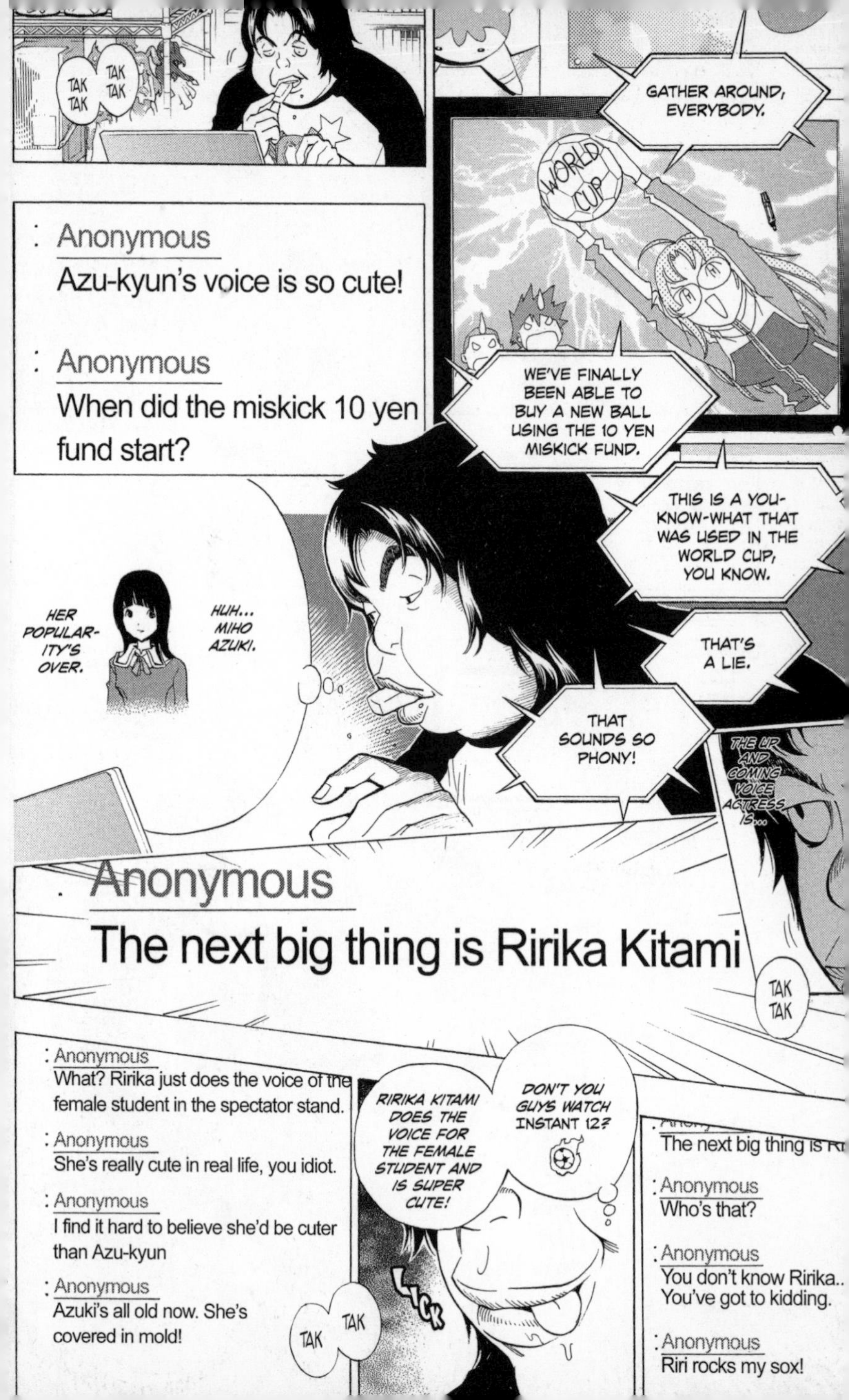
GATHER AROUND, EVERYBODY.
WORLD CUP
TAK TAK TAK TAK
WE'VE FINALLY BEEN ABLE TO BUY A NEW BALL USING THE 10 YEN MISKICK FUND.
: Anonymous
Azu-kyun's voice is so cute!
: Anonymous
When did the miskick 10 yen fund start?
THIS IS A YOU-KNOW-WHAT THAT WAS USED IN THE WORLD CUP, YOU KNOW.
THAT'S A LIE.
THAT SOUNDS SO PHONY!
HUH... MIHO AZUKI.
HER POPULAR-ITY'S OVER.
THE UP AND COMING VOICE ACTRESS IS...
: Anonymous
The next big thing is Ririka Kitami
TAK TAK
The next big thing is Ri
: Anonymous
Who's that?
: Anonymous
You don't know Ririka..
You've got to kidding.
: Anonymous
Riri rocks my sox!
DON'T YOU GUYS WATCH INSTANT 12?
RIRIKA KITAMI DOES THE VOICE FOR THE FEMALE STUDENT AND IS SUPER CUTE!
LICK
TAK TAK
: Anonymous
What? Ririka just does the voice of the female student in the spectator stand.
: Anonymous
She's really cute in real life, you idiot.
: Anonymous
I find it hard to believe she'd be cuter than Azu-kyun
: Anonymous
Azuki's all old now. She's covered in mold!

OHBA'S STORYBOARD

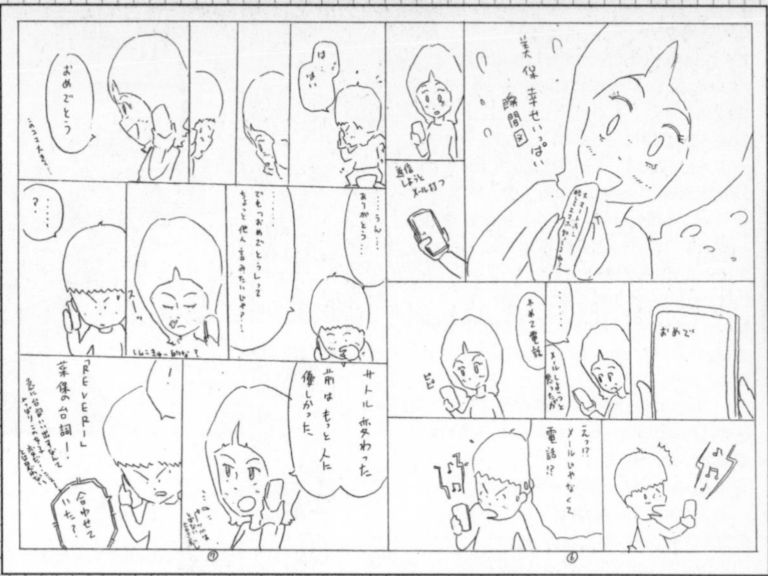
美保 幸せいっぱい 瞬間図
通信しようとメール打つ
おめで
やめて電話
えっ!? メールじゃなくて 電話!?
はっ はい
おめでとう
…うん… ありがとう…
?……
サトル 変わった 前はもっと人に優しかった
「REVERI」菜保の台詞!

OBATA'S STORYBOARD

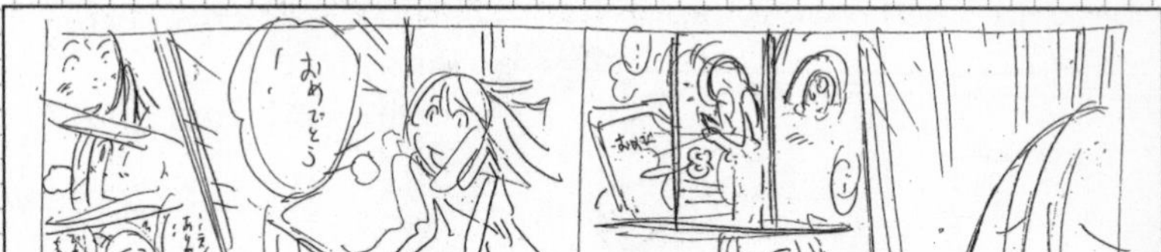
おめでとう
サトル変わった…!
はい!

COMPLETE!

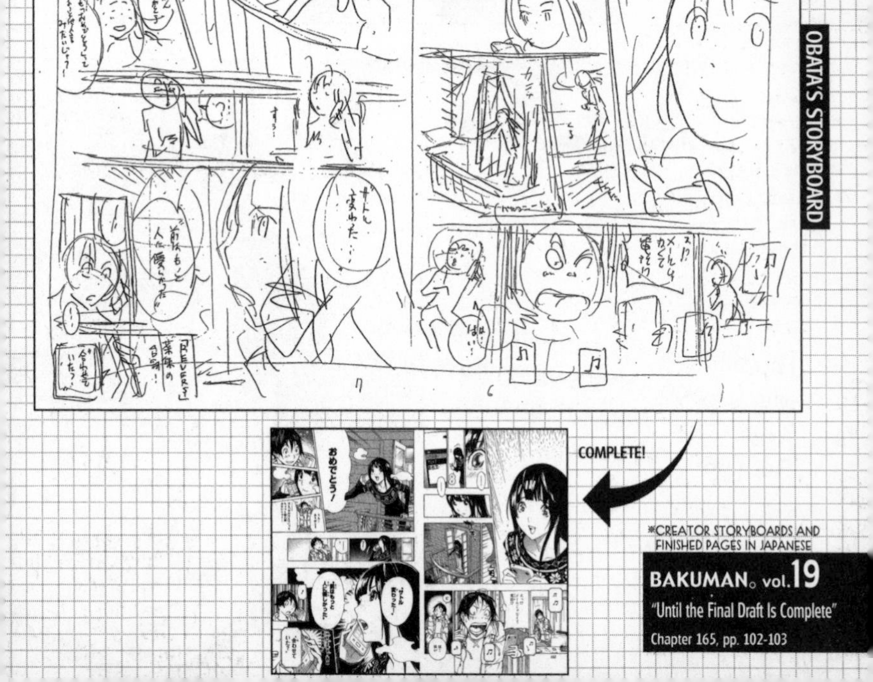
おめでとう!

※CREATOR STORYBOARDS AND FINISHED PAGES IN JAPANESE

BAKUMAN。 vol.19

"Until the Final Draft Is Complete"

Chapter 165, pp. 102-103

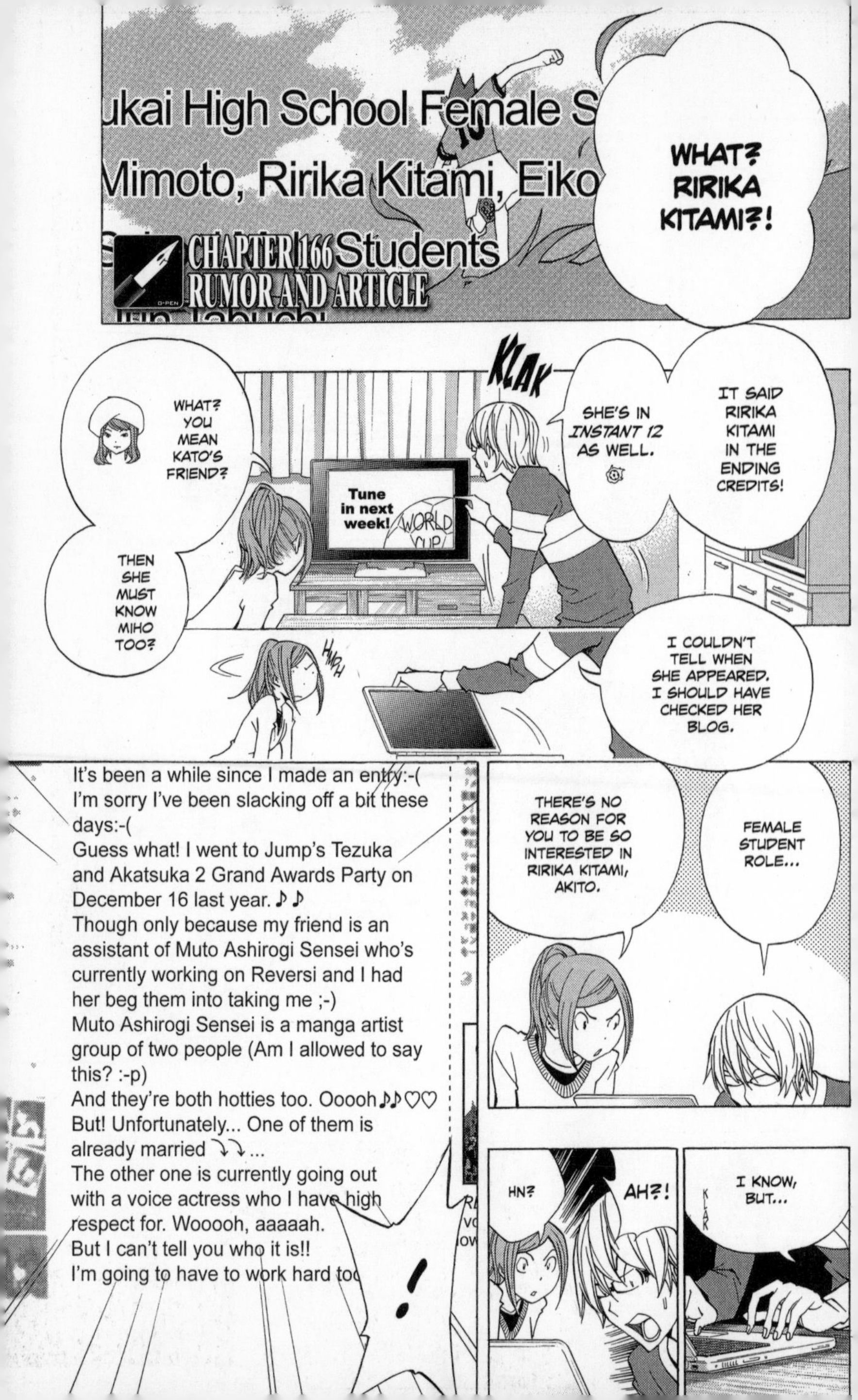
ukai High School Female S
Mimoto, Ririka Kitami, Eiko
Students
CHAPTER 166
RUMOR AND ARTICLE
WHAT⁈ RIRIKA KITAMI⁈!
IT SAID RIRIKA KITAMI IN THE ENDING CREDITS!
SHE'S IN INSTANT 12 AS WELL.
KLAK
Tune in next week!
WORLD CUP
WHAT? YOU MEAN KATO'S FRIEND?
THEN SHE MUST KNOW MIHO TOO?
HMPH
I COULDN'T TELL WHEN SHE APPEARED. I SHOULD HAVE CHECKED HER BLOG.
FEMALE STUDENT ROLE...
THERE'S NO REASON FOR YOU TO BE SO INTERESTED IN RIRIKA KITAMI, AKITO.
It's been a while since I made an entry:-(
I'm sorry I've been slacking off a bit these days:-(
Guess what! I went to Jump's Tezuka and Akatsuka 2 Grand Awards Party on December 16 last year.♪♪
Though only because my friend is an assistant of Muto Ashirogi Sensei who's currently working on Reversi and I had her beg them into taking me ;-)
Muto Ashirogi Sensei is a manga artist group of two people (Am I allowed to say this? :-p)
And they're both hotties too. Ooooh♪♪♡♡
But! Unfortunately... One of them is already married ⤵⤵...
The other one is currently going out with a voice actress who I have high respect for. Wooooh, aaaaah.
But I can't tell you who it is!!
I'm going to have to work hard too
I KNOW, BUT...
KLAK
AH⁈!
HN?

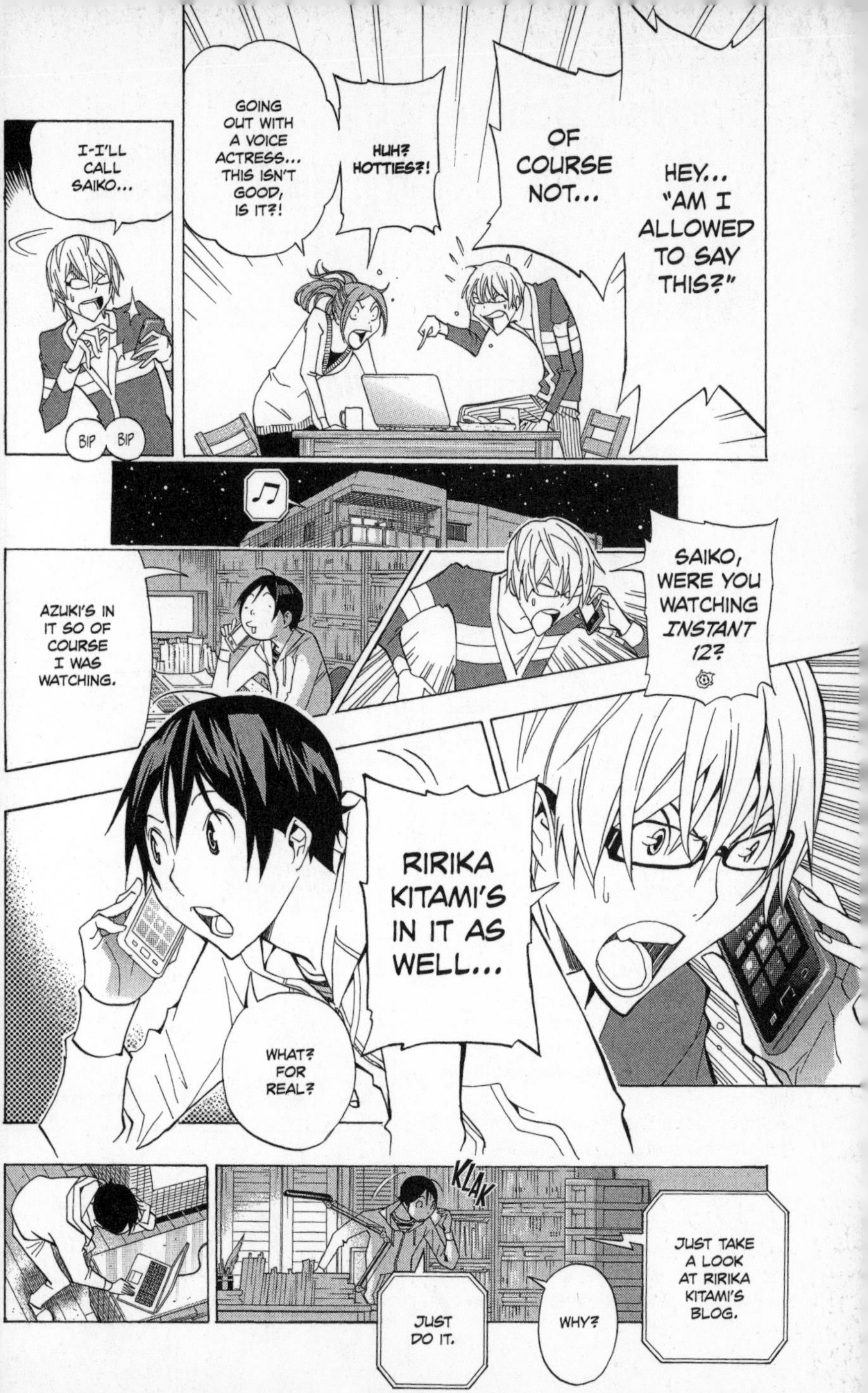
HEY... "AM I ALLOWED TO SAY THIS?"
OF COURSE NOT...
HUH? HOTTIES?!
GOING OUT WITH A VOICE ACTRESS... THIS ISN'T GOOD, IS IT?!
I-I'LL CALL SAIKO...
BIP BIP
♫
SAIKO, WERE YOU WATCHING INSTANT 12?
AZUKI'S IN IT SO OF COURSE I WAS WATCHING.
RIRIKA KITAMI'S IN IT AS WELL...
WHAT? FOR REAL?
JUST TAKE A LOOK AT RIRIKA KITAMI'S BLOG.
WHY?
JUST DO IT.
KLAK

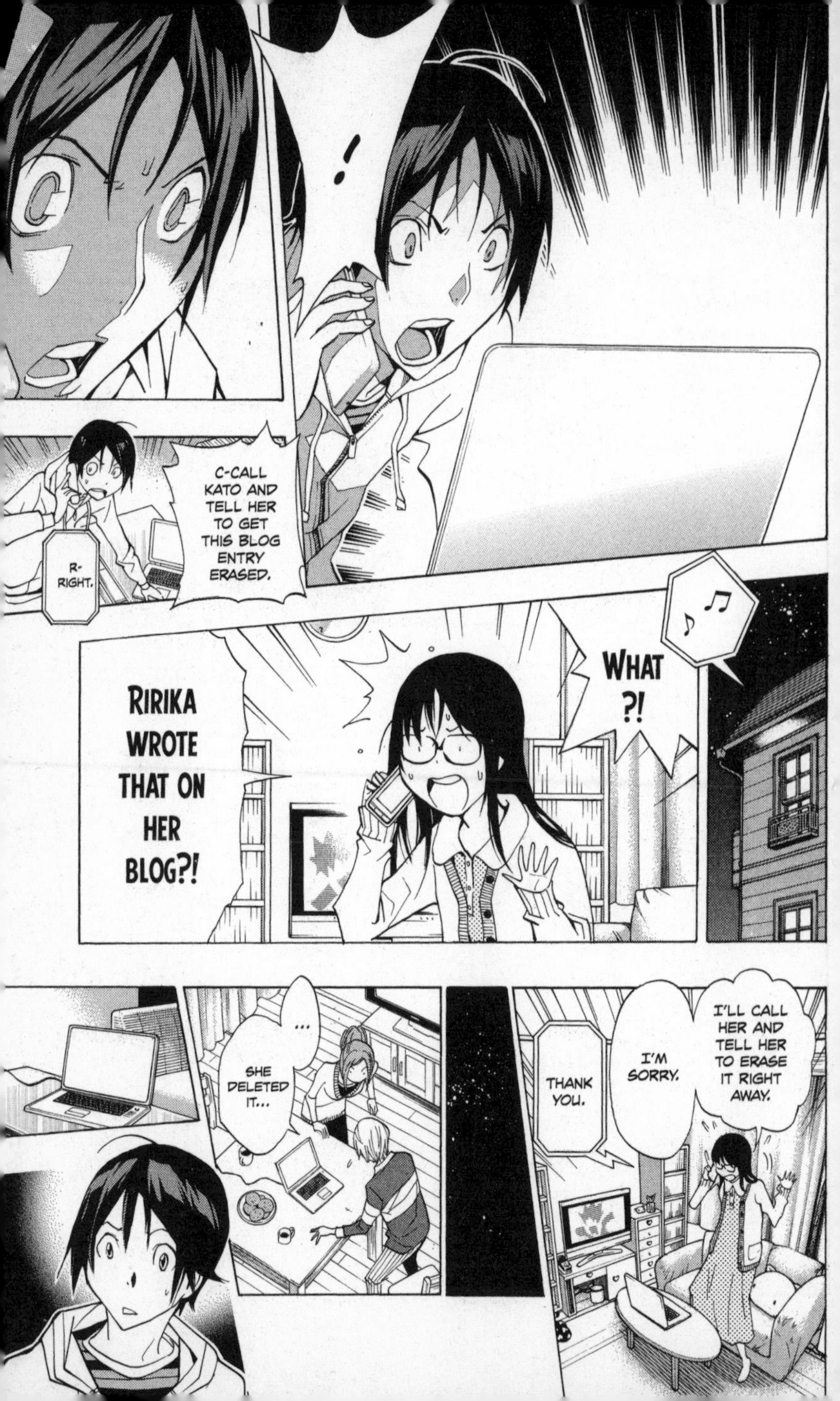
!
C-CALL KATO AND TELL HER TO GET THIS BLOG ENTRY ERASED.
R-RIGHT.
♪ ♫
WHAT ?!
RIRIKA WROTE THAT ON HER BLOG?!
I'LL CALL HER AND TELL HER TO ERASE IT RIGHT AWAY.
I'M SORRY.
THANK YOU.
...
SHE DELETED IT...

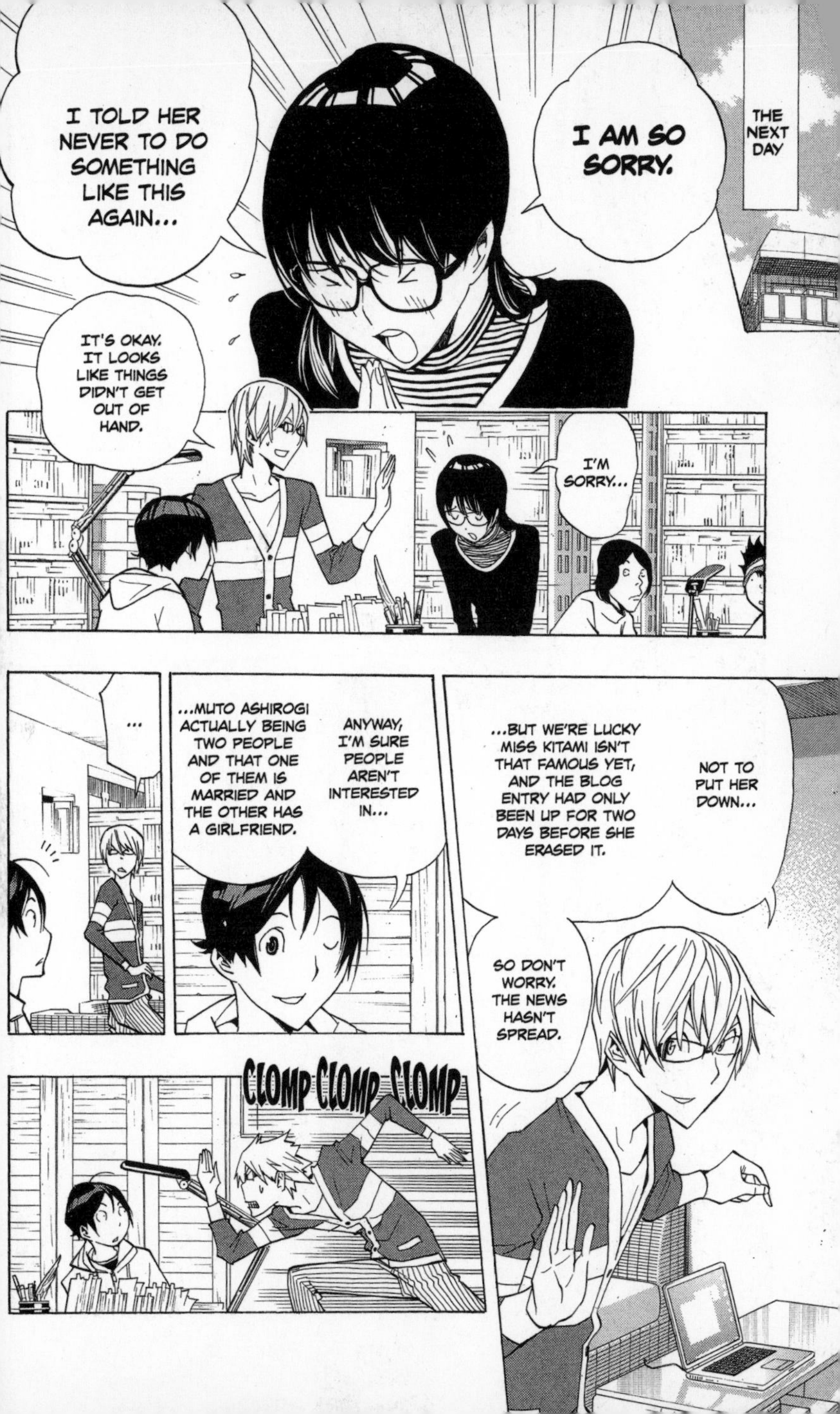
THE NEXT DAY
I AM SO SORRY.
I TOLD HER NEVER TO DO SOMETHING LIKE THIS AGAIN...
I'M SORRY...
IT'S OKAY. IT LOOKS LIKE THINGS DIDN'T GET OUT OF HAND.
NOT TO PUT HER DOWN...
...BUT WE'RE LUCKY MISS KITAMI ISN'T THAT FAMOUS YET, AND THE BLOG ENTRY HAD ONLY BEEN UP FOR TWO DAYS BEFORE SHE ERASED IT.
SO DON'T WORRY. THE NEWS HASN'T SPREAD.
ANYWAY, I'M SURE PEOPLE AREN'T INTERESTED IN...
...MUTO ASHIROGI ACTUALLY BEING TWO PEOPLE AND THAT ONE OF THEM IS MARRIED AND THE OTHER HAS A GIRLFRIEND.
...
CLOMP CLOMP CLOMP

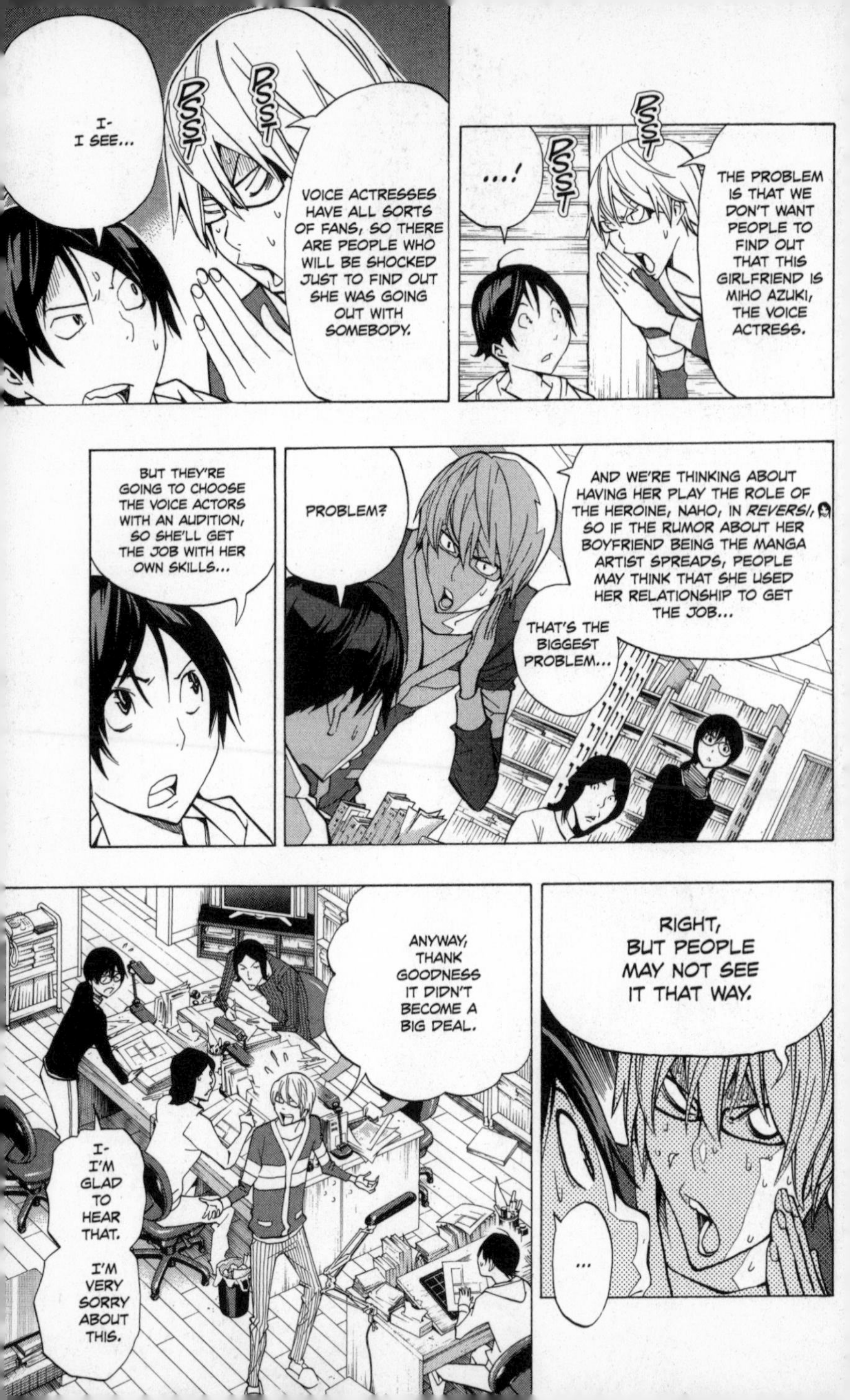

THE PROBLEM IS THAT WE DON'T WANT PEOPLE TO FIND OUT THAT THIS GIRLFRIEND IS MIHO AZUKI, THE VOICE ACTRESS.
PSST
...!
PSST
VOICE ACTRESSES HAVE ALL SORTS OF FANS, SO THERE ARE PEOPLE WHO WILL BE SHOCKED JUST TO FIND OUT SHE WAS GOING OUT WITH SOMEBODY.
PSST
PSST
I- I SEE...
AND WE'RE THINKING ABOUT HAVING HER PLAY THE ROLE OF THE HEROINE, NAHO, IN REVERSI, SO IF THE RUMOR ABOUT HER BOYFRIEND BEING THE MANGA ARTIST SPREADS, PEOPLE MAY THINK THAT SHE USED HER RELATIONSHIP TO GET THE JOB...
THAT'S THE BIGGEST PROBLEM...
PROBLEM?
BUT THEY'RE GOING TO CHOOSE THE VOICE ACTORS WITH AN AUDITION, SO SHE'LL GET THE JOB WITH HER OWN SKILLS...
RIGHT, BUT PEOPLE MAY NOT SEE IT THAT WAY.
...
ANYWAY, THANK GOODNESS IT DIDN'T BECOME A BIG DEAL.
I- I'M GLAD TO HEAR THAT.
I'M VERY SORRY ABOUT THIS.

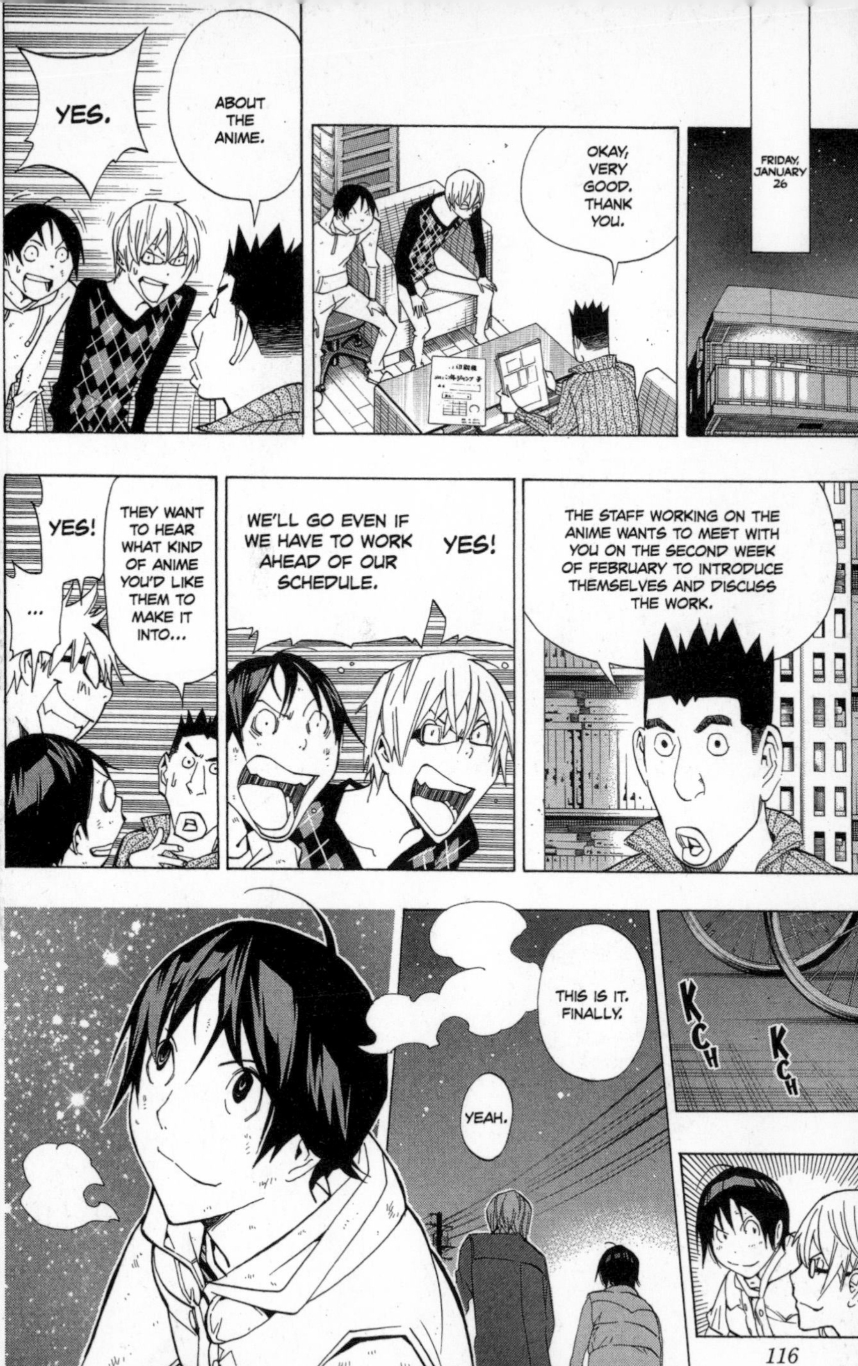
FRIDAY, JANUARY 26
OKAY, VERY GOOD. THANK YOU.
ABOUT THE ANIME.
YES.
THE STAFF WORKING ON THE ANIME WANTS TO MEET WITH YOU ON THE SECOND WEEK OF FEBRUARY TO INTRODUCE THEMSELVES AND DISCUSS THE WORK.
YES!
WE'LL GO EVEN IF WE HAVE TO WORK AHEAD OF OUR SCHEDULE.
THEY WANT TO HEAR WHAT KIND OF ANIME YOU'D LIKE THEM TO MAKE IT INTO...
YES!
...
KCH
KCH
THIS IS IT. FINALLY.
YEAH.

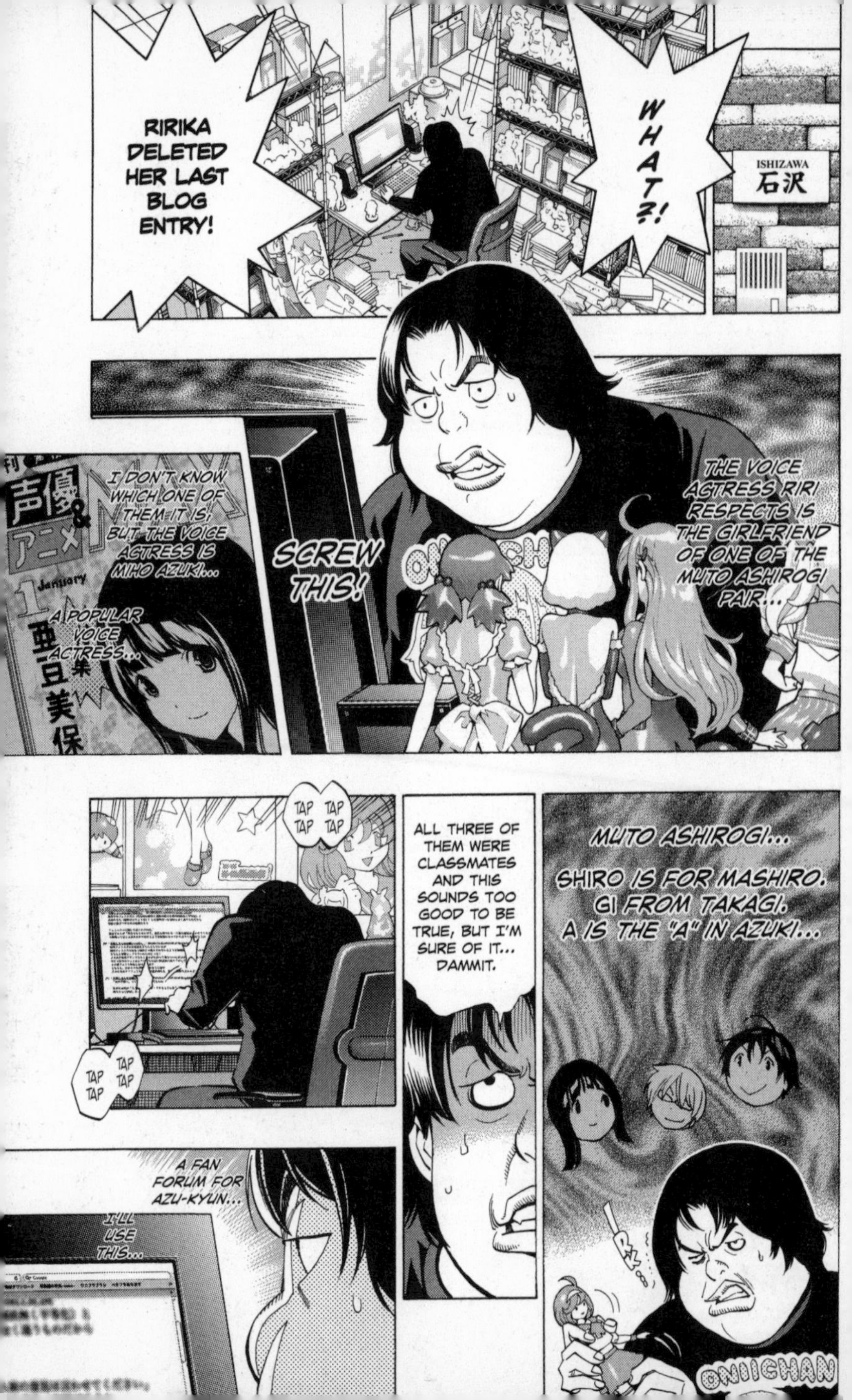
ISHIZAWA
石沢
WHAT?!
RIRIKA DELETED HER LAST BLOG ENTRY!
THE VOICE ACTRESS RIRI RESPECTS IS THE GIRLFRIEND OF ONE OF THE MUTO ASHIROGI PAIR...
SCREW THIS!
I DON'T KNOW WHICH ONE OF THEM IT IS, BUT THE VOICE ACTRESS IS MIHO AZUKI...
声優&アニメ
January
1
A POPULAR VOICE ACTRESS...
亜豆美保
MUTO ASHIROGI...
SHIRO IS FOR MASHIRO. GI FROM TAKAGI. A IS THE "A" IN AZUKI...
ONIICHAN
ALL THREE OF THEM WERE CLASSMATES AND THIS SOUNDS TOO GOOD TO BE TRUE, BUT I'M SURE OF IT... DAMMIT.
TAP TAP TAP TAP
TAP TAP TAP TAP
A FAN FORUM FOR AZU-KYUN...
I'LL USE THIS...

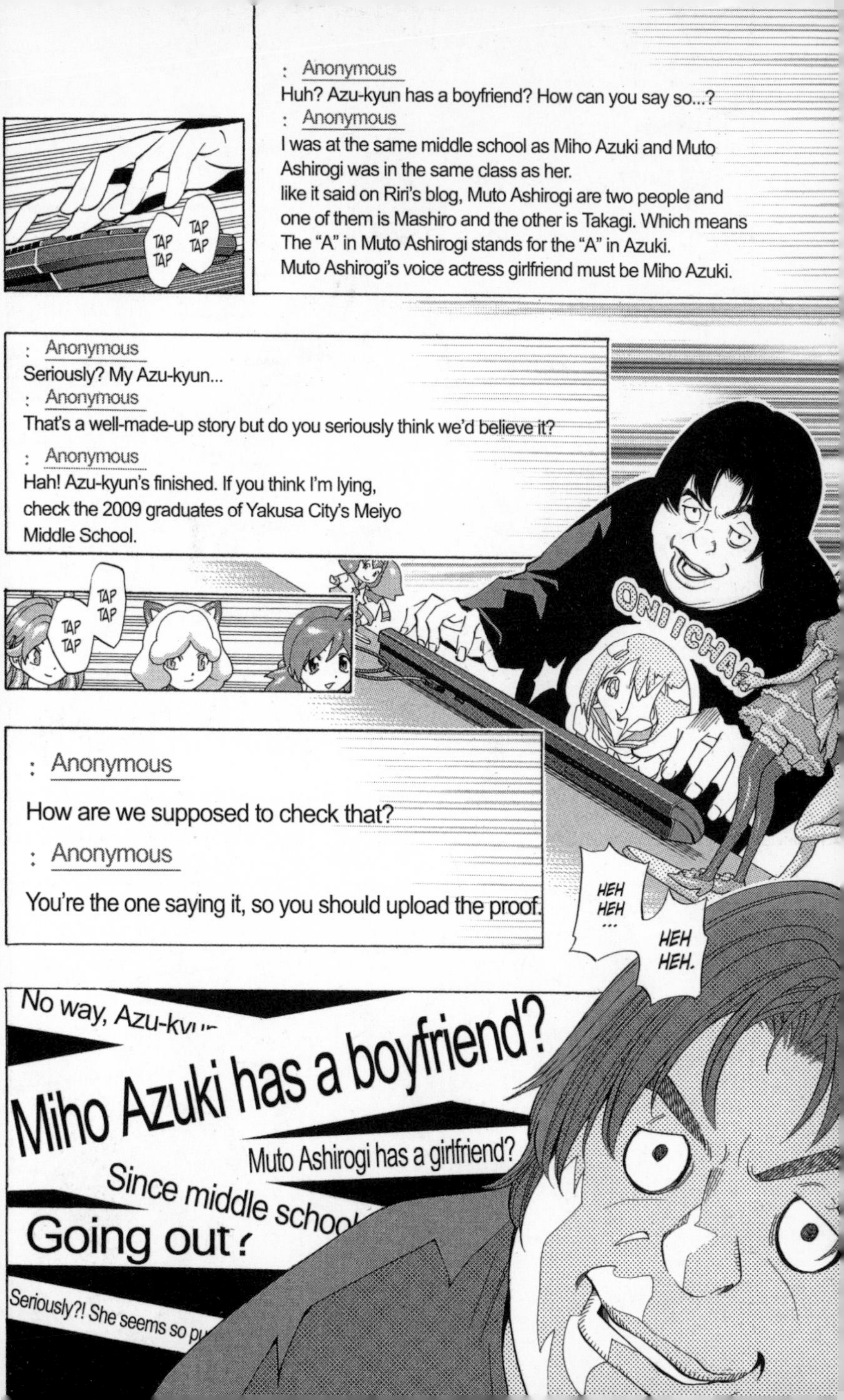
: Anonymous
Huh? Azu-kyun has a boyfriend? How can you say so...?
: Anonymous
I was at the same middle school as Miho Azuki and Muto Ashirogi was in the same class as her.
like it said on Riri's blog, Muto Ashirogi are two people and one of them is Mashiro and the other is Takagi. Which means The "A" in Muto Ashirogi stands for the "A" in Azuki.
Muto Ashirogi's voice actress girlfriend must be Miho Azuki.
TAP TAP TAP TAP
: Anonymous
Seriously? My Azu-kyun...
: Anonymous
That's a well-made-up story but do you seriously think we'd believe it?
: Anonymous
Hah! Azu-kyun's finished. If you think I'm lying, check the 2009 graduates of Yakusa City's Meiyo Middle School.
ONI I CHAN
TAP TAP
TAP TAP
: Anonymous
How are we supposed to check that?
: Anonymous
You're the one saying it, so you should upload the proof.
HEH HEH...
HEH HEH.
No way, Azu-kyu
Miho Azuki has a boyfriend?
Muto Ashirogi has a girlfriend?
Since middle schoo
Going out
Seriously?! She seems so pu

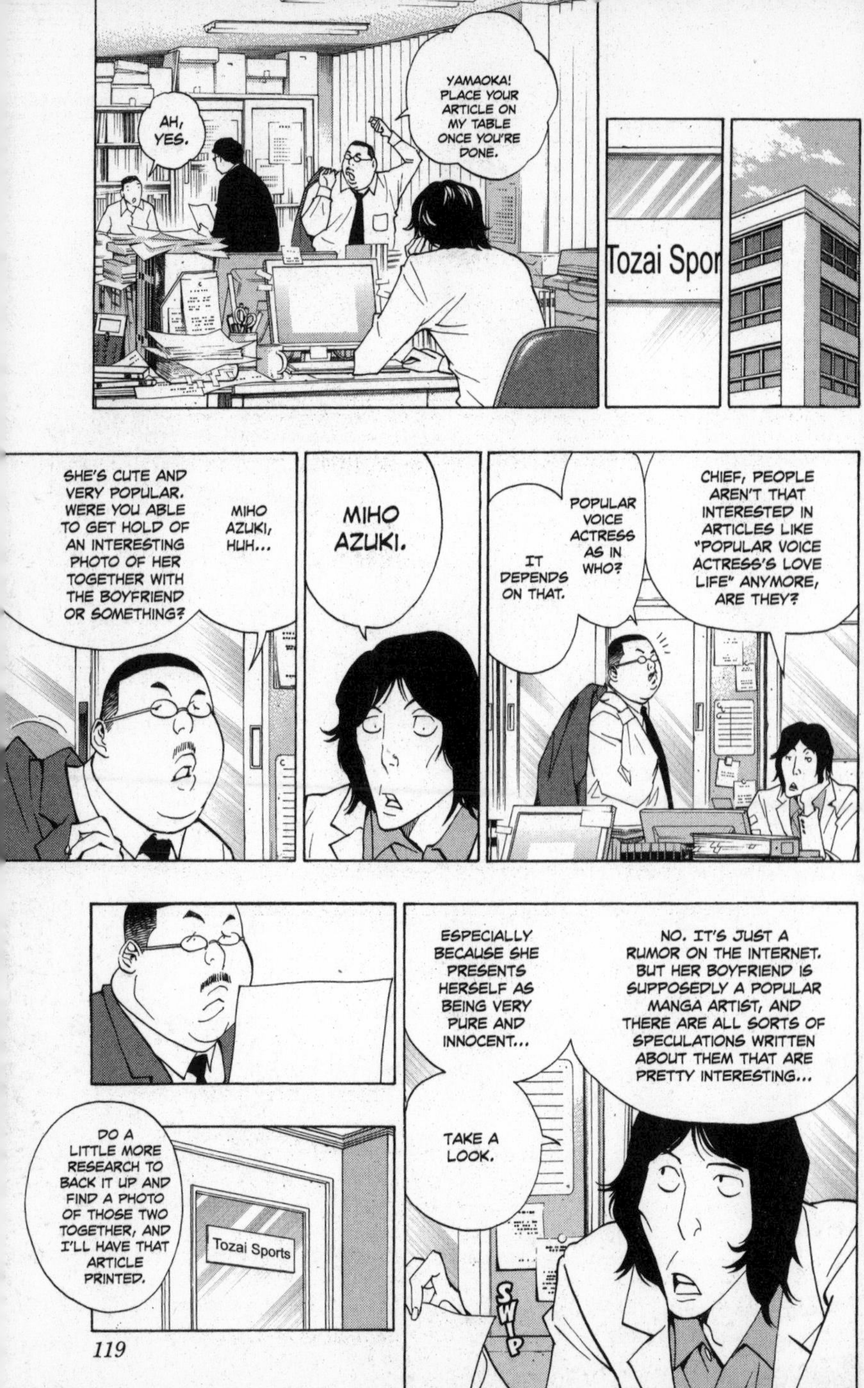
Tozai Spor
YAMAOKA! PLACE YOUR ARTICLE ON MY TABLE ONCE YOU'RE DONE.
AH, YES.
CHIEF, PEOPLE AREN'T THAT INTERESTED IN ARTICLES LIKE "POPULAR VOICE ACTRESS'S LOVE LIFE" ANYMORE, ARE THEY?
POPULAR VOICE ACTRESS AS IN WHO?
IT DEPENDS ON THAT.
MIHO AZUKI.
MIHO AZUKI, HUH...
SHE'S CUTE AND VERY POPULAR. WERE YOU ABLE TO GET HOLD OF AN INTERESTING PHOTO OF HER TOGETHER WITH THE BOYFRIEND OR SOMETHING?
NO. IT'S JUST A RUMOR ON THE INTERNET. BUT HER BOYFRIEND IS SUPPOSEDLY A POPULAR MANGA ARTIST, AND THERE ARE ALL SORTS OF SPECULATIONS WRITTEN ABOUT THEM THAT ARE PRETTY INTERESTING...
ESPECIALLY BECAUSE SHE PRESENTS HERSELF AS BEING VERY PURE AND INNOCENT...
TAKE A LOOK.
SWIP
Tozai Sports
DO A LITTLE MORE RESEARCH TO BACK IT UP AND FIND A PHOTO OF THOSE TWO TOGETHER, AND I'LL HAVE THAT ARTICLE PRINTED.

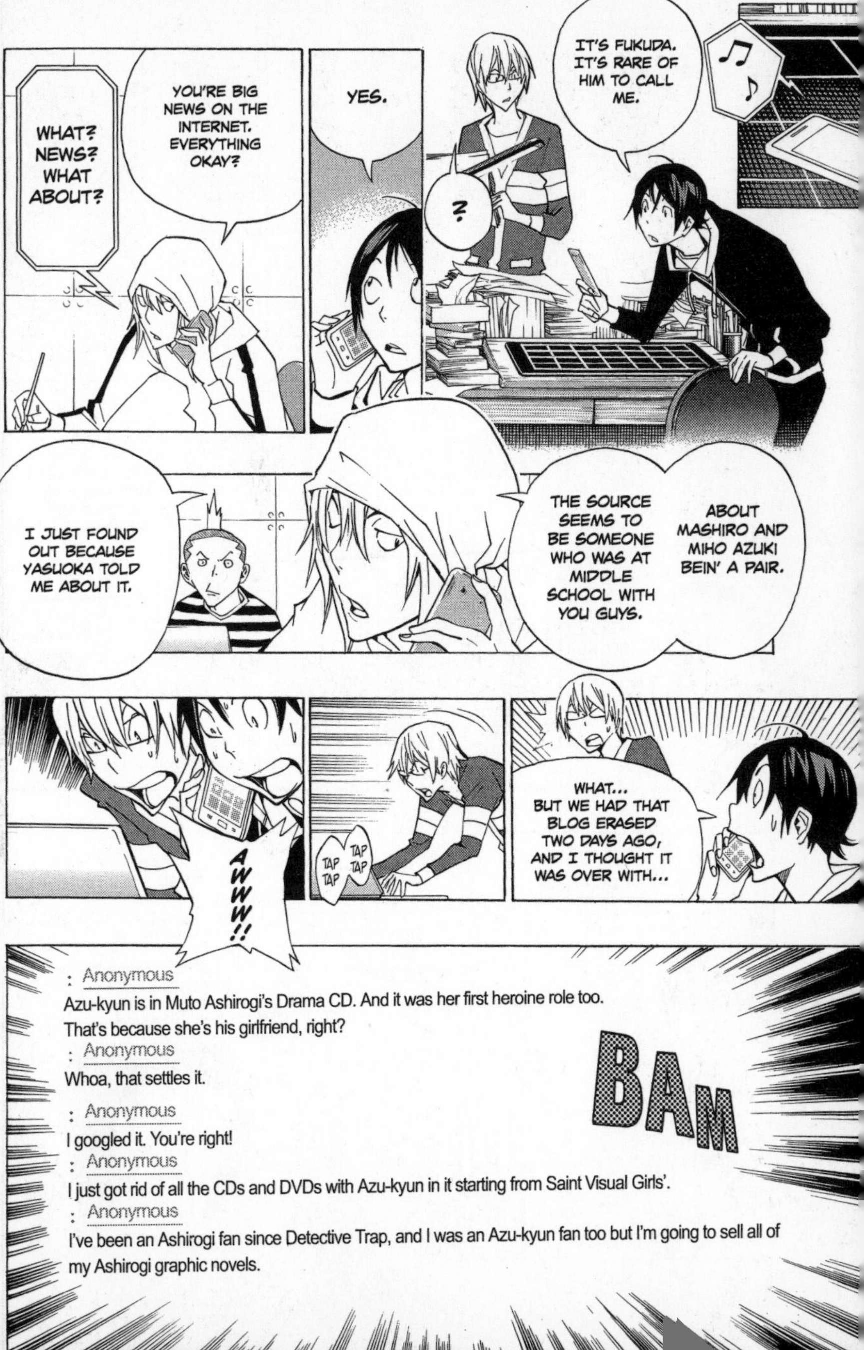
♫ ♪
IT'S FUKUDA. IT'S RARE OF HIM TO CALL ME.
?
YES.
YOU'RE BIG NEWS ON THE INTERNET. EVERYTHING OKAY?
WHAT? NEWS? WHAT ABOUT?
ABOUT MASHIRO AND MIHO AZUKI BEIN' A PAIR.
THE SOURCE SEEMS TO BE SOMEONE WHO WAS AT MIDDLE SCHOOL WITH YOU GUYS.
I JUST FOUND OUT BECAUSE YASUOKA TOLD ME ABOUT IT.
WHAT... BUT WE HAD THAT BLOG ERASED TWO DAYS AGO, AND I THOUGHT IT WAS OVER WITH...
TAP TAP TAP TAP
AWWW!!
: Anonymous
Azu-kyun is in Muto Ashirogi's Drama CD. And it was her first heroine role too.
That's because she's his girlfriend, right?
: Anonymous
Whoa, that settles it.
: Anonymous
I googled it. You're right!
: Anonymous
I just got rid of all the CDs and DVDs with Azu-kyun in it starting from Saint Visual Girls'.
: Anonymous
I've been an Ashirogi fan since Detective Trap, and I was an Azu-kyun fan too but I'm going to sell all of my Ashirogi graphic novels.
BAM

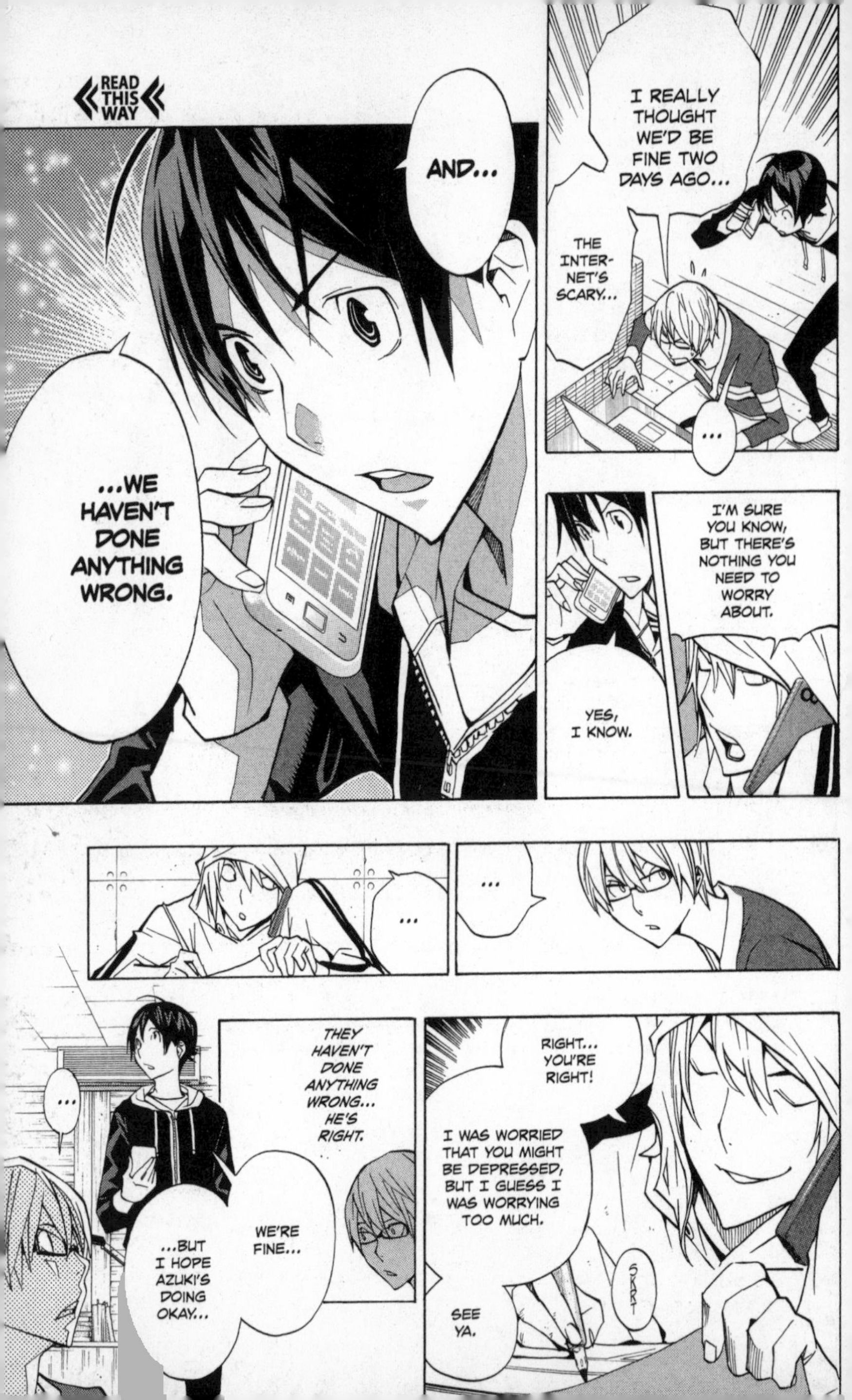
READ THIS WAY
I REALLY THOUGHT WE'D BE FINE TWO DAYS AGO...
THE INTER-NET'S SCARY...
...
I'M SURE YOU KNOW, BUT THERE'S NOTHING YOU NEED TO WORRY ABOUT.
YES, I KNOW.
AND...
...WE HAVEN'T DONE ANYTHING WRONG.
...
...
RIGHT... YOU'RE RIGHT!
I WAS WORRIED THAT YOU MIGHT BE DEPRESSED, BUT I GUESS I WAS WORRYING TOO MUCH.
SKRT
SEE YA.
THEY HAVEN'T DONE ANYTHING WRONG... HE'S RIGHT.
...
WE'RE FINE...
...BUT I HOPE AZUKI'S DOING OKAY...

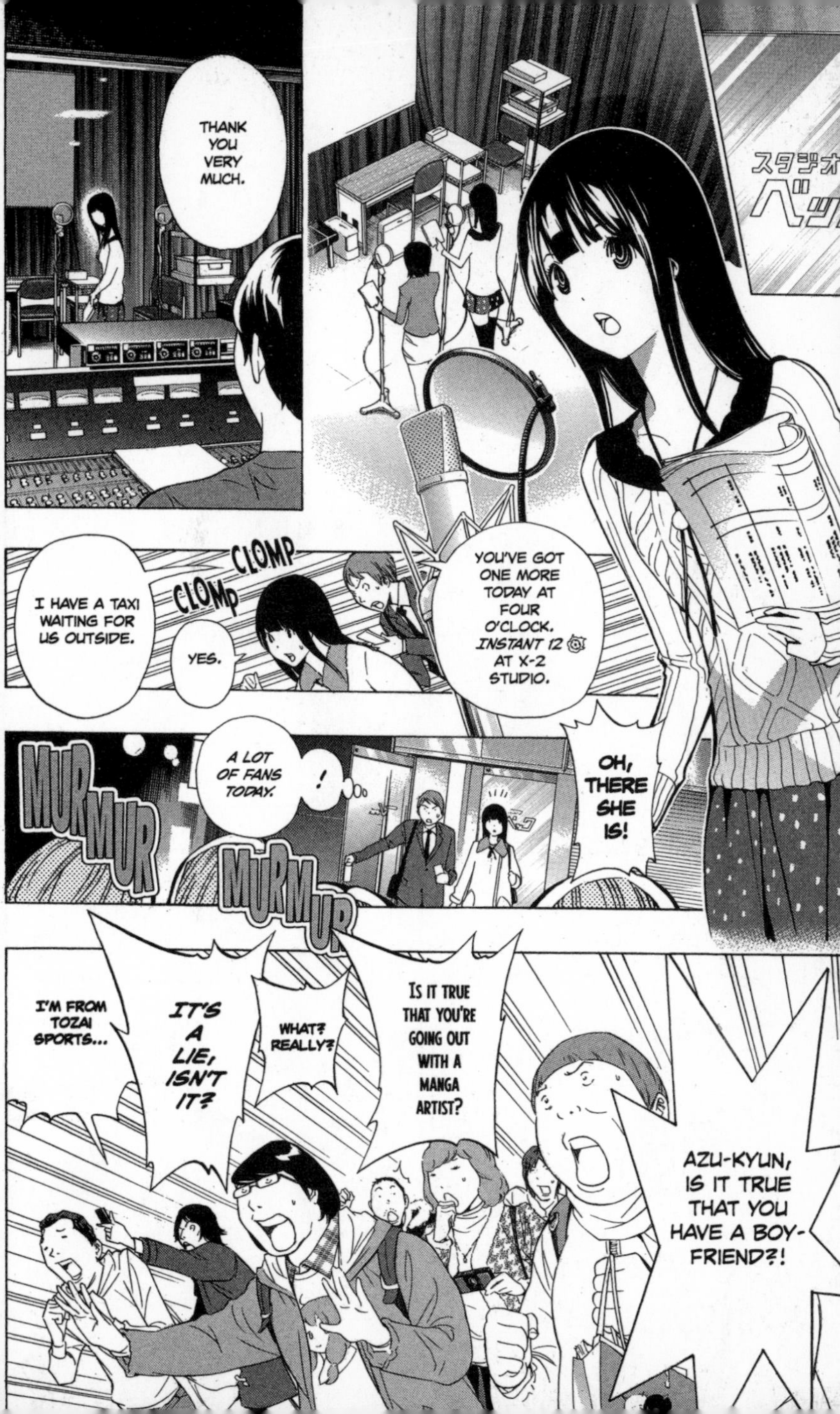
スタジオ
YOU'VE GOT ONE MORE TODAY AT FOUR O'CLOCK. INSTANT 12 AT X-2 STUDIO.
THANK YOU VERY MUCH.
CLOMP
CLOMP
I HAVE A TAXI WAITING FOR US OUTSIDE.
YES.
OH, THERE SHE IS!
!
A LOT OF FANS TODAY.
MURMUR
MURMUR
AZU-KYUN, IS IT TRUE THAT YOU HAVE A BOY-FRIEND?!
IS IT TRUE THAT YOU'RE GOING OUT WITH A MANGA ARTIST?
WHAT? REALLY?
IT'S A LIE, ISN'T IT?
I'M FROM TOZAI SPORTS...

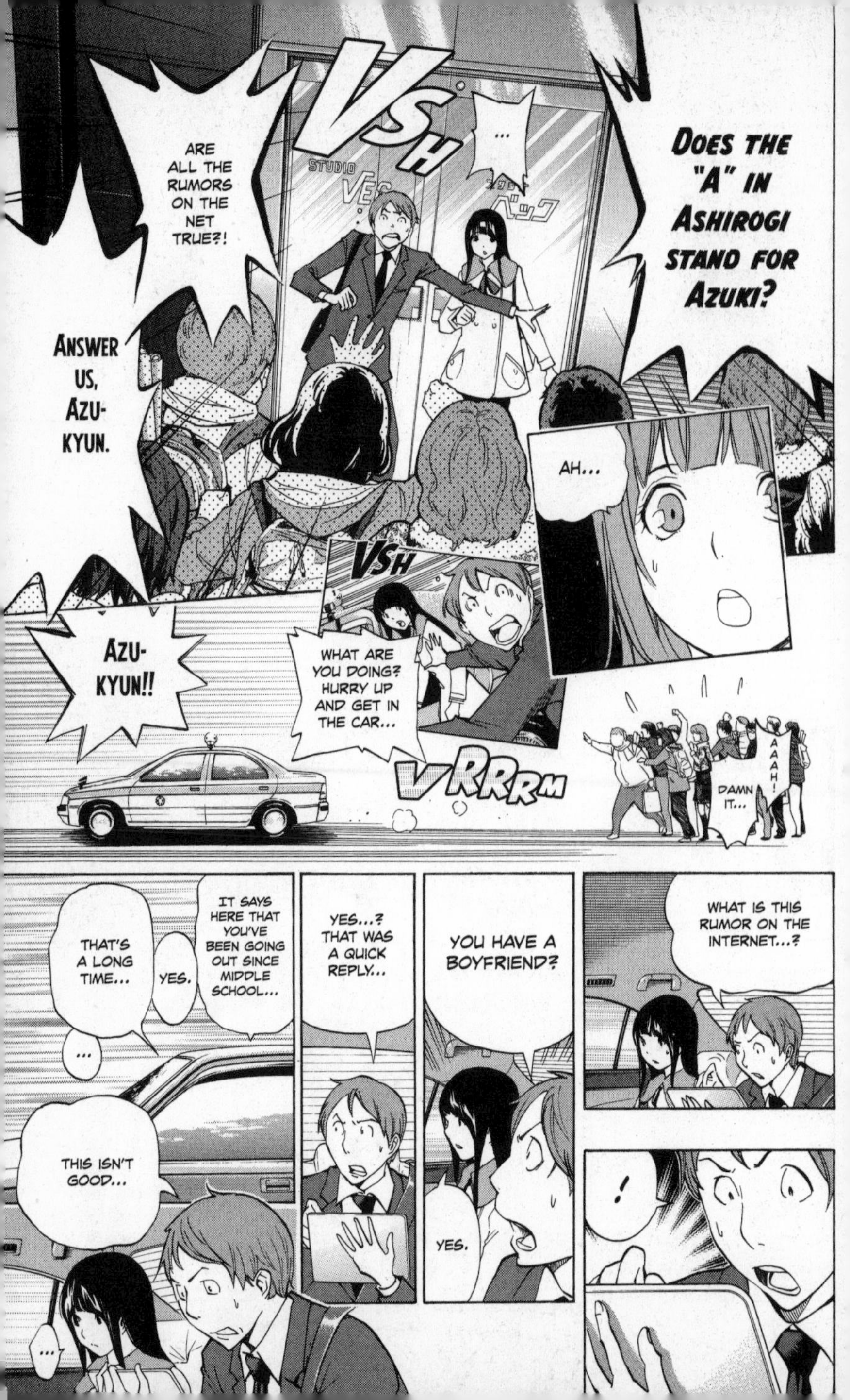
Does the "A" in Ashirogi stand for Azuki?
VSH
...
ARE ALL THE RUMORS ON THE NET TRUE?!
ANSWER US, AZU-KYUN.
AH...
VSH
WHAT ARE YOU DOING? HURRY UP AND GET IN THE CAR...
AZU-KYUN!!
DAMN IT...
AAAH!
VRRRM
WHAT IS THIS RUMOR ON THE INTERNET...?
!
YOU HAVE A BOYFRIEND?
YES.
YES...? THAT WAS A QUICK REPLY...
IT SAYS HERE THAT YOU'VE BEEN GOING OUT SINCE MIDDLE SCHOOL...
YES.
THAT'S A LONG TIME...
...
THIS ISN'T GOOD...
...

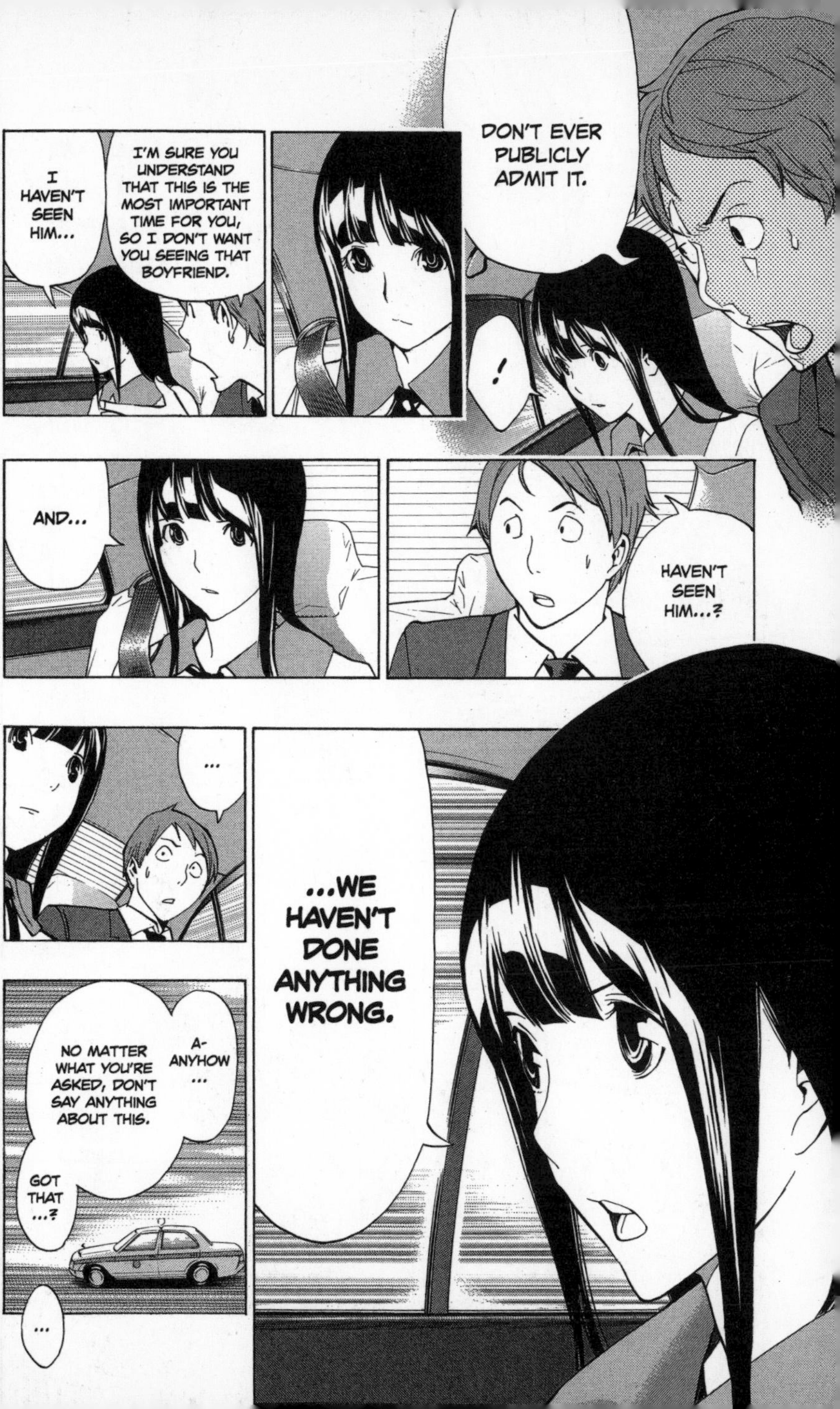
DON'T EVER PUBLICLY ADMIT IT.
!
I'M SURE YOU UNDERSTAND THAT THIS IS THE MOST IMPORTANT TIME FOR YOU, SO I DON'T WANT YOU SEEING THAT BOYFRIEND.
I HAVEN'T SEEN HIM...
HAVEN'T SEEN HIM...?
AND...
...WE HAVEN'T DONE ANYTHING WRONG.
...
A-ANYHOW ...
NO MATTER WHAT YOU'RE ASKED, DON'T SAY ANYTHING ABOUT THIS.
GOT THAT ...?
...

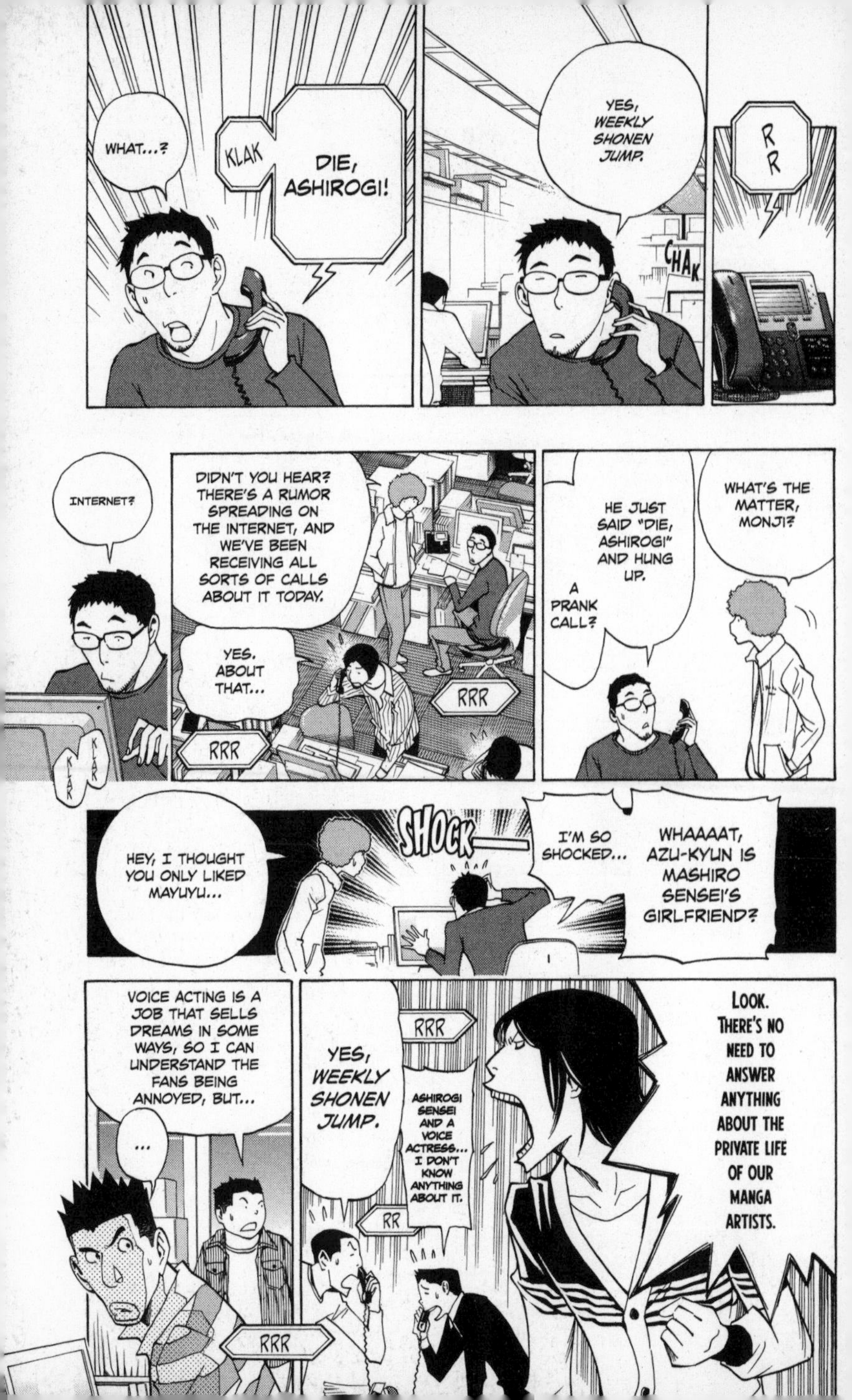
R R
YES, WEEKLY SHONEN JUMP.
CHAK
DIE, ASHIROGI!
KLAK
WHAT...?
WHAT'S THE MATTER, MONJI?
HE JUST SAID "DIE, ASHIROGI" AND HUNG UP.
A PRANK CALL?
DIDN'T YOU HEAR? THERE'S A RUMOR SPREADING ON THE INTERNET, AND WE'VE BEEN RECEIVING ALL SORTS OF CALLS ABOUT IT TODAY.
YES. ABOUT THAT...
RRR
RRR
INTERNET?
KLAK
KLAK
WHAAAAT, AZU-KYUN IS MASHIRO SENSEI'S GIRLFRIEND?
I'M SO SHOCKED...
SHOCK
HEY, I THOUGHT YOU ONLY LIKED MAYUYU...
LOOK. THERE'S NO NEED TO ANSWER ANYTHING ABOUT THE PRIVATE LIFE OF OUR MANGA ARTISTS.
RRR
YES, WEEKLY SHONEN JUMP.
ASHIROGI SENSEI AND A VOICE ACTRESS... I DON'T KNOW ANYTHING ABOUT IT.
RR
VOICE ACTING IS A JOB THAT SELLS DREAMS IN SOME WAYS, SO I CAN UNDERSTAND THE FANS BEING ANNOYED, BUT...
...
RRR

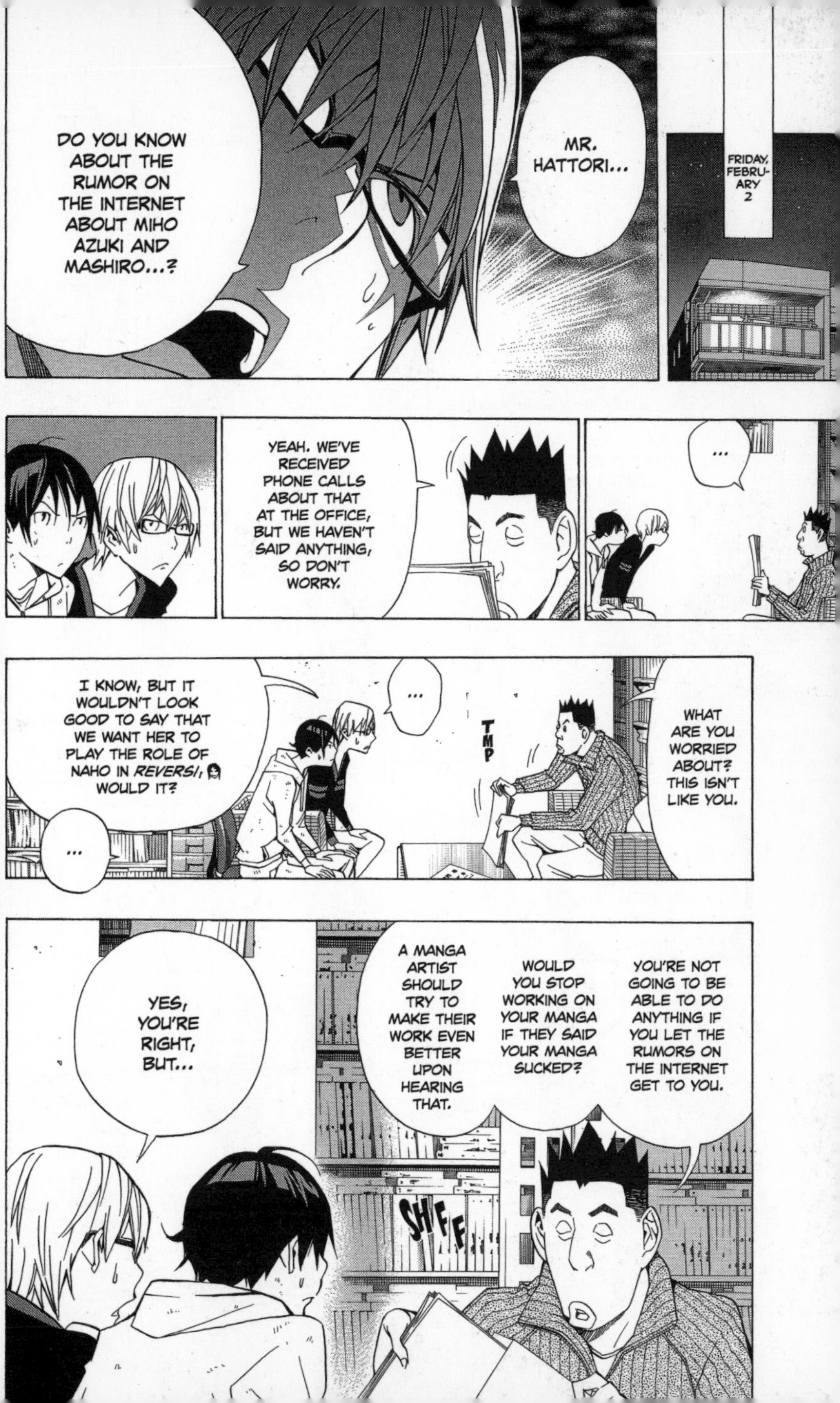
FRIDAY, FEBRUARY 2
MR. HATTORI...
DO YOU KNOW ABOUT THE RUMOR ON THE INTERNET ABOUT MIHO AZUKI AND MASHIRO...?
...
YEAH. WE'VE RECEIVED PHONE CALLS ABOUT THAT AT THE OFFICE, BUT WE HAVEN'T SAID ANYTHING, SO DON'T WORRY.
WHAT ARE YOU WORRIED ABOUT? THIS ISN'T LIKE YOU.
TMP
...
I KNOW, BUT IT WOULDN'T LOOK GOOD TO SAY THAT WE WANT HER TO PLAY THE ROLE OF NAHO IN REVERSI, WOULD IT?
...
YOU'RE NOT GOING TO BE ABLE TO DO ANYTHING IF YOU LET THE RUMORS ON THE INTERNET GET TO YOU.
WOULD YOU STOP WORKING ON YOUR MANGA IF THEY SAID YOUR MANGA SUCKED?
A MANGA ARTIST SHOULD TRY TO MAKE THEIR WORK EVEN BETTER UPON HEARING THAT.
SHFF
YES, YOU'RE RIGHT, BUT...

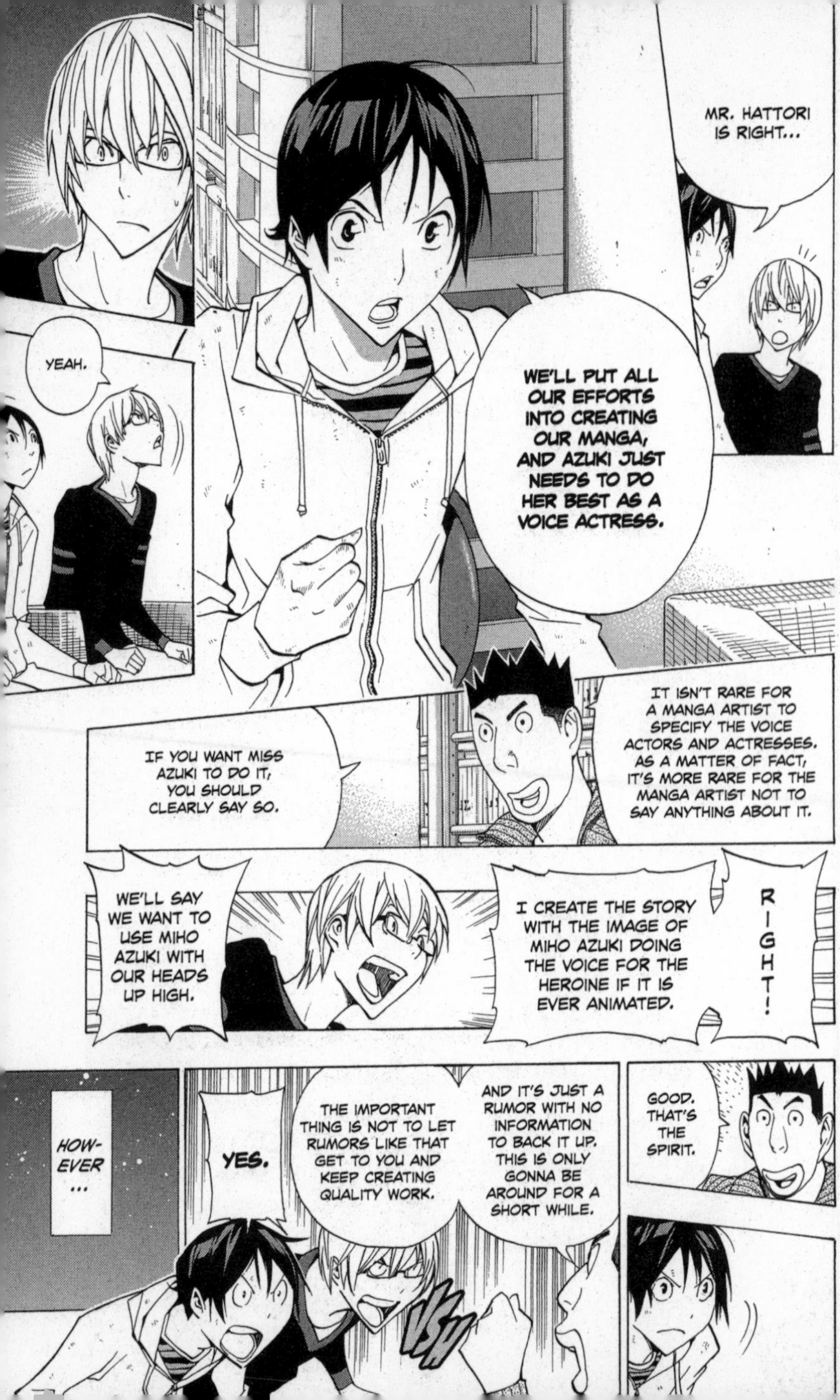
MR. HATTORI IS RIGHT...
WE'LL PUT ALL OUR EFFORTS INTO CREATING OUR MANGA, AND AZUKI JUST NEEDS TO DO HER BEST AS A VOICE ACTRESS.
YEAH.
IT ISN'T RARE FOR A MANGA ARTIST TO SPECIFY THE VOICE ACTORS AND ACTRESSES. AS A MATTER OF FACT, IT'S MORE RARE FOR THE MANGA ARTIST NOT TO SAY ANYTHING ABOUT IT.
IF YOU WANT MISS AZUKI TO DO IT, YOU SHOULD CLEARLY SAY SO.
R-I-G-H-T-!
I CREATE THE STORY WITH THE IMAGE OF MIHO AZUKI DOING THE VOICE FOR THE HEROINE IF IT IS EVER ANIMATED.
WE'LL SAY WE WANT TO USE MIHO AZUKI WITH OUR HEADS UP HIGH.
GOOD. THAT'S THE SPIRIT.
AND IT'S JUST A RUMOR WITH NO INFORMATION TO BACK IT UP. THIS IS ONLY GONNA BE AROUND FOR A SHORT WHILE.
THE IMPORTANT THING IS NOT TO LET RUMORS LIKE THAT GET TO YOU AND KEEP CREATING QUALITY WORK.
YES.
VSH
HOW-EVER ...

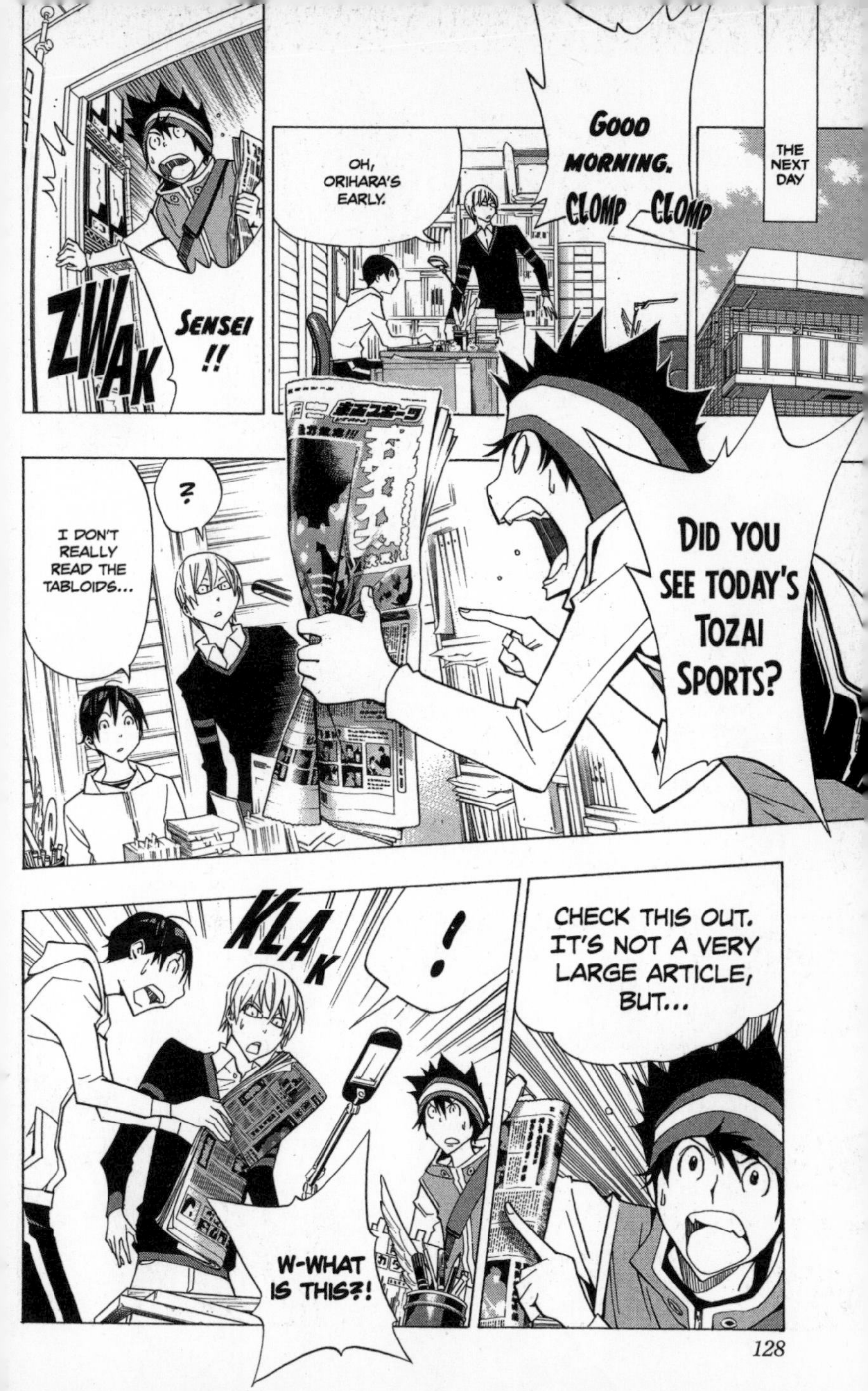
THE NEXT DAY
GOOD MORNING.
CLOMP CLOMP
OH, ORIHARA'S EARLY.
SENSEI !!
ZWAK
DID YOU SEE TODAY'S TOZAI SPORTS?
?
I DON'T REALLY READ THE TABLOIDS...
CHECK THIS OUT. IT'S NOT A VERY LARGE ARTICLE, BUT...
!
KLAK
W-WHAT IS THIS?!

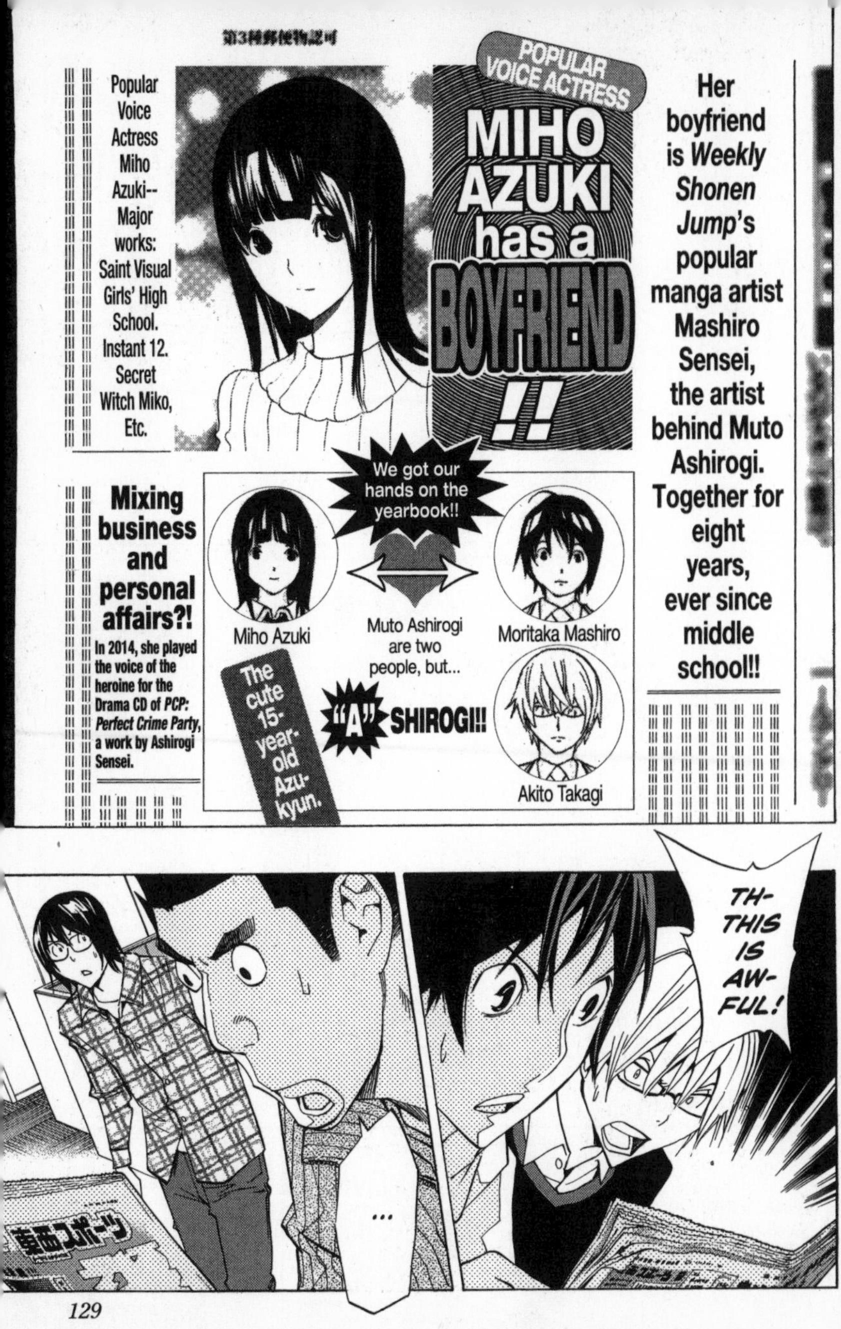
POPULAR VOICE ACTRESS
MIHO AZUKI has a BOYFRIEND!!
Her boyfriend is *Weekly Shonen Jump*'s popular manga artist Mashiro Sensei, the artist behind Muto Ashirogi. Together for eight years, ever since middle school!!
Popular Voice Actress Miho Azuki-- Major works: Saint Visual Girls' High School. Instant 12. Secret Witch Miko, Etc.
We got our hands on the yearbook!!
Miho Azuki
Moritaka Mashiro
Akito Takagi
Muto Ashirogi are two people, but...
"A" SHIROGI!!
The cute 15-year-old Azu-kyun.
Mixing business and personal affairs?!
In 2014, she played the voice of the heroine for the Drama CD of *PCP: Perfect Crime Party*, a work by Ashirogi Sensei.
TH-THIS IS AW-FUL!
...
東西スポーツ

※CREATOR STORYBOARDS AND FINISHED PAGES IN JAPANESE

BAKUMAN。vol. 19

"Until the Final Draft Is Complete"

Chapter 166, pp. 120-121

COMPLETE!

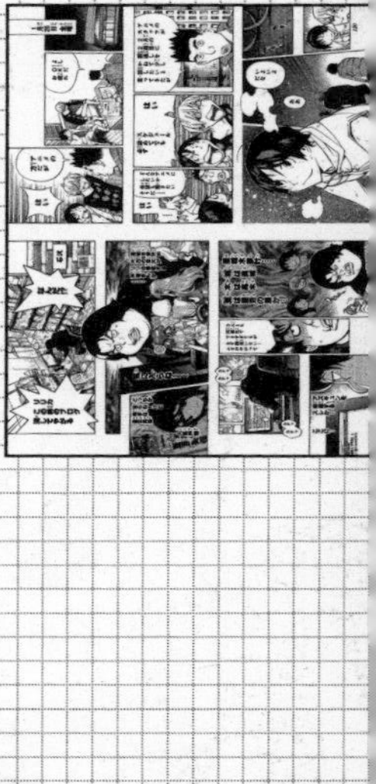

OBATA'S STORYBOARD

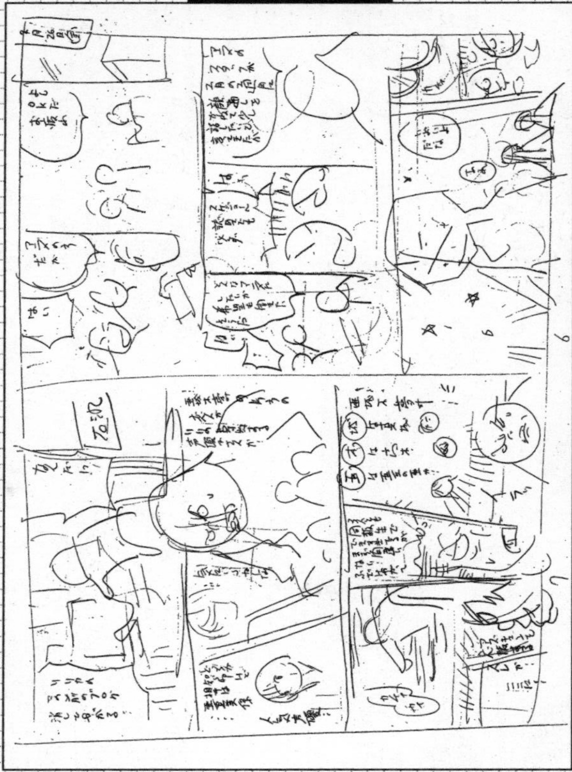

OHBA'S STORYBOARD

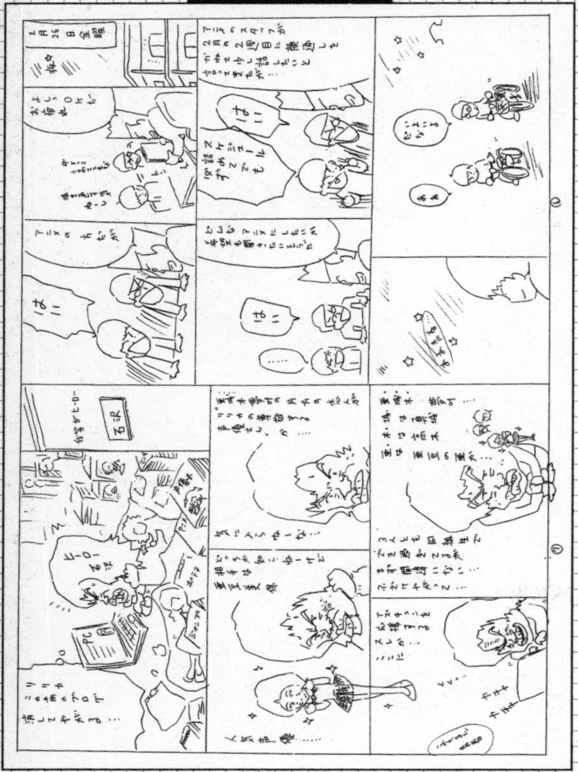

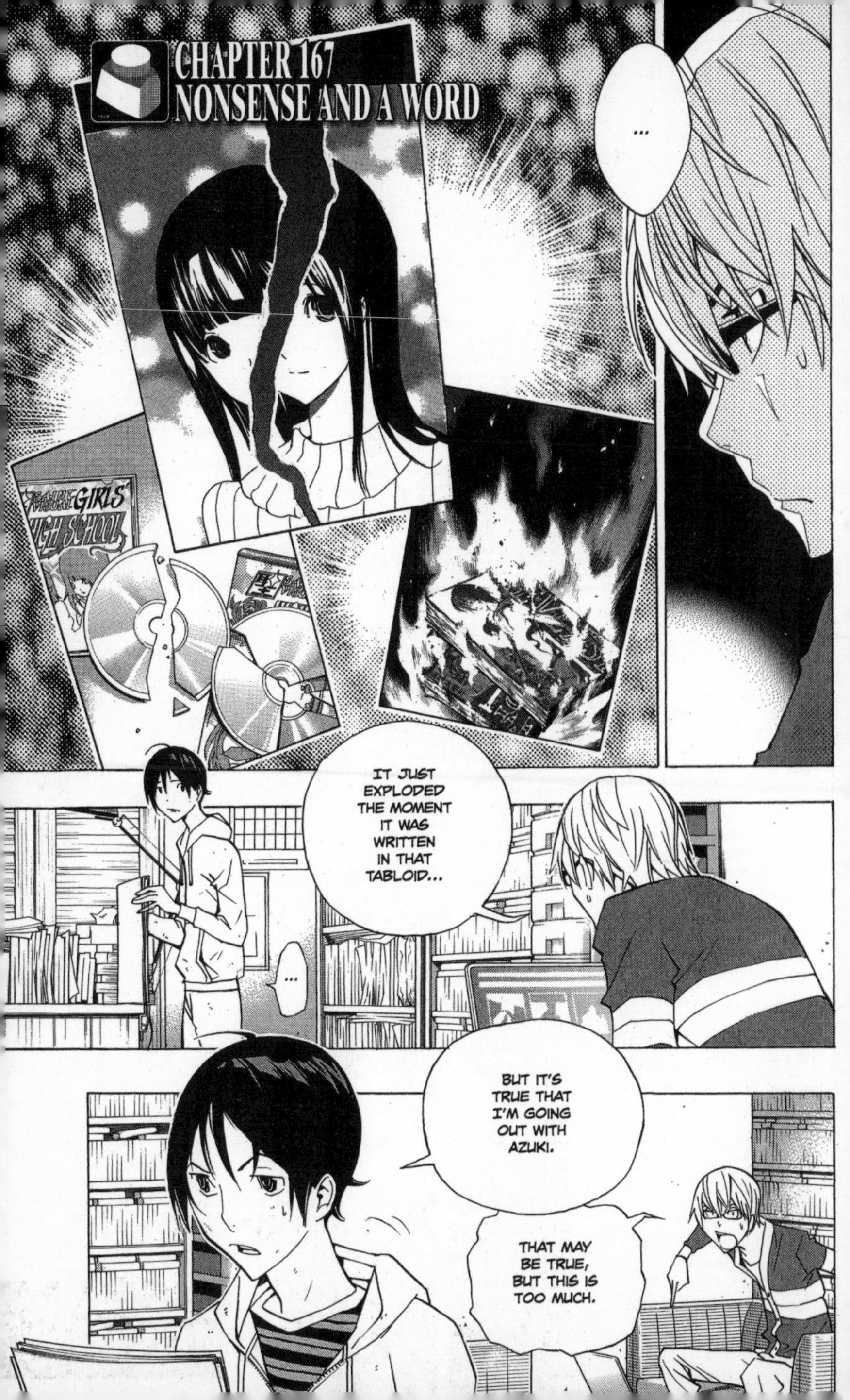
...
CHAPTER 167
NONSENSE AND A WORD
IT JUST EXPLODED THE MOMENT IT WAS WRITTEN IN THAT TABLOID...
...
BUT IT'S TRUE THAT I'M GOING OUT WITH AZUKI.
THAT MAY BE TRUE, BUT THIS IS TOO MUCH.

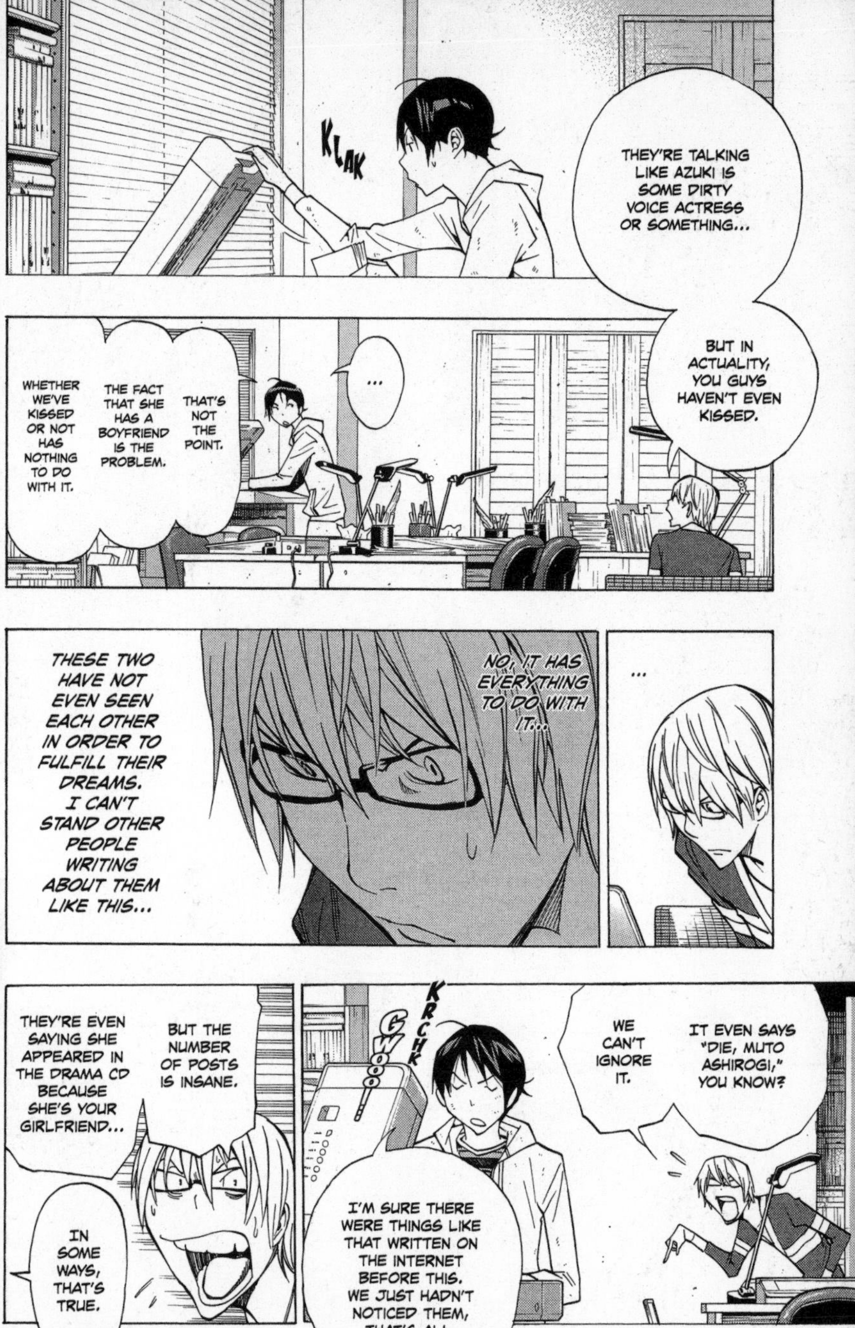
THEY'RE TALKING LIKE AZUKI IS SOME DIRTY VOICE ACTRESS OR SOMETHING...
KLAK
BUT IN ACTUALITY, YOU GUYS HAVEN'T EVEN KISSED.
...
THAT'S NOT THE POINT.
THE FACT THAT SHE HAS A BOYFRIEND IS THE PROBLEM.
WHETHER WE'VE KISSED OR NOT HAS NOTHING TO DO WITH IT.
...
NO, IT HAS EVERYTHING TO DO WITH IT...
THESE TWO HAVE NOT EVEN SEEN EACH OTHER IN ORDER TO FULFILL THEIR DREAMS. I CAN'T STAND OTHER PEOPLE WRITING ABOUT THEM LIKE THIS...
IT EVEN SAYS "DIE, MUTO ASHIROGI," YOU KNOW?
WE CAN'T IGNORE IT.
KRCHK
GWOOO
I'M SURE THERE WERE THINGS LIKE THAT WRITTEN ON THE INTERNET BEFORE THIS. WE JUST HADN'T NOTICED THEM, THAT'S ALL.
BUT THE NUMBER OF POSTS IS INSANE.
THEY'RE EVEN SAYING SHE APPEARED IN THE DRAMA CD BECAUSE SHE'S YOUR GIRLFRIEND...
IN SOME WAYS, THAT'S TRUE.

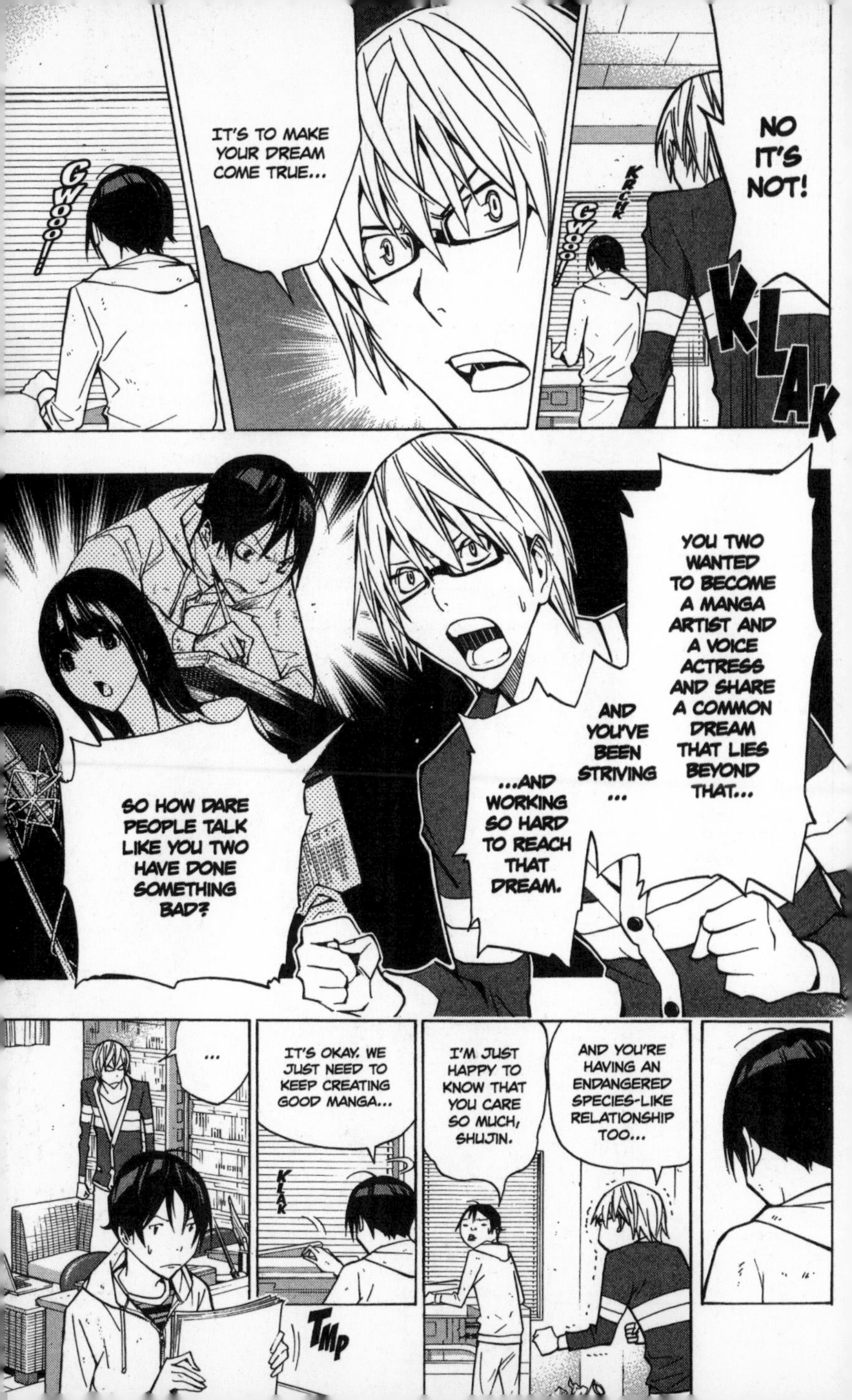
NO IT'S NOT!
KRCHK
GWOOO
KLAK
IT'S TO MAKE YOUR DREAM COME TRUE...
GWOOO
YOU TWO WANTED TO BECOME A MANGA ARTIST AND A VOICE ACTRESS AND SHARE A COMMON DREAM THAT LIES BEYOND THAT...
AND YOU'VE BEEN STRIVING ...
...AND WORKING SO HARD TO REACH THAT DREAM.
SO HOW DARE PEOPLE TALK LIKE YOU TWO HAVE DONE SOMETHING BAD?
AND YOU'RE HAVING AN ENDANGERED SPECIES-LIKE RELATIONSHIP TOO...
I'M JUST HAPPY TO KNOW THAT YOU CARE SO MUCH, SHUJIN.
IT'S OKAY. WE JUST NEED TO KEEP CREATING GOOD MANGA...
KLAK
...
TMP

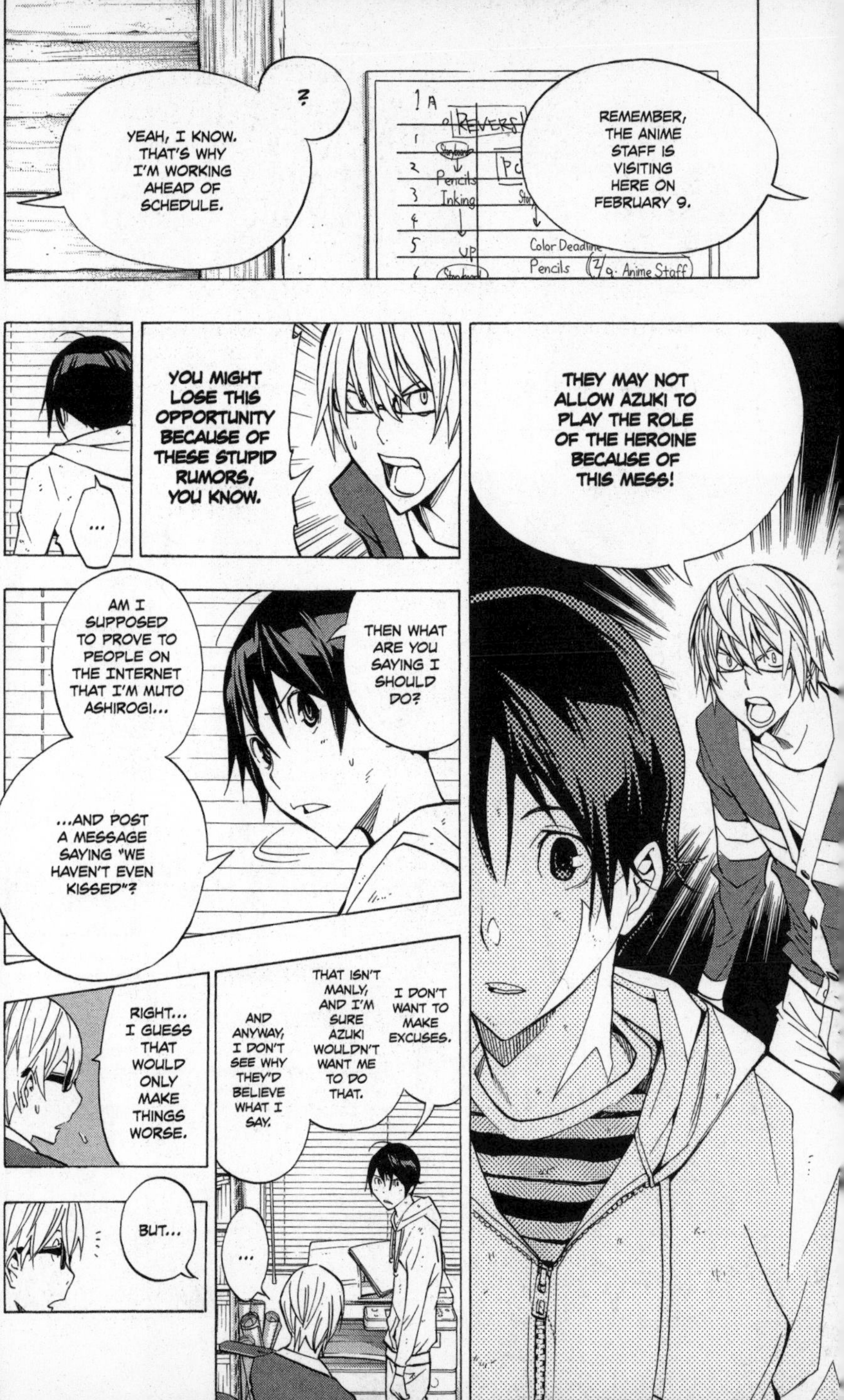
REMEMBER, THE ANIME STAFF IS VISITING HERE ON FEBRUARY 9.
1A
REVERSI
Storyboards
Pencils
Inking
UP
Color Deadline
Pencils
2/9 Anime Staff
YEAH, I KNOW. THAT'S WHY I'M WORKING AHEAD OF SCHEDULE.
?
THEY MAY NOT ALLOW AZUKI TO PLAY THE ROLE OF THE HEROINE BECAUSE OF THIS MESS!
YOU MIGHT LOSE THIS OPPORTUNITY BECAUSE OF THESE STUPID RUMORS, YOU KNOW.
...
THEN WHAT ARE YOU SAYING I SHOULD DO?
AM I SUPPOSED TO PROVE TO PEOPLE ON THE INTERNET THAT I'M MUTO ASHIROGI...
...AND POST A MESSAGE SAYING "WE HAVEN'T EVEN KISSED"?
I DON'T WANT TO MAKE EXCUSES.
THAT ISN'T MANLY, AND I'M SURE AZUKI WOULDN'T WANT ME TO DO THAT.
AND ANYWAY, I DON'T SEE WHY THEY'D BELIEVE WHAT I SAY.
...
RIGHT... I GUESS THAT WOULD ONLY MAKE THINGS WORSE.
BUT...

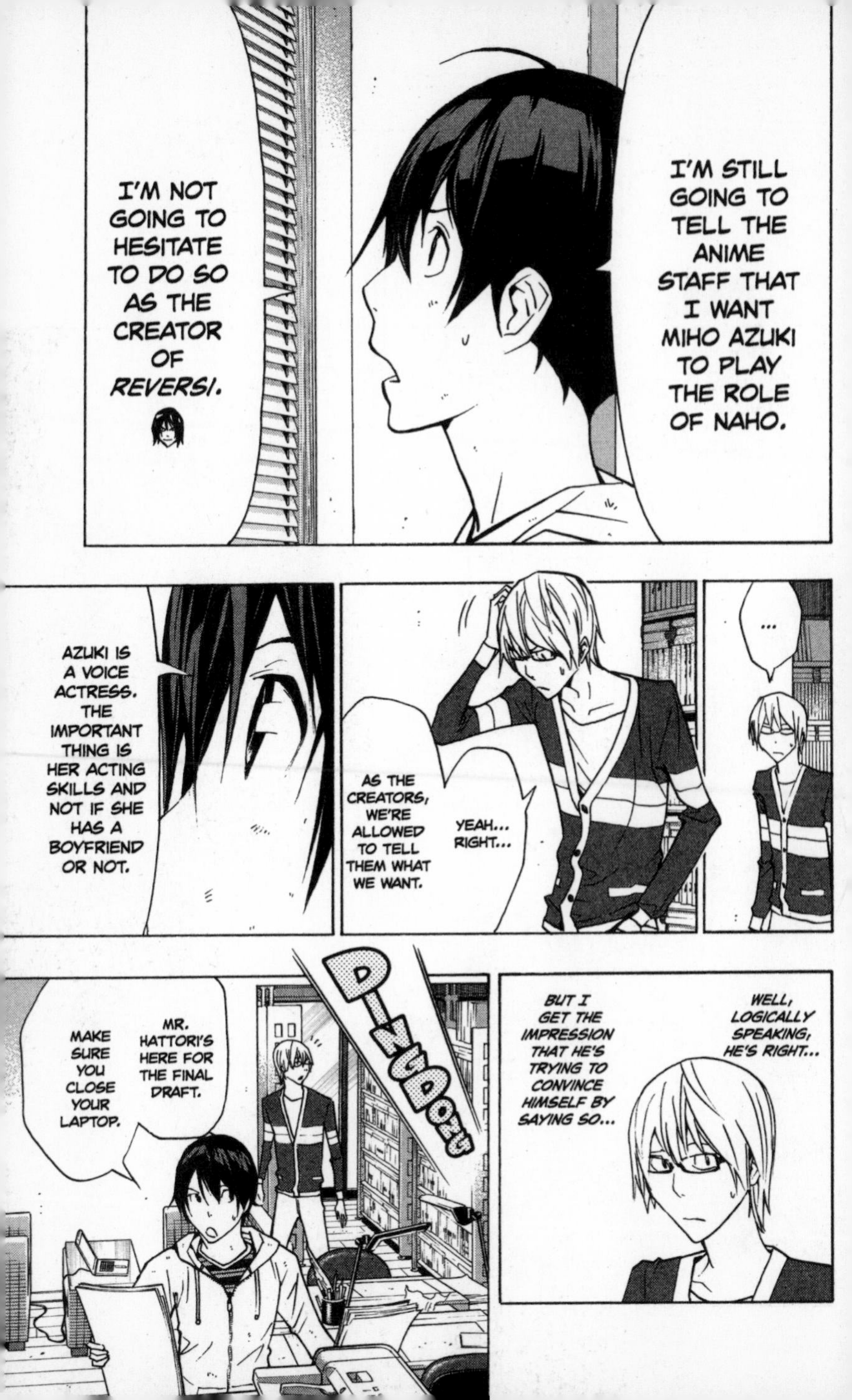
I'M STILL GOING TO TELL THE ANIME STAFF THAT I WANT MIHO AZUKI TO PLAY THE ROLE OF NAHO.
I'M NOT GOING TO HESITATE TO DO SO AS THE CREATOR OF REVERSI.
...
YEAH... RIGHT...
AS THE CREATORS, WE'RE ALLOWED TO TELL THEM WHAT WE WANT.
AZUKI IS A VOICE ACTRESS. THE IMPORTANT THING IS HER ACTING SKILLS AND NOT IF SHE HAS A BOYFRIEND OR NOT.
WELL, LOGICALLY SPEAKING, HE'S RIGHT...
BUT I GET THE IMPRESSION THAT HE'S TRYING TO CONVINCE HIMSELF BY SAYING SO...
DINGDONG
MR. HATTORI'S HERE FOR THE FINAL DRAFT.
MAKE SURE YOU CLOSE YOUR LAPTOP.

OKAY, THE FINAL DRAFT LOOKS FINE.
MR. HATTORI, WE'LL BE OKAY, WON'T WE?
HN? WHAT DO YOU MEAN?
HAVING MIHO AZUKI DO THE VOICE OF NAHO.
...
OH, THAT.
...
YOU'VE DONE NOTHING WRONG, SO YOU DON'T HAVE TO WORRY ABOUT IT.
...
...
BUT THINGS HAVE GOTTEN SO OUT OF HAND...

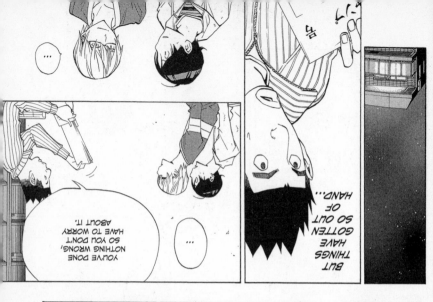

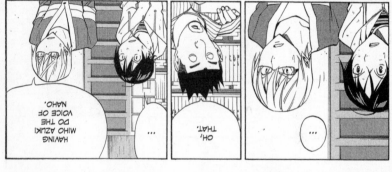

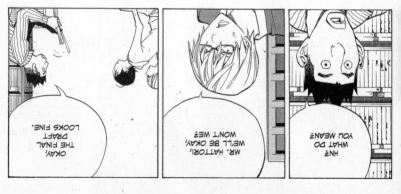

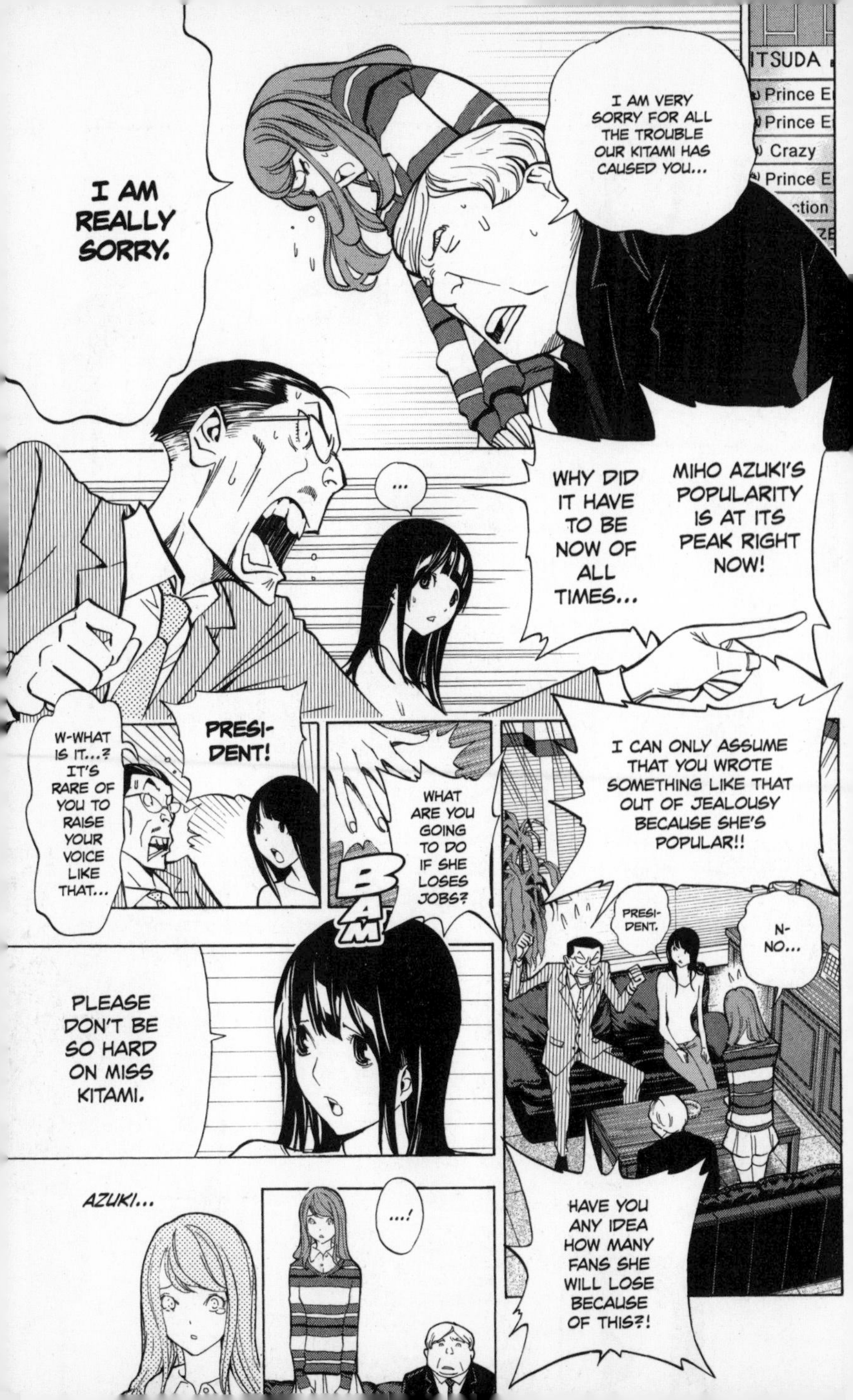
I AM VERY SORRY FOR ALL THE TROUBLE OUR KITAMI HAS CAUSED YOU...
I AM REALLY SORRY.
ITSUDA
Prince E
Prince E
Crazy
Prince E
MIHO AZUKI'S POPULARITY IS AT ITS PEAK RIGHT NOW!
WHY DID IT HAVE TO BE NOW OF ALL TIMES...
...
I CAN ONLY ASSUME THAT YOU WROTE SOMETHING LIKE THAT OUT OF JEALOUSY BECAUSE SHE'S POPULAR!!
N-NO...
PRESI-DENT.
HAVE YOU ANY IDEA HOW MANY FANS SHE WILL LOSE BECAUSE OF THIS?!
WHAT ARE YOU GOING TO DO IF SHE LOSES JOBS?
BAM
PRESI-DENT!
W-WHAT IS IT...? IT'S RARE OF YOU TO RAISE YOUR VOICE LIKE THAT...
PLEASE DON'T BE SO HARD ON MISS KITAMI.
...!
AZUKI...

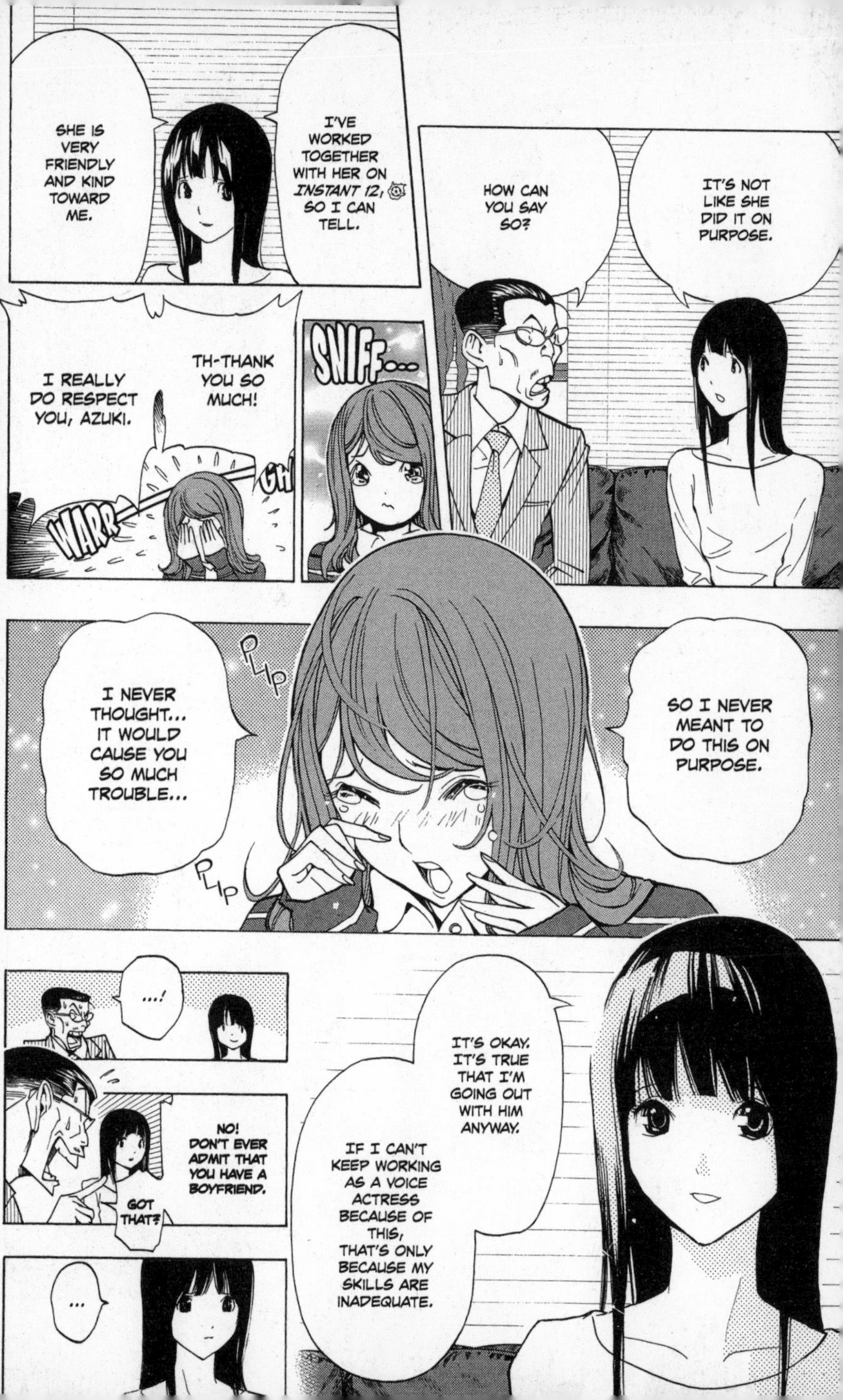
IT'S NOT LIKE SHE DID IT ON PURPOSE.
HOW CAN YOU SAY SO?
I'VE WORKED TOGETHER WITH HER ON *INSTANT 12*, SO I CAN TELL.
SHE IS VERY FRIENDLY AND KIND TOWARD ME.
SNIFF...
TH-THANK YOU SO MUCH!
I REALLY DO RESPECT YOU, AZUKI.
GH
WARR
SO I NEVER MEANT TO DO THIS ON PURPOSE.
PLIP
I NEVER THOUGHT... IT WOULD CAUSE YOU SO MUCH TROUBLE...
PLIP
IT'S OKAY. IT'S TRUE THAT I'M GOING OUT WITH HIM ANYWAY.
IF I CAN'T KEEP WORKING AS A VOICE ACTRESS BECAUSE OF THIS, THAT'S ONLY BECAUSE MY SKILLS ARE INADEQUATE.
...!
NO! DON'T EVER ADMIT THAT YOU HAVE A BOYFRIEND.
GOT THAT?
...

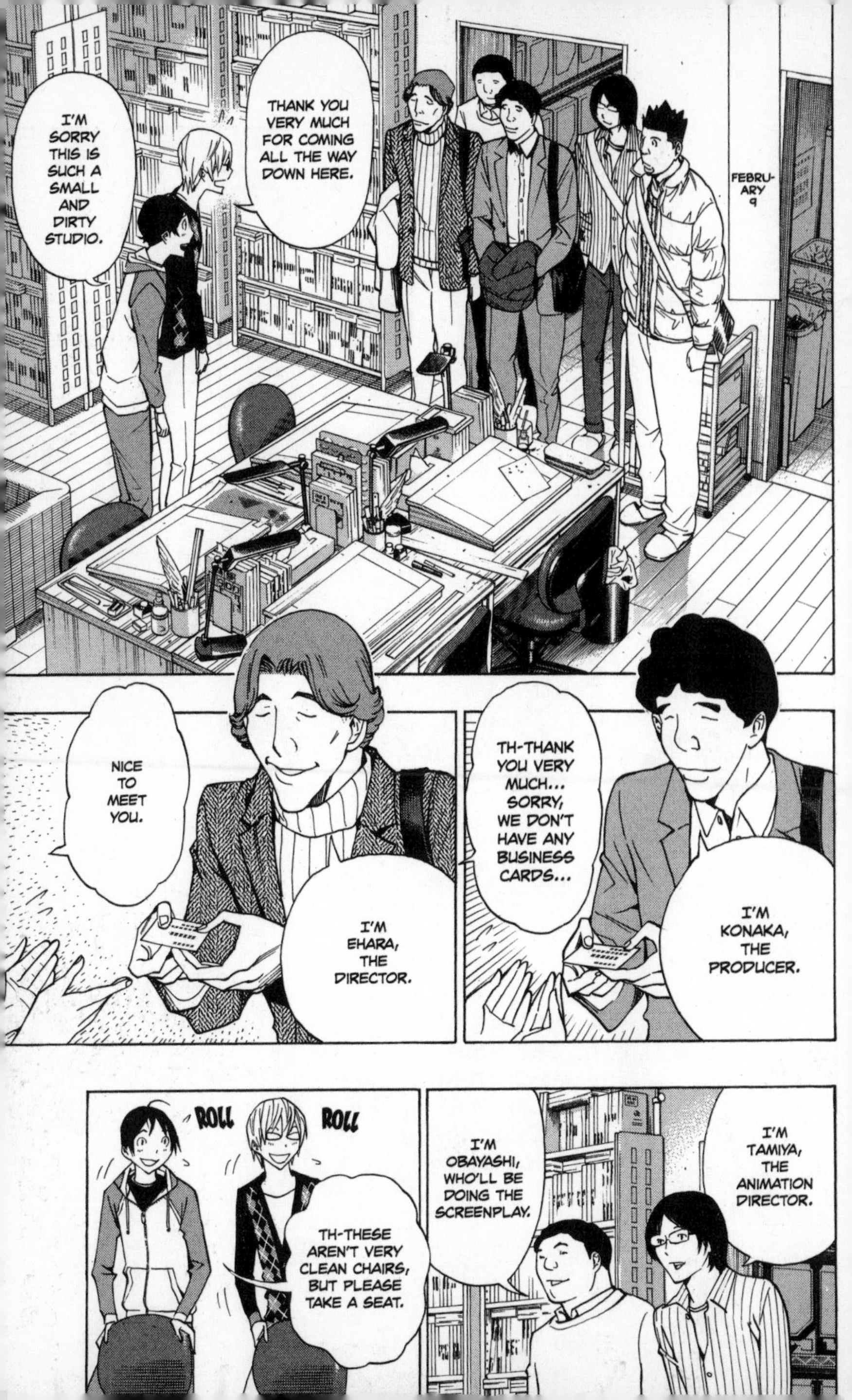
FEBRUARY 9
THANK YOU VERY MUCH FOR COMING ALL THE WAY DOWN HERE.
I'M SORRY THIS IS SUCH A SMALL AND DIRTY STUDIO.
I'M KONAKA, THE PRODUCER.
TH-THANK YOU VERY MUCH... SORRY, WE DON'T HAVE ANY BUSINESS CARDS...
I'M EHARA, THE DIRECTOR.
NICE TO MEET YOU.
I'M TAMIYA, THE ANIMATION DIRECTOR.
I'M OBAYASHI, WHO'LL BE DOING THE SCREENPLAY.
ROLL
ROLL
TH-THESE AREN'T VERY CLEAN CHAIRS, BUT PLEASE TAKE A SEAT.

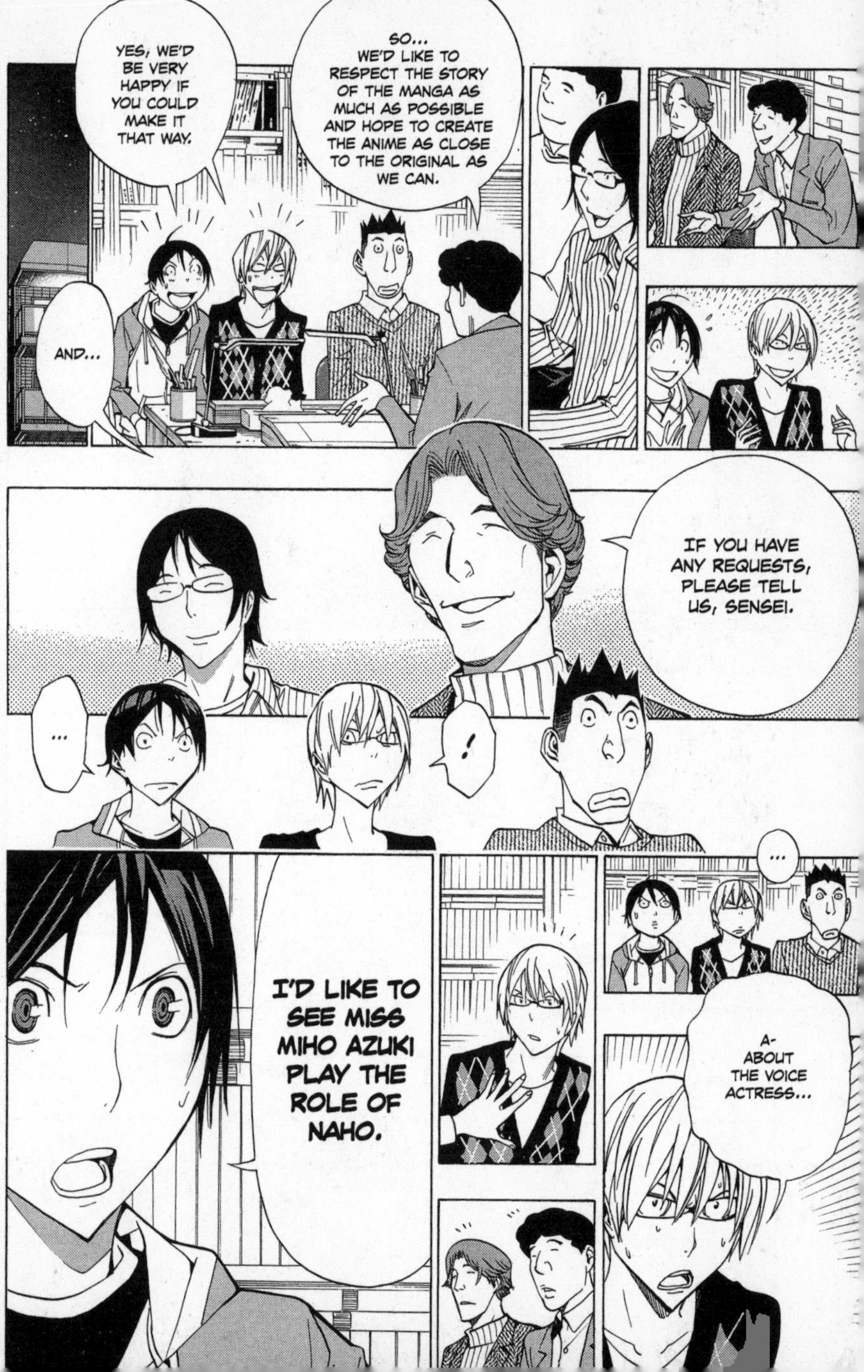
SO...
WE'D LIKE TO RESPECT THE STORY OF THE MANGA AS MUCH AS POSSIBLE AND HOPE TO CREATE THE ANIME AS CLOSE TO THE ORIGINAL AS WE CAN.
YES, WE'D BE VERY HAPPY IF YOU COULD MAKE IT THAT WAY.
AND...
IF YOU HAVE ANY REQUESTS, PLEASE TELL US, SENSEI.
!
...
...
A- ABOUT THE VOICE ACTRESS...
I'D LIKE TO SEE MISS MIHO AZUKI PLAY THE ROLE OF NAHO.

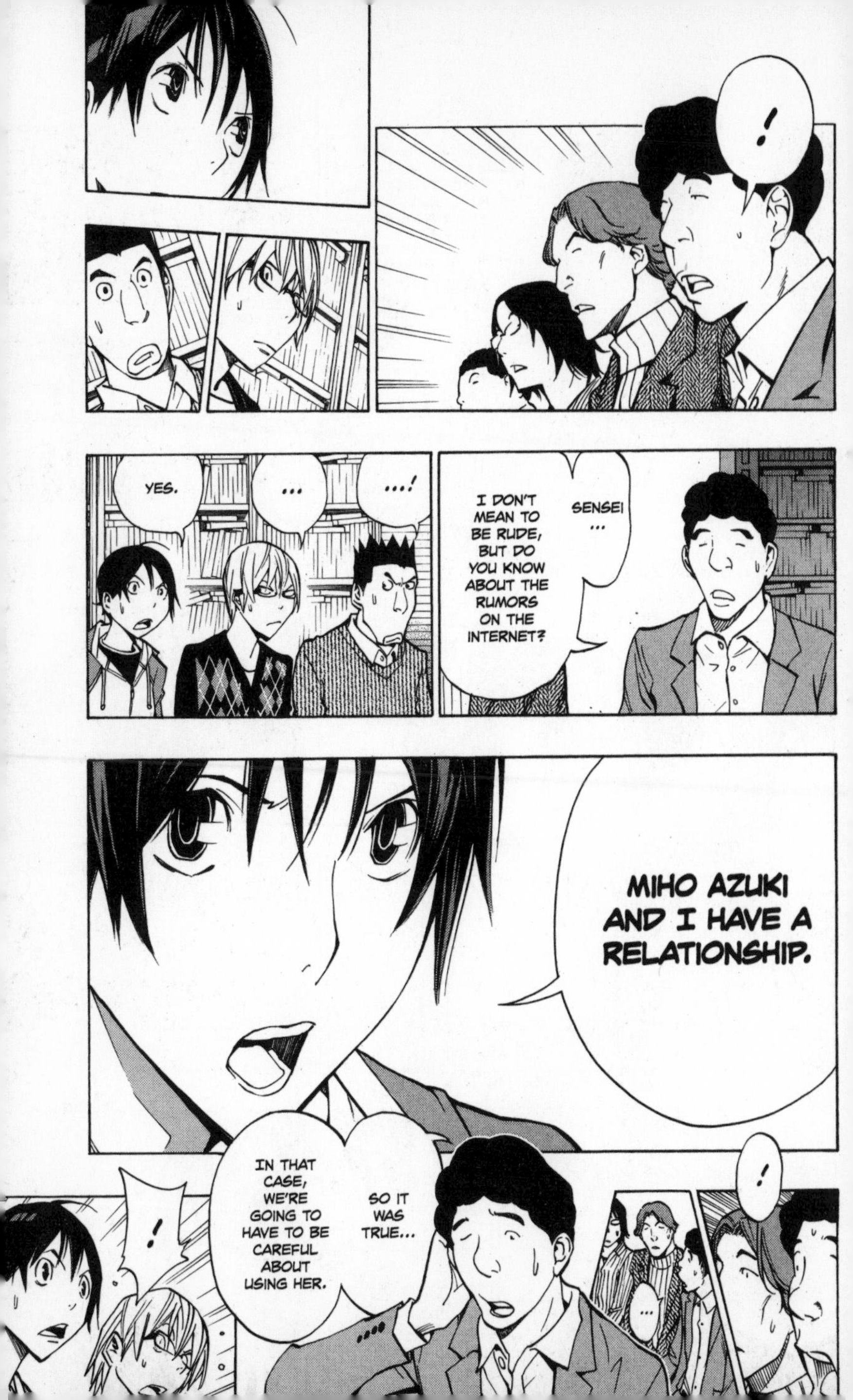
!
SENSEI ...
I DON'T MEAN TO BE RUDE, BUT DO YOU KNOW ABOUT THE RUMORS ON THE INTERNET?
...!
...
YES.
MIHO AZUKI AND I HAVE A RELATIONSHIP.
!
...
SO IT WAS TRUE...
IN THAT CASE, WE'RE GOING TO HAVE TO BE CAREFUL ABOUT USING HER.
!

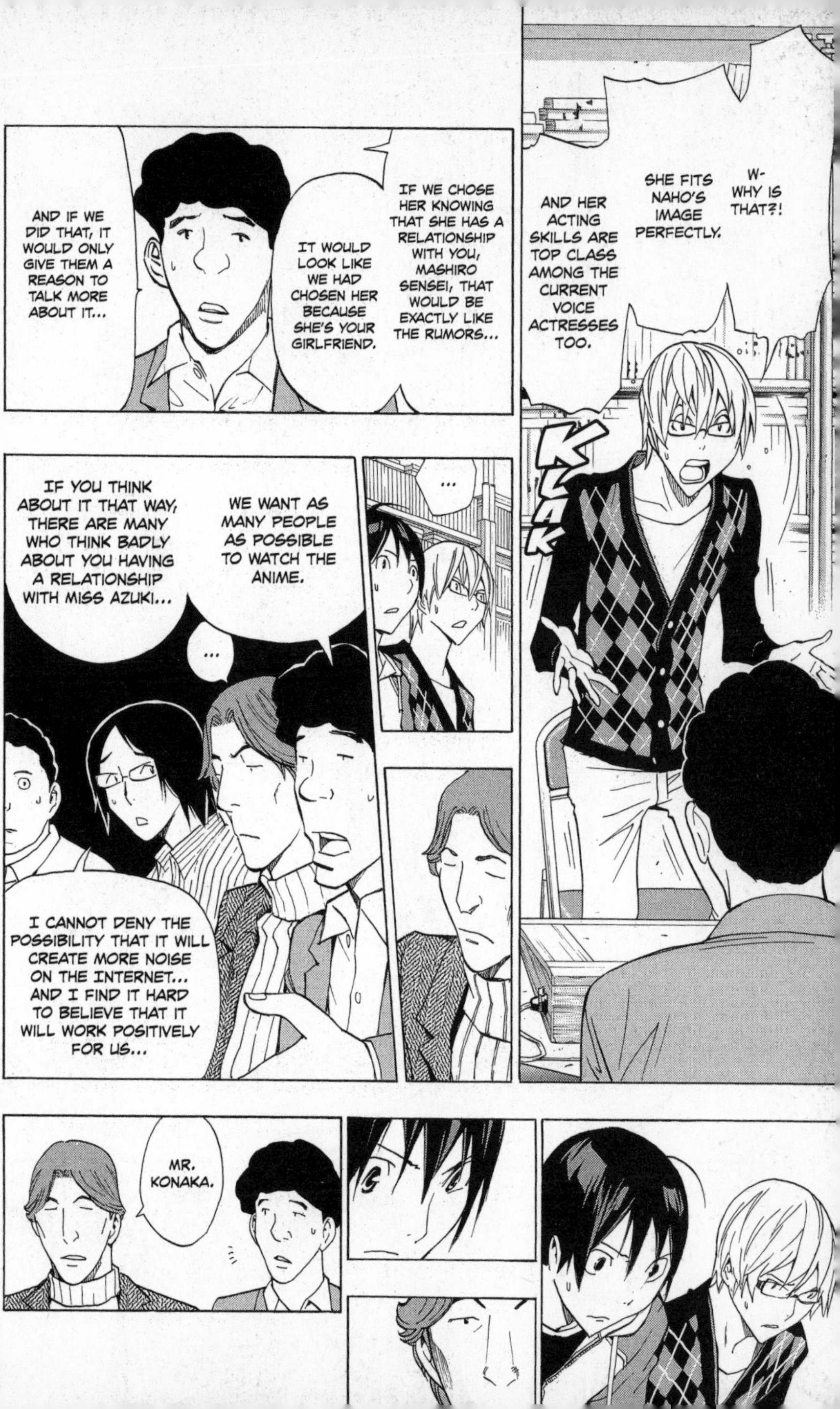
W- WHY IS THAT?!
SHE FITS NAHO'S IMAGE PERFECTLY.
AND HER ACTING SKILLS ARE TOP CLASS AMONG THE CURRENT VOICE ACTRESSES TOO.
KLAK
IF WE CHOSE HER KNOWING THAT SHE HAS A RELATIONSHIP WITH YOU, MASHIRO SENSEI, THAT WOULD BE EXACTLY LIKE THE RUMORS...
IT WOULD LOOK LIKE WE HAD CHOSEN HER BECAUSE SHE'S YOUR GIRLFRIEND.
AND IF WE DID THAT, IT WOULD ONLY GIVE THEM A REASON TO TALK MORE ABOUT IT...
...
WE WANT AS MANY PEOPLE AS POSSIBLE TO WATCH THE ANIME.
IF YOU THINK ABOUT IT THAT WAY, THERE ARE MANY WHO THINK BADLY ABOUT YOU HAVING A RELATIONSHIP WITH MISS AZUKI...
...
I CANNOT DENY THE POSSIBILITY THAT IT WILL CREATE MORE NOISE ON THE INTERNET... AND I FIND IT HARD TO BELIEVE THAT IT WILL WORK POSITIVELY FOR US...
MR. KONAKA.

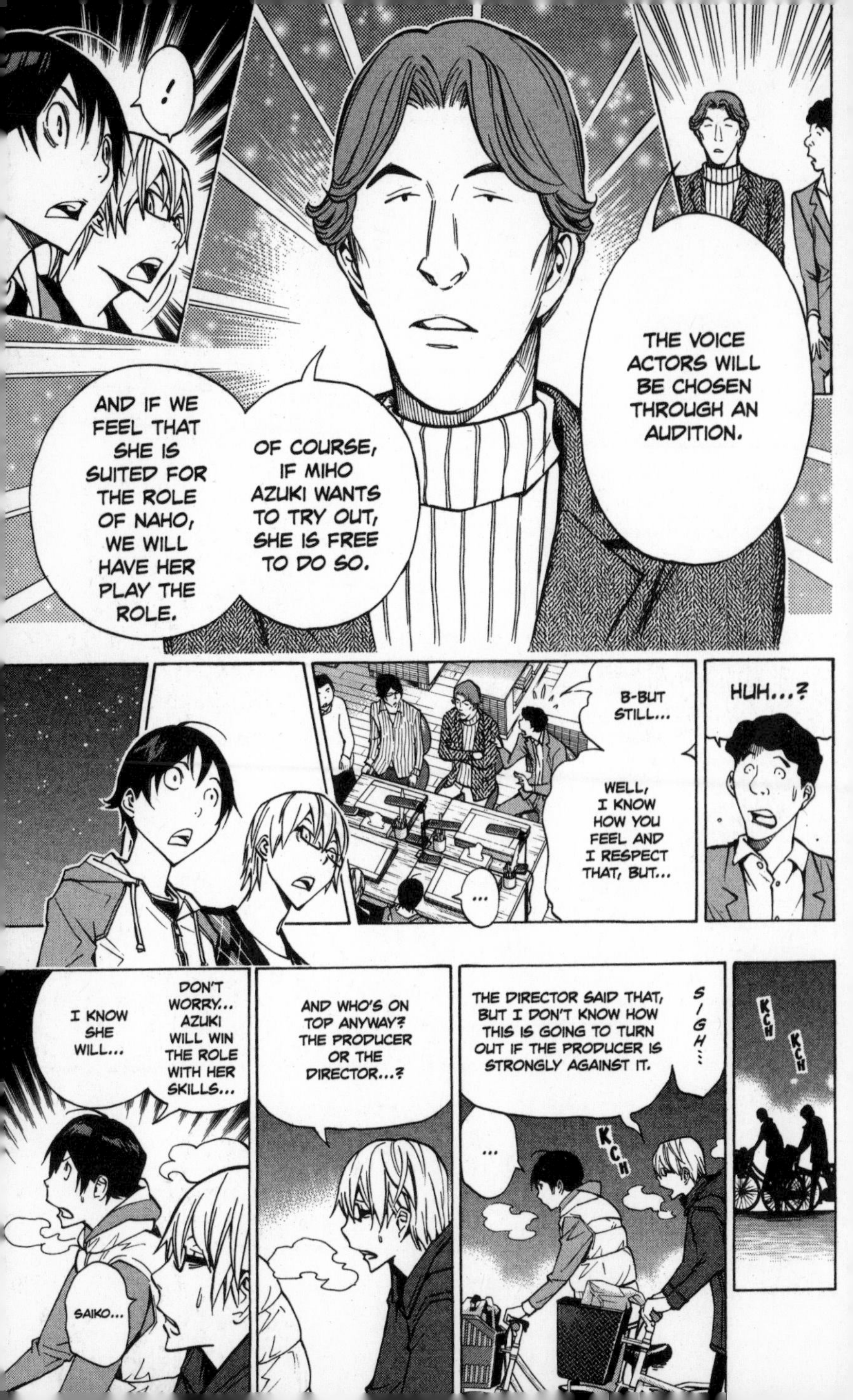
THE VOICE ACTORS WILL BE CHOSEN THROUGH AN AUDITION.
OF COURSE, IF MIHO AZUKI WANTS TO TRY OUT, SHE IS FREE TO DO SO.
AND IF WE FEEL THAT SHE IS SUITED FOR THE ROLE OF NAHO, WE WILL HAVE HER PLAY THE ROLE.
!
HUH...?
B-BUT STILL...
WELL, I KNOW HOW YOU FEEL AND I RESPECT THAT, BUT...
...
KCH
KCH
THE DIRECTOR SAID THAT, BUT I DON'T KNOW HOW THIS IS GOING TO TURN OUT IF THE PRODUCER IS STRONGLY AGAINST IT.
S/GH...
KCH
...
AND WHO'S ON TOP ANYWAY? THE PRODUCER OR THE DIRECTOR...?
DON'T WORRY... AZUKI WILL WIN THE ROLE WITH HER SKILLS...
I KNOW SHE WILL...
SAIKO...

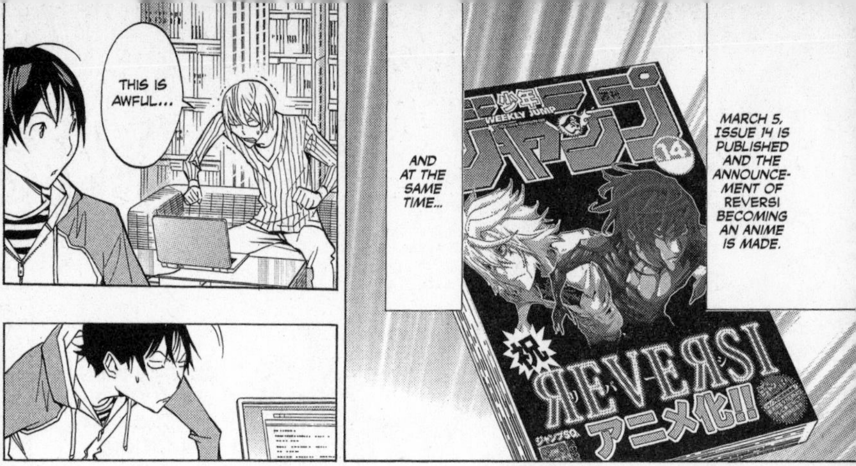
MARCH 5, ISSUE 14 IS PUBLISHED AND THE ANNOUNCE-MENT OF REVERSI BECOMING AN ANIME IS MADE.
AND AT THE SAME TIME...
WEEKLY JUMP
14
REVERSI
祝
アニメ化!!
THIS IS AWFUL...

: Anonymous
He got his personal anime made, huh. His wife Miho's gonna play Naho.
: Anonymous
The adult world is so dirty.
: Anonymous
It's not the adult world that'd dirty, it's Azuki. Dirty voice actress Azu-kyun.
: Anonymous
Ashirogi's the one to blame. They've got to be stupid if they really choose Azu-kyun after all of this.
: Anonymous
But Azu-kyun is actually cutting back on her work so she can be in his anime.
: Anonymous
She probably lost work because they found out she has a BF.
: Anonymous
I'm never gonna watch the Reversi anime.
: Anonymous
I used to be an Azu-kyun fan too. Voice actresses who succeeded in presenting themselves as being that pure are rare.
: Anonymous
Azu-kyun has changed her name to Bitch-kyun.
: Anonymous
Bitch-kyun, that's funny.

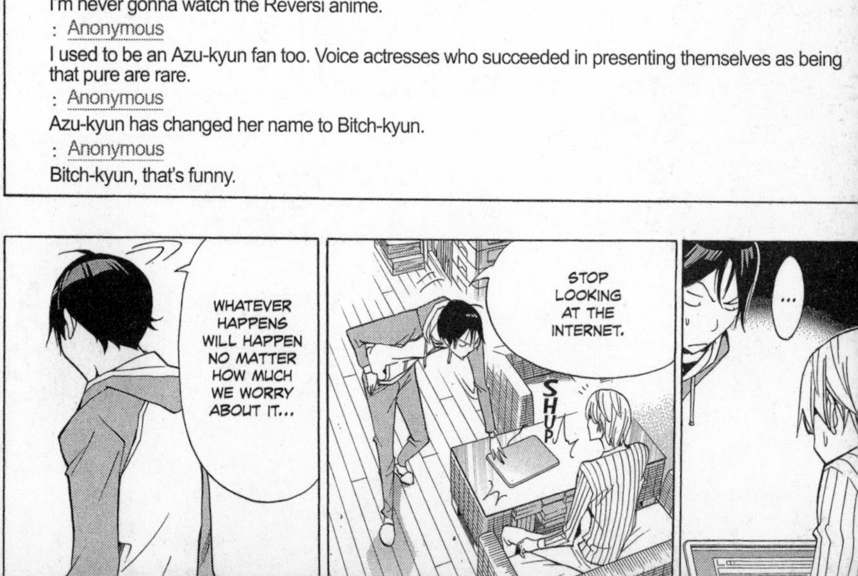
...
STOP LOOKING AT THE INTERNET.
SHUP
WHATEVER HAPPENS WILL HAPPEN NO MATTER HOW MUCH WE WORRY ABOUT IT...

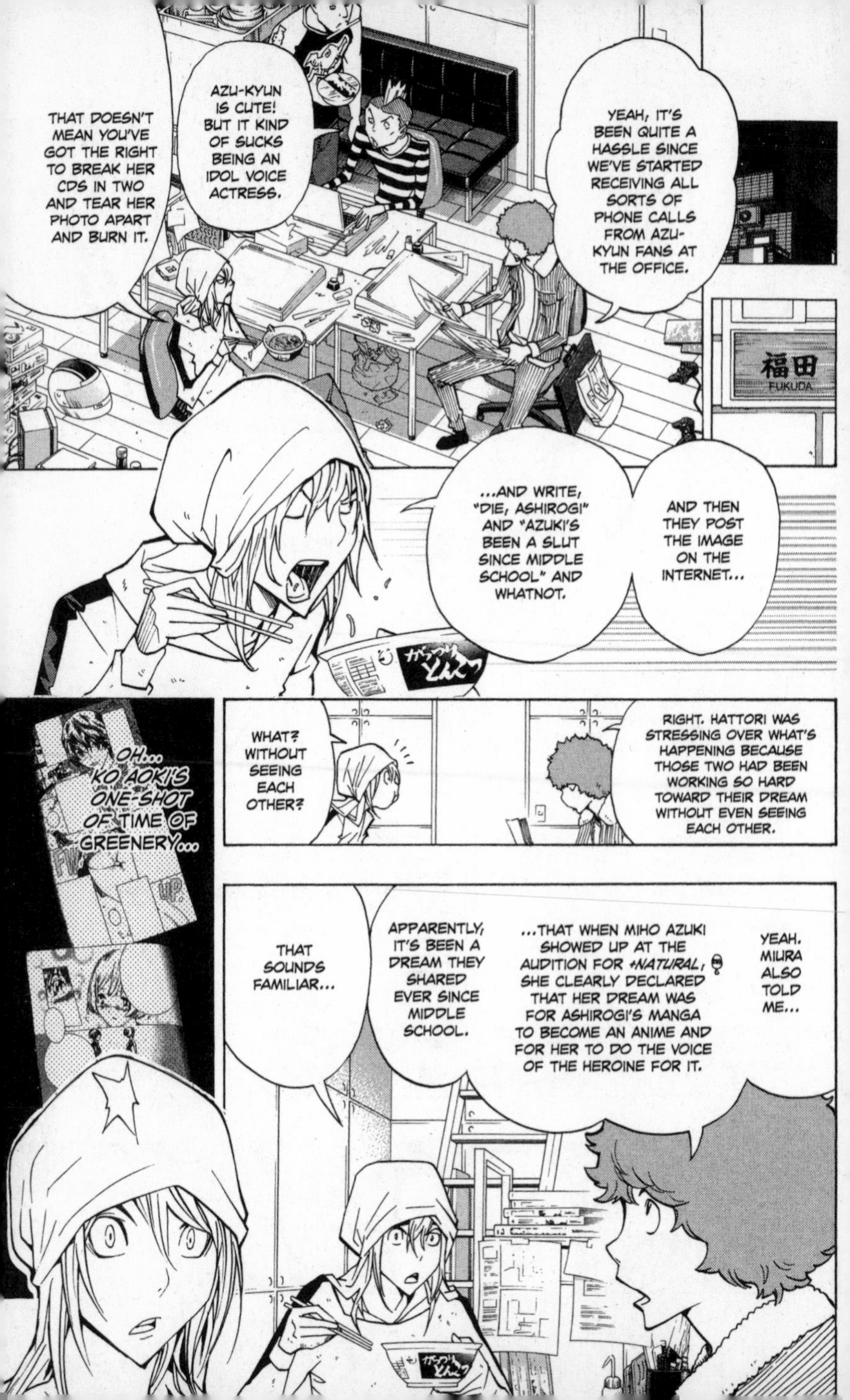
YEAH, IT'S BEEN QUITE A HASSLE SINCE WE'VE STARTED RECEIVING ALL SORTS OF PHONE CALLS FROM AZU-KYUN FANS AT THE OFFICE.
福田
FUKUDA
AZU-KYUN IS CUTE! BUT IT KIND OF SUCKS BEING AN IDOL VOICE ACTRESS.
THAT DOESN'T MEAN YOU'VE GOT THE RIGHT TO BREAK HER CDS IN TWO AND TEAR HER PHOTO APART AND BURN IT.
AND THEN THEY POST THE IMAGE ON THE INTERNET...
...AND WRITE, "DIE, ASHIROGI" AND "AZUKI'S BEEN A SLUT SINCE MIDDLE SCHOOL" AND WHATNOT.
RIGHT. HATTORI WAS STRESSING OVER WHAT'S HAPPENING BECAUSE THOSE TWO HAD BEEN WORKING SO HARD TOWARD THEIR DREAM WITHOUT EVEN SEEING EACH OTHER.
WHAT? WITHOUT SEEING EACH OTHER?
OH... KO AOKI'S ONE-SHOT OF TIME OF GREENERY...
YEAH. MIURA ALSO TOLD ME...
...THAT WHEN MIHO AZUKI SHOWED UP AT THE AUDITION FOR +NATURAL, SHE CLEARLY DECLARED THAT HER DREAM WAS FOR ASHIROGI'S MANGA TO BECOME AN ANIME AND FOR HER TO DO THE VOICE OF THE HEROINE FOR IT.
APPARENTLY, IT'S BEEN A DREAM THEY SHARED EVER SINCE MIDDLE SCHOOL.
THAT SOUNDS FAMILIAR...

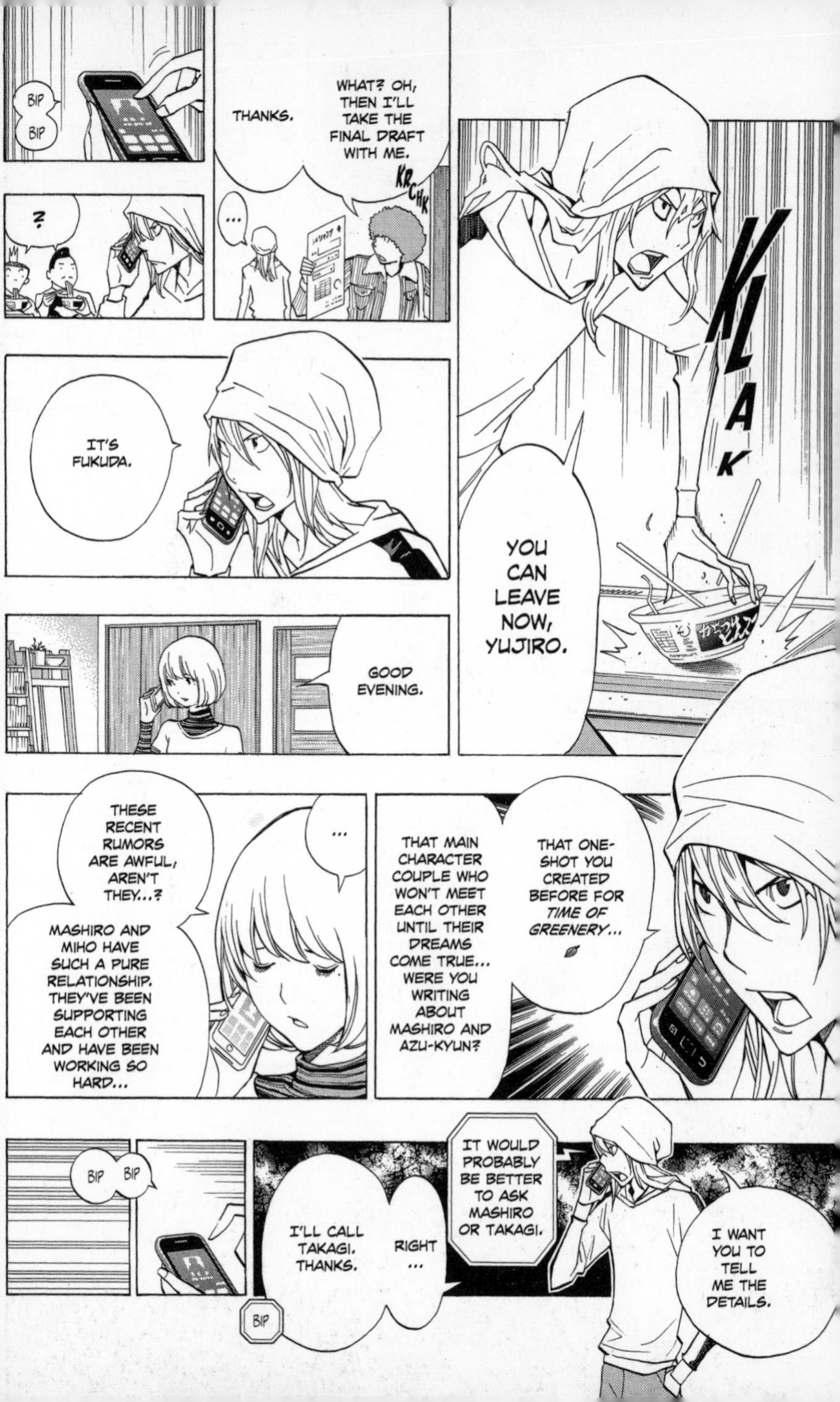
WHAT? OH, THEN I'LL TAKE THE FINAL DRAFT WITH ME.
THANKS.
KRCHK
BIP
BIP
...
?
KLAK
YOU CAN LEAVE NOW, YUJIRO.
IT'S FUKUDA.
GOOD EVENING.
THAT ONE-SHOT YOU CREATED BEFORE FOR *TIME OF GREENERY*...
THAT MAIN CHARACTER COUPLE WHO WON'T MEET EACH OTHER UNTIL THEIR DREAMS COME TRUE... WERE YOU WRITING ABOUT MASHIRO AND AZU-KYUN?
...
THESE RECENT RUMORS ARE AWFUL, AREN'T THEY...?
MASHIRO AND MIHO HAVE SUCH A PURE RELATIONSHIP. THEY'VE BEEN SUPPORTING EACH OTHER AND HAVE BEEN WORKING SO HARD...
I WANT YOU TO TELL ME THE DETAILS.
IT WOULD PROBABLY BE BETTER TO ASK MASHIRO OR TAKAGI.
RIGHT...
I'LL CALL TAKAGI. THANKS.
BIP
BIP
BIP

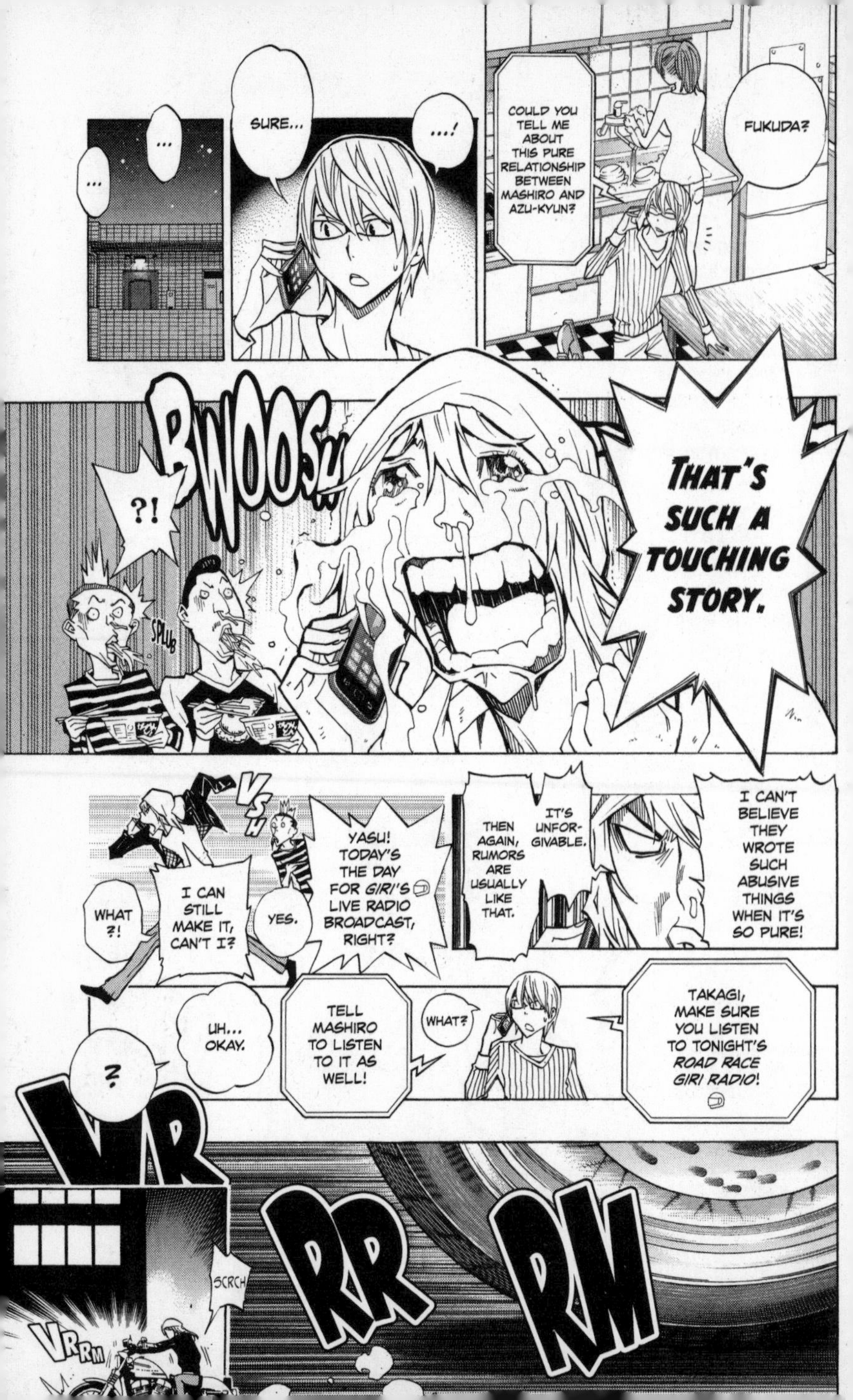

FUKUDA?
COULD YOU TELL ME ABOUT THIS PURE RELATIONSHIP BETWEEN MASHIRO AND AZU-KYUN?
...!
SURE...
...
...
THAT'S SUCH A TOUCHING STORY.
BWOOSH
?!
SPLUB
I CAN'T BELIEVE THEY WROTE SUCH ABUSIVE THINGS WHEN IT'S SO PURE!
IT'S UNFORGIVABLE.
THEN AGAIN, RUMORS ARE USUALLY LIKE THAT.
YASU! TODAY'S THE DAY FOR GIRI'S LIVE RADIO BROADCAST, RIGHT?
YES.
VSH
I CAN STILL MAKE IT, CAN'T I?
WHAT?!
TAKAGI, MAKE SURE YOU LISTEN TO TONIGHT'S ROAD RACE GIRI RADIO!
WHAT?
TELL MASHIRO TO LISTEN TO IT AS WELL!
UH... OKAY.
?
VRRRRM
SCRCH
VRRM

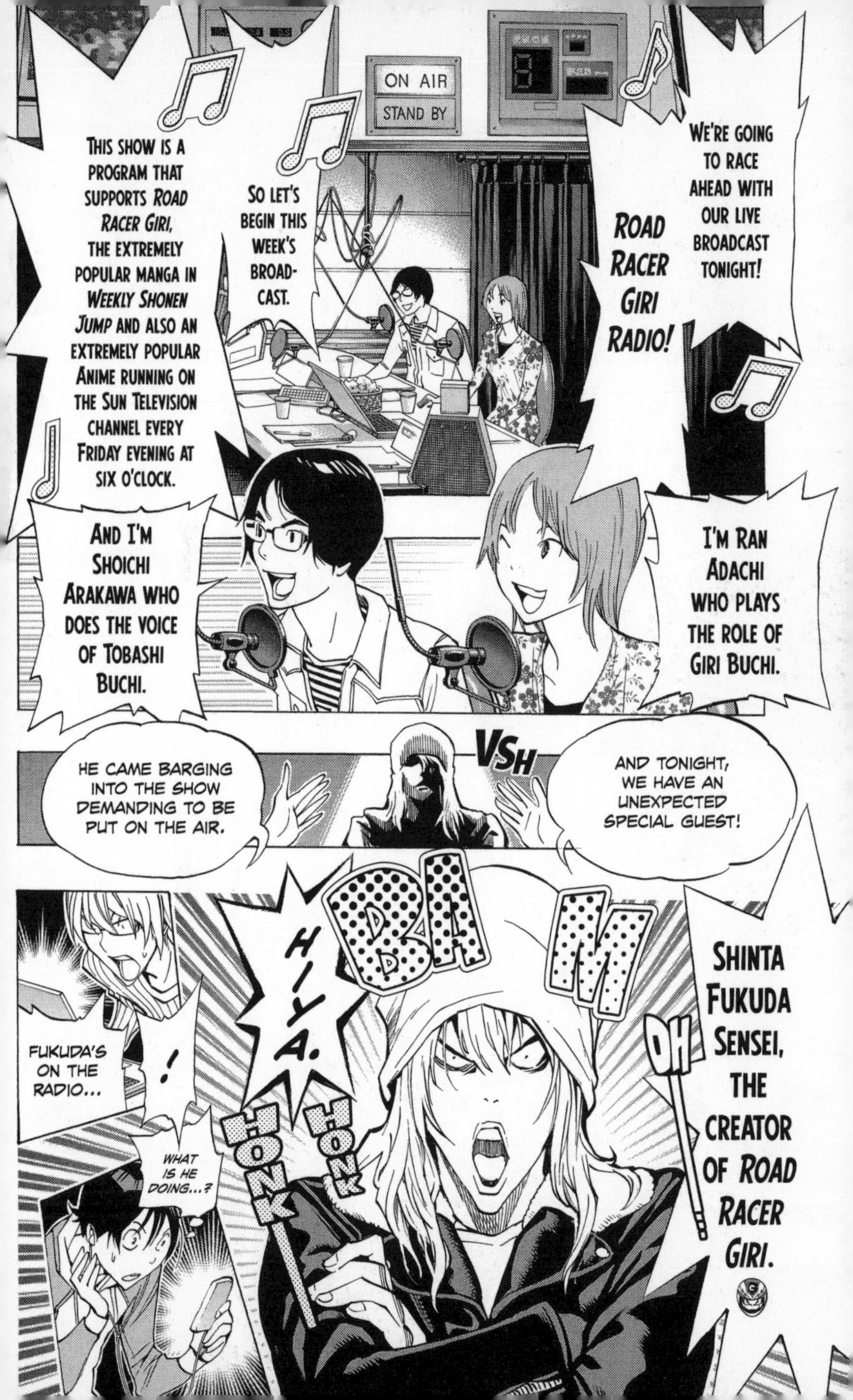
ON AIR
STAND BY
ROAD RACER GIRI RADIO!
WE'RE GOING TO RACE AHEAD WITH OUR LIVE BROADCAST TONIGHT!
SO LET'S BEGIN THIS WEEK'S BROAD-CAST.
THIS SHOW IS A PROGRAM THAT SUPPORTS *ROAD RACER GIRI*, THE EXTREMELY POPULAR MANGA IN *WEEKLY SHONEN JUMP* AND ALSO AN EXTREMELY POPULAR ANIME RUNNING ON THE SUN TELEVISION CHANNEL EVERY FRIDAY EVENING AT SIX O'CLOCK.
I'M RAN ADACHI WHO PLAYS THE ROLE OF GIRI BUCHI.
AND I'M SHOICHI ARAKAWA WHO DOES THE VOICE OF TOBASHI BUCHI.
AND TONIGHT, WE HAVE AN UNEXPECTED SPECIAL GUEST!
VSH
HE CAME BARGING INTO THE SHOW DEMANDING TO BE PUT ON THE AIR.
BAM
SHINTA FUKUDA SENSEI, THE CREATOR OF *ROAD RACER GIRI*.
OH
HI-YA.
HONK HONK
!
FUKUDA'S ON THE RADIO...
WHAT IS HE DOING...?

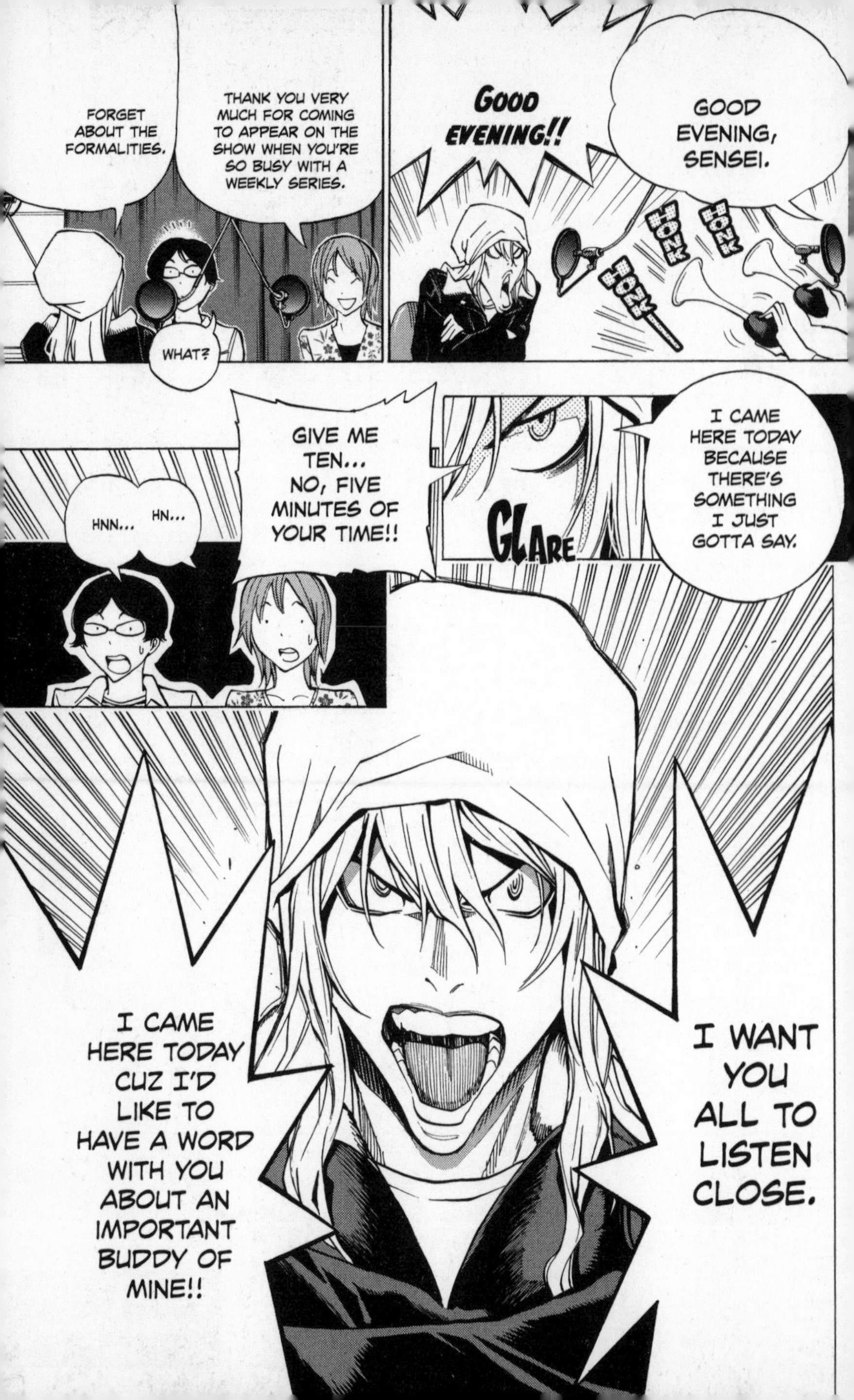
GOOD EVENING, SENSEI.
HONK
HONK
HONK
GOOD EVENING!!
THANK YOU VERY MUCH FOR COMING TO APPEAR ON THE SHOW WHEN YOU'RE SO BUSY WITH A WEEKLY SERIES.
FORGET ABOUT THE FORMALITIES.
WHAT?
I CAME HERE TODAY BECAUSE THERE'S SOMETHING I JUST GOTTA SAY.
GLARE
GIVE ME TEN... NO, FIVE MINUTES OF YOUR TIME!!
HN...
HNN...
I WANT YOU ALL TO LISTEN CLOSE.
I CAME HERE TODAY CUZ I'D LIKE TO HAVE A WORD WITH YOU ABOUT AN IMPORTANT BUDDY OF MINE!!

OHBA'S STORYBOARD

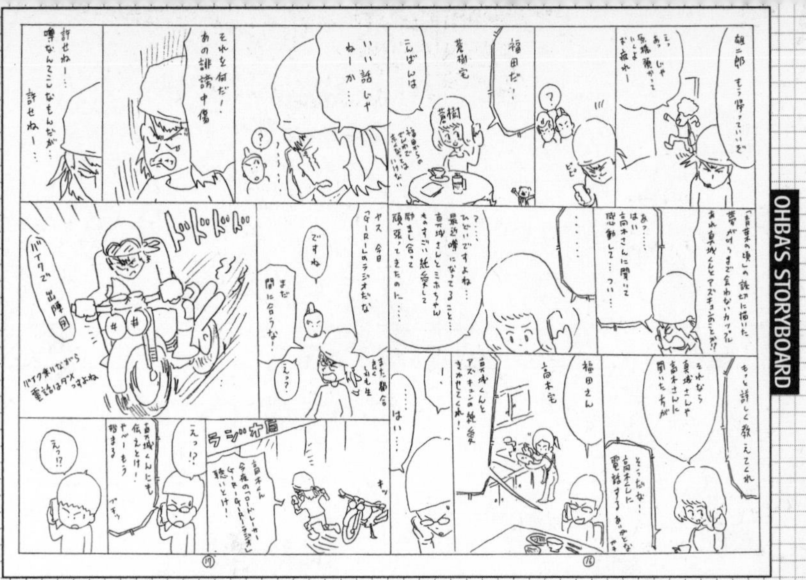

OBATA'S STORYBOARD

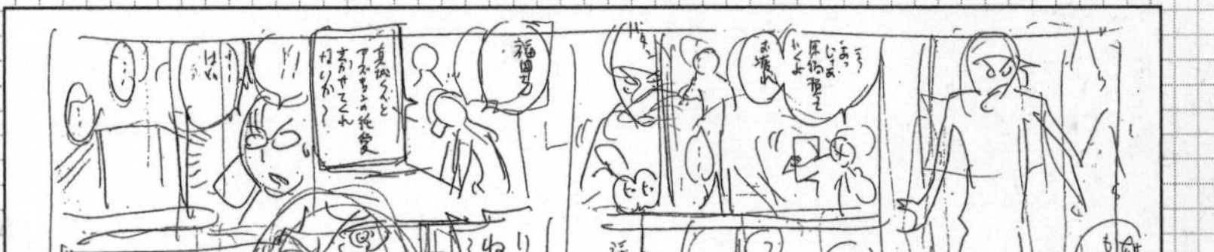

COMPLETE!

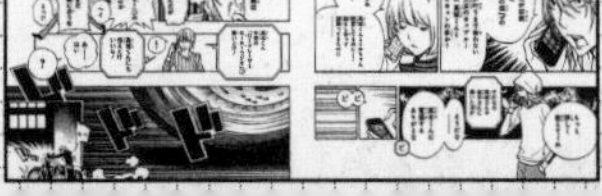

※CREATOR STORYBOARDS AND FINISHED PAGES IN JAPANESE

BAKUMAN。 vol.19

"Until the Final Draft Is Complete"

Chapter 167, pp. 150-151

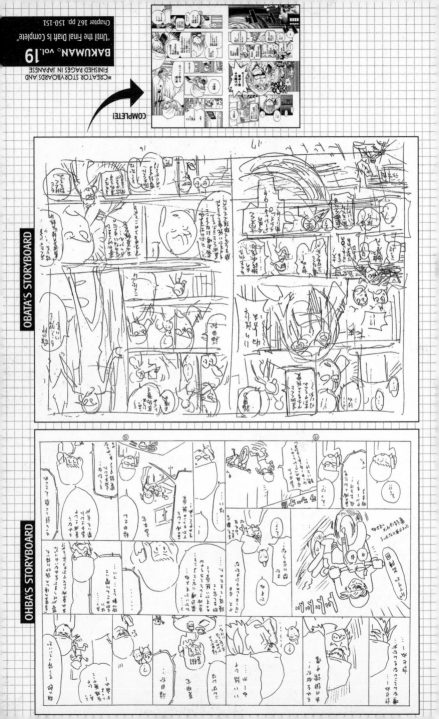

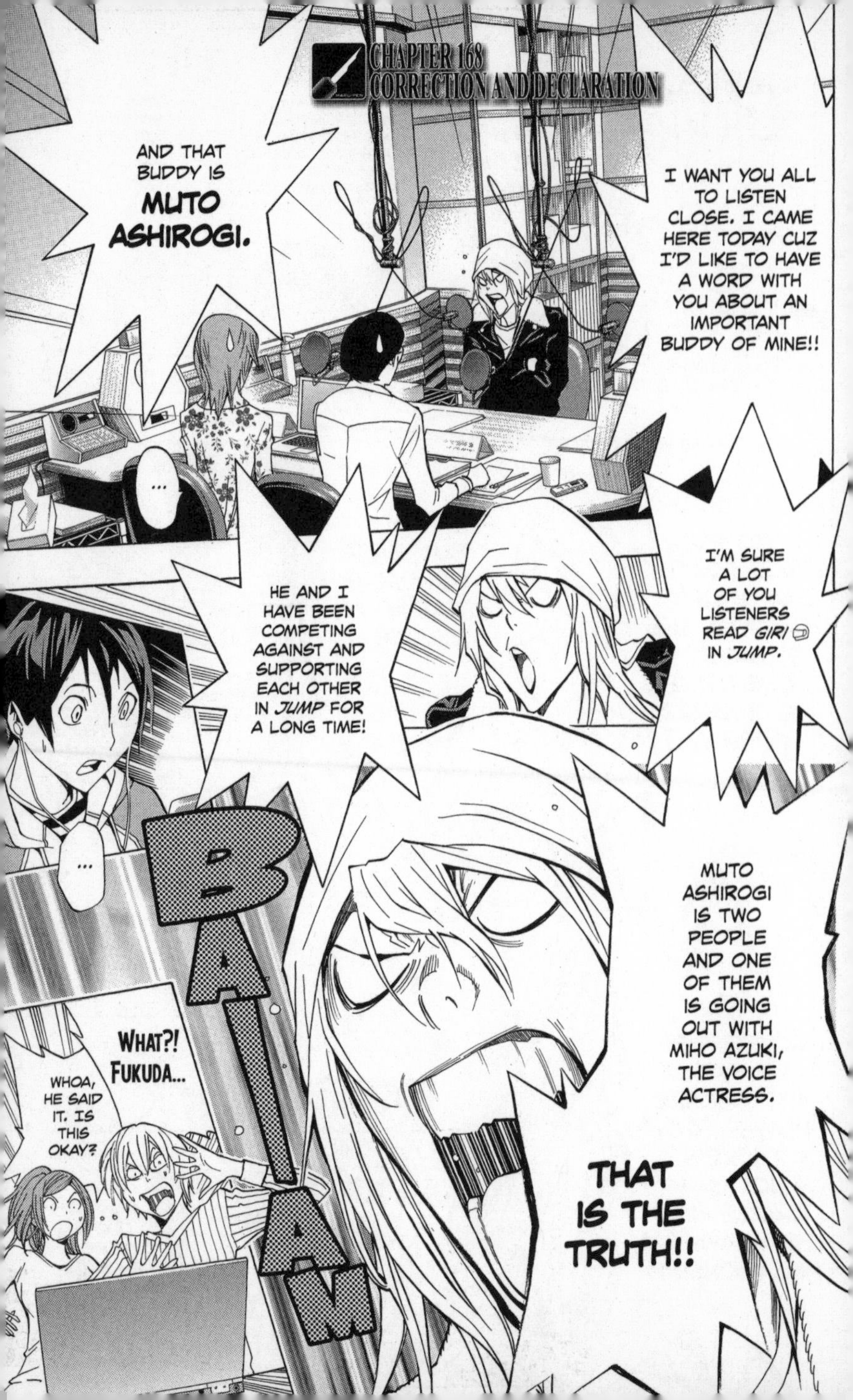
CHAPTER 168 CORRECTION AND DECLARATION
I WANT YOU ALL TO LISTEN CLOSE. I CAME HERE TODAY CUZ I'D LIKE TO HAVE A WORD WITH YOU ABOUT AN IMPORTANT BUDDY OF MINE!!
AND THAT BUDDY IS MUTO ASHIROGI.
...
I'M SURE A LOT OF YOU LISTENERS READ GIRI IN JUMP.
HE AND I HAVE BEEN COMPETING AGAINST AND SUPPORTING EACH OTHER IN JUMP FOR A LONG TIME!
MUTO ASHIROGI IS TWO PEOPLE AND ONE OF THEM IS GOING OUT WITH MIHO AZUKI, THE VOICE ACTRESS.
THAT IS THE TRUTH!!
BAAAM
...
WHAT?! FUKUDA...
WHOA, HE SAID IT. IS THIS OKAY?

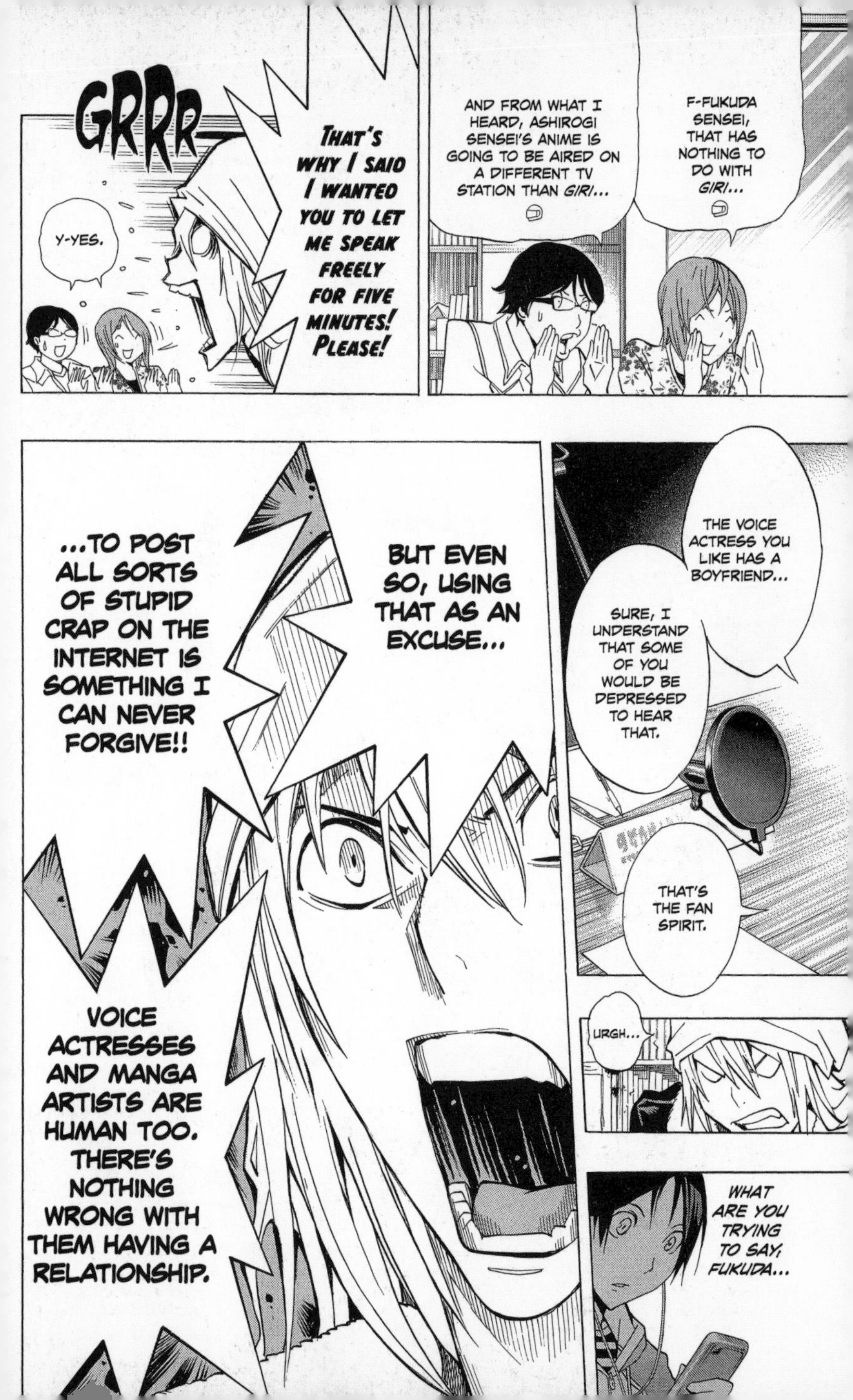
F-FUKUDA SENSEI, THAT HAS NOTHING TO DO WITH GIRI...
AND FROM WHAT I HEARD, ASHIROGI SENSEI'S ANIME IS GOING TO BE AIRED ON A DIFFERENT TV STATION THAN GIRI...
GRRR
THAT'S WHY I SAID I WANTED YOU TO LET ME SPEAK FREELY FOR FIVE MINUTES! PLEASE!
Y-YES.
THE VOICE ACTRESS YOU LIKE HAS A BOYFRIEND...
SURE, I UNDERSTAND THAT SOME OF YOU WOULD BE DEPRESSED TO HEAR THAT.
THAT'S THE FAN SPIRIT.
URGH...
WHAT ARE YOU TRYING TO SAY, FUKUDA...
BUT EVEN SO, USING THAT AS AN EXCUSE...
...TO POST ALL SORTS OF STUPID CRAP ON THE INTERNET IS SOMETHING I CAN NEVER FORGIVE!!
VOICE ACTRESSES AND MANGA ARTISTS ARE HUMAN TOO. THERE'S NOTHING WRONG WITH THEM HAVING A RELATIONSHIP.

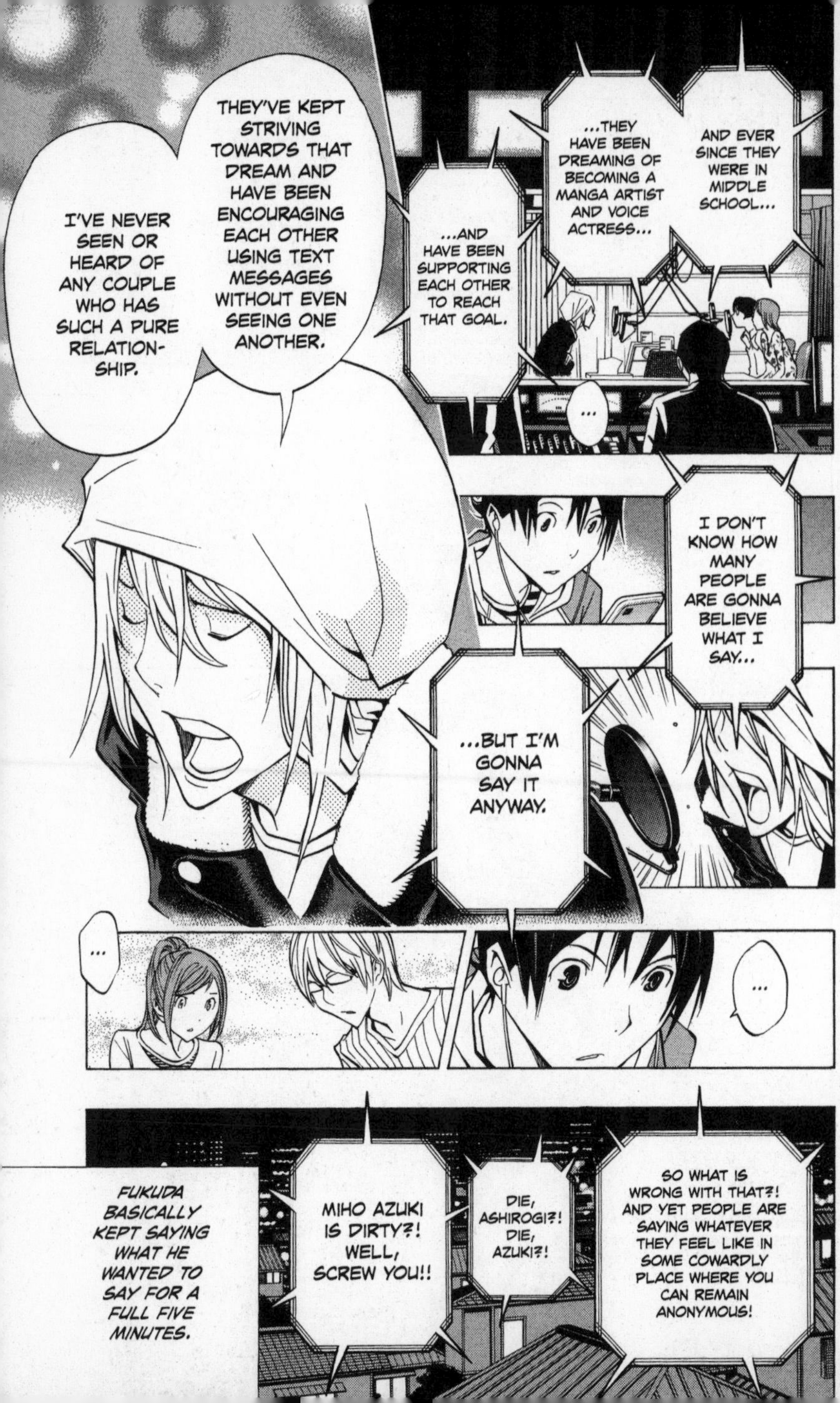
AND EVER SINCE THEY WERE IN MIDDLE SCHOOL...
...THEY HAVE BEEN DREAMING OF BECOMING A MANGA ARTIST AND VOICE ACTRESS...
...AND HAVE BEEN SUPPORTING EACH OTHER TO REACH THAT GOAL.
...
THEY'VE KEPT STRIVING TOWARDS THAT DREAM AND HAVE BEEN ENCOURAGING EACH OTHER USING TEXT MESSAGES WITHOUT EVEN SEEING ONE ANOTHER.
I'VE NEVER SEEN OR HEARD OF ANY COUPLE WHO HAS SUCH A PURE RELATION-SHIP.
I DON'T KNOW HOW MANY PEOPLE ARE GONNA BELIEVE WHAT I SAY...
...BUT I'M GONNA SAY IT ANYWAY.
...
...
SO WHAT IS WRONG WITH THAT?! AND YET PEOPLE ARE SAYING WHATEVER THEY FEEL LIKE IN SOME COWARDLY PLACE WHERE YOU CAN REMAIN ANONYMOUS!
DIE, ASHIROGI?! DIE, AZUKI?!
MIHO AZUKI IS DIRTY?! WELL, SCREW YOU!!
FUKUDA BASICALLY KEPT SAYING WHAT HE WANTED TO SAY FOR A FULL FIVE MINUTES.

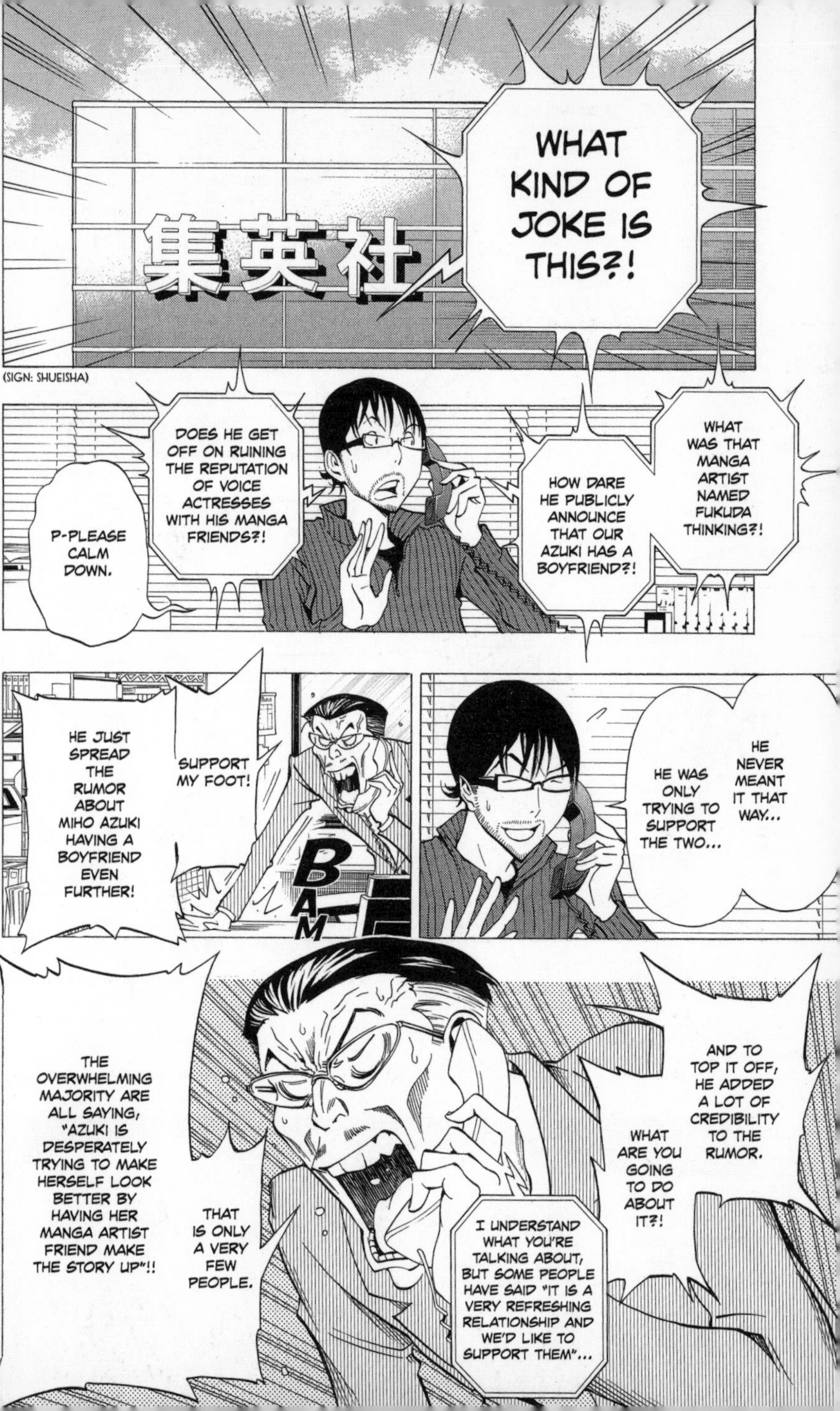
集英社
WHAT KIND OF JOKE IS THIS?!
(SIGN: SHUEISHA)
WHAT WAS THAT MANGA ARTIST NAMED FUKUDA THINKING?!
HOW DARE HE PUBLICLY ANNOUNCE THAT OUR AZUKI HAS A BOYFRIEND?!
DOES HE GET OFF ON RUINING THE REPUTATION OF VOICE ACTRESSES WITH HIS MANGA FRIENDS?!
P-PLEASE CALM DOWN.
HE NEVER MEANT IT THAT WAY...
HE WAS ONLY TRYING TO SUPPORT THE TWO...
SUPPORT MY FOOT!
BAM
HE JUST SPREAD THE RUMOR ABOUT MIHO AZUKI HAVING A BOYFRIEND EVEN FURTHER!
AND TO TOP IT OFF, HE ADDED A LOT OF CREDIBILITY TO THE RUMOR.
WHAT ARE YOU GOING TO DO ABOUT IT?!
I UNDERSTAND WHAT YOU'RE TALKING ABOUT, BUT SOME PEOPLE HAVE SAID "IT IS A VERY REFRESHING RELATIONSHIP AND WE'D LIKE TO SUPPORT THEM"...
THAT IS ONLY A VERY FEW PEOPLE.
THE OVERWHELMING MAJORITY ARE ALL SAYING, "AZUKI IS DESPERATELY TRYING TO MAKE HERSELF LOOK BETTER BY HAVING HER MANGA ARTIST FRIEND MAKE THE STORY UP"!!

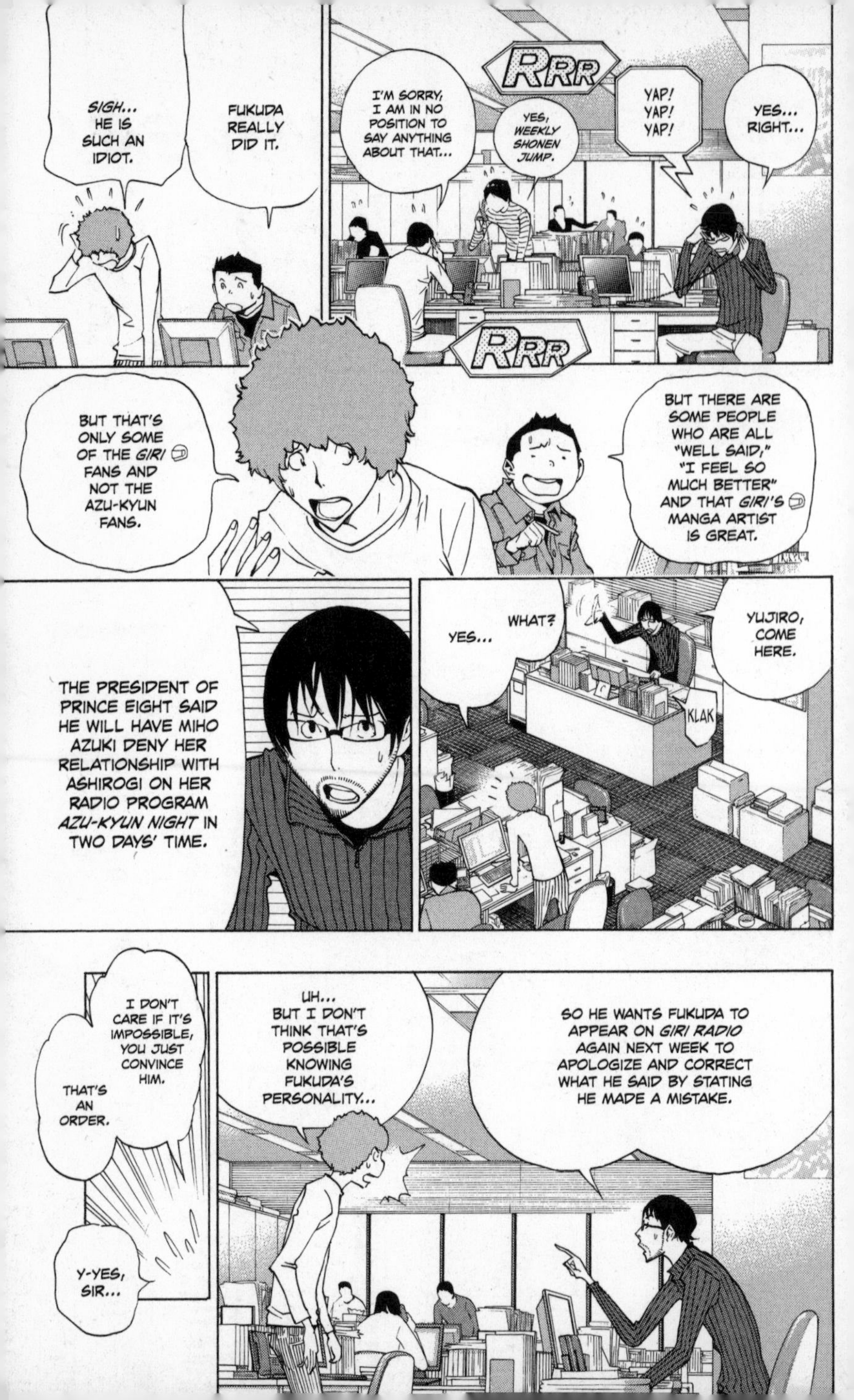
YES... RIGHT...
YAP! YAP! YAP!
RRR
YES, WEEKLY SHONEN JUMP.
I'M SORRY, I AM IN NO POSITION TO SAY ANYTHING ABOUT THAT...
RRR
FUKUDA REALLY DID IT.
SIGH... HE IS SUCH AN IDIOT.
BUT THERE ARE SOME PEOPLE WHO ARE ALL "WELL SAID," "I FEEL SO MUCH BETTER" AND THAT GIRI'S MANGA ARTIST IS GREAT.
BUT THAT'S ONLY SOME OF THE GIRI FANS AND NOT THE AZU-KYUN FANS.
YUJIRO, COME HERE.
KLAK
WHAT?
YES...
THE PRESIDENT OF PRINCE EIGHT SAID HE WILL HAVE MIHO AZUKI DENY HER RELATIONSHIP WITH ASHIROGI ON HER RADIO PROGRAM AZU-KYUN NIGHT IN TWO DAYS' TIME.
SO HE WANTS FUKUDA TO APPEAR ON GIRI RADIO AGAIN NEXT WEEK TO APOLOGIZE AND CORRECT WHAT HE SAID BY STATING HE MADE A MISTAKE.
UH... BUT I DON'T THINK THAT'S POSSIBLE KNOWING FUKUDA'S PERSONALITY...
I DON'T CARE IF IT'S IMPOSSIBLE, YOU JUST CONVINCE HIM.
THAT'S AN ORDER.
Y-YES, SIR...

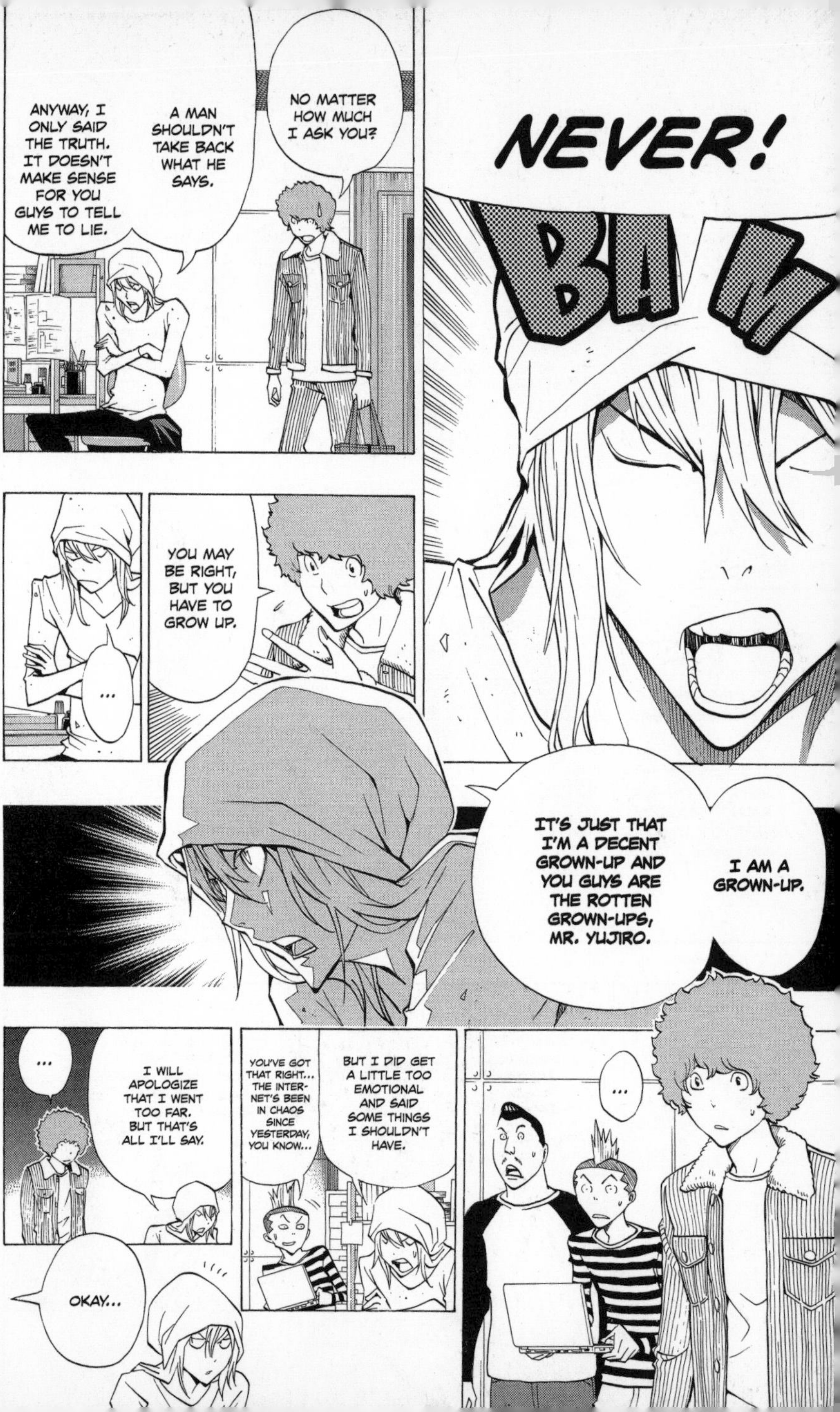
NEVER!
BAM
NO MATTER HOW MUCH I ASK YOU?
A MAN SHOULDN'T TAKE BACK WHAT HE SAYS.
ANYWAY, I ONLY SAID THE TRUTH. IT DOESN'T MAKE SENSE FOR YOU GUYS TO TELL ME TO LIE.
YOU MAY BE RIGHT, BUT YOU HAVE TO GROW UP.
...
I AM A GROWN-UP.
IT'S JUST THAT I'M A DECENT GROWN-UP AND YOU GUYS ARE THE ROTTEN GROWN-UPS, MR. YUJIRO.
...
BUT I DID GET A LITTLE TOO EMOTIONAL AND SAID SOME THINGS I SHOULDN'T HAVE.
YOU'VE GOT THAT RIGHT... THE INTER-NET'S BEEN IN CHAOS SINCE YESTERDAY, YOU KNOW...
I WILL APOLOGIZE THAT I WENT TOO FAR. BUT THAT'S ALL I'LL SAY.
...
OKAY...

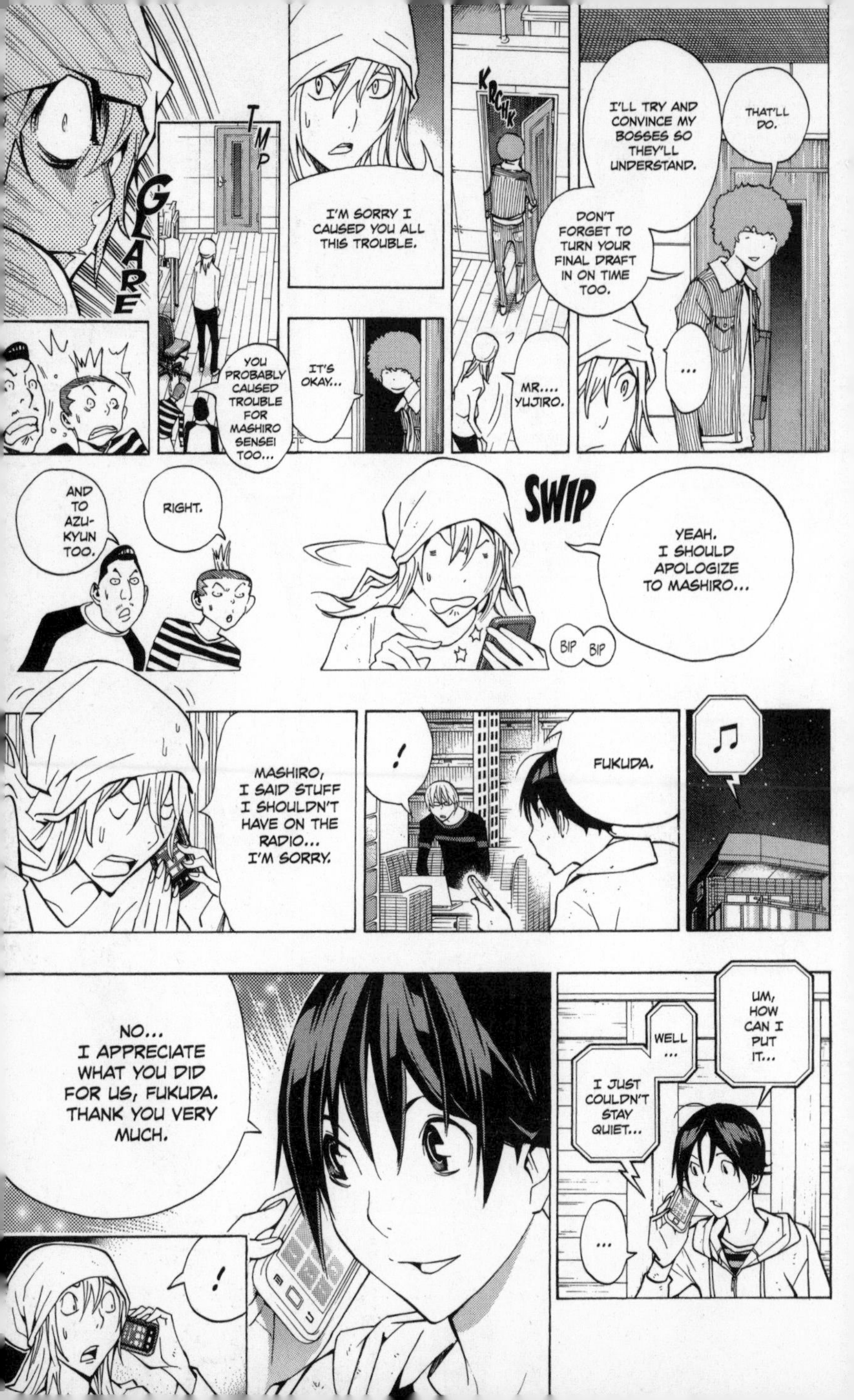
THAT'LL DO.
I'LL TRY AND CONVINCE MY BOSSES SO THEY'LL UNDERSTAND.
DON'T FORGET TO TURN YOUR FINAL DRAFT IN ON TIME TOO.
...
KRCHK
MR.... YUJIRO.
I'M SORRY I CAUSED YOU ALL THIS TROUBLE.
IT'S OKAY...
TMP
YOU PROBABLY CAUSED TROUBLE FOR MASHIRO SENSEI TOO...
GLARE
YEAH. I SHOULD APOLOGIZE TO MASHIRO...
BIP BIP
SWIP
RIGHT.
AND TO AZU-KYUN TOO.
♫
FUKUDA.
!
MASHIRO, I SAID STUFF I SHOULDN'T HAVE ON THE RADIO... I'M SORRY.
UM, HOW CAN I PUT IT...
WELL...
I JUST COULDN'T STAY QUIET...
...
NO... I APPRECIATE WHAT YOU DID FOR US, FUKUDA. THANK YOU VERY MUCH.
!

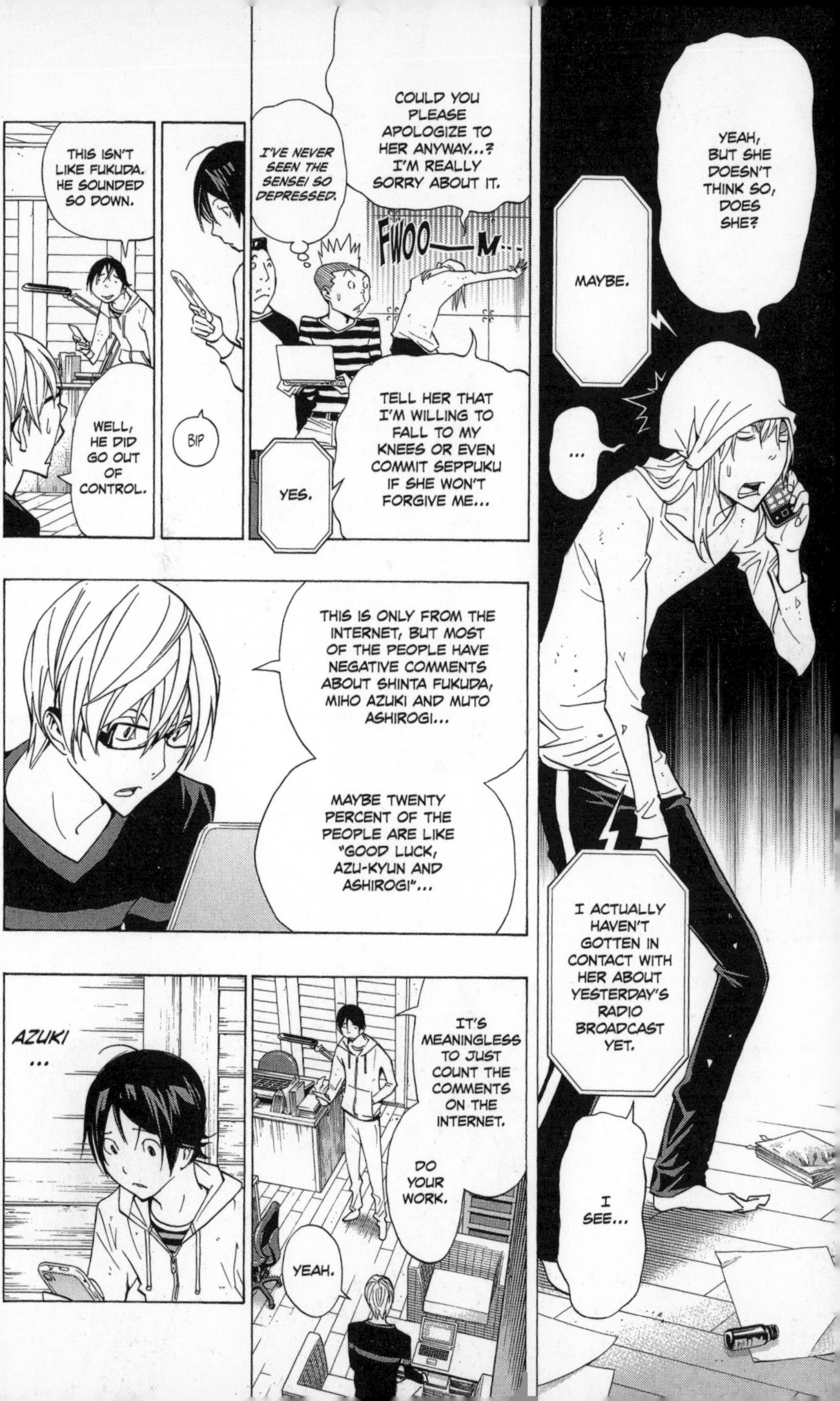
YEAH, BUT SHE DOESN'T THINK SO, DOES SHE?
MAYBE.
...
I ACTUALLY HAVEN'T GOTTEN IN CONTACT WITH HER ABOUT YESTERDAY'S RADIO BROADCAST YET.
I SEE...
COULD YOU PLEASE APOLOGIZE TO HER ANYWAY...? I'M REALLY SORRY ABOUT IT.
FWOO—M...
I'VE NEVER SEEN THE SENSEI SO DEPRESSED.
TELL HER THAT I'M WILLING TO FALL TO MY KNEES OR EVEN COMMIT SEPPUKU IF SHE WON'T FORGIVE ME...
YES.
BIP
THIS ISN'T LIKE FUKUDA. HE SOUNDED SO DOWN.
WELL, HE DID GO OUT OF CONTROL.
THIS IS ONLY FROM THE INTERNET, BUT MOST OF THE PEOPLE HAVE NEGATIVE COMMENTS ABOUT SHINTA FUKUDA, MIHO AZUKI AND MUTO ASHIROGI...
MAYBE TWENTY PERCENT OF THE PEOPLE ARE LIKE "GOOD LUCK, AZU-KYUN AND ASHIROGI"...
IT'S MEANINGLESS TO JUST COUNT THE COMMENTS ON THE INTERNET.
DO YOUR WORK.
YEAH.
AZUKI ...

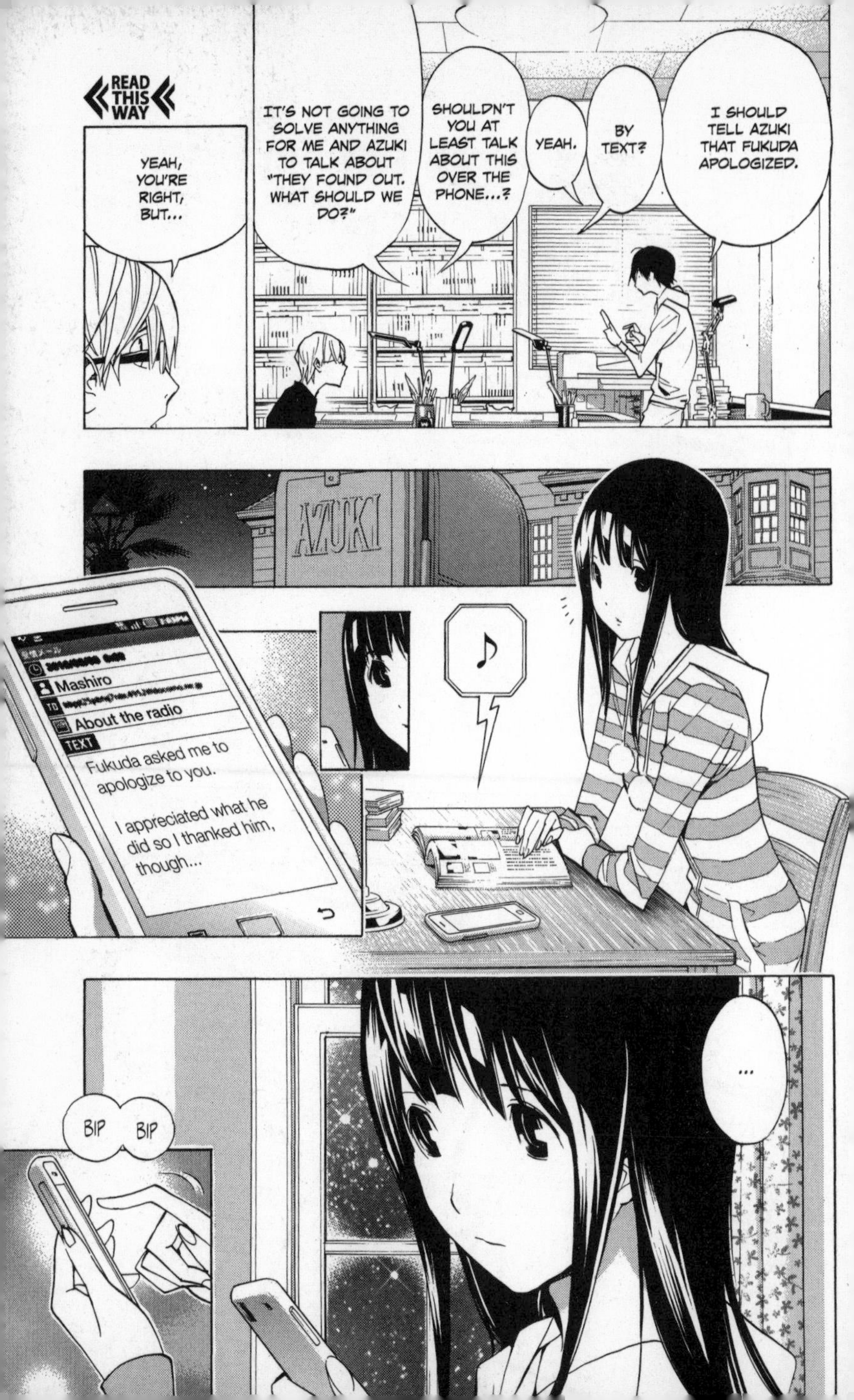
READ THIS WAY
I SHOULD TELL AZUKI THAT FUKUDA APOLOGIZED.
BY TEXT?
YEAH.
SHOULDN'T YOU AT LEAST TALK ABOUT THIS OVER THE PHONE...?
IT'S NOT GOING TO SOLVE ANYTHING FOR ME AND AZUKI TO TALK ABOUT "THEY FOUND OUT. WHAT SHOULD WE DO?"
YEAH, YOU'RE RIGHT, BUT...
AZUKI
♪
Mashiro
About the radio
TEXT
Fukuda asked me to apologize to you.
I appreciated what he did so I thanked him, though...
...
BIP BIP

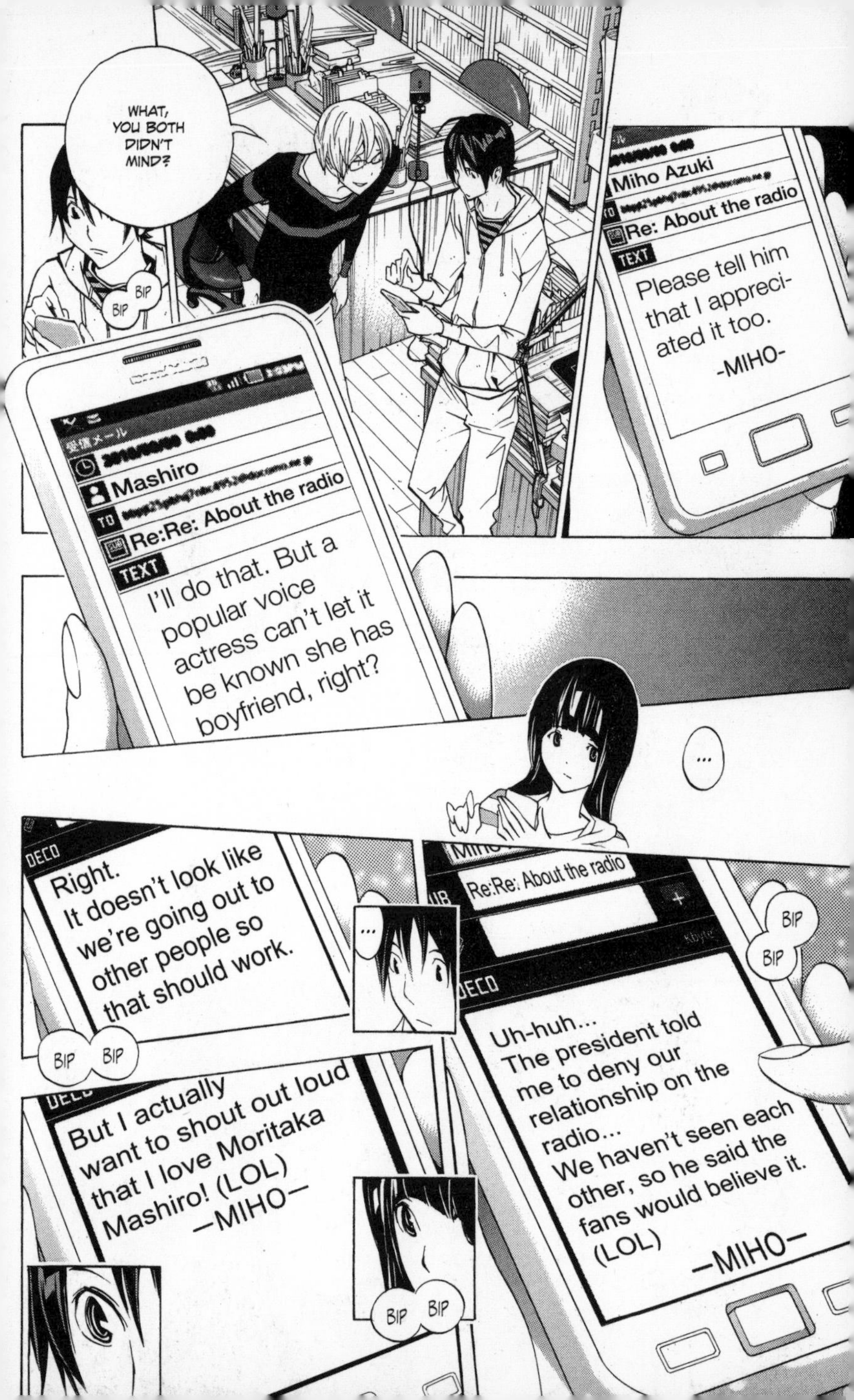
Miho Azuki
Re: About the radio
TEXT
Please tell him that I appreciated it too.
-MIHO-
WHAT, YOU BOTH DIDN'T MIND?
BIP BIP
Mashiro
TO
Re:Re: About the radio
TEXT
I'll do that. But a popular voice actress can't let it be known she has boyfriend, right?
...
Re:Re: About the radio
BIP BIP
DECO
Uh-huh...
The president told me to deny our relationship on the radio...
We haven't seen each other, so he said the fans would believe it. (LOL)
—MIHO—
BIP BIP
...
DECO
Right.
It doesn't look like we're going out to other people so that should work.
BIP BIP
But I actually want to shout out loud that I love Moritaka Mashiro! (LOL)
—MIHO—

READ THIS WAY

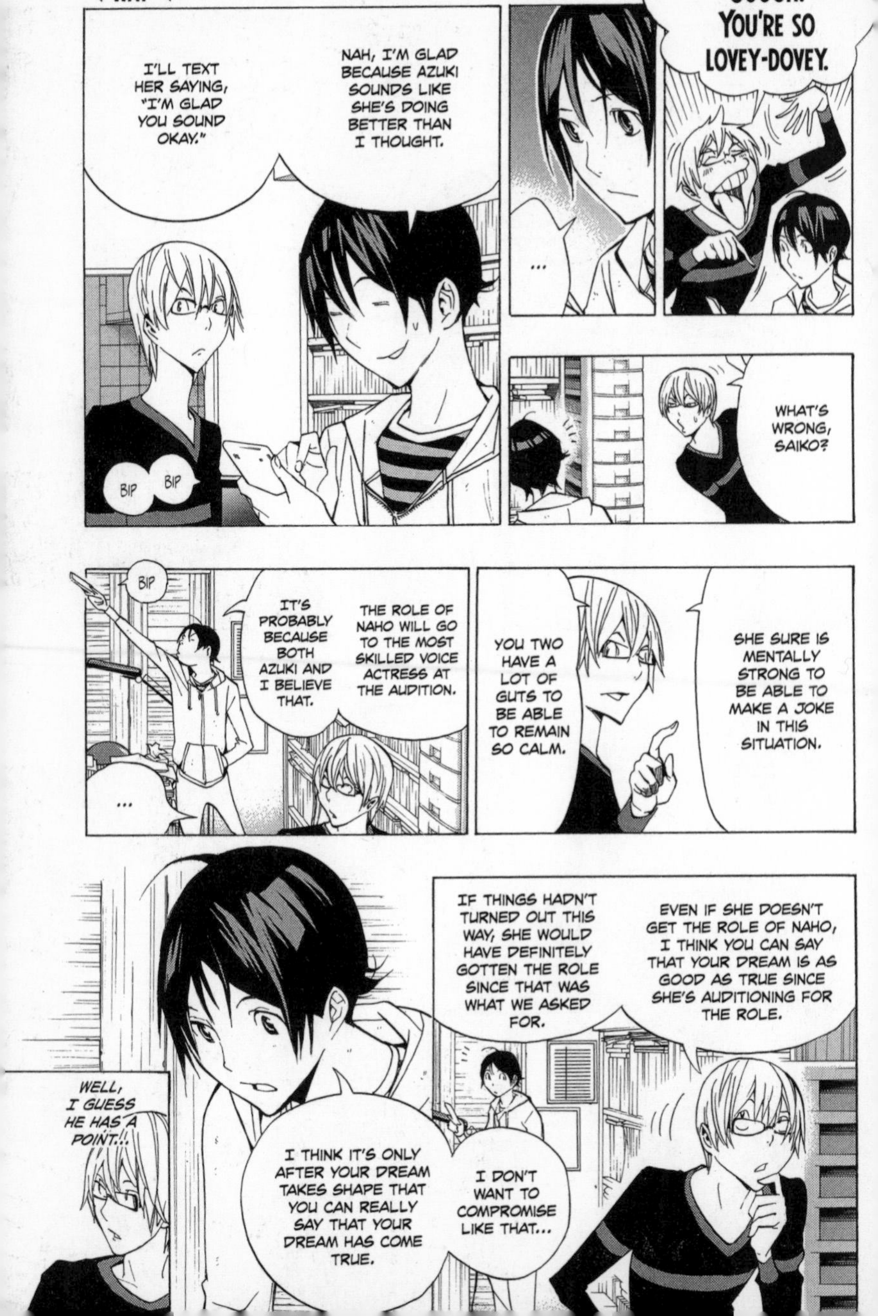
OOOOH. YOU'RE SO LOVEY-DOVEY.
...
WHAT'S WRONG, SAIKO?
NAH, I'M GLAD BECAUSE AZUKI SOUNDS LIKE SHE'S DOING BETTER THAN I THOUGHT.
I'LL TEXT HER SAYING, "I'M GLAD YOU SOUND OKAY."
BIP
BIP
SHE SURE IS MENTALLY STRONG TO BE ABLE TO MAKE A JOKE IN THIS SITUATION.
YOU TWO HAVE A LOT OF GUTS TO BE ABLE TO REMAIN SO CALM.
THE ROLE OF NAHO WILL GO TO THE MOST SKILLED VOICE ACTRESS AT THE AUDITION.
IT'S PROBABLY BECAUSE BOTH AZUKI AND I BELIEVE THAT.
BIP
...
EVEN IF SHE DOESN'T GET THE ROLE OF NAHO, I THINK YOU CAN SAY THAT YOUR DREAM IS AS GOOD AS TRUE SINCE SHE'S AUDITIONING FOR THE ROLE.
IF THINGS HADN'T TURNED OUT THIS WAY, SHE WOULD HAVE DEFINITELY GOTTEN THE ROLE SINCE THAT WAS WHAT WE ASKED FOR.
I DON'T WANT TO COMPROMISE LIKE THAT...
I THINK IT'S ONLY AFTER YOUR DREAM TAKES SHAPE THAT YOU CAN REALLY SAY THAT YOUR DREAM HAS COME TRUE.
WELL, I GUESS HE HAS A POINT...

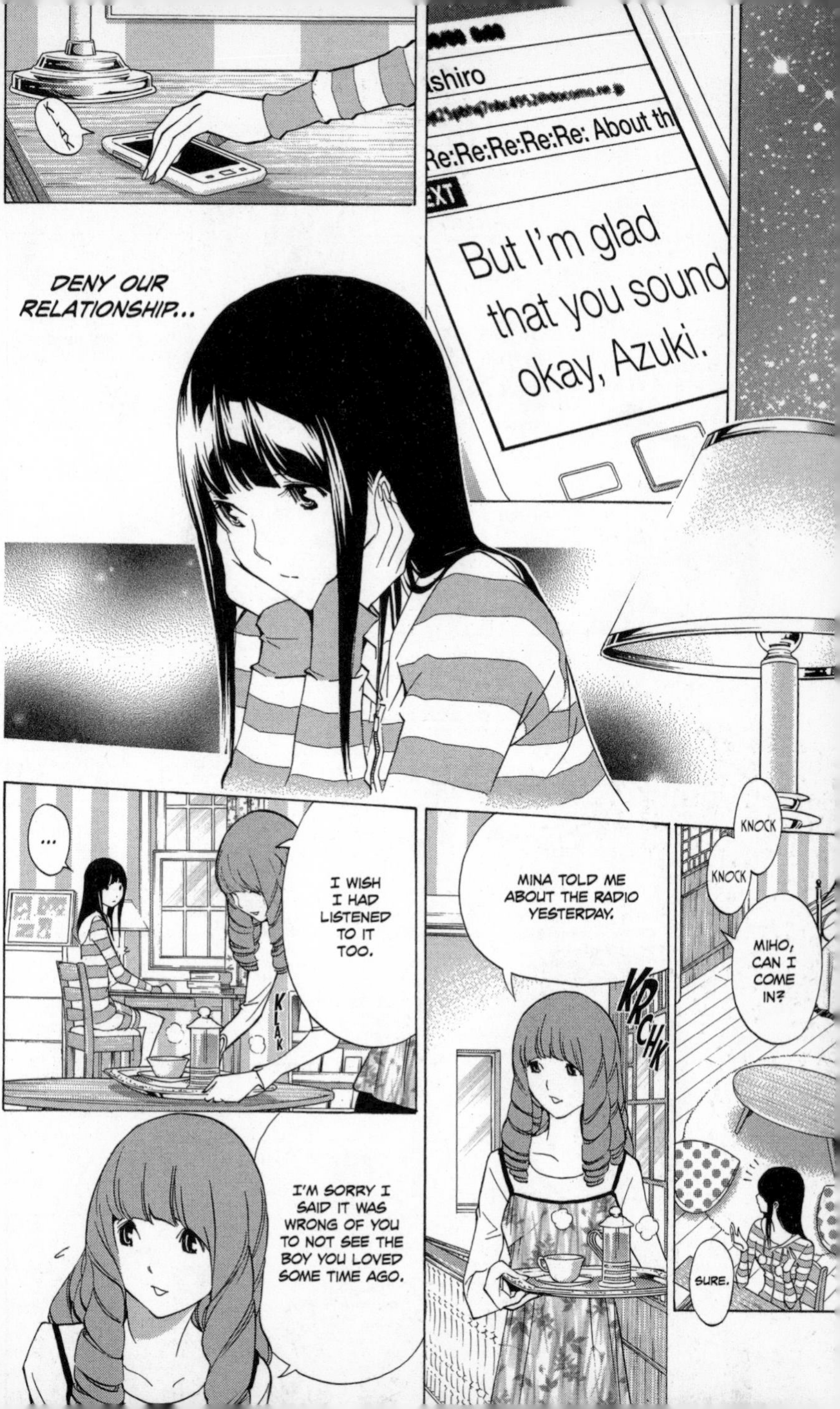
shiro
Re:Re:Re:Re:Re: About th
EXT
But I'm glad that you sound okay, Azuki.
KLAK
DENY OUR RELATIONSHIP...
KNOCK
KNOCK
MIHO, CAN I COME IN?
SURE.
KRCHK
MINA TOLD ME ABOUT THE RADIO YESTERDAY.
I WISH I HAD LISTENED TO IT TOO.
KLAK
...
I'M SORRY I SAID IT WAS WRONG OF YOU TO NOT SEE THE BOY YOU LOVED SOME TIME AGO.

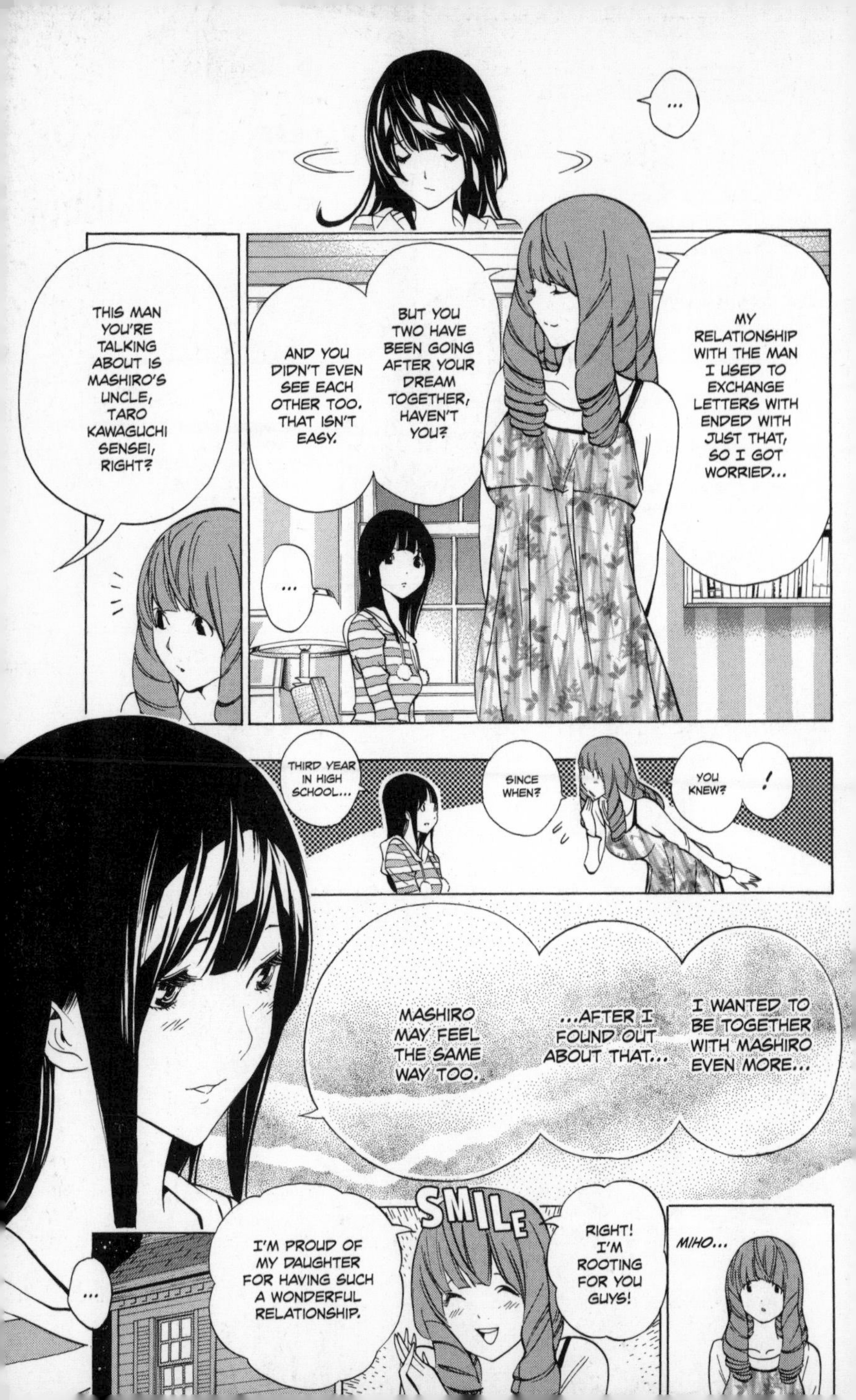
...
MY RELATIONSHIP WITH THE MAN I USED TO EXCHANGE LETTERS WITH ENDED WITH JUST THAT, SO I GOT WORRIED...
BUT YOU TWO HAVE BEEN GOING AFTER YOUR DREAM TOGETHER, HAVEN'T YOU?
AND YOU DIDN'T EVEN SEE EACH OTHER TOO. THAT ISN'T EASY.
...
THIS MAN YOU'RE TALKING ABOUT IS MASHIRO'S UNCLE, TARO KAWAGUCHI SENSEI, RIGHT?
!
YOU KNEW?
SINCE WHEN?
THIRD YEAR IN HIGH SCHOOL...
I WANTED TO BE TOGETHER WITH MASHIRO EVEN MORE...
...AFTER I FOUND OUT ABOUT THAT...
MASHIRO MAY FEEL THE SAME WAY TOO.
MIHO...
RIGHT! I'M ROOTING FOR YOU GUYS!
SMILE
I'M PROUD OF MY DAUGHTER FOR HAVING SUCH A WONDERFUL RELATIONSHIP.
...

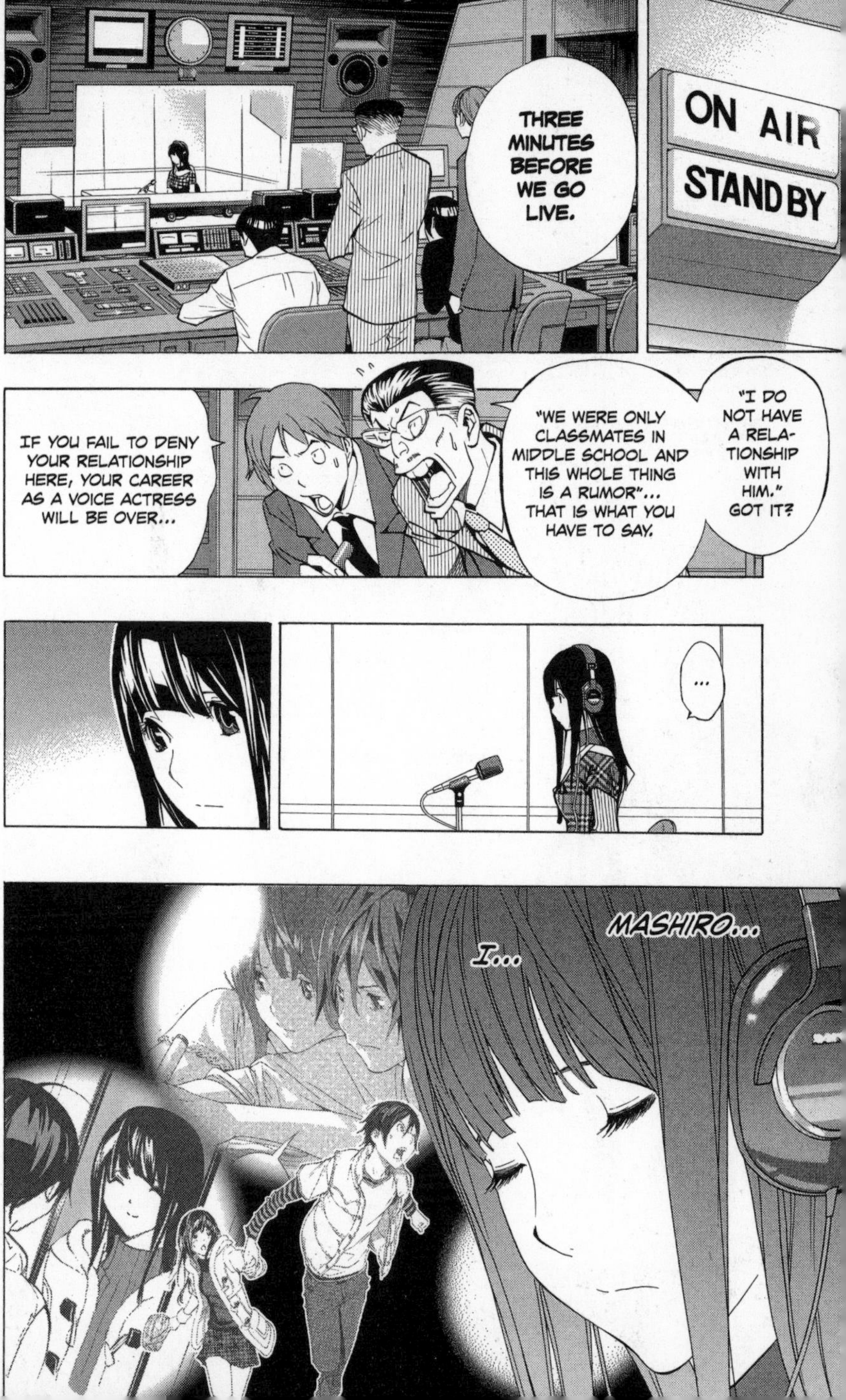
ON AIR
STAND BY
THREE MINUTES BEFORE WE GO LIVE.
"I DO NOT HAVE A RELATIONSHIP WITH HIM." GOT IT?
"WE WERE ONLY CLASSMATES IN MIDDLE SCHOOL AND THIS WHOLE THING IS A RUMOR"... THAT IS WHAT YOU HAVE TO SAY.
IF YOU FAIL TO DENY YOUR RELATIONSHIP HERE, YOUR CAREER AS A VOICE ACTRESS WILL BE OVER...
...
MASHIRO...
I...

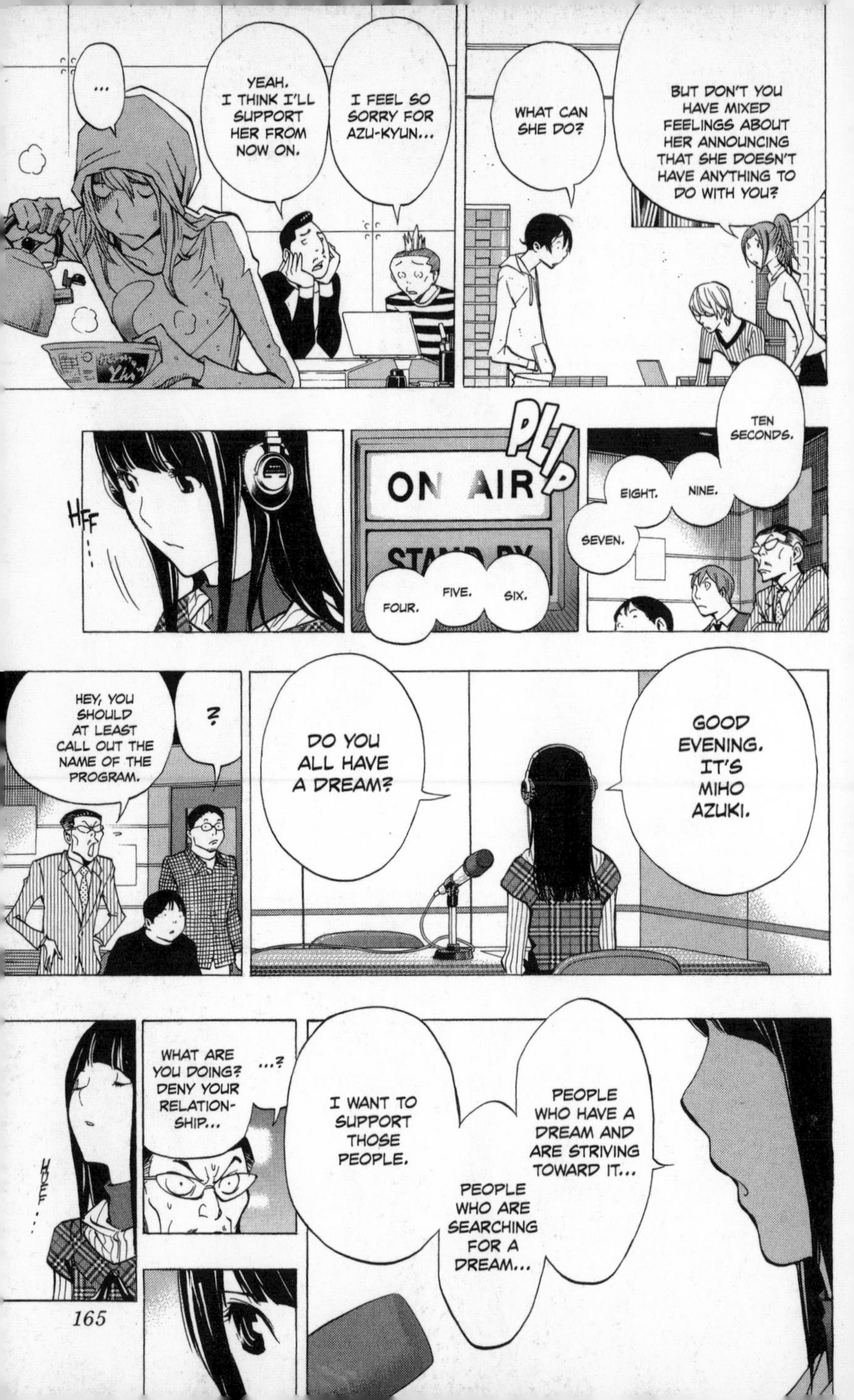
BUT DON'T YOU HAVE MIXED FEELINGS ABOUT HER ANNOUNCING THAT SHE DOESN'T HAVE ANYTHING TO DO WITH YOU?
WHAT CAN SHE DO?
I FEEL SO SORRY FOR AZU-KYUN...
YEAH. I THINK I'LL SUPPORT HER FROM NOW ON.
...
TEN SECONDS.
NINE.
EIGHT.
SEVEN.
PLIP
ON AIR
SIX.
FIVE.
FOUR.
HFF...
GOOD EVENING. IT'S MIHO AZUKI.
DO YOU ALL HAVE A DREAM?
?
HEY, YOU SHOULD AT LEAST CALL OUT THE NAME OF THE PROGRAM.
PEOPLE WHO HAVE A DREAM AND ARE STRIVING TOWARD IT...
PEOPLE WHO ARE SEARCHING FOR A DREAM...
I WANT TO SUPPORT THOSE PEOPLE.
...?
WHAT ARE YOU DOING? DENY YOUR RELATION-SHIP...
HUFF...

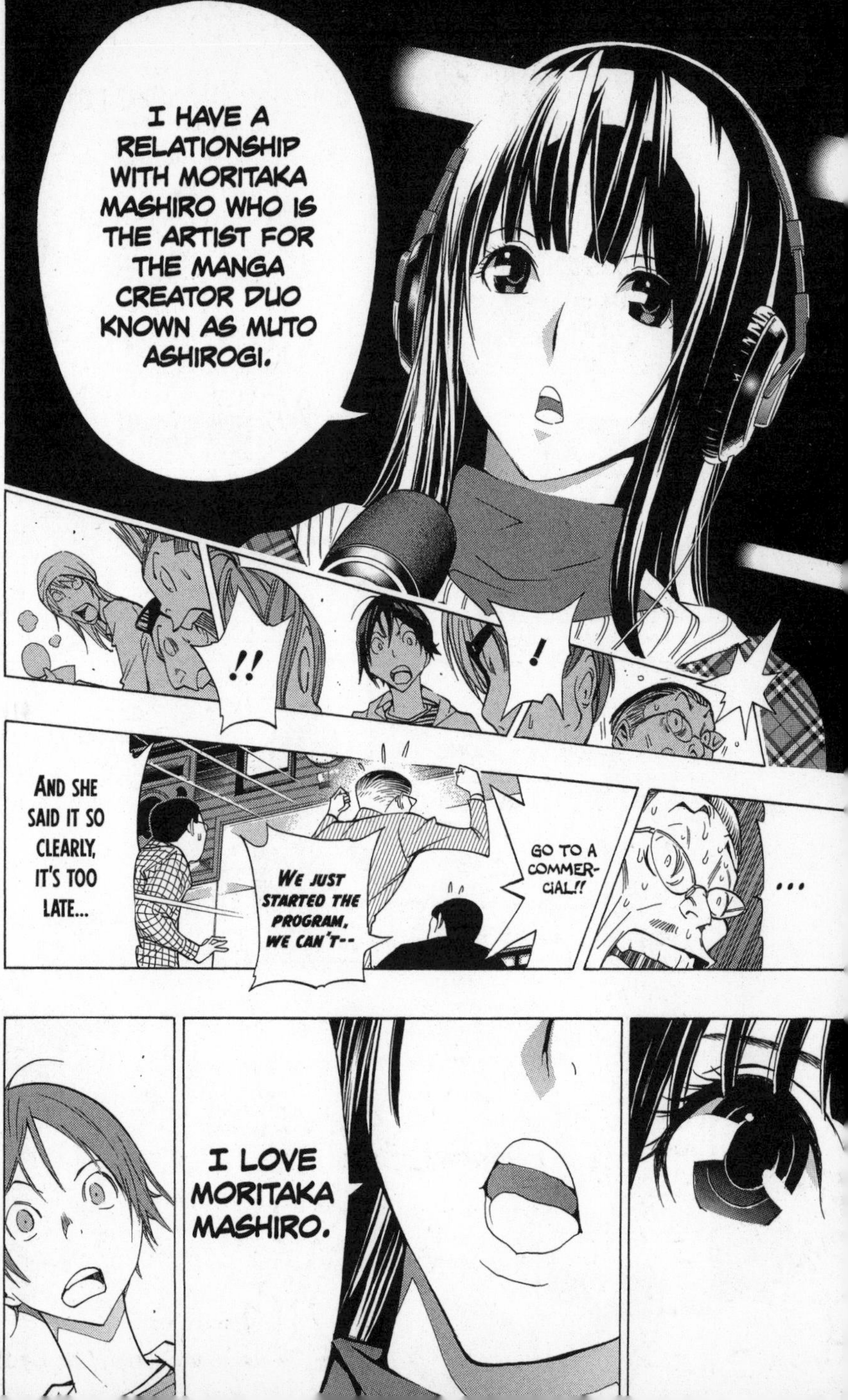
I HAVE A RELATIONSHIP WITH MORITAKA MASHIRO WHO IS THE ARTIST FOR THE MANGA CREATOR DUO KNOWN AS MUTO ASHIROGI.
!
!!
...
GO TO A COMMER-CIAL!!
WE JUST STARTED THE PROGRAM, WE CAN'T--
AND SHE SAID IT SO CLEARLY, IT'S TOO LATE...
I LOVE MORITAKA MASHIRO.

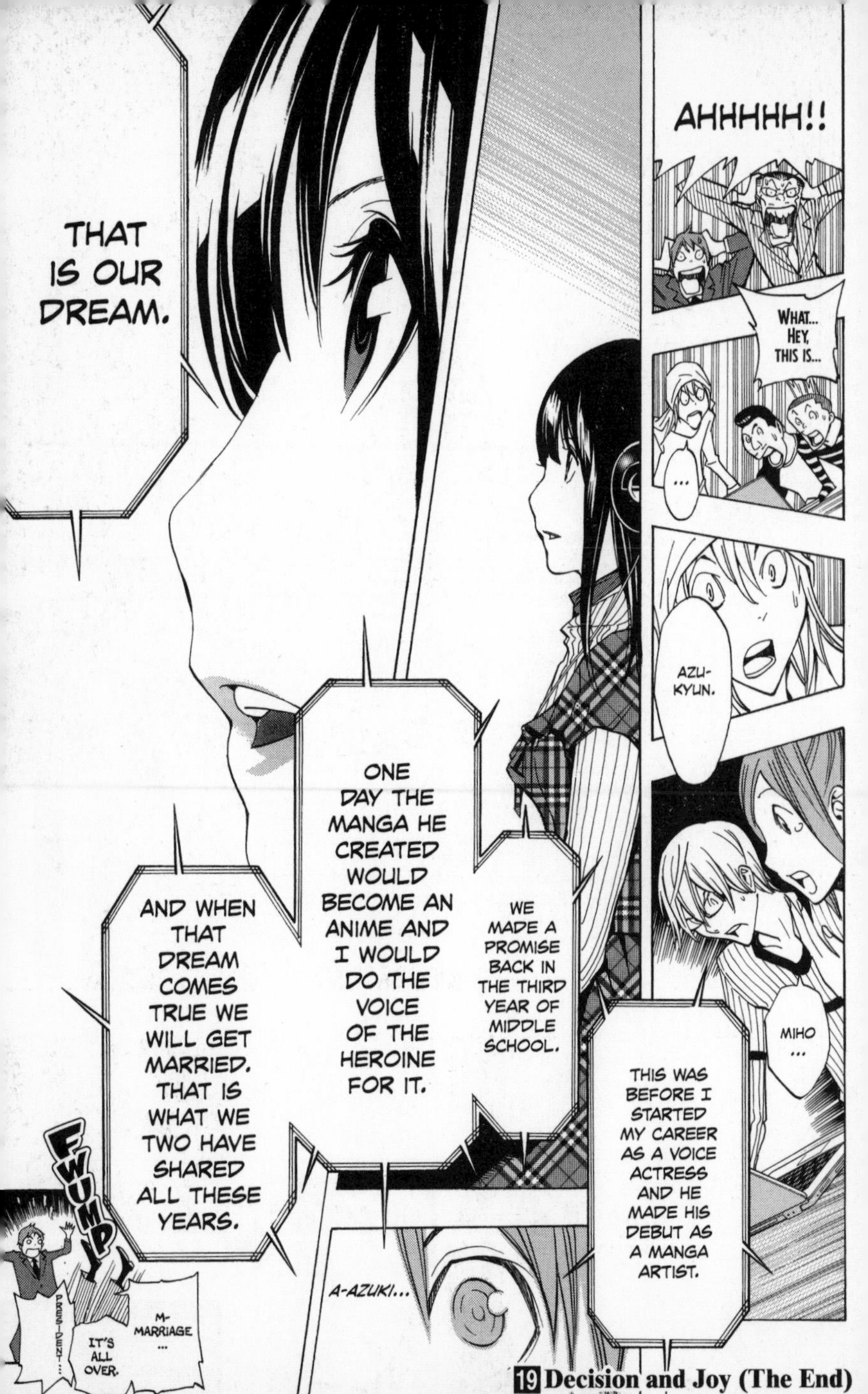
AHHHHH!!
WHAT... HEY, THIS IS...
...
AZU-KYUN.
MIHO ...
THIS WAS BEFORE I STARTED MY CAREER AS A VOICE ACTRESS AND HE MADE HIS DEBUT AS A MANGA ARTIST.
WE MADE A PROMISE BACK IN THE THIRD YEAR OF MIDDLE SCHOOL.
ONE DAY THE MANGA HE CREATED WOULD BECOME AN ANIME AND I WOULD DO THE VOICE OF THE HEROINE FOR IT.
AND WHEN THAT DREAM COMES TRUE WE WILL GET MARRIED. THAT IS WHAT WE TWO HAVE SHARED ALL THESE YEARS.
THAT IS OUR DREAM.
A-AZUKI...
FWUMP
M-MARRIAGE ...
PRESIDENT... IT'S ALL OVER.

OHBA'S STORYBOARD

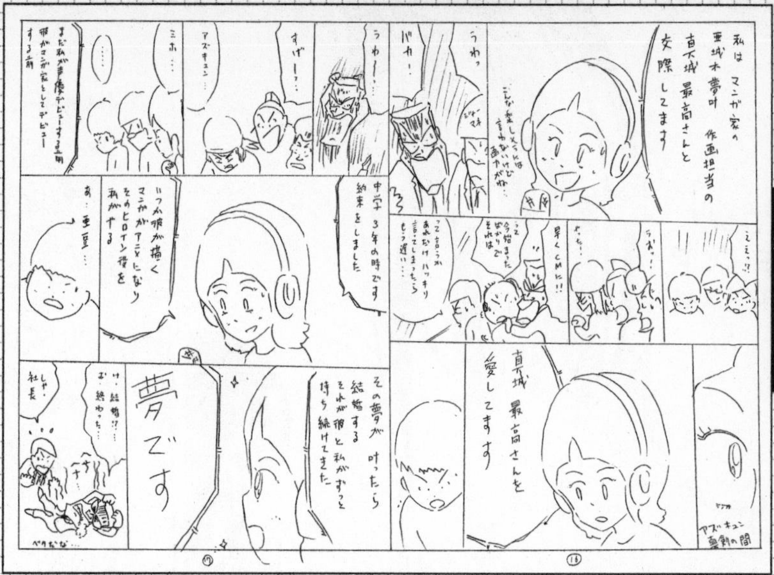
私は マンガ家の 亜城木夢叶 作画担当の 真城最高さんと 交際してます
うわっ
バカ!
ええっ!?
うおっ
早くCMに!!
って今始まったばかりでそれは
ってここまであれだけハッキリ言ってしまったらもう遅い…
アズキュン真剣の間
真城最高さんを愛してます
うわ〜!
すげー…
アズキュン…
ミホ…
……
まだ私が声優デビューする前 彼がマンガ家としてデビューする前
中学3年の時です 約束をしました
いつか彼が描くマンガがアニメになりそのヒロイン役を私がする
あ…亜豆…
その夢が叶ったら結婚する それが彼と私がずっと持ち続けてきた
夢です
け…結婚!?… お…終わった…
しゃ…社長…

OBATA'S STORYBOARD

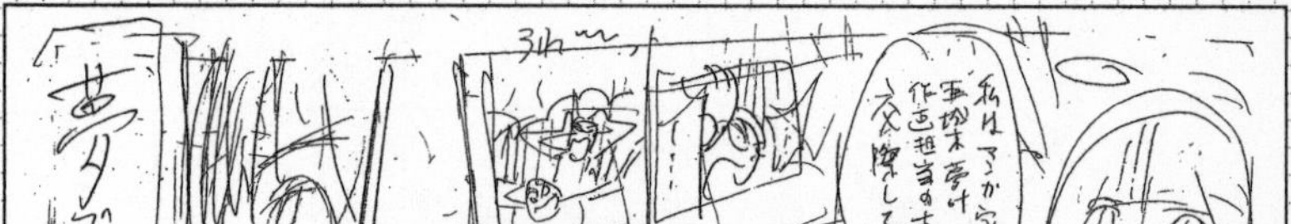

COMPLETE!

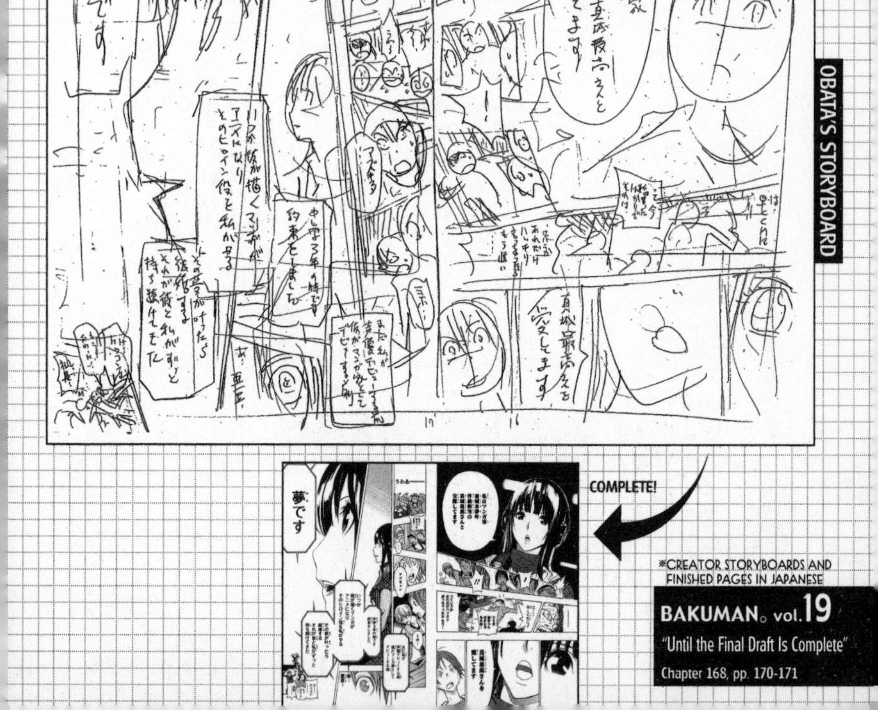
夢です

※CREATOR STORYBOARDS AND FINISHED PAGES IN JAPANESE

BAKUMAN。 vol.19
"Until the Final Draft Is Complete"
Chapter 168, pp. 170-171

BAKUMAN

In the NEXT VOLUME

For ten years, Moritaka and Azuki have believed in each other as they worked hard in search of their dreams. Can they finally make it a reality? See for yourself in the final volume of *Bakuman*。!

Available August 2013!

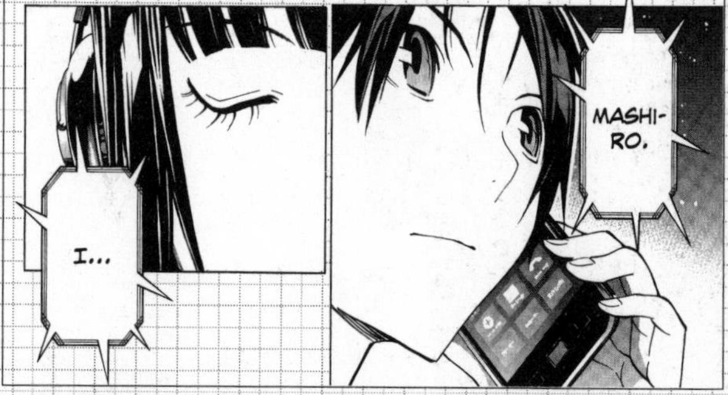
MASHI-RO.
I...

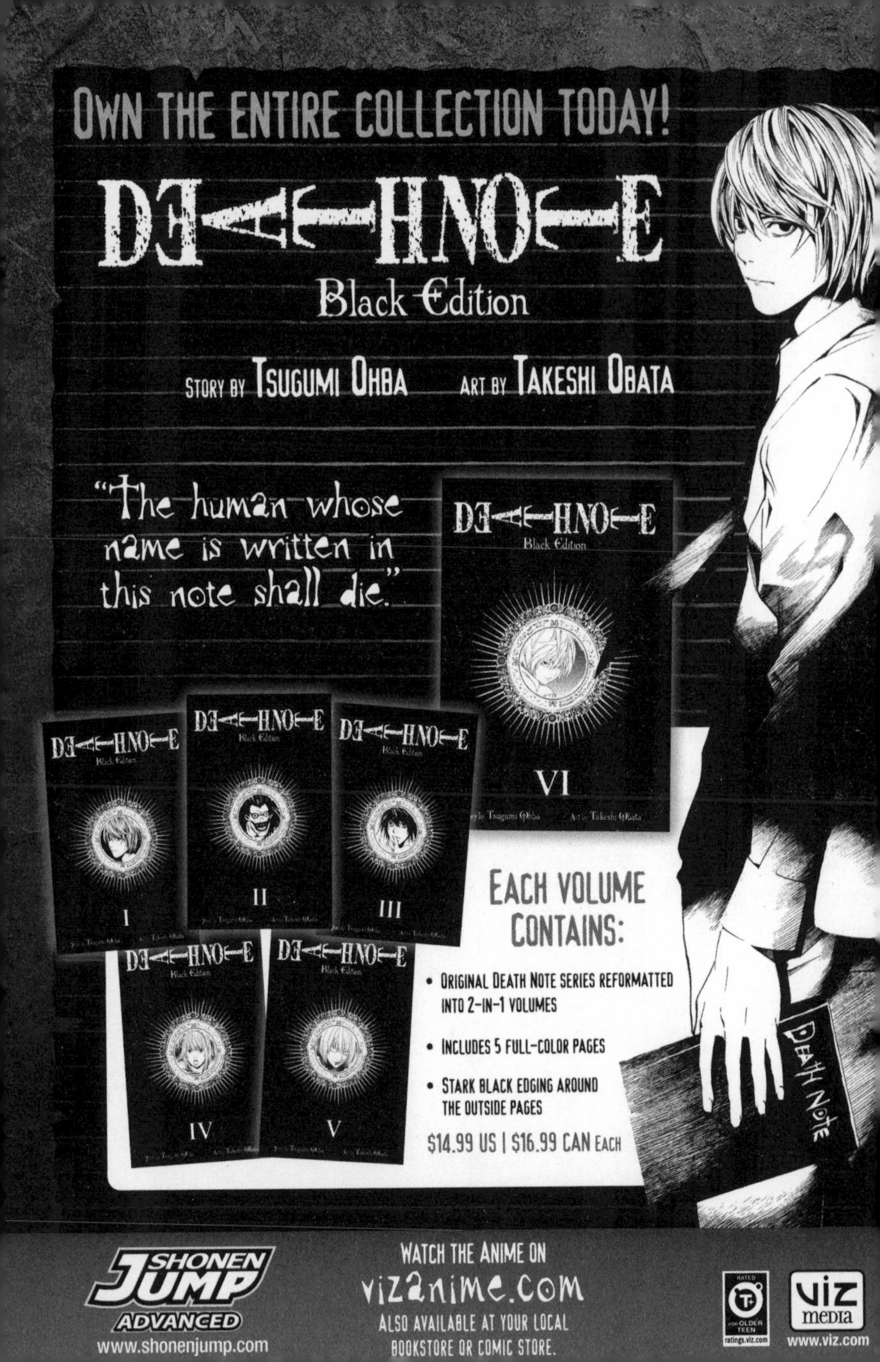

OWN THE ENTIRE COLLECTION TODAY!
DEATH NOTE
Black Edition
STORY BY TSUGUMI OHBA ART BY TAKESHI OBATA
"The human whose name is written in this note shall die."
DEATH NOTE Black Edition VI
EACH VOLUME CONTAINS:
• ORIGINAL DEATH NOTE SERIES REFORMATTED INTO 2-IN-1 VOLUMES
• INCLUDES 5 FULL-COLOR PAGES
• STARK BLACK EDGING AROUND THE OUTSIDE PAGES
$14.99 US | $16.99 CAN EACH
DEATH NOTE
SHONEN JUMP ADVANCED
www.shonenjump.com
WATCH THE ANIME ON
vizanime.com
ALSO AVAILABLE AT YOUR LOCAL BOOKSTORE OR COMIC STORE.
RATED T+ FOR OLDER TEEN
ratings.viz.com
VIZ media
www.viz.com

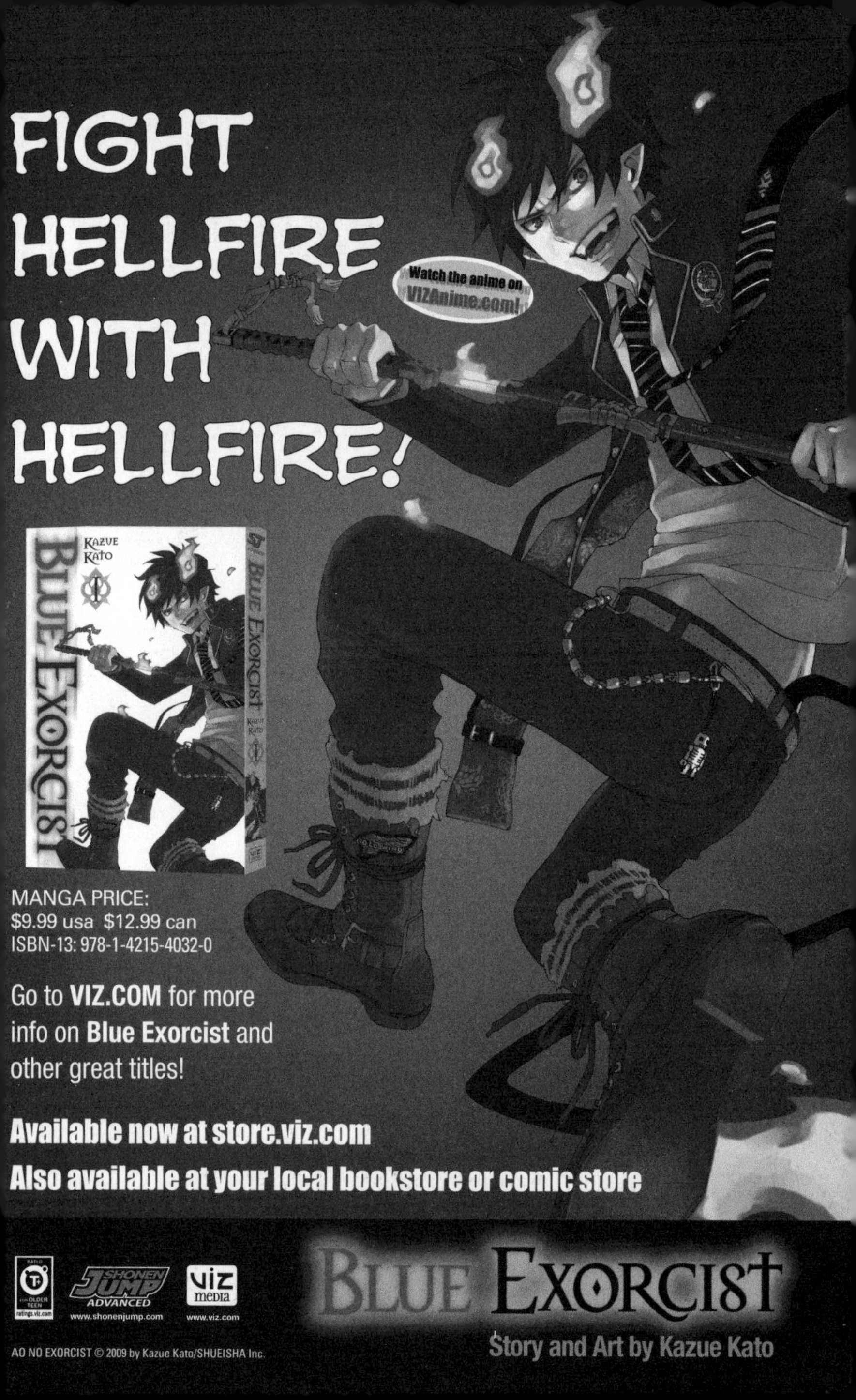
FIGHT HELLFIRE WITH HELLFIRE!
Watch the anime on VIZAnime.com!
KAZUE KATO
BLUE EXORCIST
MANGA PRICE:
$9.99 usa $12.99 can
ISBN-13: 978-1-4215-4032-0
Go to VIZ.COM for more info on Blue Exorcist and other great titles!
Available now at store.viz.com
Also available at your local bookstore or comic store
OLDER TEEN
ratings.viz.com
SHONEN JUMP ADVANCED
www.shonenjump.com
viz media
www.viz.com
BLUE EXORCIST
Story and Art by Kazue Kato
AO NO EXORCIST © 2009 by Kazue Kato/SHUEISHA Inc.

This is the LAST PAGE.

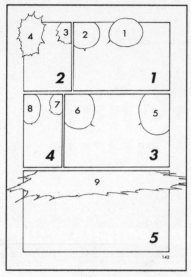

142

← Follow the action this way.

BAKUMAN。 has been printed in the original Japanese format in order to preserve the orientation of the original artwork.

Please turn it around and begin reading from right to left. Unlike English, Japanese is read right to left. Japanese comics are re[ad in] order from the way E[nglish is] typically read. Have [fun!]